SOCIAL JUSTICE

Strategies for National Renewal

THE REPORT OF THE COMMISSION
ON SOCIAL JUSTICE

VINTAGE

Published by Vintage 1994

2 4 6 8 10 9 7 5 3

Vintage
Random House, 20 Vauxhall Bridge Road
London SW1V 2SA

Random House Australia (Pty) Limited
20 Alfred Street, Milsons Point, Sydney
New South Wales 2061, Australia

Random House New Zealand Limited
18 Poland Road, Glenfield, Auckland 10
New Zealand

Random House South Africa (Pty) Limited
PO Box 337, Bergvlei, South Africa

Random House UK Limited Reg. No. 954009

A CIP catalogue record for this book
is available from the British Library

ISBN 0 09 951141 X

Printed and bound in Great Britain by
The Guernsey Press Co. Ltd., Guernsey, Channel Islands

A VINTAGE ORIGINAL

SOCIAL JUSTICE

STRATEGIES FOR NATIONAL RENEWAL

With conservative ~~~~~~~~~~~~~~ the opposition parties striving to offer credible alternatives, *Social Justice* ~~~~~~~~~ important and influential book of the year. Radically confronting the bankrupt dogmas of the free-market economy, *Social Justice* presents a forward-thinking programme for social and economic reform, showing how intelligent welfare and new economic opportunities can be the driving force for national renewal. The Commission on Social Justice is an independent body set up by the late Rt Hon John Smith MP under the auspices of the Institute for Public Policy Research (IPPR). Chaired by Sir Gordon Borrie, former Director-General of Fair Trading, its mission is to develop a practical vision of economic and social reform for the 21st century. The Commission's final report is a challenge to politicians and citizens alike.

'The scourges of poverty, unemployment and low skills are barriers, not only to opportunities for people, but to the creation of a dynamic and prosperous society. It is simply unacceptable to continue to waste our most precious resource – the extraordinary skills and talents of ordinary people.'

Rt Hon John Smith QC, MP
1938–1994

Contents

Preface   ix

Abbreviations   xii

List of Figures and Tables   xv

Acknowledgements   xvii

Executive Summary   1

Introduction   15

Part I: The UK Today

1. The State of the Nation   27

Part II: What's Wrong? What Can Be Done?

2. Diagnosis: The UK in a Changing World   61
3. Prescription: A Tale of Three Futures   94

Part III: Strategies for the Future

4. Investment: Adding Value Through Lifelong Learning   119
5. Opportunity: Working for a Living   151
6. Security: Building an Intelligent Welfare State   221
7. Responsibility: Making a Good Society   306
8. Taxation: Investing in Ourselves   374

    Conclusion: The Need for Change   397

Written and Oral Evidence	400
Commission Terms of Reference	412
Commission Publications	413
Commission Outreach Visits	415

PREFACE

The Commission on Social Justice was set up in December 1992 at the instigation of the late Rt Hon John Smith QC MP, then Leader of the Labour Party. John Smith allied a passion for social justice with a vision of economic renewal; his early death robbed his party and the country of a principled advocate of change. We hope this report will be seen as one legacy of the time and energy he devoted to public life.

The Commission was launched in 1992, the fiftieth anniversary of the pathbreaking Beveridge Report *Social Insurance and Allied Services*, which became the foundation of the welfare state in the UK. The Commission's job was to carry out an independent inquiry into social and economic reform in the UK; the terms of reference are listed on page 412. Commissioners served in a personal, part-time, unpaid capacity; their names are listed below.

The Commission was based at the Institute for Public Policy Research, the independent, left-of-centre think-tank. It met sixteen times. Detailed work was done in three panels of Commissioners, covering 'work and wages', 'money and wealth', and 'services and communities'. The first panel was greatly assisted by the expertise of Hilary Metcalf of the Policy Studies Institute. The Commission undertook eleven outreach visits around the UK; details of these visits can be found on pages 415–418. We are grateful to all the people who helped make this part of our work so successful.

In addition to two interim reports published in July 1993, the Commission also published thirteen 'issue papers'. These were very important in helping us to develop ideas and to stimulate debate. We are grateful for the time and effort put in by the people who agreed to write these papers; the full list of titles appears on pages 413–414.

The Commission was staffed by its Secretary, David Miliband; two Research Fellows, Richard Thomas and Dr James McCormick; an Administrator, Irene Faluyi (until September 1994); a Press Officer, Lucie Carrington, who joined the staff in November 1993; and Katherine Edwards, who co-ordinated the Commission's work in the run-up to publication of our final report. We are most grateful to all our staff for their enthusiasm, hard work and unflagging patience.

Funding for the Commission was generously provided by the Andersen Foundation, the Follett Trust, the Gatsby Charitable Foundation, Glaxo Pharmaceuticals (UK), the Inland Revenue Staff Federation, UNISON, and individual donors. We gratefully acknowledge the financial support given by the Council of Civil Service Unions (CCSU), which contributed to the costs of the background research for this report. The CCSU, whilst remaining firmly non-party political, wished to ensure that the Commission, and the readers of this report, could reach their conclusions on the basis of sound research. The Centre for Housing Research and Urban Studies at the University of Glasgow kindly provided an office for James McCormick. A separate project on 'social justice from the bottom up', directed by Professor David Donnison, was funded by the Joseph Rowntree Charitable Trust, with additional help from the Barrow and Geraldine S. Cadbury Trust.

Numerous organisations and individuals from all parts of the UK, as well as from many countries abroad, contributed in writing and orally to our enquiry; they are listed on pages 400–411. We are extremely grateful to all those who made the Commission's work possible.

This book constitutes the final report of the Commission, which was unanimously agreed at the last meeting of the Commission on 25 July 1994.

Sir Gordon Borrie QC (Chairman)

Professor A.B. Atkinson FBA
Warden, Nuffield College, Oxford

Anita Bhalla
Asian Resource Centre, Birmingham

Professor John Gennard
Professor of Industrial Relations, Strathclyde University

The Very Reverend John Gladwin
Provost of Sheffield and Bishop-Elect of Guildford

Christopher Haskins
Chairman, Northern Foods Plc

Patricia Hewitt (Deputy Chair)
Director of Research, Andersen Consulting
Deputy Director, IPPR (until September 1994)

Dr Penelope Leach
Fellow, British Psychological Society

Professor Ruth Lister
Professor of Social Policy and Administration,
Loughborough University

Professor David Marquand
Professor of Politics and Director,
Political Economy Research Centre, University of Sheffield

Bert Massie
Director, Royal Association for Disability and Rehabilitation

Emma MacLennan
Vice-Chair, Low Pay Unit

Dr Eithne McLaughlin
Reader in Social Policy, Queen's University of Belfast

Steven Webb
Economist, Institute for Fiscal Studies

Margaret Wheeler
Director of Organisation Development, UNISON

Professor Bernard Williams, FBA
White's Professor of Moral Philosophy, University of Oxford

Abbreviations

AEEU	Amalgamated Engineering and Electrical Union
ALBSU	Adult Literacy and Basic Skills Unit
A Levels	Advanced Levels
ANC	African National Congress
BA	British Airways
BBC	British Broadcasting Corporation
BSI	British Standards Institution
CAB	Citizens Advice Bureaux
CAT	Credit Accumulation & Transfer
CBI	Confederation of Business Industry
CDF	Community Development Fund
CLES	Centre for Local Economic Strategies
CNAA	Council for National Academic Awards
CPAG	Child Poverty Action Group
CRE	Commission for Racial Equality
CSVs	Community Service Volunteers
DM	Deutschmark
DSS	Department of Social Security
DTI	Department of Trade and Industry
EC	European Community
ECU	European Currency Unit
EMA	Education Maintenance Allowance
EOC	Equal Opportunities Commission
ERM	Exchange Rate Mechanism
ESOPs	Employee Share Ownership Plans
ET	Employment Training
EU	European Union
FE	Further Education
FT	*Financial Times*

FTSE	Financial Times Stock Exchange 100 Index
G7	Group of Seven Major Industrialised Countries
GATT	General Agreement on Tariffs and Trade
GCSE	General Certificate of Secondary Education
GDP	Gross Domestic Product
GLC	Greater London Council
GNP	Gross National Product
GNVQs	General National Vocational Qualifications
GPs	General Practitioners
HAG	Housing Association Grant
HE	Higher Education
HPAEs	High Performing Asian Economies
ICA	Invalid Care Allowance
IFS	Institute for Fiscal Studies
ILA	Individual Learning Account
ILMs	Intermediate Labour Markets
JET	Jobs, Education and Training Programme
LA	Local Authority
LB	Learning Bank
LEA	Local Education Authority
LEC	Local Enterprise Company
LEL	Lower Earnings Limit
LETS	Local Exchange Trading Systems
LPU	Low Pay Unit
LSE	London School of Economics
MIRAS	Mortgage Interest Relief at Source
MITR	Mortgage Interest Tax Relief
MMC	Monopolies and Mergers Commission
NACRO	National Association for the Care and Resettlement of Offenders
NAFTA	North American Free Trade Agreement
NAO	National Audit Office
NATO	North Atlantic Treaty Organisation
NCE	National Commission on Education
NCRA	National Community Regerneration Agency
NCVO	National Council for Voluntary Organisations
NCVQ	National Council of Vocational Qualifications
NHS	National Health Service
NI	National Insurance
NICs	National Insurance Contributions
NIT	Negative Income Tax

NSPP	National Savings Pension Plan
NVQs	National Vocational Qualifications
OECD	Organisation for Economic Co-operation and Development
OPCS	Office of Population Censuses and Surveys
PSBR	Public Sector Borrowing Requirement
PSI	Policy Studies Institute
R & D	Research and Development
RSA	Royal Society of Arts
SERPS	State Earnings Related Pension Scheme
SMP	Statutory Maternity Pay
SRB	Single Regeneration Budget
SSAC	Social Service Advisory Committee
SSP	Statutory Sick Pay
TAPs	Training Access Points
TECs	Training and Enterprise Councils
TGWU	Transport and General Workers' Union
TPAS	Tenant Participation Advisory Schemes
TUC	Trades Union Congress
UB	Unemployment Benefit
UCW	Union of Communication Workers
UEL	Upper Earnings Limit
USDAW	Union of Shop, Distributive and Allied Workers
VAT	Value Added Tax
WHO	World Health Organisation
YT	Youth Training

LIST OF FIGURES AND TABLES

Figures

1.1	A Few Get Richer	29
1.2	Something for Nothing: Top Pay Rockets	30
1.3	Inequality is Rising	31
1.4	Poverty is Rising	32
1.5	Diverse Fortunes: Pensioner Inequality is Rising	33
1.6	Men Not at Work	34
1.7	More Unemployed, for Longer	35
1.8	Women at Work	37
1.9	Bottom of the Learning League	40
1.10	Learning Improves Earning	41
1.11	Infant Mortality: Class Still Counts in Britain	43
1.12	Killed by Class: Children Killed in Traffic Accidents and Social Class	44
1.13	Dying from Poverty?	45
1.14	Inequality is Bad for Your Health	46
1.15	Richer Economy, Poorer Society?	47
1.16	Streets Ahead: Homelessness in Europe 1991/2	48
1.17	Crime Rises ... and Rises	49
2.1	Catching Up: Later Growth is Faster Growth	68
2.2	The UK Cannot Compete on Low Wages	69
3.1	The Link Between Investment and Productivity	100
4.1	Rich Pickings	137
4.2	The Learning Bank	142
5.1	Regulation and Prosperity Can Go Together	163
5.2	Work and Wealth Creation	168
6.1	No Better Off on £10,000 a Year	246
8.1	The Growth Dividend	375

8.2 Where the Money Goes   377
8.3 Employer Social Contributions in Europe   388

Tables

5.1 UK Employment Trends by Sex   153
5.2 The Decline of Collective Bargaining   198
8.1 Tax at the Top   390

ACKNOWLEDGEMENTS

In addition to the many people who wrote papers and answered queries, the Commission are indebted to a number of people who were especially helpful during the course of the Commission's work. Among IPPR staff, we would like to thank former Director James Cornford, the publications team of Ros Burton, Helena Scott and Joanne Bailey, Senior Economist Dan Corry, Hamlyn Fellow in Social Policy Anna Coote, Research Fellow Sarah Spencer and our graphic designer James Sparling. Susan Harkness provided invaluable help in the preparation of chapter 1. We have also been greatly helped by a number of interns and volunteers: Rachel Abrams, Rachel Foran, Dominic Johnson, Daniel Pearl, Simon Preston and Hyong Yi.

We are very grateful to the authors of the Commission's 13 issue papers. In addition, a number of people were kind enough to help with our visits around the country: thanks to Dr David Donnison (Glasgow), Professor Nicholas Deakin (Birmingham), Dr Andy Pithouse (Cardiff), Professor Bryan Robson (Manchester), Professor Denis Kavanagh (Nottingham), Professor John Veit Wilson (Newcastle), Dr Ian Forbes (Southampton), Bryan Heading (East Anglia), and Alan Sinclair of the Wise Group (Glasgow). The Department of Trade Union Studies, MANCAT, provided invaluable help in the preparation of the Commission's discussion pack.

The Commission was established independently of the Labour Party, but the Shadow Secretary of State for Social Security, Donald Dewar, provided encouragement throughout the 18 months of our deliberations.

Thanks are due to the Union of Communication Workers, and especially Dave and Pat Ward, for providing us with excellent facilities for a weekend meeting in Bampton, Oxfordshire.

Last but not least, Sarah Westcott led a helpful and friendly team at Vintage. She also secured the time of Pascal Cariss, who provided invaluable editorial help when it was most needed.

EXECUTIVE SUMMARY

Introduction

This book explains how the strengths of this country, and above all the untapped talent of its people, can be the basis of national renewal. It sets out a long-term strategy, designed to build a radical consensus for change; it is not a manifesto for one Parliament or one party.

We start from the proposition that the UK need not be the tired, resentful, divided and failing country it is today. The problem is not just that poverty, unemployment, poor education and ill health are a blight on so many lives. There is a wider malaise to be addressed which concerns our capacity as a nation to understand and to reverse what seems to many people to be inexorable decline.

The values of social justice are for us essential (pages 17–20). They are: the equal worth of all citizens, their equal right to be able to meet their basic needs, the need to spread opportunities and life chances as widely as possible, and finally the requirement that we reduce and where possible eliminate unjustified inequalities. Social justice stands against fanatics of the free market economy; but it also demands and promotes economic success. The two go together.

Four propositions run through our policy proposals in chapters 4 to 8:

- We must transform the welfare state from a safety net in times of trouble to a springboard for economic opportunity.

- We must radically improve access to education and training, and invest in the talent of all our people.
- We must promote real choices across the life-cycle for men and women in the balance of employment, family, education, leisure and retirement.
- We must reconstruct the social wealth of our country. Social institutions, from the family to local government, must be nurtured to provide a dependable social environment in which people can lead their lives.

Chapter 1: The State of the Nation

For generations, we have grown up to believe that our children would be better off than ourselves. But today, for many people, that assumption has been shattered. Old evils of homelessness and pauperism have returned; new evils of insecurity have emerged. The causes for concern are clear, the need for change unanswerable:

- Nearly two-thirds of people live in households where income is less than the average, and one in three children now grows up in poverty (pages 28–33).
- One in five men of working age are not in employment, more than one million people are long-term unemployed, and earnings inequality is greater than at any time since 1886 (pages 33–39).
- One in five 21-year-olds has problems with basic maths and one in seven with basic reading and writing; Japanese and German students are twice as likely to achieve the equivalent of two A levels as an English student (pages 39–42).
- The poorest children in Britain are twice as likely to die from respiratory illness and more than four times as likely to be killed by a car as those from the top social class (pages 42–47).
- Crime is now the UK's fourth largest industry; the number of drug addicts has gone up 14 fold since 1973 (pages 47-50); and racially-motivated violence is estimated to have risen faster than almost all other forms of crime over the last decade (pages 50–52).

Chapter 2: Diagnosis: the UK in a Changing World

For 15 years, the Conservative Party has tried to reverse UK decline through the application of free-market economics. The result has been a vicious circle of economic weakness, social division and political centralisation. But the UK's problems are not simply the fault of the Conservatives; the causes stretch back before 1979.

The UK is suffering from a failure to keep up with three great revolutions that are transforming our world. There is no going back to the stability and security of the 1950s and 1960s.

The *economic revolution* is a global revolution of finance, competition, skill and technology (pages 64–77). Macroeconomic power is now shared at the European level rather than held by individual nations. Competition is based on innovation and 'value-added', which depends on the skills of every person in an organisation. The notion of a 'job for life' has disappeared, and employment insecurity affects us all.

The *social revolution* is a revolution of women's life-chances, of family structures and of demography, and it has enormous implications for men as well (pages 77–84). Employers and government need to catch up with the changes. Social renewal demands that we build an inclusive society, where rights carry responsibilities, and individuals have the chance to realise their potential.

The *political revolution* is a challenge to old assumptions of Parliamentary sovereignty, and to the growing centralisation of government power (pages 84–90). Political renewal demands that government be decentralised and democratised – people want to have more say about the things that are important in their lives, from schools to pensions, and government should use its power to devolve responsibility to individuals and communities. But the UK must also play an active and positive role in shaping the European Union.

Chapter 3: Prescription: A Tale of Three Futures

We need to decide a new direction for our country. Only then will the detailed policy questions fit into a coherent framework. There are three options on offer: we could be Investors, Deregulators or Levellers.

Investors' Britain: Investors combine the ethics of community with the dynamics of a market economy (pages 96–106). They believe that the extension of economic opportunity is not only the source of economic prosperity but also the basis of social justice. This demands strong social institutions, strong families and strong communities, which enable people and companies to grow, adapt and succeed. Investment in people is the top priority. Investors see security, not fear, as the basis for renewal. They argue we must engage with change – in the home or at work, in local government or in Europe – if we are to extend social justice.

Deregulators' Britain: Deregulators dream of a future in which dynamic entrepreneurs, unshackled by employment laws or social responsibilities, create new businesses and open up new markets (pages 106–110). Theirs is a future of extremes, where the rich get richer and the poor get poorer, and where the rewards for success are matched only by the risks of failure. Economically, it depends upon the unceasing drive for competitiveness through ever-cheaper production and the pursuit of short-term profit; socially, upon the reduction of public services and public spending; politically, on a logic of centralisation, destroying institutions that stand between law-making government and individual decisions in the marketplace.

Levellers' Britain: The Levellers are pessimists, who do not see how we can turn the economy round, and in any case argue that economic renewal should not be the concern of a Commission on Social Justice (pages 110–113). They say our job is to protect the poor from economic decay. The Levellers share many of the aspirations of the Investors, but they have different strategies to achieve these ambitions. They believe that we should try to achieve social justice primarily through the tax and benefits systems.

- We must radically improve access to education and training, and invest in the talent of all our people.
- We must promote real choices across the life-cycle for men and women in the balance of employment, family, education, leisure and retirement.
- We must reconstruct the social wealth of our country. Social institutions, from the family to local government, must be nurtured to provide a dependable social environment in which people can lead their lives.

Chapter 1: The State of the Nation

For generations, we have grown up to believe that our children would be better off than ourselves. But today, for many people, that assumption has been shattered. Old evils of homelessness and pauperism have returned; new evils of insecurity have emerged. The causes for concern are clear, the need for change unanswerable:

- Nearly two-thirds of people live in households where income is less than the average, and one in three children now grows up in poverty (pages 28–33).
- One in five men of working age are not in employment, more than one million people are long-term unemployed, and earnings inequality is greater than at any time since 1886 (pages 33–39).
- One in five 21-year-olds has problems with basic maths and one in seven with basic reading and writing; Japanese and German students are twice as likely to achieve the equivalent of two A levels as an English student (pages 39–42).
- The poorest children in Britain are twice as likely to die from respiratory illness and more than four times as likely to be killed by a car as those from the top social class (pages 42–47).
- Crime is now the UK's fourth largest industry; the number of drug addicts has gone up 14 fold since 1973 (pages 47-50); and racially-motivated violence is estimated to have risen faster than almost all other forms of crime over the last decade (pages 50–52).

Chapter 2: Diagnosis: the UK in a Changing World

For 15 years, the Conservative Party has tried to reverse UK decline through the application of free-market economics. The result has been a vicious circle of economic weakness, social division and political centralisation. But the UK's problems are not simply the fault of the Conservatives; the causes stretch back before 1979.

The UK is suffering from a failure to keep up with three great revolutions that are transforming our world. There is no going back to the stability and security of the 1950s and 1960s.

The *economic revolution* is a global revolution of finance, competition, skill and technology (pages 64–77). Macroeconomic power is now shared at the European level rather than held by individual nations. Competition is based on innovation and 'value-added', which depends on the skills of every person in an organisation. The notion of a 'job for life' has disappeared, and employment insecurity affects us all.

The *social revolution* is a revolution of women's life-changes, of family structures and of demography, and it has enormous implications for men as well (pages 77–84). Employers and government need to catch up with the changes. Social justice demands that we build an inclusive society, where rights responsibilities, and individuals have the chance to realise potential.

The *political revolution* is a challenge to old assumptions of Parliamentary sovereignty, and to the growing centralisation of government power (pages 84–90). Political renewal requires that government be decentralised and democratised. People want to have more say about the things that affect their lives, from schools to pensions, and government must use its power to devolve responsibility to individuals and communities. But the UK must also play an active and constructive role in shaping the European Union.

The policy chapters detail how we think a future of economic opportunity, social cohesion and political renewal – the Investors' future – can be achieved.

Chapter 4: Investment:
Adding Value Through Lifelong Learning

Lifelong learning is at the heart of our vision of a better country. By investing in skills, we help people realise their potential, raise their capacity to add value to the economy, take charge of their own lives and contribute to their families and communities. 'Thinking for a living' is not a choice but an imperative. We set out six priorities for policy:

- **Universal pre-school education** for 3- and 4-year-olds, coupled with new investment in childcare. 85 per cent of 3-year-olds and 95 per cent of 4-year-olds should be in good quality, pre-school education (pages 122–128).
- **Basic skills** for all children through literacy and numeracy targets for 7-year-olds. Basic skills programmes should also target people who are long-term unemployed (pages 128–130).
- **High achievement for every young person** through a unified qualifications system that ends the divide between education and training for 14- to 19-year-olds and allows every young person to balance academic and vocational study according to aptitude and interest (pages 131–134).
- **Training investment** by employers. All but the smallest organisations should be required to invest a minimum proportion of total payroll in training (pages 134–136).
- **Expansion of university education**, with a new and fairer funding system (pages 136–141).
- **A Learning Bank** to support lifelong learning. The long-term goal should be to ensure that over the course of their life every individual has access to the equivalent of 3 years' education and training beyond A level or its equivalent. The Learning Bank would raise public and private capital, and fund education and training from contributions by government, employers and individuals (pages141–147).

Chapter 5: Opportunity: Working for a Living

Paid or unpaid, work is central to our lives. The unpaid work of parents and carers underpins the economy, paid work is inseparable from individual opportunity. We explain why government must commit itself to a modern form of full employment and explain the conditions for achieving it (pages 153–158). We set out proposals to achieve three goals: more demand for labour, a fairer and more efficient distribution of employment and unemployment, and fairer rewards for employment.

Increasing the demand for labour. The UK government should pursue policies at international, European and national levels to increase demand in a sustainable way, particularly by increasing both public and private investment (pages 163–165). In the tradeable sector, high productivity growth will mean low employment growth. It is in the non-tradeable sector where job growth must come, and on which our quality of life depends; there is no shortage of work to be done (pages 165–170).

Fair and efficient distribution of unemployment and employment. We propose a new Jobs, Education and Training strategy (JET) to get the long-term unemployed and lone mothers back to work (pages 172–182). JET would have six goals:

- To create a re-employment service to match employee aspirations and employment opportunities.
- To use training and education to improve people's employability.
- To sponsor 'micro-entrepreneurs' with the talent to move from unemployment to self-employment.
- To help lone parents find good childcare facilities.
- To encourage intermediate labour markets in areas of economic hardship.
- To use wage subsidies to reconnect the registered long-term unemployed to rewarding jobs.

Men and women must be able to balance work and family at different stages in the life-cycle. We must:

- Reduce the segregation between 'men's jobs' and 'women's jobs' (pages 185–188).
- Promote family-friendly employment for men and women (pages 188–191).
- Encourage a reduction in working hours for full-time workers (pages 191–194).
- Combat discrimination and promote equal opportunities (pages 194–197).

Rewarding employment. Paid work should be – but too often is not – a route to an adequate income, social networks and personal fulfilment. Intelligent regulation can help make the workplace and the economy more efficient and more just.

We consider the problem of the UK's uncoordinated pay bargaining system and warn of the danger earnings inflation poses to employment. A national minimum hourly wage is vital for four reasons: it would stop exploitation, save money on benefits, properly value poorly paid workers' skills, and promote investment in people (pages 200–207). Minimum legal rights at work will promote 'fair flexibility' and level out the playing-field for part-time workers (pages 207–209). We argue the case for greater democracy at the workplace, to create the trust necessary for greater efficiency. Trade unions have a vital role to play in defending individuals and creating successful enterprises (pages 209–212). We also argue the case for the development of works councils and employee share-ownership trusts (pages 213–216). As the basis for a labour market which is both fair and flexible, the UK should opt in to the Social Chapter.

Chapter 6: Security: Building an Intelligent Welfare State

The post-war welfare state offered security against the risks of industrial society, primarily the loss of the male breadwinner's wages through unemployment or retirement. Economic and social change creates a new need for the security which only a welfare state can offer: but it must be an intelligent welfare state, able to help people negotiate unpredictable changes within both family and workplace. The welfare state must enable people to achieve self-improvement and self-support. It must offer a hand-up, not just a hand-out.

Objectives for Social Security. The social security system is part of a mixed economy of welfare. The system of benefits, tax allowances and private provision should serve six objectives:

- Prevent poverty where possible and relieve it where necessary.
- Protect people against risks arising in the labour market and from family change.
- Redistribute resources from richer to poorer members of society.
- Redistribute resources of time and money over people's life-cycles.
- Encourage personal independence.
- Promote social cohesion.

Financial security for people of working age. Work and welfare go together. It is essential to enable both men and women to move from welfare to work. In place of a benefits system which helps to keep poor people poor, we need a transformation in welfare to enable people to earn their way out of poverty and find security in an increasingly insecure world. Means-testing, the Deregulators' panacea, will not work: means-tested benefits are not claimed, they are expensive to administer, they encourage dependence on benefits by trapping people on welfare, they penalise saving, and they provide disincentives for women to take paid work. A Minimum Income Standard should be set as a benchmark for employment and social security policy (page 225).

Welfare reform can promote personal independence and produce significant savings to the Exchequer. But it requires a revolution in the benefits system and building up a **modern social insurance system** (pages 226–245) tailored to changing employment risks and family needs. Modern social insurance will offer help during unemployment (part-time as well as full-time), maternity leave, sickness and retirement; and it will eventually offer help with lifelong learning and parental leave. Social insurance is more efficient and fair than private insurance; it rewards personal effort; balances rights with responsibilities; and has a unique role in helping people distribute income across increasingly varied life-cycles.

A part-time unemployment benefit should be set up to match the needs of part-time workers. We examine ways to reform availability for work tests, including the requirement that, providing there is adequate childcare, mothers of school-age children should be available for at least part-time work if they want to claim benefit. We look at the why and how of social insurance for family responsibilities, and the future of benefits for disabled people.

In the medium term, improvements to means-tested benefits can help our welfare to work strategy (pages 245–258). The interaction of Income Support and Family Credit makes work a risk not worth taking. We show how government can change the welfare state to make work pay.

Wholesale tax benefit integration or negative income tax does not offer a way forward (pages 258–261), but we consider the case for a Citizen's Income and for the development of a Participation Income alongside modern Social Insurance (pages 261–265).

Security for Retirement and Older Age. The traditional approach to the eradication of pensioner poverty – raising the basic pension – is expensive. It would help pensioners who do not claim Income Support, but not the 1.5 million already on Income Support. We propose a new **pension guarantee**, a form of tax-benefit integration for pensioners to supplement the basic pension and raise pensioner income to a guaranteed level (pages 267–272). The guarantee could be based on pension income alone, or it could also take account of income from other savings.

For future pensioners, we propose a **universal second pension** (pages 272–281):

- Every employee or self-employed person would belong to a second pension scheme of their choice.
- Working people and their employer would make a minimum pension contribution.

- The universal second pension could be based on extending and improving the State Earnings Related Pension Scheme (SERPS) or a range of pensions including a new National Savings Pensions Plan (NSPP).
- Better regulation of personal and occupational pensions is essential (pages 281–283).

A common basic pension age of 65 for men and women should be gradually phased in, with savings used to help the most vulnerable groups (pages 283–285).

Health and Community Care. The health gap between social classes, regions and communities is neither inevitable nor acceptable. Enabling everyone to enjoy the best possible health, and to receive the treatment and care they need, is an important part of a just society. We support measures to promote good health and reduce health inequalities, including improved equality of access. We explain why we reject proposals for an earmarked 'health tax' (page 292) and argue that the question of priorities within inevitably limited resources must be properly addressed (pages 292–295). Finally, we consider the growing need for community care, proposing a fairer funding system now and more adequate insurance against the need for long-term care in the future.

Chapter 7: Responsibility: Making a Good Society

A good society depends not just on the economic success of the individual, but the 'social capital' of the community. Investment in social institutions, including good quality public services, is as important as investment in economic infrastructure. Communities do not become strong because they are rich; they become rich because they are strong. At the centre of the Investors' strategy is the belief not only that we owe something to each other, but that we gain from giving to each other. This is the heart of a moral community.

We start with the smallest social institutions, families. Government should develop policies for families to ensure that children grow up in an environment that meets their needs, that women are able to share financial responsibility for their children, and men to share the emotional and practical responsibilities of parenthood (pages 310–313). We explain why **Child Benefit** should be increased, but also taxed for parents paying income tax at the higher rate (pages 313–317). We propose reforms to the child-support system (pages 317–320) and a new statement of parents' responsibilities (pages 320-322).

Community Regeneration. Building strong communities must start from the bottom up (pages 323–340). Disadvantaged people living in disadvantaged places pay the highest price for economic and social failure. The best approach is to build linkages between economic, physical and social capital, through the talent of local people. A National Community Regeneration Agency should coordinate local efforts; Community Development Trusts should build capacity in the local community; and small-scale credit unions must nurture community capital, while community action must make larger-scale investment work for local people.

Housing. It is a disgrace that nearly half a million people are homeless, over a million more people live in homes which are officially unfit for habitation, and 800,000 homes are standing empty. We discuss the gradual release of local authorities' receipts from council house sales; the establishment of Local Housing Companies to develop and manage social rented housing; the creation of a national Housing Bank; and the development of a more flexible housing market to match new workplace and family conditions (pages 340–350). We argue for sustained efforts to refurbish unfit properties, and for the encouragement of tenant participation and management.

Local democracy and civic leadership are the roots of a thriving civic culture. Government in the UK is over-centralised and unaccountable. Power must be decentralised to Scotland and Wales, and where appropriate to the English regions. Local authorities must be able to exercise effective power and invest resources, but must themselves devolve power too. Power must wherever possible be returned from unelected quangos to elected bodies, and unelected bodies must be made accountable. Public services, which are a vital foundation of opportunity and security, must be strengthened and new rights for citizens matched by a recognition of the role of public-service professionals (pages 350–361).

Citizens' Service. A national voluntary community service scheme primarily for people aged between 16 and 25 should be set up. It would promote education for citizenship, break down social barriers, and develop participants' self-confidence and abilities. Participants should include young employees seconded by their employers, students between school and higher or further education and people who are unemployed. Volunteers should receive a weekly allowance and credits to pay for further learning (pages 361–369).

Chapter 8: Taxation: Investing in Ourselves

Only when questions of principle, objectives and structure have been resolved can detailed issues of finance be decided. There are many ways to fund the investment this country needs – economic growth, changing priorities, getting people off welfare and into work, public/private partnerships, and sharing costs with users and employers (pages 374–376).

Taxation will remain an important source of funding for public action; taxes are the contribution we all make towards building a better society. But we are conscious that low- and middle-income families are facing higher tax rises than ever before. It is not our job to make short-term suggestions about tax policy; we are concerned with the structure.

We have not proposed a new tax system. We believe government should set ten principles for tax policy (pages 378–384). Taxes must be necessary, fair, acceptable, clear, and levied on a broad base. They must contribute to economic performance and employment, respect individuals' independence and be easy to understand and collect. The tax system must also take account of capital, business and labour mobility across the global economy.

We also examine five important structural problems with the tax system, and what can be done about them (pages 384–391). We look at the problems of high tax on low pay; unfair tax allowances; disincentives to employment; high tax rates paid by the majority and low tax paid by the richest; and unfair taxation of inheritance.

There is growing debate about 'hypothecated taxes' (pages 391–393). We support reforms to the national accounts to identify investment clearly. We are, however, sceptical about plans to hypothecate recurrent expenditure, but propose the establishment of a hypothecated **National Renewal Fund**, containing a proportion of tax revenues, to fund important capital-investment projects.

Throughout the European Union, there is growing interest in shifting taxation from earnings to environmental pollution – taxing 'bads' like pollution and not 'goods' like labour (pages 393–395). The case is strong, although the effects on people with below-average income must be carefully considered. However, there is scope for a major energy-efficiency drive to protect the environment.

Conclusion: The Need for Change

The UK needs new direction. We need to be clear about our values, understand the forces shaping change, create our own vision of the future – and then set out to achieve it. Our fate is not determined; we can bridge the gap between the country we are and the country we would like to be.

INTRODUCTION

*'I know the Government have made a mess
of things ... but is there any alternative?'*

That question, asked by a sixth-former in Birmingham, embodies
the reasons why the Commission on Social Justice needed to be
set up, and the substance of what it has tried to do. Wherever we
have travelled over the last eighteen months, from Southampton
to Belfast to Newcastle to Glasgow, we have heard one thing
clearly and constantly: people believe that the country is on the
wrong track, and want to know how things could be better.

Some of the problems that concern people can be straightfor-
wardly expressed in figures. One in three children grows up in
poverty; one in five men of working age is not working; one in
seven 21-year-olds has trouble with basic reading; more than one
million pensioners live on Income Support or less. But beyond
such data – and there are many alarming facts of this kind in the
pages that follow – there is a less definite disquiet and depression
widespread in Britain. Many people who have the chance to
work hard and to make themselves and their families better off
are insecure about the future for themselves and their children,
anxious about their jobs, scared about crime, worried about old
age, and disillusioned with politics. Although nearly three times
wealthier as a nation than we were in 1950, we are certainly not
three times happier as a society.

Our aims have been to give an account of things as they are
and of the problems that our country faces; to develop a vision of
social reform and economic renewal that will be fit for the new

century; and to suggest strategies that will help to make that design a reality. This report offers the results of our work.

Two things became clear to us at the outset. One was the size of the problem. There is no simple solution, a 'quick fix', for the UK's difficulties, and if politicians or others suggest that there is, no one should believe them. The other very clear fact is that our world is so different from that which William Beveridge addressed fifty years ago, and it is now changing so fast, that there is no way in which the prescriptions that suited an earlier time can merely be renewed, however much goodwill, money or technical sophistication one might hope to call up in their support. Beveridge counted on more or less steady and full employment; today, we face mass structural unemployment and underemployment. Beveridge assumed that a woman's place was in the home; today, women form nearly half the workforce. Fifty years ago, most elderly people were poor; today, there is a widening gulf between the significant number of elderly people who are reasonably well off and those wholly dependent on state support. In addition, after the experience of the Second World War people were prepared to accept that Whitehall knew best – or, at least, it was not unreasonable of Whitehall to think that they did. Today, people do not want to see themselves as simply the recipients of planners' benevolence and ingenuity, but to make more decisions for themselves.

Beyond all the many changes within the UK, it is also vital to stress that the future of this country is even more radically affected than it used to be by what happens elsewhere. In terms of the economic environment, for instance, one billion Chinese are entering the international labour market for the first time, two-thirds of our trade is with other countries in the European Union, and the power of financial speculators cannot be tackled by one country alone. The idea that Britain can 'go it alone' in comfortable, or even austere, self-sufficiency is no more than a desperate dream.

This report and its schemes for national renewal are directed to the longer term. The proposed strategies look ahead to 2010 and beyond; it would be impossible to try to put them all into effect immediately. This time-scale affects our proposals. As an independent Commission, set up by the Opposition but with no official standing within the Labour Party, we have not tried to create a detailed programme of spending and revenue-raising for the next few years. To do so would in any case be inappropriate, given our long-term perspective: our attempt has been to develop a strategy strong enough to give the country a new direction, but flexible enough to cope with rapidly changing conditions. No one should trivialise the serious questions we discuss by trying to pretend that our ideas for change over ten to fifteen years are in fact proposals which we believe should be implemented immediately and simultaneously.

We have not written a programme for one parliament; we offer a design, not a manifesto. On the other hand, we have seen it as part of our task to go into some detail about key reforms. In trying to conceive a better future for Britain, we consider it a mark of good faith to offer practicable designs and not merely righteous aspirations.

What is Social Justice?

In Chapter 3 of this report we lay out three different styles of economic and social strategy for the coming decade and after, and among these we believe the most attractive is also the most optimistic and the most ambitious. This choice certainly rests on more than economic forecasts and analyses of pension plans. It is based on a conviction which we share among ourselves and, we hope, with many others, that the UK need not be a tired, resentful, divided, failing country. We believe that under more imaginative policies it can be both fairer and more successful: indeed, that it must be both fairer and more successful if it is to be either. We are a commission on social justice, not on economic success, but it is a constant theme of this report that there is not an opposition between these two aims. On the contrary, each demands the other.

In the first of our interim reports, *The Justice Gap*, we discussed the content of the ideal of social justice, and we claimed that it could be defined in terms of a hierarchy of four ideas. First, the belief that the foundation of a free society is the equal worth of all citizens, expressed most basically in political and civil liberties, equal rights before the law, and so on. Second, the argument that everyone is entitled, as a right of citizenship, to be able to meet their basic needs for income, shelter and other necessities. Basic needs can be met by providing resources or services, or helping people acquire them: either way, the ability to meet basic needs is the foundation of a substantive commitment to the equal worth of all citizens. Third, self-respect and equal citizenship demand more than the meeting of basic needs: they demand opportunities and life chances. That is why we are concerned with the primary distribution of opportunity, as well as its redistribution. Finally, to achieve the first three conditions of social justice, we must recognise that although not all inequalities are unjust (a qualified doctor should be paid more than a medical student), unjust inequalities should be reduced and where possible eliminated.

One important question is how far such a vision of social justice can coexist with economic success, or even with economic survival, in a competitive world. Social justice is indeed an ideal in its own right, but we believe in addition that the economic success of our country requires a greater measure of social justice. Our report bears witness to this at every turn. Squalor and crime carry enormous economic as well as social costs; unemployment uses resources simply to sustain people who might sustain themselves and contribute to the economy. Even in times of fuller employment the UK has wasted, as it continues to waste, much potential achievement through an inefficient and divisive education system which offers little to the very young, fails to educate most youngsters to A-level standard, and sorts people as soon as it can into social classes in which, for the most part, they stay for the rest of their lives. For these and many other reasons which this report makes clear, there will be no solid economic success without more social justice.

At the same time, it is also true that we cannot have social justice without a decent measure of economic success. Social benefits have to be paid for, and the economy will not sustain limitless transfers from a diminishing section of society to an increasing class of the destitute. More fundamentally, what has most power to sustain a general desire for social justice and for the common good is hope, and a widely shared sense of security. Of course, there can be justice in shared suffering, and social solidarity can flourish under deprivation in face of an external enemy. But this is not an appropriate recipe for the UK's future. In the coming years, the spirit that favours a more just society is likely to flourish only if we can free ourselves from the resentment and frustration that stem from economic failure.

Granted all this, we do not see social justice as an ideal that condemns modern commercial society and people's aspirations for a more comfortable and interesting life for themselves and for their families. But there are various ideas and outlooks that social justice stands against. It is opposed, for instance, to the lazy cynicism which supposes that even if the poor do not actually deserve to be poor, it is probably safer to treat them as though they did; and to the stupid respect for greed which helps some to believe (despite the evidence) that talented top managers will do their best only if they are paid fifty or a hundred times more than their employees. Social justice stands against fanatics of the market economy, who forget that a market is a social reality which itself requires trust, order, goodwill and other forms of support – support that people will very reasonably withhold unless they believe that the order under which they live has some concern for them and offers them chances that are, within the limits of the possible, fair.

There is also, however, another image, only too familiar, of social justice as a subtractive and inhibiting force which busies itself, for reasons ranging from asceticism to sheer envy, in taking away things from successful people and giving them to the unsuccessful (minus the considerable bureaucratic costs of doing so). This is not social justice as we understand it. Social justice does indeed attend to the needy – that is part of its point – but in doing so it can be an enabling force for everybody. It is, moreover, something that society requires because everyone's quality of life is dependent in part on a high degree of social well-being. This conclusion, that social justice is not simply a moral ideal but an economic necessity, is at the heart of this report.

This conclusion is not a product of sociological theory, nor is it a piece of political rhetoric. It is a plain fact, obvious to anyone who has recognised the discouragement, the cynicism and the anger which seep through the structure of our society, and which make people uneasy even if they are themselves more successful than others. They are uneasy because they fear for their own and their children's future in such a society, and because, whatever their personal prospects, they do not really want to run their lives or their enterprises in a brightly lit and heavily guarded tent, surrounded by a wasteland of bitterness and disappointment.

Four Propositions on Social Justice

Four propositions are central to our analysis and our recommendations. We believe that they must be at the centre of any serious attempt to tackle the UK's problems.

1. *We must transform the welfare state from a safety net in times of trouble to a springboard for economic opportunity. Paid work for a fair wage is the most secure and sustainable way out of poverty.*

We need a new definition of welfare. The post-war welfare state was passive when people were active – above all when they (or in the case of married women, their husbands) were at work. It provided cash benefits to the unemployed, on the assumption that an economic upswing would restore full employment. Today, however, the welfare state needs to be active throughout people's lives, helping them to make and take opportunities, to extend security, and to promote responsibility. The welfare state is as much about high-quality services as adequate cash benefits. It must help develop a new relationship between paid and unpaid work, where the value of caring for children and other family members is properly recognised. People want to earn a living and the job of the welfare state is to help people who are in a position to do paid work to get off welfare. A high social security budget is a sign of economic underperformance, not social justice.

20

2. We must radically improve access to education and training, and invest in the talent of all our people.

Mass education is still Britain's greatest failure. It simply cannot be true that while eight out of ten Korean or French schoolchildren can reach university entrance standard, only three or four out of ten children in the UK can. We have an education and training system designed for an élite, not the majority; we now, finally, need to insist that high standards of performance can be stimulated from all children, and that opportunities for lifelong learning should be available to everyone. Education and skills are the route to opportunity, employability and security.

3. We must promote real choices across the life-cycle in the balance of employment, family, education, leisure and retirement.

The post-war generation assumed stable and predictable life-cycles: education followed by paid work and retirement for men, education followed by motherhood as well as (or instead of) employment for women. This assumption has now broken down. Education must last longer than ever before and be taken up at different points in life. Men must take on some of the caring responsibilities previously carried by women. People must be able to strike new balances between paid work, education and family responsibility at different stages in their lives. That requires structures of social insurance, employment and pensions that promote choice and security.

4. We must reconstruct the social wealth of our country. Social institutions, from the family to local government, must be nurtured to provide a dependable social environment in which people can lead their lives. Renewal must come from the bottom up as well as from the top down.

The UK is more divided now than at any time since the 1930s. This emerges in all kinds of indicators: dental care and diet, infant mortality and the risk of suicide, exam results and family break-up. It hurts us all. Socially, crime and the fear of crime diminish our lives. Economically, inequality is very inefficient, whether measured in the costs of unemployment, poor health, or inadequate education. Whatever the strides to extend personal independence, the reality is that we are more and more interdependent. It is by what we do together, as well as what we do on our own, that we determine our future. Our quality of life depends on the quality of the communities in which we live: safe public spaces and affordable transport, respected local government and thriving community organisations, leisure opportunities and cultural development all represent social capital, and that capital has perilously dwindled away. The centralisation of power at Westminster is itself a major obstacle to national renewal. We need to build from the bottom up, by creating structures of power that release the talents and potential of ordinary people. What central government can do for people is limited, but there is no limit to what people and communities can be enabled to do for themselves.

Structure of the Report

In the pages that follow, we examine the state of Britain today, and try to explain it; we chart the new challenges facing this country, and the options for meeting them; and we set out a strategy for national renewal which, while it is neither easy nor painless, does offer the prospect of a country that will be better and not merely different – a country in which the widely shared values of social justice are given practical meaning.

There are, however, two important restrictions on our work. First, although our analysis goes well beyond the borders of the UK, our policy prescriptions do not. We live in what in global terms is a well-off country: the social safety net of the industrial countries helps 100 million people with annual incomes less than about $5,000, but the 1.3 billion poor people in developing countries have average incomes less than $300 per year. International injustice dwarfs the arguments that take place within the industrialised world, but our remit is confined to justice and injustice within the UK. The UK is, however, a member of the European Union, and we must be concerned with developments at the European level.

Second, it was not our job to consider in detail ecological questions of what we should provide and save for posterity. Although we have been very much aware of the ecological constraints on economic development, we could not hope to deal with all the issues raised by the principle of sustainable development, and we do not do so.

The Report is divided into three parts:

Chapter 1 sets out the cause for concern – our inability to remove from the whole population the fear of the 'six great evils' of want, idleness, ignorance, disease, squalor and discrimination, and to extend universal opportunities for financial independence, work, lifelong learning, good health, a safe environment and equal opportunities.

Chapters 2 and 3 examine causes and remedies. Chapter 2 looks at the ways in which the economic, social and political revolutions of our time have left the UK tied down by economic inequality, social anachronism and political centralism. Chapter 3 sets out three different directions for our country, offered by three outlooks we label as those of the Investors, the Deregulators, and the Levellers.

Chapters 4 to 8 set out our policy strategies. Chapter 4 examines the most vital investment of all – in the education and training of all our citizens. Chapter 5 goes to the heart of economic opportunity, and looks at the future of work. Chapter 6 takes up the enduring value of security, and shows how we can build an intelligent welfare state offering security in our fast-changing world. Chapter 7 tackles the question of responsibility, and of how we can strengthen the social institutions that are the basis of a good society. Chapter 8 looks at how we can generate resources to invest in ourselves, and at the principles which should guide taxation policy in future.

In the UK today, economic inequality makes us all poorer, out-of-date social attitudes deny too many people the chance to develop their talents, and political centralism cripples our ability to manage change. The cure is not easy or quick, but it is available. Our standard of living and quality of life depend on new opportunities to earn, learn, save and own; on the security provided by an intelligent welfare state which is designed to help people manage economic and social change; and on the responsibility we owe each other to build strong families and strong communities. This report shows how we can achieve these things.

PART ONE

The UK Today

1

THE STATE OF THE NATION

In January 1994, a 28-year-old Birmingham engineer sent us his payslip. He earns £2.50 an hour – £101 a week. 'I am scared to put the heating on as I would not be able to afford the electric bill,' he told us. 'Please do not tell my employer I wrote to you as I would be straight on the dole.'

In July 1994, water and electricity companies revealed in their annual reports that senior managers' rewards had rocketed since privatisation. Sir Desmond Pitcher, the chairman of North West Water, whose predecessor was earning £47,000 per year four years ago, is now paid £338,000 – £6,500 a week. Share options are often worth even more than salaries, producing paper profits of more than £1 million for Henry Casley, the chief executive, and two other directors of Southern Electricity.[1]

For those at the top, these are the best of times. For those at the bottom, horizons are even narrower than they were a decade ago and the gap between rich and poor is greater than at any time since the 1930s. For most people – those in the middle – insecurity and anxiety are rife.

Comparison with the past is important. In many respects, almost everyone living in the United Kingdom today is better off than their parents and grandparents were.[2] But not in every respect – and we have analysed exactly where the condition of the UK has declined. As important as the comparison with our own past, however, is the comparison with other countries. More young people in the UK today have the chance to go to university than at any time in the past. But newly industrialising countries like Taiwan and Korea, as well as mature economies like Germany and Japan, make an even larger investment in education. Doing better than we used to is not good enough when others set their sights far higher.

But the real comparison – the comparison to shock anyone concerned with the future of this country – is the one between what we are and what we have it in ourselves to become, the gap between potential and performance. Most people in this country are doing less well than they want to and less well than they could, if only they were able to learn more, work more productively (or work at all), live more safely, more securely and more healthily. Too often, opportunities are distributed not on the basis of ability, but on the basis of ability to pay; not because of who you are but of who your parents were; not on what you can offer but on where you live; not on the basis of merit, but on grounds of race or gender. This is what the sixth-form students whom we met at a Birmingham secondary school had in mind when, with only one exception, they said that Britain was an unfair society – and that the first unfairness was class.

We must complete the attack launched by William Beveridge on the 'five great evils' of want, idleness, ignorance, squalor and disease; and we must root out a sixth evil, racial discrimination. But there is a broader agenda, centred on the extension of six great opportunities – opportunities for financial independence, work, lifelong learning, a safe environment, good health and equal treatment. As we measure the evils which remain and the opportunities not yet created, we can begin to judge the scale of the task ahead.

The Evil of Want and the Goal of Financial Independence

For nearly forty years after the Second World War, the income gap between the richest and the poorest in the UK gradually narrowed. That progress has now been reversed.[3] Today, the gap between the earnings of the highest-paid and those of the lowest-paid workers is greater than at any time since records were first kept in 1886.[4] While the best-off have increased their share of total national income, the proportion going to the poorest is

Figure 1.1 – A Few Get Richer
Percentage of total disposable income, adjusted for household size

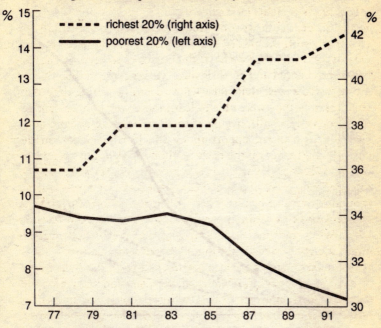

Source: Karen Gardiner 'The Scale of Injustice' *New Economy* Vol 1 Issue 1
(London: IPPR/The Dryden Press, 1994)

shrinking, as Figure 1.1 shows. The bottom half of the population, who received a third of our national income in 1979, now only receive a quarter.[5] Nearly two-thirds of people live in households whose income is below the average.

By contrast, the lucky few have done well. Over the five years to 1992, the average pay of the top directors of the FTSE 100 companies rose by 133 per cent to £535,000 a year, while average earnings rose by only 48 per cent. But high pay does not necessarily reflect high performance: Figure 1.2 shows that as companies' profits fell after 1988, company directors' salaries went on rising.[6]

Under the rule of free-market economics, the so-called 'trickle-down effect' has not happened. In fact, as Figure 1.3 demonstrates, the poor have become poorer. Between 1979 and 1991/2,

Figure 1.2 – Something for Nothing: Top Pay Rockets
1983 = 100

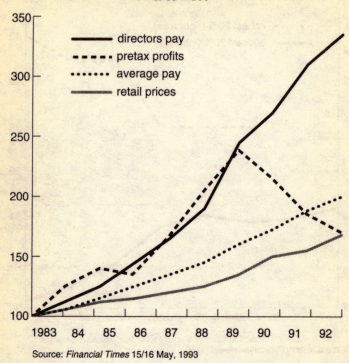

Source: *Financial Times* 15/16 May, 1993

the poorest 10 per cent saw their real incomes *fall* by 17 per cent, from £74 to £61 a week.[7] Despite the recession, the very highest-paid people in London and the South-East increased their earnings by an average of £22,000 a year between 1989 and 1991, while the bottom 50 per cent of earners took an average pay *cut* of more than £200 a year.[8] Men in the bottom tenth of the earnings league are now earning less per hour in real terms than in 1975.[9]

Growing inequalities in pay have been compounded by increasingly unfair taxes. Over the last decade, the poorest 10 per cent of households have lost £156 a year – £3 a week – as a result of increased VAT, National Insurance Contributions and other taxes; the wealthiest 10 per cent have gained £31 a week – £1,612

Figure 1.3 – Inequality is Rising

Change in income 1979–1991/2, adjusted for household size, after housing costs

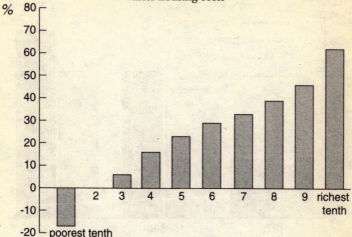

Source: *Households Below Average Income:* a statistical analysis 1979–1991/2 (London, HMSO, 1994)

a year – as a result of income tax cuts.[10] The biggest gains have gone to the top 1 per cent of the population – people with average incomes of more than £120,000 a year – for whom the cumulative gain from tax cuts since 1979 has been a staggering £75-billion.[11] When all taxes are taken into account – VAT and other indirect as well as direct taxes – the poorest tenth of the population pay a *higher* proportion of their income in tax than the richest tenth, 43 per cent versus 32 per cent respectively.[12]

By any measure, poverty has risen fast, as Figure 1.4 shows. Families with children have suffered worst, particularly compared with couples with two earners and no children. In 1979, one in ten children was living in a low-income family; today, poverty hits one in three.[13] Although some on the political Right claim that real poverty no longer exists in this country, Income Support levels are very low indeed: in 1994, two parents with one child aged 10 and another of 14 are expected to pay for everything except the rent from £120.40 a week (£6,260 a year).

Figure 1.4 – Poverty is Rising
Percentage below half average (mean) income, adjusted for household size, after housing costs

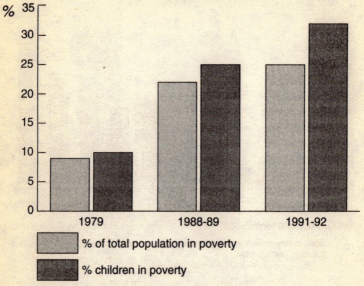

Source: *Households Below Average Income* op cit.

Fifty years ago, being old meant being poor. That is no longer the case: inequality between pensioners is growing fast. Occupational pensions and other savings have produced a substantial rise in the incomes of better-off elderly people: the top two-fifths have seen their real incomes rise by two thirds since 1979, compared to 10 per cent for the bottom tenth[14], as Figure 1.5 shows.

By any measurement, about one-fifth of our population lives in poverty. But doing without is not confined to them. The London Weekend Television *Breadline Britain* survey in 1991 found that at least one of the necessities which make life worth living – hobbies, a holiday, the occasional celebration (each rated 'necessary' by between half and three-quarters of the public) – is simply too expensive for some 21 million people.[15] The average family now has a debt equal to seven weeks' wages, nearly double the level in 1980.[16]

Figure 1.5 – Diverse Fortunes: Pensioner Inequality is Rising
Income change 1979–1992, after housing costs

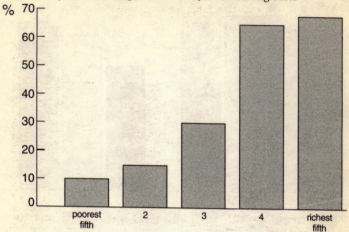

Source: Dilnot et al Pensions Policy in the UK (London: Institute for Fiscal Studies, (1994)

The Evil of Idleness and the Prize of Fulfilling Employment

Over the last forty years the United Kingdom has moved from full employment (for men) to high and lasting levels of unemployment; from a labour market dominated by manufacturing industry and blue-collar jobs to one dominated by services and white-collar jobs; from a workforce that was two-thirds men to one that is nearly half women. In the last twenty years alone, the number of men in full-time employment has dropped by 3.4 million; the number of women in part-time employment increased by over a million.[17]

With the average cost of each unemployed person now estimated at approximately £9,000 a year in benefit payments and lost income tax and contributions,[18] unemployment is costing the nation some £24 billion a year. In July 1994, 2.6 million people were registered as unemployed. Even though registered unemployment has been falling for over eighteen consecutive months, it still remains massively higher than it has during most

Figure 1.6 – Men Not at Work
Working age men in employment, 1977 and 1992

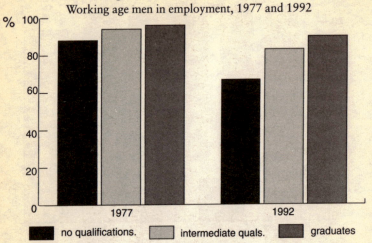

Source: Paul Gregg 'Jobs and Justice', in Edward Balls and Paul Gregg
Work and Welfare (London: IPPR, 1993)

of the post-war period. Unemployment averaged around one third of a million in the 1950s, less than half a million in the 1960s and nearly one million in the 1970s. Throughout the 1980s, however, it averaged 2.7 million.

But registered unemployment only tells part of the story. By the end of 1993, one in four men aged between sixteen and sixty-four was economically inactive, although fewer than half of those not in work were officially registered as unemployed.[19] Although governments treat every decrease in the unemployment numbers as progress, not everyone leaves unemployment for a job: half the unqualified unemployed between the ages of 22 and 54 leave unemployment only to become inactive.[20] In September of 1993, according to some surveys, only half the men of working age were in full-time employment.[21] The speed of change is extraordinary: just twenty years ago, more than three-quarters of men aged between 16 and 64 were in full-time employment. As researchers Stephen Machin and Jane Waldfogel of the London School of Economics concluded: 'the single most dramatic change, and the most important factor driving

Figure 1.7 – More Unemployed, for Longer

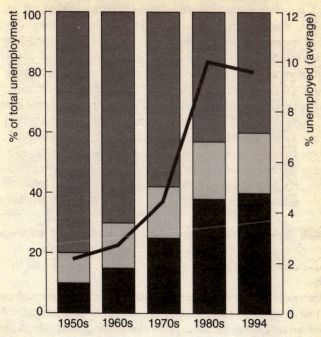

the increased inequality of family incomes from the late 1970s to the early 1990s, is the decline of the male breadwinner.'[22]

Although employment rates have fallen among every group of men, including the best-educated, the decline has been worst among those with no qualifications at all, as Figure 1.6 shows. Less than twenty years ago, nearly nine out of ten men who had left school without qualifications were in employment; today, it is below seven out of ten, and falling.[23]

Most disturbing of all is the growth in long-term unemployment. Between April 1993 and April 1994 unemployment fell by a third of a million, 9 per cent. But long-term unemployment (those without work for more than a year) remained almost static, falling only 30,000 to just over one million. And the number of people unemployed for more than two years *rose* by 47 per cent over the period.[24] As Figure 1.7 demonstrates, the concentration of joblessness is rising as it affects the same people for longer periods.[25] Over the last fifteen years, the chances of an unemployed, unskilled man moving into employment have dropped markedly. The single biggest risk factor in determining whether or not a man will be unemployed this year is not his education, his previous occupation or where he lives, but whether or not he was unemployed in the last year.[26] Women's unemployment, of course, is hidden and much more difficult to define: women looking after children or elderly dependents may not see themselves as unemployed, even though they might want to work, and they are certainly not treated as unemployed by the authorities.

Although unskilled workers are most likely to be unemployed, job insecurity affects all classes. Many management jobs have disappeared as a result of corporate restructuring, and one in three middle-class earners fears that he or she will be made redundant over the next year.[27] Although some managers can take early retirement on a comfortable pension, others find that their only hope is to slide down the occupational ladder. A 51-year-old man who wrote to us from Kent was previously a manager in a large company. He is now on Income Support, taking every training opportunity and seeking help with the job search – but to no avail. He cannot sell his house without incurring enormous debts because its value is less than the outstanding mortgage.

While employment among men is falling rapidly, employment among most women has been growing steadily – as Figure 1.8 shows – with the exception being women without any educational qualifications, those bringing up children on their own and women married to unemployed men. With the exception of Denmark, the UK (together with France and Portugal) now has the highest level of women's employment in the EU.[28]

Figure 1.8 – Women at Work
Working age women in employment, 1977 and 1992

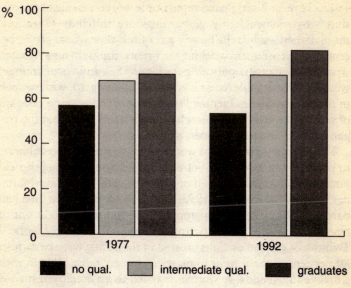

Source: Paul Gregg op cit.

But women are still under-represented in good jobs: whereas 60 per cent of graduate men work as managers or professionals, 60 per cent of graduate women are employed in administrative or clerical jobs. Between 1991 and 2000, another two-thirds of a million women are expected to enter employment, most of it in administrative and professional jobs but almost none of it in management.[29] As the Equal Opportunities Commission stressed to us, however, women from the Afro-Caribbean and Asian communities are unlikely to share in this job growth because they are concentrated in lower-skill jobs. And only one in two lone mothers is in employment; indeed, the UK is the only country in the European Union where lone mothers are *less* likely to be in employment than women with a partner.[30]

British women are also more likely to work part-time than in most other European countries; in 1994, 46 per cent of employed women worked part-time,[31] most of them in low-paid jobs with few pension rights and little prospect of training or promotion. Indeed, there are slightly fewer women working full-time than in 1973.[32] Lower hourly pay for part-time workers is one of the reasons why women's average earnings are still only two-thirds those of men – while the hourly pay of full-time women is 79 per cent of that of men working full-time, for part-time women workers the figure is only 59 per cent.[33] The earnings of younger women without children are, however, catching up, with women in their early thirties earning 90 per cent of the average earnings of men of the same age: it is when children are born that the pay gap between women and men really opens up.[34]

The changes in men's and women's employment are combining to produce a new problem – a widening gap between 'work-rich' families, with one and a half or two jobs, and 'work-poor' families, with no job at all. By 1992, six out of ten employed men had partners who were also in employment; but nearly eight out of ten unemployed men had partners who were also out of work.[35] Two-thirds of the new jobs created in the 1980s were part-time; 80 per cent of them went to married women, most of them with employed husbands. A woman married to an employed man is almost *three times* as likely to be in a job herself as a woman married to a man without a job.[36] The problem is not women taking men's jobs but the combination of a decline in men's employment, new jobs emerging in sectors traditionally dominated by women, and the structure of the benefit system.

Although most people in employment have continued to enjoy increased real earnings, the low-paid have been hit hard, and other conditions at work have often deteriorated. Within retailing thousands of full-time workers have found themselves forced to cut their hours, their pay and their entitlements, or face redundancy. The most effective form of worker representation – trade union membership and recognition – has declined to 31 per cent of all employees in 1993.[37] Fewer workplaces have consultative committees today than in 1984.[38]

These deteriorations have been accompanied by a reduction in employees' legal rights. In 1980, the qualifying period for protection against unfair dismissal and redundancy was raised to two years – it had previously been six months. The result has been a rapid increase in the number of people sacked just before they have been in the job for two years. Citizens' Advice Bureaux found that in order to avoid paying for maternity leave employers were sacking pregnant women with less than two years' service.[39] This practice has now been stopped by legislation bringing the UK into line with European Community standards.

Disabled people are further disadvantaged in the labour market. When the Spastics Society sent two identical CVs to a group of employers, one declaring a disability and the other not, the able-bodied applicant was twice as likely to obtain an interview as the disabled applicant.[40] Although organisations employing at least twenty people have been required for the last fifty years to achieve a quota of 3 per cent of disabled employees, in 1994 fewer than one in three met this target.[41]

The Evil of Ignorance and the Opportunity to Learn

Designed for an élite, the British education system still offers world-class standards to the top 20 per cent of pupils. But despite fifty years of attempted reform, it continues to fail many others.

The problems start before children reach school age. Along with Portugal, the UK has the lowest level of educational provision for under-fives in the European Union. Only one in three British 3- and 4-years olds has access to a publicly funded nursery place, compared with 95 per cent of French children.[42] There are also wide variations from one part of the country to another. In Cleveland, more than nine out of ten 3- and 4-year-olds are in nursery schools or primary classes, while in Bromley fewer than one in five children enjoy similar opportunities.[43]

At primary school, where children are taught in classes larger than in almost any other modern industrial country, the average class size in England rose during the 1980s to nearly twenty-seven.[44] Within the 24-nation Organisation for Economic Cooperation and Development (OECD), only Turkey, Ireland and Japan have equally crowded classrooms. In private schools, however, attended by only 7 per cent of British children, there is one teacher for every eleven pupils.

Figure 1.9 – Bottom of the Learning League

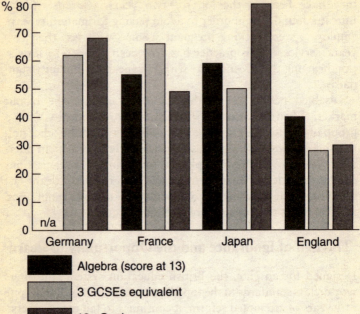

Algebra (score at 13)

3 GCSEs equivalent

18+ Qual.

note: the algebra score is for England and Wales

Sources: Andrew Green and Hilary Steedman *Educational provision, educational attainment and the needs of industry: a review of research for Germany, France, Japan, the USA and Britain* (London: NIESR, 1993); and *The East Asian Miracle* (Oxford: OUP, 1993)

Compared with an 18-year-old in England, Japanese and German students are at least twice as likely to reach the standard of two A levels or more.[45] And, once again, the regional differences in this country are shocking. In Northern Ireland and Wales in 1993, one in six young men left school with no graded exam results; the figure in the South-West was only one in twenty.[46]

In 1991, one in five 21-year-olds had trouble with basic maths, and one in seven with basic reading and writing.[47] People know this costs them dear. As one unemployed man put it: 'I went for a job as an ambulance driver and the writing and spelling let me down on it. It stops me getting a better job, a more secure one.'

Figure 1.10 – Learning Improves Earning

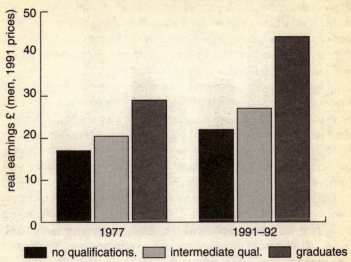

Source: John Schmitt and Jonathan Wadsworth 'The Rise in Economic Inactivity' in Andrew Glyn and David Miliband (eds) *Paying for Inequality* (London: IPPR, 1994)

Poor basic skills cost British companies an estimated £5 billion every year, through clerical errors or cancelled orders.[48]

We refuse to believe that our children are less intelligent than those in other countries. Indeed, Scotland – which has a different education system – produces better results than England, Wales and Northern Ireland. Seven out of ten pupils in English schools fail to achieve better than Grade C in three core subjects (English, maths and science) at the age of sixteen, although more than six out of ten French and German pupils achieve the equivalent grade.[49] Figure 1.9 compares French, German, English and Japanese children in algebra skills at the age of 13, and in examinations at 16 and 18.

Only one in four of Britain's eighteen-year-olds is still in full-time education, compared with more than 60 per cent in Japan and France.[50] Universities continue to be the destination of a disproportionately high number of children from well-off families and private schools.

Although there are now more women than men entering higher education, the legacy of the past can be seen in the educational level of men and women already in the labour force. Four out of ten men whose fathers were in the top social class have a degree, but only one in a hundred of the women whose fathers were unskilled manual workers.[51]

The gap between ourselves and our competitors continues into the workforce. Two-thirds of British workers have no vocational or professional qualification, compared with only one quarter of the German workforce.[52] But those who need training most are least likely to get it: only one-third of those with no educational qualifications have received any recent training, compared with nearly 80 per cent of graduates.[53]

Today, as Figure 1.10 demonstrates, people's life-chances are even more powerfully affected by their education than in the past. Not only are people without qualifications far more likely to be out of work, but the earnings gap between people with a university degree or its equivalent, and those without, is rapidly growing wider.[54]

The Evil of Disease and the Chance of Good Health

Average life expectancy rose by two years between 1981 and 1991, infant mortality continues to fall and preventable diseases have been virtually eradicated. But Scotland and Northern Ireland have the worst heart-disease rates in Western Europe[55] – and women in Glasgow and Belfast have the highest death rates from heart disease of 38 cities and regions in 21 countries studied by the World Health Organisation.[56] British workers appear to have very much higher rates of sickness than their counterparts in competitor countries such as Japan and Germany. In 1986 the Confederation of British Industry (CBI) estimated that absence from work cost UK industry at least £5 billion a year.[57] And throughout the United Kingdom, growing inequality of income is being matched by growing inequality of health. From cradle to grave, social class affects people's health.

Figure 1.11 – Infant Mortality: Class still Counts in Britain

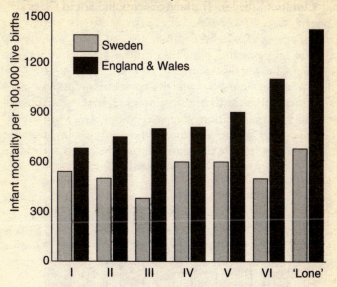

note: 'Lone' refers to births registered in mother's name only
Social classes from I (professional) to VI (unskilled manual)

Source: D Leon, D Vagero and P Otterbiad 1992 'Social class differences
in infant mortality in Sweden: Comparisons with England and Wales'
British Medical Journal Vol 305, 1992

A baby whose father is an unskilled manual worker is one and a half times more likely to die before the age of 1 as the baby of a manager or professional employee. Yet a mortality gap between rich and poor is not inevitable: in Sweden, infant mortality rates are very similar in all social classes, and the worst rate there is still better than the best here, as Figure 1.11 shows.[58] If all British children had the same chance of living as those born to non-manual employees, there would be 700 fewer stillbirths and 1,500 fewer infant deaths each year.[59]

As British children grow up, the poorest children are twice as likely as those from social class I to die from a respiratory illness, more than four times as likely to be killed in a traffic accident – as Figure 1.12 shows – and more than six times as likely to die in a house fire.[60]

Figure 1.12 – Killed by Class:
Children Killed in Traffic Accidents and Social Class

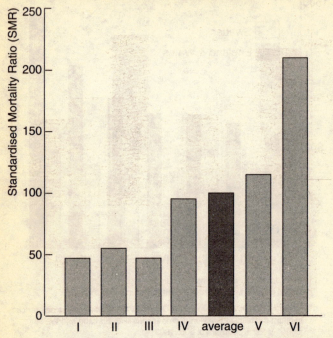

Source: OPCS Occupational Mortality Childhood Supplement DS No. 8 (1988)

Among men aged between 45 and 64, unskilled manual work-ers are nearly three times as likely as professionals to suffer from a longstanding illness which limits their activity.[61] Angina is nearly twice as common among middle-aged manual workers as among non-manual.[62] In Sheffield and Glasgow, people living in the most affluent areas can expect to live eight years longer than those in the most deprived areas.[63]

Poverty should carry a government health warning. In some of the poorest parts of Britain, death rates are now as high as they were forty years ago.[64] Figure 1.13 shows the trend. The damage done by unemployment is also clear. Not only are unemployed people much more likely to suffer a chronic illness or disability, but a middle-aged man made redundant or taking early retire-

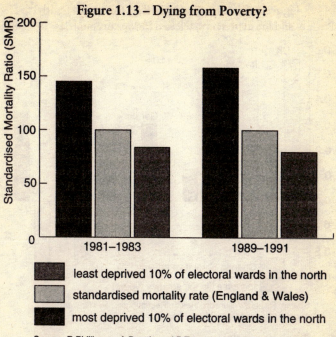

Figure 1.13 – Dying from Poverty?

least deprived 10% of electoral wards in the north

standardised mortality rate (England & Wales)

most deprived 10% of electoral wards in the north

Source: P Phillimore, A Beattie and P Townsend 'Widening inequality of health in Northern England' *British Medical Journal* Vol 308, 1994

ment is twice as likely to die within five years as a man who stays in work.[65] Research leaves no doubt that unemployment also causes, and does not simply result from, deteriorating psychological health. According to studies in Edinburgh and Oxford, unemployed men are between ten and fifteen times more likely to attempt suicide. Most horrifying is the fact that the suicide rate among young men doubled between 1983 and 1990.[66]

But it is not only poverty and unemployment which affect health, and it is not only the poor and unemployed who are suffering. Over the last fifteen years the United Kingdom has slipped from 10th to 17th position in the life-expectancy league of OECD countries[67] – and the widening gap between rich and poor cannot be ignored. Figure 1.14 shows that, in different countries, reduced poverty is associated with improved life expectancy. Dr Richard Wilkinson of the University of Sussex has calculated that

Figure 1.14 – Inequality is Bad for your Health
Poverty and life expectancy, selected European countries, 1975–85

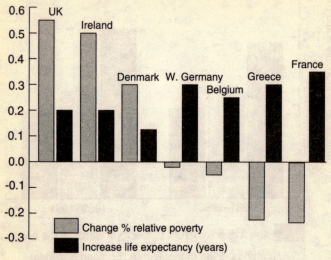

Source: Richard Wilkinson, 'Health, Redistribution and Growth' in
Andrew Glyn and David Miliband op cit.

if income inequality in the UK was reduced to continental levels, we could expect average life expectancy to rise by two years.[68]

The amount spent directly on health care, however, does not appear to affect life expectancy; the USA, for example, devotes a far higher share of national income to medical treatment than Japan,[69] but has a lower life-expectancy. Preventing ill-health is often simple and may save money. Eye-tests, for example, can be used to identify undiagnosed neurological problems as well as eyesight difficulties. Yet the number of people taking a test fell by more than a third after charges were introduced in 1989. Nor is it only the health services that can improve people's health. In Easthall in Glasgow, we learnt about Rosie, a 35-year-old chronic asthma sufferer whose damp council flat had been reno-vated by HeatWise, a charitable company which trains young people in energy efficiency services. Proper insulation cut her fuel bills from £16 to £3 a week, her asthma improved and she suc-ceeded in finding a job.

Figure 1.15 – Richer Economy, Poorer Society?

Source: T Jackson and N Marks Measuring Sustainable Economi
A Pilot Index: 1950–1990 (Stockholm: Stockholm Environment
New Economics Foundation, 1994)

The Evil of Squalor and the Need for a Safe Environment

The economic growth we have achieved has been at the cost of environmental decline. Amongst children, asthma has increased so much that in 1994 one in seven children suffer from it.[70] In order to measure aspects of the social and environmental health of the nation, the New Economics Foundation and the Stockholm Environment Institute have developed an Index of Sustainable Economic Welfare.[71] Between 1950 and 1974, they found that Gross National Product (GNP) in the UK rose in line with welfare. Since 1974, however, the two have diverged, as Figure 1.15 shows. Once pollution, traffic congestion and ill-health are taken into account, Britain's welfare in 1990 was no greater than it was forty years earlier.

In 1992, the private sector built only 144,000 homes, while local authorities and new towns built fewer than 3,000 (and fewer than 200 in London).[72] When the Beveridge Report was

Figure 1.16 – Streets Ahead: Homelessness in Europe 1991/2

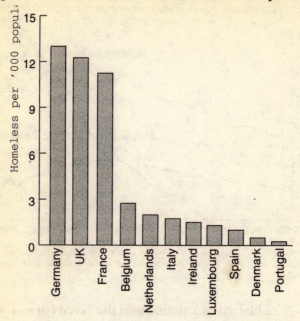

Source: M Daly *Abandoned: Profile of Europe's Homeless People*
(Brussels: FEANTSA, 1993) (Figure for Greece not available)

published, about four in ten households were buying their own home. Today, home ownership is 70 per cent – higher than in most other European Union countries. But during the 1980s, well over one million households were registered as homeless by local authorities.[73] A third of a million people were still registered as homeless in 1992. More than 150,000 young people are homeless; nearly half of them have been in care, and nearly half of the young women had left home because of sexual abuse.[74] The UK is nearly top of the homelessness league shown in Figure 1.16. The extent of homelessness, both registered and hidden, reflects various factors, including the failure to replace council housing stock and the removal of benefit entitlement from 16- and 17-year-olds, as well as the fact that the UK has nearly 4 million more households than it did 30 years ago (in part the prod-

Figure 1.17 – Crime Rises ... and Rises

Notifiable offences per thousand population recorded by the police
(England and Wales)

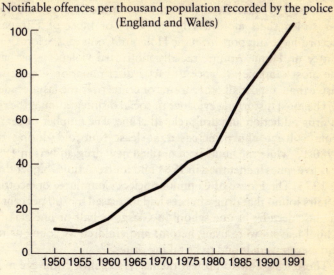

Source: Home Office *Criminal Statistics* (London: Home Office, 1993)

uct of family changes, including later marriage and higher divorce levels).

Home ownership, of course, does not solve every problem. At least 1.3 million homes in Britain, although occupied, are officially 'unfit for human habitation', including one in twenty owner-occupied homes. Despite signs of recovery in the housing market, in early 1994 more than 1.2 million families were still trapped in negative equity, with a mortgage worth more than their home. A third of a million families are in arrears with their mortgage, and over the last three years 145,000 families have had their homes repossessed.[75]

Meanwhile, crime just seems to rise and rise, as the data in Figure 1.17 reveal. In 1991, 1.35 million home burglaries were reported. Crime is now the United Kingdom's fourth largest industry, and its fastest growing, with an estimated annual turnover of £14 billion.[76] One estimate says that one in ten married or cohabiting women suffers from domestic violence, and the number of violent crimes generally has doubled over the last decade.[77] A survey of crime in twenty countries showed that motorists in England and Wales are now more likely to have their car stolen than motorists in the USA or most of Europe.[78] According to a report from the House of Commons Select Committee on Home Affairs, racially motivated violence – perhaps the most tangible evidence of racial discrimination – has risen faster than almost all other forms of crime over the last decade.

The most disturbing evidence of social disintegration is the rise in drug addiction and drug-related crime. The number of deaths from solvent abuse increased at least four-fold during the 1980s,[79] while the number of notified new drug addicts in 1993 was five times higher than in 1981 and fourteen times higher than in 1973. The House of Commons Select Committee on Scottish Affairs found that drug offences had increased by 700 per cent in the last decade; in one school in Glasgow, half of one class of school-leavers were using heroin, and children as young as ten and eleven were found to be taking drugs.[80]

Those least able to protect themselves against crime are most likely to suffer. People living on the poorest council estates are four times more likely to be a victim of crime than people living in affluent suburbs.[81] The average insurance premium in what the insurance companies call 'red-line' areas is £600 a year, compared with £239 for a quiet, affluent part of the same city.[82]

Unemployment does not turn a law-abiding citizen into a criminal. But whatever other factors are at work in rising crime, there now seems to be a clear association between unemployment and crime among young men between the ages of 17 and 25, who account for 70 per cent of all adults convicted or cautioned for a criminal offence.[83] One study of offenders found that only 20 per cent of them were employed at the time of the offence, while 42 per cent of prisoners aged under 21 were unemployed when they were arrested.[84]

In the most disadvantaged parts of the United Kingdom, poverty, unemployment, ill-health and squalor combine to wreck people's chances. It is hardly surprising that communities which are disconnected from the mainstream often do not even bother to vote: in parts of the UK, the turnout for local council elections has fallen to around one in seven people.

The Evil of Racial Discrimination and the Ambition of Equal Opportunities

Racial discrimination is a significant element in economic, social and political injustice in the United Kingdom today: it is a drain on our progress. Whether it takes the form of violent attacks on Asian families or the stereotyped assumptions that some people make about the potential of Afro-Caribbean youngsters, racism wastes people's talent and prospects, creating bitter feelings of resentment and alienation. But racial discrimination and disadvantage are complex problems which affect different groups in different ways. They interrelate with the far larger picture of class and gender inequalities; and they take various forms. The simple divide between black and white – in relation to unemployment or housing – is shocking, but it is not the whole story. Racism is wider than colour-racism and includes discrimination and prejudice against groups defined by their cultures and religions.[85] Yet despite the evidence that it still exists, discrimination does not always succeed; some individuals and groups manager to prosper in spite of it.

An indication of the complexity of class and race differences is that by 1990, white children had become the least likely to remain in full-time education after the age of 16, with Afro-Caribbean and then Bangladeshi children doing a little better, and Chinese, African Asian and African children the most likely to continue their education.[86] Most ethnic minority children from manual workers' families are at least as likely to stay on in education as most middle-class white children. But only one in five Pakistanis aged between 16 and 24, and only one in twenty Bangladeshis, had at least an A level or equivalent qualification, compared with a third of the age-group as a whole.[87] Afro-Caribbean pupils are not only more likely to be excluded for bad behaviour from schools in England and Wales,[88] but also far less likely to go to university.[89]

With the exception of the Chinese and African Asian communities, unemployment hits ethnic minorities even harder than it does white people. In 1992, one in eight Pakistanis who usually worked in white-collar jobs was unemployed, compared with one in fourteen Afro-Caribbeans and only one in thirty-three whites with the same occupational background. Bangladeshis in manual jobs were almost three times more likely to be made redundant than Chinese, African Asian or white manual workers.[90] In a South Glamorgan survey of employment training schemes, white trainees were 50 per cent more likely to get a job on leaving the scheme than black trainees.[91]

While there is evidence that, during the 1980s, East African Asians, Indians and Chinese made real progress in self-employment, educational qualifications, and entry into higher education and the professions, the position of several minority groups is much worse than the national average. White people with at least an A-Level or equivalent are 14 per cent more likely than equally well-qualified Afro-Caribbeans to join the top two occupational groups. While about half of all male employees are in manual work, for Caribbeans, Pakistanis and Bangladeshis the proportion is two-thirds or more, with Bangladeshis grossly over-represented in semi-skilled and unskilled manual work.[92]

One important issue outside the scope of this report concerns immigration policy, which can and too often does have a negative impact on race relations. An unjust approach undermines the security of families from ethnic minority communities who have often been in this country for generations, and exacerbates hostility and prejudice among some white people. The solution is not to remove all immigration controls, but to reform them to stop discrimination on the grounds of race.

Conclusion

No one is satisfied with the state of the UK today – and with good reason. In economic and social terms, the gap between this country and our foreign neighbours is shaming. More important, the gap between what we are and what we could be is a source of frustration and depression. But this report is not just a chronicle of decay; it is also addressed to the causes of and remedies for national malaise. In the next chapter, we explore the roots of economic underperformance and social fragmentation.

Notes

1. 'It's better when you're private', *Financial Times*, 17 July 1994
2. In 1940, of every 1,000 births, 56 babies died; today, the figure is 8. In 1951 four out of ten homes had no bath; today, 99 per cent have one. In 1950 only 30 per cent of 15-year-olds were at school, compared with over 95 per cent today. See Stephen Constantine *Social Conditions 1918–1939* (London: Methuen, 1983)
3. John Hills *Changing Tax* (London: Child Poverty Action Group, 1988). Also Alissa Goodman and Steven Webb *For Richer for Poorer* (London: Institute for Fiscal Studies, 1994)
4. Calculations by the Low Pay Unit. Sources: *British Labour Statistics Historical Abstract: 1886–1968* (London: HMSO, 1971); *New Earnings Surveys* (London: HMSO, 1970–91)
5. Department of Social Security *Households Below Average Income: a statistical analysis 1979–1991/2* (London: HMSO, 1994)
6. Paul Gregg *et al The Disappearing Relationship between Directors' Pay and Company Performance* (London: LSE Centre for Economic Performance, Working Paper 282, 1993)
7. Department of Social Security *Households* op cit
8. Parliamentary Written Answers January 12 1994 (Hansard Vol 235, Cols 190–193) and January 27 1994 (Hansard Vol 236, Cols 353–354)
9. Amanda Gosling, Stephen Machin and Costa Meghir *What Has Happened to Wages?* (London: Institute for Fiscal Studies, 1994)
10. Gordon Brown *Fair is Efficient – a socialist agenda for fairness* (London: Fabian Society, Pamphlet 563, 1994)
11. Ibid
12. *Economic Trends* (London: HMSO, April 1993)
13. Department of Social Security *Households* op cit. These figures do not take account of the hidden poverty experienced by children and their mothers when income is not shared fairly within the family.
14. Andrew Dilnot *et al Pensions Policy in the UK: an economic analysis* (London: Institute for Fiscal Studies, 1994)
15. London Weekend Television *Breadline Britain 1990* (1991)
16. Bank of England *Banking Act Report*, unpublished, 1993
17. Department of Employment *Employment Gazette* (London: HMSO, May 1994)
18. Dennis Snower in the *Financial Times*, 20 April 1994
19. Department of Employment *Employment Gazette* (London: HMSO, April 1994)

20. John Schmitt and Jonathan Wadsworth 'The Rise in Economic Activity' in Andrew Glyn and David Miliband (eds) *Paying for Inequality: The Economic Costs of Social Injustice* (London: IPPR/Rivers Oram Press, 1994)

21. Department of Employment *Employment* op cit (April 1994)

22. Stephen Machin and Jane Waldfogel *The Decline of the Male Breadwinner* (London: LSE Welfare State Programme 103, 1994)

23. Paul Gregg 'Jobs and Justice' in Edward Balls and Paul Gregg *Work and Welfare: Tackling the Jobs Deficit* (London: IPPR, 1993)

24. Unemployment Unit *Working Brief* Issue 55 (London: Unemployment Unit and Youthaid, 1994)

25. Paul Gregg 'Jobs' op cit

26. Jonathan Gershuny and Catherine Marsh 'Unemployment in Work Histories' in Duncan Gallie, Catherine Marsh and Carolyn Vogler (eds) *Social Change and the Experience of Unemployment* (London: Oxford University Press, 1993)

27. *Sunday Times*, 26 June 1994

28. European Commission *Employment in Europe* (Brussels: Commission of the European Communities, 1993)

29. Equal Opportunities Commission *Labour Market Prospects for Women* (Manchester: EOC, 1993)

30. Jo Roll *Lone-Parent Families in the European Communities* (London: European Family and Social Policy Unit, 1992)

31. Department of Employment *Employment Gazette* (London: HMSO, July 1994)

32. Department of Employment *Employment* op cit

33. Department of Employment *New Earnings Survey 1993* (London: HMSO, 1993)

34. Jane Waldfogel *Women Working for Less* (London: LSE Welfare State Programme /93, 1993)

35. Paul Gregg 'Jobs' op cit

36. Ibid

37. Department of Employment *Employment Gazette* (London: HMSO, June 1994)

38. Neil Millward *The New Industrial Relations?* (London: Policy Studies Institute, 1994)

39. National Association of Citizens Advice Bureaux *Job Insecurity: CAB evidence on employment problems in the recession* (London: NACAB, 1993)

40. Eileen Fry *An Equal Chance for Disabled People? A study of discrimination in employment* (London: The Spastics Society, 1986)

41. Bert Massie *Disabled People and Social Justice* (London: IPPR, 1994)
42. Kathy Sylva and Peter Moss 'Learning Before School' in National Commission on Education *Briefings* (London: Heinemann, 1993)
43. Department for Education *Pupils under five years in age in schools in England and Wales* (London: DFE Statistical Bulletin Issue No. 11/93, 1993)
44. Peter Mortimore and Peter Blachford 'The Issue of Class Size' in National Commission on Education *Briefings* (1993) op cit.
45. Andrew Green and Hilary Steedman *Educational provision, educational attainment and the needs of industry: a review of research for Germany, France, Japan, the USA and Britain* (London: National Institute for Economic and Social Research, Report Series No 5, 1993)
46. *Social Trends 1994* (London: HMSO, 1994)
47. Adult Literacy and Basic Skills Unit *The Basic Skills of Young Adults* (London: ALBSU, 1993)
48. Adult Literacy and Basic Skills Unit *The Cost to Industry: Basic skills and the UK workforce* (London: ALBSU, 1993)
49. Green and Steedman *Educational* op cit
50. Ibid
51. Ann Bridgwood and David Savage *General Household Survey* No.22 (London: HMSO, 1993)
52. Green and Steedman *Educational* op cit
53. Duncan Gallie and Michael White *Employee Commitment and the Skills Revolution* (London: Policy Studies Institute, 1993)
54. Schmitt and Wadsworth 'The Rise' op cit
55. British Heart Foundation *Coronary Heart Disease Statistics* (London: BHF, 1994)
56. Report of Monica study conducted by the World Health Organisation, published in *Circulation* (1994). See also the *Guardian*, 12 July 1994
57. Confederation of British Industry *Absence from work: a survey of absence and non-attendance* (London: CBI, 1987)
58. D. Leon, D. Vagero and P. Otterblad 'Social class differences in infant mortality in Sweden: comparisons with England and Wales', *British Medical Journal*, 305 (1992)
59. T. Delamothe 'Social Inequalities in Health', *British Medical Journal*, 303, pp 1046–50 (1991)
60. OPCS Occupational Mortality tables, quoted in Caroline Woodruffe *et al Children, Teenagers and Health: The Key Data* (Buckingham: Open University Press, 1993)

61. E. Breeze, G. Trever and A. Wilmot (eds) *General Household Survey*, OPCS Series GHS 20 (London: HMSO, 1991)

62. S. Pocock *et al* 'Social Class Differences in Ischaemic Heart Disease in British Men', *Lancet ii*, pp 197-201 (1987)

63. Commission on Social Justice *The Justice Gap* (London: IPPR, 1993)

64. P. Phillimore, A. Beattie and P. Townsend 'Widening inequality of health in northern England', *British Medical Journal*, 308 (1994)

65. S. Pocock *et al* 'Social' op cit

66. Richard Wilkinson *Unfair Shares* (London: Barnardo's, 1994)

67. Ibid

68. Richard Wilkinson 'Health, Redistribution and Growth' in Andrew Glyn and David Miliband (eds) *Paying for Inequality: The Economic Cost of Social Injustice* (London: Rivers Oram / IPPR, 1994)

69. John Hills *The Future of Welfare – A guide to the debate* (York: Joseph Rowntree Foundation, 1993)

70. Data from the National Asthma Campaign

71. T. Jackson and N. Marks *Measuring Sustainable Economic Welfare – A Pilot Index: 1950 – 1990* (Stockholm: Stockholm Environment Institute and New Economics Foundation, 1994)

72. Shelter 'The costs of temporary accommodation relative to new build for local authorities' unpublished report (London: Shelter, 1993)

73. Robina Goodlad *et al* 'Making Housing Work' in *Housing and Social Justice*, Commission on Social Justice Issue Paper 9 (London: IPPR, 1994)

74. National Children's Home *The NCH Factfile* (London: NCH, 1993)

75. Kenneth Gibb et al 'Making Housing Pay' in *Housing and Social Justice*, Commission on Social Justice Issue Paper 9 (London: IPPR, 1994)

76. Union of Communication Workers, submission to Commission on Social Justice (January 1994)

77. Violence against the person rose from 100,200 in 1981 to 201,800 in 1991. See *Social Trends 1994* (London: HMSO, 1994)

78. Commission on Criminal Justice *Crime and Prejudice* (London: Channel Four Television, 1993). Data taken from 1989 International Crime Survey

79. Richard Wilkinson *Unfair Shares* (London: Barnardo's, 1994)

80. House of Commons Scottish Affairs Committee *Drug Abuse in Scotland* Volume 1 (London: HMSO, 1994)

81. Home Office *Research Findings Bulletin* (London: Home Office, 1992)
82. Association of London Authorities *At a Premium* (London: ALA, 1994)
83. D. Dickinson 'Crime and Unemployment' (unpublished paper 1994)
84. National Children's Home *British Children in Need 1993* (London: NCH, 1993)
85. Tariq Modood *Racial Equality: Colour, Culture and Justice*, Commission on Social Justice Issue Paper 5 (London: IPPR, 1994)
86. Trevor Jones *Britain's Ethnic Minorities* (London: Policy Studies Institute, 1993)
87. The attitude of some Muslims to the education of girls may be thought to affect this statistic, but we have also seen in our visits around the country a strong education ethic among boys and girls in Muslim communities. Among Pakistanis and Bangladeshis, boys are twice as likely as girls to get an A level equivalent or better (25 per cent and 7 per cent versus 12 per cent and 4 per cent). Among whites, the figures for boys and girls are 37 per cent and 29 per cent respectively. Trevor Jones *Britain's Ethnic Minorities* op cit
88. Department for Education 'A New Deal for "Out of Schools" Pupils', press release 23 April, 1993
89. Tariq Modood *Not Easy Being British: Colour, Culture and Citizenship*, (London: Runnymede Trust and Trentham Books, 1992)
90. Trevor Jones *Britain's Ethnic Minorities* op cit
91. E. Ogbanna *Ethnic Minorities, Employment Training and Business Start-up Schemes* (Cardiff: Cardiff Business School, 1992)
92. Trevor Jones *Britain's Ethnic Minorities* op cit

PART TWO

WHAT'S WRONG?
WHAT CAN BE DONE?

2

DIAGNOSIS: THE UK IN A CHANGING WORLD

'The Conservative government elected in May 1979 was
more than a change of government; in terms of economic
and political philosophy, it was a revolution.'[1]

Sir Leo Pliatzky, former Second Permanent Secretary,
HM Treasury and Permanent Secretary,
Department of Trade and Industry

● ● ●

The Conservatives' election victory in 1979 marked a fundamental departure from the governing philosophy of the post-war years. Under Mrs Thatcher, the Conservatives were ambitious and bold: they argued that the United Kingdom was trapped in a cycle of decline, advanced a radical diagnosis of this decline, and sought a mandate to reverse it.

The Thatcherites argued that the post-war drive for a fairer society had produced high taxes, over-powerful trade unions and a bloated public sector. As a result, they said, incentives to entrepreneurship were weak, management could not restructure business or increase efficiency, and the public sector 'crowded out' private-sector expansion. There was relatively slow growth, and slowly increasing equality, and the second caused the first. The argument from the Right was that the state had to be rolled back and the market extended, the public sector had to be disciplined and the private sector set free, collectivism reined in and the individual rewarded. Lower direct taxation, less trade union power, and a new emphasis on personal initiative and enterprise would, the Conservatives claimed, build both economic strength and a more responsible society.

This neo-liberal argument was to become conventional wisdom across North America and much of Europe (east as well as west) in the 1980s, but in the UK in 1979 it was a daring and radical credo. For the first time in more than a generation, a political party was trying to challenge, rather than accommodate, the assumptions of the post-war consensus. The Conservatives genuinely believed that they had found the cure for the UK's decline. But they were wrong.

The neo-liberals' medicine has proved worse than the disease. Slow growth continues; taxes have gone up; millions more people depend upon benefits; the state has become more centralised; and crime and the fear of crime have shot up. The dangers of deregulation and untrammelled individualism are increasingly recognised on the Right as well as the Left of the political spectrum. Right-wing intellectuals diagnose a crisis of conservatism.[2] The free market weekly *The Economist* has lamented the government's failure to take responsibility for projects that are crucial to national renewal.[3] The Treasury has launched an investigation into the most sacred of free markets – that governing the supply of finance to industry.

But the UK's problems are not simply the product of Conservative mistakes. The causes reach back well before the onset of Conservative administration in 1979, and they will not be tackled by trying to recreate the country that existed before then.

In 1979, the UK was struggling both to compete internationally and to co-operate domestically. After the war, the UK had relied on a combination of national economic management, a mildly redistributive welfare state, and a mixed economy of public and private sectors. The system had seemed to work well enough until 1970, but during the next decade this post-war settlement came under intense strain. The symptoms were clear: the economy suffered 'stagflation' (the previously unknown combination of rising unemployment and rising inflation); the state could no longer resolve conflicts between employers and labour, even when it was itself the employer; and public services and public housing, which had transformed people's lives after the war, had too often come to be seen as dreary and confining.

The reality was that the foundations of the post-war settlement had been destroyed by national and international change. The international economic conditions included the maintenance of free trade, with access to the USA's consumer and capital markets; the creation of a relatively open and stable international financial system agreed at the Bretton Woods conference in 1946; the availability of secure and cheap Middle East oil supplies. In the last 20 years, however, we have seen the breakdown of the Bretton Woods system; growing instability in world financial markets; the loss of control over oil supplies by the main Western consumers (the UK's North Sea Oil has been a temporary windfall); the rapid industrialisation of the Pacific Rim; the increasing recognition that on environmental as well as moral grounds the fate of the Third World is a pressing issue; and the collapse of the Communist 'second' world, with the end of the Cold War.

The *national* conditions were transformed too. The welfare capitalist states that developed in Europe after the Second World War sought to combine social justice and economic prosperity on the basis of a common set of values. However, the ways in which they expressed these values depended on three specific factors: full employment, the nuclear family, and the interventionist national state. The relations between these three elements took different forms in different countries, the product of particular cultural, institutional and political traditions. In Sweden, for example, an active labour market policy, highly egalitarian policies towards women, and universal public-sector services combined to produce – until recently – a virtuous circle of low unemployment, high investment and extensive social provision. In Germany, by contrast, the economic miracle of the 1950s and 1960s was based on high-wage and high-skill employment for men, a traditional family structure, and a corporatist partnership between public and private sectors in the organisation of the economy.[4]

In comparison with these countries, the UK was a hybrid. In part, our welfare institutions and practices were at the leading edge of radical social reform (in their creation of a national insurance system to cover people from cradle to grave), in part they lagged behind (in their ambition only to set a minimum floor on the basics of citizenship); in part they were collectivist (council housing for example), in part individualist (for example redistributing individual earnings across the life-cycle); in part they were based on social citizenship (the NHS), in part rooted in a contributory system (unemployment benefit); in part the provision was 'universal' (family allowances and, later, child benefit), in part it was means-tested (national assistance and now Income Support).

The tragedy of the 1960s and 1970s in the UK was that the Left, which had created the successful post-war settlement, failed to come to terms with these forces of change. The tragedy of the 1980s was that the Right, which grasped the need for change, failed to understand what was really needed. Bill Morris, General Secretary of the Transport and General Workers' Union, wrote to the Commission: 'While we cannot afford to indulge in nostalgia for a supposed bygone era of welfarism which never really existed, it is nevertheless true that many of the principles on which the post-war welfare state was based still hold good today.' If the values of the welfare state – opportunity, security, responsibility – are to have real meaning in future, then they will require new institutions and policies to give them practical effect. We have no option but to engage with the three great revolutions – economic, social, and political – which are changing our lives, and those of people in every other industrialised country.

The Economic Revolution

The economic revolution is a global revolution of finance, competition, skill and technology in which the United Kingdom is being left behind.

The economic revolution affects every industrialised country. But the United Kingdom, by virtue of its past structures and present policies, is sadly ill-equipped to confront the challenge. First, economic globalisation is constraining the power of individual nation-states, putting a premium on international co-operation:

but the UK government carries little weight within the European Union and uses what influence it has there and internationally to promote deflation and deregulation. Second, the new competitive conditions of the global economy demand that we raise our productivity if we are to maintain, let alone improve, our living standards and quality of life: neither protectionism, nor the low-cost, low value-added strategy offers a way forward. Third, the revolution of technology, skill and organisation which is transforming the demand for and nature of work means that economic success increasingly depends upon investment in human, physical and social capital – precisely the factors which have been most seriously neglected in this country.

Economic globalisation and national sovereignty

The changing economic power of nation states starts from the massive increase in the last two decades in the volume of international financial flows. The *daily* turnover on foreign-exchange markets is $1 trillion. Twenty years ago, 90 per cent of currency flows were based on trade and only 10 per cent on speculation; today, the proportions have been reversed. Deregulation of financial markets, the growth of international telecommunications and the creation of highly sophisticated computer software have not only encouraged aggressive speculation in new financial instruments but have effectively created an international market in government policies. Speculators who doubt the ability of a national government to maintain a particular exchange rate can destroy the government's position by betting against the currency, as George Soros did to great effect in 1992. The search for market credibility has already imposed a deflationary straight-jacket on European economies, led by high interest rates across Europe in the last 15 years, and the power of individual economies to buck these trends is severely restricted.

Foreign direct investment is also on the rise. Among the OECD countries, it has grown from $440 billion only ten years ago to $1,720 billion in 1990. Between 1986 and 1991, the holdings by foreigners of companies registered in the US, Japan and Europe increased from $800 billion to $1,300 billion.

Professor Fritz Scharpf, a leading German political economist, explains the diminishing power of nation-states in blunt terms:

National governments in highly industrialised countries in the 1970s lost the ability to maintain or regain full employment through demand reflation; in the 1980s they have lost (or abdicated) the power to protect their own industries against intensified competition from other first-world countries; and they are now for the first time confronted with the possibility that world markets may be captured by high-quality industrial goods (and services) produced at very low costs in what used to be third-world or second-world countries.[5]

But single countries are not the only economic powers. For European countries today, it is at the pan-European level that effective macroeconomic sovereignty resides. The EU is a significant player in the world economy. Not only does it contain a wealthy market of 320 million citizens (345 million with the entry in 1995 of Austria, Finland, Sweden and Norway), but 93 per cent of European investment and trade takes place between EU countries, and the Union as a whole is broadly in current-account balance with the rest of the world. In the last thirty years, trade within the EU has doubled as a share of European GDP, while the share of European GDP taken up by global trade has remained constant. The European Union now offers its members the scope to do together what no European nation, except Germany, can do alone: increase economic growth without crashing into unsustainable trade deficits.

Of course, it is not only economic interdependence that is a striking feature of the modern world. Ecological interdependence is no less obvious. The present terms of world trade are desperately disadvantageous to countries that rely on their natural resources, while the pursuit of economic growth without regard to ecological constraints is likely to prove disastrous, possibly to ourselves and certainly to our children and grandchildren. Nationally and internationally, markets need to be shaped by environmental regulation and taxation, providing constant incentives to business to find cleaner ways of producing cleaner goods.

Economic decline can be as disastrous for the environment as economic growth – as is witnessed by the ecological difficulties of the former Soviet Union – and disengagement from world trade will not serve the best interests of the developing world. Rather than try to persuade people in India or China to do without cars, in the interests of holding down CO_2 emissions and protecting the global environment, we would do better to try to develop, for them and for us, cleaner forms of private *and* public transport. Not only is this the ecologically responsible route to follow, there is ample evidence that companies and countries which lead the way in raising environmental standards gain a competitive advantage in increasingly environmentally-aware markets. Environmental protection is now big business, amounting to over 2.5 per cent of national income (at least £12 billion a year).[6]

Competition: the new global marketplace

The World Bank's analysis of growth rates in the twenty-five years after 1960 provides surprising reading. Botswana was the fastest-growing economy in the period, followed by Taiwan, Indonesia, Hong Kong, Singapore, Korea and Japan. Egypt was 10th, Greece 13th, Italy and Spain 22nd and 23rd respectively, with the US and UK 32nd and 33rd.[7]

Of course, these figures do not reveal the size of each economy. None the less, the figures show something important about changes in international wealth and power. Technological change is fuelling growth in developing economies at a scarcely believable pace. Figure 2.1 shows that while it took the UK sixty years to double national output at the end of the eighteenth century (at a growth rate of about 1.2 per cent per year), the Chinese economy doubled its output in the ten years from 1977. If South Korea and Taiwan continue to grow as fast as they have over the past decade, they could overtake America's income per head within about twenty-five years. The later a country industrialises, the faster it does so.

The result of these fast growth rates among newly-industrialising countries is a new international geography of economic strength. In the post-war period, there was one dominant, 'hege-

Figure 2.1 – Catching Up: Later growth is Faster Growth
Period over which output per person doubled

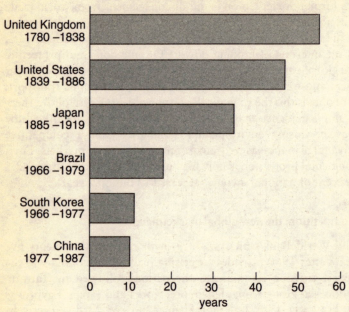

Source: John Wybrew *Global Forces for Change – The Challenge to UK Business and Society* (London: Shell UK, 1994)

monic' economic power – the United States. As a result, it was the USA that underpinned and policed the international economy. In the late 1960s and early 1970s, however, under the pressure of international entanglements and domestic economic problems, US hegemony declined. Today's international order lacks a dominant power: we are living in a multipolar economic world. Three blocs – North America (perhaps soon to be relabelled 'the Americas' to include Mexico and other countries to the south), Europe and the Far East – are emerging, and it will be in and through international forums like the G7, not within the government of any one country, that the world's economic framework will have to be hammered out

The success of the high-performing Asian economies – Japan, the 'four tigers' (Hong Kong, Taiwan, Singapore and Korea), and

Figure 2.2 – The UK Cannot Compete on Low Wages
Labour costs ($ per hour, manufacturing sector)

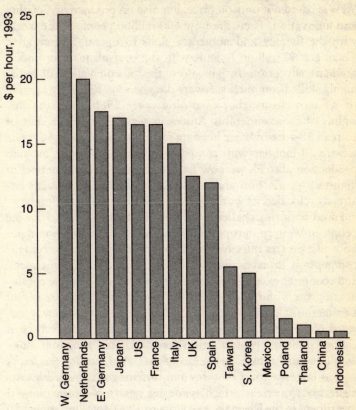

Source: John Wybrew op cit.

the new arrivals (Indonesia, Malaysia, Thailand) – has been an outstanding economic feature of the last forty years. In the next forty years or less, it will be the turn of China and India. The challenge offered by the newly industrialising countries to the old is partly based on low wage costs, as Figure 2.2. shows. It is, however, the quality and productivity of labour, not just its price, which determines the cost of production: the gap in hourly pay between Germany and Spain is compensated for by the difference in productivity. Internationally, the competitive challenge to the West is based not only on price, but also on productivity, quality and innovation. There are now 600 million people in the world with the literacy and numeracy skills to operate a computer. There are 60 million Indians with the equivalent of an undergraduate education. In Bangalore, the 'Silicon Valley' of India, highly skilled computer software designers are linked by satellite to Western clients: they earn on average $960 a month, one-eighth of the comparable American wage. Eighty per cent of Korean 18-year-olds are heading for higher education. So while we are all familiar with companies shifting low-tech, low-skill production abroad, we now have to contemplate the export of high-tech production and reasonably skilled jobs. Swissair has already relocated its worldwide accounts operation to Bombay.

Faced with this challenge to jobs and living standards, some people in Western Europe and the USA argue that we should put up walls, protect ourselves with import controls against 'unfair' competition. Protectionism can be a popular cry, and if the social and economic exclusion of significant numbers of people continues to grow within the European Union, protectionism may find a dangerous ally in xenophobia. But protectionism is no way forward. Since the vast majority of our trade is with other European Union countries, protectionism for the United Kingdom alone would require us to leave the European Union, turning our backs on our largest export markets and forfeiting the inward investment from overseas which made up nearly one-fifth of total investment in the UK in the five years to 1993, totalling some £40 billion out of £220 billion.[8]

Whether at national or European level, there are four main arguments against protectionism. First, putting up barriers to other countries' imports invites them to put up similar barriers to ours. European Union protectionism would risk a trade war with the world's two other large economic blocs – North America and the Pacific Rim. Second, import controls would either increase the price British consumers pay for imported goods, or make such goods scarce: either way, living standards would suffer, just as they did in New Zealand during its protectionist years.

Third, those concerned with social justice in the UK and in Europe should not try to achieve it at the expense of people who are even poorer than the poorest in our country. In what used to be the Third World, international trade is enabling countries like Taiwan and Brazil to raise living standards rapidly. If Poland, Hungary and the Czech Republic are to do the same, they need to be able to sell their agricultural products within the European Union, instead of being penalised by the Common Agricultural Policy. Finally, trade is not a zero sum game, in which another country's gain must be our loss: as trade increases living standards in Central and Eastern Europe, in the Pacific Rim and elsewhere, it creates new consumers for the goods and services that we can produce.

To argue against protectionism is not, however, to argue for a trade free-for-all, in which social and environmental standards are bid down in a race to the lowest cost. Child labour is becoming an important issue again, 100 years after it was banned in the UK. In China's special enterprise zones, girls under the age of ten work 14 hour days for less than $10 a month. Anita Roddick, the founder and managing director of the Body Shop, has exposed the 'species-skimming' multinational corporations which claim patent rights over indigenous people's resources. She and other advocates of fair trade argue that, just as national markets are shaped by national standards, liberalised world trade requires new international regulations to prevent the worst excesses of social and environmental dumping.[9]

Global labour standards could do something to stop the poverty of poor nations depressing the living standards of poor people in rich countries. Although those in the poorest countries often argue that today's industrialised countries became rich through precisely the same practices which we now condemn, and that we have no right to pull up the ladder behind us, there is a case for using international trade negotiations to help spread economic growth more fairly within newly industrialising countries – provided of course that wealthy countries are also willing to end practices like child labour at home. Future GATT negotiations and the work of the International Labour Organisation and other international bodies should, for instance, consider proposals for an international charter of basic workers' rights, a principle suggested to us in evidence by Professor Peter Townsend of Bristol University. It is furthermore in everyone's interests to create international regimes which will protect the world's environment by promoting sustainable development in both industrialised and industrialising countries. Far more attractive than narrow-minded protectionism is what the US Secretary of Labor, Robert Reich, has called 'outward-looking nationalism' (which in our case must include 'outward-looking Europeanism') – a conviction that building a country and a region to be proud of depends on engagement with the outside world, not retreat from it.

The new international economic order is not benign; economic and industrial change will continue to impose a painful price on those with the least educational and economic power. The challenge to all those who believe that protectionism is not the answer is to find new ways of enabling all our people to survive and to thrive in radically changed circumstances.

Change in production and work

Debates about economic sovereignty and the implications of Chinese economic development may seem a long way from the everyday concerns of people in the UK. But international competition is rapidly penetrating the domestic economies of the West, while new technologies would continue to transform every workplace even if we could cut ourselves off from international trade. The speed of change leaves many people breathless and scared. In the management jargon:

- Companies are 'delayering' – cutting out the middle-management jobs in personnel, finance and corporate planning that were the heart of middle-class security.[10]
- Companies are 'downsizing' – breaking up into self-governing units, concentrating on core functions and exporting the rest to independent contractors.
- Companies are 'networking' – joining chains of cooperation and co ordination to maximise efficiencies of organisation.

Throughout the world, many unskilled, routine jobs are being automated out of existence, while the content of jobs is being changed in a continuous process of technological upgrading. German engineering trainees spend six years in apprenticeship; but it is estimated that the 'half-life' of their skills – the time it takes for half their value to drain away – is only four years. Rapidly changing markets and technologies mean that people starting a career today can expect to change jobs between five and eight times in their lives. In a paper circulated to the Commission, David Sainsbury, Chairman of one of the UK's most successful businesses, stressed that it is 'cumulative learning' that determines the standard of living of a country:

> The world's best companies ... are using the intelligence and skills of their workers more fully than in the past, and as a result are unleashing major advances in productivity, quality, variety and speed of new product introductions.

Yet while governments in France as well as Korea and Japan are on course to have 80 per cent of young people reaching university entrance standard by the year 2000, the English, Welsh, Northern Irish, and to a lesser extent Scottish, education systems are designed to weed out all but the top third by the age of eighteen.[11] At Nissan in Sunderland, where the Commission talked to management and front-line workers, 7 out of 10 job applicants fail to score 40 per cent on the company's verbal reasoning test. Skill levels in this country are 40 per cent below those of our neighbours, and two-thirds of workers have no vocational or professional qualification at all.

It would be foolish to believe that skills alone are enough to build competitive strength. However good the skills, they will be wasted if the tools are poor. But the UK lags behind as much in investment in plant and technology as it does in education. Capital stock per worker is 94 per cent higher in Germany than in Britain, 73 per cent higher in the USA, 49 per cent higher in France and 31 per cent higher in Japan. Business investment in research and development, which was at roughly the same level as in Japan, West Germany and the USA in 1980, is now one-third less. According to the OECD, investment (measured as gross fixed capital formation) rose in the 1980s to reach 20 per cent of our national income but has now fallen back to 18 per cent, compared with 21 per cent in Germany and a massive 32 per cent in Japan and 35 per cent in Singapore. Between 1960 and 1990, total investment in the UK economy was on average 1 per cent less than in other European countries, and 10 per cent a year less than in Japan.[12]

The failure of investment is symptomatic of the short-termism that divides the Anglo-Saxon market economies – particularly the USA and the UK – from those of Continental Europe and the Pacific Rim. Over the last thirty years, while companies in Japan have been expected to show an average annual return of 3.1 per cent, in Switzerland 5.3 per cent and in Germany 6.9 per cent, the UK Stock Market has demanded an average return of 9.8 per cent.[13]

Even if the UK achieves far higher investment in skills and plant, we will still need organisations capable of using them. The potential of people and technology cannot be fulfilled in a company structured on traditional lines, with vertical hierarchies and strict demarcation of tasks. Driven by technological change and the search for competitive advantage in a crowded market, successful companies are leaving behind the systems of industrial production that powered the first industrial revolution, with their separation of manual from mental labour, where thinkers were not expected to make anything, and doers were not expected to think.

The old model is giving way to new systems of 'mass customisation', which combine the innovation and improvisation of craft production with the efficiency of mass production. That requires a fundamental reorganisation of production and, above all, a decentralisation of decision-making, the elimination of unnecessary chains of command, and the promotion of teamworking and cooperation. Firms beat off low-wage competition from other countries by moving up market: James Womack and his colleagues, whose book *The Machine that Changed the World* documents the transformation in car production, argue that what they call 'lean production' is more than a match for low-wage mass production; it raises the threshold of acceptable quality, offers a wider variety of products, responds rapidly to

---

Old economy versus New economy

Mass production	Mass customisation
Efficiency	Value added
Command and control	Empowerment/decentralisation
Conglomerates	Enterprise webs
Individuals	Teams
Assets are things	Assets are people
Trade for life	Multiskilling
Training	Learning
Contract	Trust
Us and them	Us and us

---

changes in consumer tastes, and can fully utilise automation in ways that mass production cannot.[14]

The Director of one of the major Japanese conglomerates, Konsouke Matsushita, argues forcefully that the West cannot compete through the old ways:

> Your firms are built on the Taylor model;[15] even worse, so are your heads. With your bosses doing the thinking while the workers wield the screwdrivers ... the essence of management is getting the ideas out of the heads of the bosses and into the hands of labour. We are beyond the Taylor model; business, we know, is now so complex and difficult, the survival of firms so hazardous ... the core of management is precisely the art of mobilising and pulling together the intellectual resources of all employees in the service of the firm.

Rover Cars has learnt this lesson so successfully that it is now a model for visiting Japanese managers. One of Rover's top managers explained to us that as the company struggled to survive it dawned upon the management that 'with every pair of hands, we get a free brain', and that worker involvement was the only route to company success. Unfortunately, most British companies have scarcely begun to use their workers' brains: two-thirds of employees report that they have no significant influence over changes in work organisation that could directly affect their jobs.[16]

In the best companies, managers do not just eat in the same canteen as other employees (what Professor Jeffrey Pfeffer of the Stanford Graduate School of Business calls 'symbolic egalitarianism')[17] they develop ideas with them, and share profits and stock options with them. Conflict between management and workforce is of course not dead: shareholders do not have the same priorities as employees, senior management do not lead the same lives as workers on the office or shop floor. But in the 'inclusive company' – the company which accounts for the varying interests of employees, suppliers, shareholders and the local community – various interests are at least given appropriate weight and consideration, to the benefit of all concerned.

The strategic choice between old and new was vividly illustrated for the Commission by our visit to Southampton Docks in May 1993. At Southampton Container Terminals (SCT), TGWU dockers were locked in a bitter dispute with employers who were demanding a pay freeze, longer working hours, and job flexibility, while threatening compulsory redundancies. A few hundred yards away, at Southampton Cargo Handling (SCH), TGWU dockers were their own employers, the result of an employee buy-out organised by the union three years earlier. Facing intense competition in an overcrowded industry, one firm was trying to compete by cutting costs and sub-contracting, the other by engaging every employee in the drive for higher quality.

SCH's slogan, 'every worker a shareholder', stresses that the worker/owners' commitment to quality and speed guarantees top-class service to customers. Gone are the old demarcations between white-collar and blue-collar workers: today, administrative staff drive vehicles onto waiting ships and nobody stops work until the loading is finished. Gone too are the structures of 'us and them' and the old conflicts between management and workers; the motto today is 'us and us', and the worker/owners elect the managing director. At SCT the dispute seemed set for a bitter lockout, but a few months later union and management had signed a deal which allowed the company to contract out work and make several dockers redundant – but which transferred their work and all the jobs to a new subsidiary of the employee-owned SCH. Both groups of workers earn less than they used to, but, as we were repeatedly told, better to have a job (and still a relatively well-paid one) than just a redundancy cheque, and better still, for the worker-owners who paid themselves their first bonus last year, to have the prospect of sharing future profits as well.

To pay our way in world markets today, and maintain, let alone improve, our standard of living for tomorrow, the United Kingdom needs to compete in the market for quality goods and services by combining Savile Row service, Marks and Spencer quantities and Woolworth prices. In today's global economy, wealth creation depends upon the value which companies and countries add through production. Low skills go with low investment, low productivity, low prices, low profit margins and low wages. The only way to achieve and sustain prosperity is through the high value-added production which requires skilled people using modern equipment in participative enterprises. The aim of public policy must be to help firms respond to the changing demands of global competition, instead of resisting them.

Social Revolution

The social revolution is a revolution of women's life-chances, of family structures and of demography. Although social change has been faster and gone further in the UK than in most other European countries, public policy has failed to keep up.

William Beveridge, like most policy-makers of his time, assumed that a woman's place was in the home of a two-parent family – even though he was writing during the war, when millions of married women were being mobilised into industry. 'By definition,' he wrote, 'the family is a group consisting of two parents, male and female respectively, and their offspring.' He envisaged that after the end of the war 'in the next thirty years housewives as mothers have vital work to do in ensuring the adequate continuance of the British race and of British ideals in the world'. Half a century on, the situation is very different. Above all, women must be treated as individuals, citizens seeking autonomy through economic opportunity as well as family security.

Change in families

In 1949, one in three British workers was a woman; today the proportion is nearly one in two, and in many regions women are already the majority of the workforce. A woman whose first child was born in the early 1950s spent an average of ten years out of employment, caring for the family; by the late 1980s, that time-span had dropped to nine months.[18] In most industrialised countries, growing (although still unequal) economic opportunities for women have been accompanied by a rise in separation, divorce, cohabitation and lone parenthood. A shrinking minority of the population now lives in a traditional nuclear family – male breadwinner, female caregiver. With the exception of Denmark, the United Kingdom now has the highest divorce rate – as well as the highest marriage and remarriage rates – in the European Union. In 1991, 37 per cent of all marriages involved at least one divorced partner.[19]

Today, nearly one child in five (18 per cent) is being brought up by a lone parent, usually the mother, compared to 8 per cent in 1972;[20] about half of these lone parents are divorced and a third have never been married. One child in ten lives with one natural parent and a step-parent. The majority – seven out of ten – are living with both their natural parents. A growing proportion of babies – three in ten in 1993 – are born outside marriage, three-quarters of them to couples living together.[21]

Family patterns differ significantly within different racial and ethnic groups. In the Afro-Caribbean community, for example, female-headed families are commonplace and not regarded as second best. Afro-Caribbean women with children are more likely than white mothers to be in employment. Within Asian communities, married women are less likely to have paid jobs, although when they are employed they are also more likely to work full-time. Families are often larger and three generations are more likely to live together.

Although statistics provide only a snapshot, it is clear that family life is not static. Children who start life living with their two parents may later become part of a one-parent family and, later still, part of one or more step-families. The rapid rise in the divorce rate suggests that more than one in three new marriages will end in divorce; among couples who cohabit without marrying, the separation rate is even higher.[22] Family breakdown is the trapdoor through which women and children most often fall into poverty – itself one of the most important factors in the worse outcomes which, on average, children from lone-parent families experience compared with children of two-parent families.[23]

Although the economic revolution has affected us all, its real victims are the older men who have been made redundant from old industries, and the young men with little education and few skills who have never had the chance to enter industry. The decline in manufacturing employment, which has occurred in almost every industrial country but fastest of all in the United Kingdom, has had a devastating impact on men who could have expected in the past to have acquired a well-paid and secure skilled job. New jobs have been created, but they are in the service sector, often part-time and offering far lower wages than those available to a skilled industrial worker; where they are well-paid, they generally require a high level of education. Men can increasingly expect to share the breadwinner role with women; and some have little prospect of contributing to family income in any way at all. In both cases, economic change is throwing into question traditional definitions of masculinity and what it means to support children.

The demands made by this transformation in domestic relations are wide-ranging:

- For families, a renegotiation of the relationships between mothers, fathers and children.
- For employers, new demands for flexible work patterns, support for childcare and other measures to accommodate caring work within the home.
- For the government, a fundamental review of the social security system, childcare and social services.

Women's growing participation in employment has not been matched by men's participation in the home. Despite the optimistic rhetoric of the 'new man', women are still responsible for most work in the home. As researchers Dr Jane Millar and Dr Caroline Glendinning have put it, 'women are service-sector workers in and out of the family'.[24] There are, however, some signs of change. Compared with the early 1960s, women are spending less time on routine housework, men a little more. Furthermore, 'time budget' analysis shows that both mothers and fathers are spending more time on childcare – mothers because of the drop in their housework time, fathers because of the fall in working hours throughout the 1970s and (for some workers) the 1980s.[25]

Although other European countries acknowledge fathers' importance to their families through provision for paid paternity leave, the United Kingdom still fails to do so, and the British government's only significant attempt to come to terms with family change – the introduction of the Child Support Act – has been a near-disaster in practice. Although British women are more likely to be in employment than in most other European countries, British families have less in the way of paid maternity, parental or family leave, and less access to publicly funded nursery education and childcare, than families in any other European country.

In the UK, mothers in part-time employment – despite their lower status and lower pay – consistently report higher levels of satisfaction with the balance they can achieve between employment, family and personal leisure. But full-time employment for men and part-time employment for mothers is an unstable and unsatisfactory pattern: the new challenge is to take advantage of increasingly flexible forms of employment to give men as well as women far greater choice as to how they combine employment, family, education, community activities and leisure in different ways and at different stages in their lives. In other words, we need to make flexibility work for rather than against employees, especially those with family responsibilities.

Fate, class and mobility

Among many changes in traditional structures over the last forty years, the power of deference has greatly declined. A belief in the equal worth and value of all citizens is now more widely and firmly accepted than ever before. Moreover, as the importance of tradition declines, more and more issues become matters of personal decision.[26] What we wear, how we vote, what we eat, what job we do, where we live – all these are concerns that, two generations ago, were determined for large sections of the population by their birth. This is no longer the case. The UK is more mobile and open, but it is also increasingly unequal.

Perhaps the greatest force for mobility has been greater participation and achievement in the education system. Participation in higher education has long been an assumption of a few; today it is becoming an aspiration for a significant number of the population. There are more than a million undergraduates in higher education, and one thing is almost certain: today's undergraduates will expect their children to go to university.

There are in fact three parallel processes going on – of which two are largely beneficial. The first is the decline of traditional patterns of hierarchy. The second is the development of more flexible and varied patterns of life. The linear progression from education to adult life to retirement is being supplanted by more complex processes: education and training take place throughout the life-cycle; employment is mixed with caring responsibilities through the prime working years; retirement is taken early or late, in increasing numbers of cases depending on individual choice.

The third shift is less welcome: social and economic *exclusion* – from work, transport, politics, education, housing, leisure facilities – is an increasingly obvious and depressing feature of life in many parts of the UK. In towns and cities the Commission has visited, the accumulated disadvantages of unemployment, bad housing and poor schooling combine to produce areas where there is simply no economy – no banks, no shops, no work.

We do not accept the common assertion that class is dead. Class matters – many of the statistics reviewed in the previous chapter reinforce our conviction that it is still the most important determinant of a child's life-chances. But the class map of the UK is changing. Manual workers formed over half the electorate twenty years ago; today they make up only one third. Fewer than four million people now work in manufacturing, once the heart of the industrial working class. Eight million people are now self-employed. The public sector – whose employees do not fit traditional class categories based on labour for the profit of an employer – still employs around six million people. Furthermore, traditional definitions of class structure have always assigned class position to a woman on the basis of her husband's occupation, an assumption which is no longer tenable.

Many of those who profess to see the end of class – or the makings of classlessness – also argue that the United Kingdom is developing an 'underclass' characterised by fecklessness, idleness, dependency and criminality. Fifteen years ago Mrs Thatcher talked of 'young single girls who deliberately become pregnant in order to jump a housing queue and get welfare payments'.[27] More recently, the Adam Smith Institute, in a pamphlet dedicated to 'ending' the welfare state, argued that the welfare state produces dependency.[28]

We are unconvinced by such descriptions. Of course there is increasing alienation and disaffection among many people: economic and social exclusion on a grand scale is bound to lessen the stake that people have in society. But the aspirations of the bottom 10 or 20 per cent of the population are remarkably similar to those of the next 60 or 70 per cent – better schools, action against crime, and above all revived economic prospects. The communities we have visited and the people we have met have not been passive victims of fate; they are often active people trying desperately to shore up communities and bring up families in the most deprived conditions.

The UK remains a society corrupted by inequities of class, which intersect with those of gender, race and disability; but the nature of those inequities, and their implications, are changing. In particular, Beveridge could not have anticipated that the UK would become the multicultural, multiracial, multilingual and multi-faith society that it is today. Racial discrimination and disadvantage are increasingly complex problems: some Asian communities which are achieving considerable success in education and the economy may nonetheless find their lives threatened by racist violence. A simple analysis of differences between black and white populations, though they do exist in employment, education and the like, has to be supplemented by a more sophisticated understanding of cultural as well as colour discrimination.[29]

Demographic change

In terms of our population, the United Kingdom is a slow-growth country in a slow-growth region of a very rapidly growing world. Today, the twelve countries of the European Union have 6 per cent of the world's population of 5.5 billion. By 2025, the same twelve countries are likely to account for only 4 per cent of a global population of 8.5 billion. The UK's fertility rate, which was 2.7 in 1960, has now dropped to 1.8. In Germany, the fertility rate is down to 1.3 – implying that unless the birth rate recovers, its native population will be extinct in 300 years![30]

A slowly growing or even shrinking population must, of course, mean an ageing population. The 18 Western European states of the OECD, now home to 50 million people over the age of sixty-five, will by 2030 have 70 million older citizens. In the UK, which had one million people aged over eighty in 1961, there are already more than two million, including 250,000 over the age of ninety.

Although many older people remain active and healthy, governments are increasingly concerned about the 'burden' placed upon the working population by older people's entitlement to pensions, health care and other services. The UK, however, has less reason to be worried than other industrialised countries. The 'support ratio', comparing the number of people of working age with those over sixty-five, was low in 1980 by international standards (at around 4:1), but it is expected to fall more slowly than in other countries. Fifty years from now, it is predicted that the UK will have one of the highest ratios (around 3:1), while Germany, Japan and the Netherlands will have among the lowest ratios (each just more than 2:1). As Dr John Hills of the LSE has shown, the projected cost of ageing over the next twenty-five years amounts to a smaller increase than during the last ten years.[31]

None the less, the care of the old presents a significant challenge. In the early 1950s, 20 per cent of NHS resources was spent on people over 65; now it is nearly 50 per cent.[32] Moreover, in 1900 for every person aged over 85, there were 24 women in their 50s (the group which carries out most informal care); by 2000 there will be only three.[33] As the woefully inadequate state of community care services suggests, we have scarcely begun to face up to the financial and social arithmetic of care. Retired people already do a great deal of productive work outside the paid economy (much of it as carers themselves), but as the number of elderly people in our population grows, so the questions of who does the caring, and of how it is paid for, become more acute.

The Political Revolution

The political revolution is a challenge to the UK's old assumptions of parliamentary sovereignty and to its growing centralisation of government power; it involves a fundamental reorientation of the relationship between those who govern and those who are governed.

Economic and social reform must be supported in the political sphere. Political factors – power, popular attitudes, institutional structures – make change possible, or serve to block it. The 1990s, however, are a time of particular political openness.

The collapse of Soviet Communism and the limitations of both Keynesian social democracy and Thatcherite neo-liberalism have left a political vacuum. The communist experiment, far from eliminating inefficiency and waste, fuelled both. Keynesian social democracy promised to smooth the business cycle, and for thirty years after the Second World War did so, but in an interdependent world economy found its prescription less and less reliable:

Keynes had not solved the problem of production after all. And the neo-liberal answer to the limitations of the 1945 settlement, a return to the laissez-faire economics of the minimal state and free markets, has in turn produced a cycle of debt, recession and social polarisation in the countries where it has been most vigorously pursued. The polarities of the post-war period – individual versus collective, state versus market, public versus private – are giving way to a new recognition of their interdependence. Since old ideas do not work, it is a good time to develop new ones: 'This is the time to *make the future* – precisely because everything is in flux,' says the American economist Peter Drucker.[34]

The welfare state of fifty years ago was built on the expertise of professionals. Too often, people were treated as passive recipients of services and benefits deemed appropriate by government. Today, people who are active and well-informed consumers of private goods and services want to make more decisions for themselves in the public sphere: about the nature of social services, traffic planning in their neighbourhood, or the future of local schools. Because people have diverse needs, and because they are almost always the best judges of their own needs, they must have a greater say in determining how needs are met. But there is also a need to address the cynicism that afflicts popular attitudes to politics. The celebration of democratic suffrage in South Africa was a timely reminder of the power of the free ballot, and the extent to which its potential has been corrupted in many countries. A new politics is needed in Europe, and nowhere more so than in the UK.

Reinventing government

There are growing and changing demands on politics and government and growing constraints on what they can achieve. In the 1970s, the Right used the idea that advanced and complex democracies were 'ungovernable' to argue that the answer was *less* government. Today, the search is for *better* government.

David Osborne, co-author of the American bestseller *Reinventing Government*, has identified four factors that explain the pressures on public services across the industrialised world: the pace of social and technological change, and the difficulties this poses for traditional, top-down government bureaucracies; the expectations of the public, for quality and choice; the impact of the global marketplace, and the need to attract mobile capital; and finally, the sheer expense of government.[35] To these should be added a fifth, the growing demand from previously excluded groups – women, ethnic minorities, disabled people – for a political system that includes them and better reflects their concerns and demands.

Further demands on government are made by, for example, technical innovation and by medical advance. It has been estimated, for instance, that spending on personal social services needs to grow by 2.5 per cent per annum to meet demand, and that if the NHS were to try to keep pace with the advances of medical technology, it would need to grow by 2 per cent per annum in real terms.[36] There are constraints on the supply side of government spending because the electorate is sceptical about increased taxation, and there is international pressure for a convergence of tax levels.

In addition, public services suffer from a 'relative price effect'. Although doctors, nurses and other staff in the NHS have recently achieved substantial increases in productivity, it is always more difficult to achieve and to measure rising productivity in services than it is in traditional manufacturing. Service-sector activities like teaching children or helping elderly people look after themselves necessarily involve a high input of labour. Because wages rise fairly consistently across the economy, the faster productivity is increased in the trading sector in the face of world competition, the faster the relative costs of services grow.

Political leadership

Just when imaginative political and civic leadership is most needed, people feel great distrust in the designs – grand or otherwise – of politicians. One councillor in Newcastle summed up the situation very succinctly for the Commission: 'The issue on the doorstep is not "Why should I vote Labour?", but "Why should I vote at all?"'

This is in part a legacy of the 1980s, when the dominant ideology was that economic and social decline were the products of government intervention, and that markets, not politics, held the solution to our problems. But the decline of people's faith in politics goes deeper: the claims and actions of politicians seem increasingly distant from the people who vote for them. One source of this is to be found in the structure of politics at Westminster.

The functions, structures and powers of the UK Parliament are peculiar. The sovereignty of the Crown in Parliament, the UK's unwritten constitution, an electoral system which tends to give very great power to the winning party, and the power of party whips and prime ministerial patronage combine to make the British system uniquely centralised, unusually confrontational in its debates, and notably weak in its ability to implement policy in a flexible and effective way. The problems that have in the last five years arisen with alarming regularity – the confusion of democracy with majority rule, the equating of public interest with ministerial interest, the neglect of local diversity and difference, the failure to consult on legislation – come from the top of the system. This is why there is such widespread demand for constitutional reform. 'High-performance government', government which is a catalyst for renewal and change, is alien in a system that revolves around administration and legislation, not persuasion and negotiation.

The policies of the post-war period were largely conceived in terms of the national state, but the national arena is increasingly too small for the large problems, and too large for the small problems. The Conservative government has passed dozens of Acts of Parliament dealing with local government, which have promised to shift power away from local government to the users of services; yet power has in fact been transferred from local government to central government and to unelected quangos. There will be 7,700 unelected quangos by 1996, with 40,000 appointees. The irony of this centralisation of power is that there is unremitting outside pressure for the transfer of responsibility away from the national level. In some matters, such as transport policy, there are calls for decentralisation to local government at regional and city level; by contrast, in the case of environmental or macroeconomic policy, a European level of debate is essential. This is the 'double-shift' faced by all advanced industrial societies.

It is not only the peculiarities of the Westminster system that make the UK increasingly hard to govern from the top down. The welfare state developed after 1945 has been undermined politically, as well as economically and socially, because it failed, with the exception of the NHS, to make citizens feel that it was theirs. The traditional Fabian conception of society was one in which people were profoundly dependent on government. Problems were to be solved by experts, and there were few mechanisms for ordinary people to participate in decisions affecting their own lives. Perhaps most revealing is the treatment of disabled people: the concept of 'need' is central, but its definition has been controlled by professionals, too often to the exclusion of disabled people themselves. There was in various public-service activities a powerful ethos of 'government knows best'.

The Government's response to this situation has been to try to impose market disciplines on public services – through contracting out, market-testing, Next Steps and a number of other initiatives. Whatever the details of the various policies that have been established, at their heart has been a view of the individual as *consumer* in the marketplace – a consumer of healthcare, refuse collection or social services, in much the same way as he or she consumes ice-cream, cars or clothes. The problem with this view is that it takes into account only a part of the relationship between the users of public services and the people who provide them. Individuals are sometimes joint producers of public services: in the case of education, for example, parental input is one essential complement to good teaching in the development of successful schooling. It is vitally important that individuals are seen not just as consumers but as citizens. While we are not particularly affected by our neighbour's choice of holiday, we are profoundly affected if neighbouring children are poorly educated. Good public services for all who use them are in all our interests.

In its attempt to change the structure of public service, the Government has been right to emphasise the needs and views of individuals. But it has neglected the potential of public-service workers to contribute constructively to change. And choice, real or imaginary, is not the whole answer: people do not have equal power to choose from equally satisfactory alternatives, and high-quality public services depend on supply-side action as well as demand-side strength. The important point is to provide responsive and efficient services, and their design must be grounded not in paternalism but in participation and democracy. Citizens should be able to shape the service, not merely buy it and complain about it.

There is a final paradox in the current debate about the renewal of social policy. Everyone agrees that expenditure of £80 billion per year on social security is not halting the increase in poverty and social division; few people believe that anyone actually likes paying taxes; yet the polls suggest that a substantial and (more significantly) increasing majority of the population says that it is in favour of spending more on social welfare and public action. *British Social Attitudes* surveys report that the number of people supporting an increase in taxation to provide better public services doubled between 1983 and 1991.[37] A *Breadline Britain* survey for London Weekend Television showed that in 1983 25 per cent of people were willing to pay an extra 5p in the pound in tax to help everyone afford items agreed to be necessities, while 59 per cent rejected the idea; by 1991, 44 per cent supported the idea, although 44 per cent were still against it.[38]

The UK today does not, in J.K. Galbraith's phrase, display a 'culture of contentment'.[39] We are a nation hungry for the satisfaction of aspirations rather than bloated by contentment; we are increasingly insecure rather than benignly content. Greater personal independence, paradoxically, means increasing social interdependence. Whether the issue is environmental protection, teamwork in the workplace, or the promotion of safety in local communities, we are more and more dependent on others for what we are able to do. The challenge is to develop new mechanisms of collective action which will at the same time meet common goals and liberate individual talent. Far from living through the death of politics, we depend on its resurrection for national renewal.

The UK and the New World Order

The economic, social and political revolutions that we have described define the conditions of change that apply to all advanced industrialised societies. But what are the conditions for success – economically, socially, and politically – today?

Economic viability depends upon creating wealth in a strong and competitive tradeable sector based upon modern industries. This is the only way to pay our way in the world economy. We must produce goods and services that we are prepared to buy ourselves, as well as sell abroad.

Social viability depends upon building a society based on inclusion. This demands an end to structural unemployment, a sustained attack on the accumulated disadvantages of deprived parts of the UK and effective support for families of all kinds. But it also demands a recognition that building a good society depends on the efforts of us all, that rights carry responsibilities.

Finally, political viability, without which economic and social viability will not be achieved, depends on a new settlement between governors and governed. This requires a new distribution of power between cities and localities as centres of economic and political power, and between national and supranational institutions. And it requires a new distribution of power between the users and providers of public services – in the interests of an empowering and enabling democracy, one that is more profound than that generated by a vote every five years.

The end of communism has not meant the end of ideology. In the liberal democracies of Western Europe, economic and social differences persist because of the peculiarities of history, culture, politics and fortune that mark each country. But the differences also mark the effect of political choices – choices not just by governments but by interest groups, businesses and millions of citizens. Despite common challenges of technology, demography and policy, political decisions can shape nations.

The UK is a middle-sized country on the edge of Europe with a relatively weak economy. But it has resources of people, ideas and expertise that are invaluable and irreplaceable. In various ways, the UK does 'punch above its weight', as Foreign Secretary

Douglas Hurd said recently. Hurd was talking about our role in international diplomacy, our seat on the UN Security Council, and our influence in and through the Commonwealth. However, in the post-war period we have also punched above our weight ideologically: the welfare state was in some ways in the vanguard of social reform, and the Thatcherite view of society and its prescriptions in the 1980s also influenced, for good or ill, a broader historical movement.

Today, while the Right is intellectually exhausted after fifteen years of permanent revolution, the Left has yet to convince people that it has the confidence and competence to set the country on a new course. That is both the challenge facing the Commission, and its opportunity. In our interim reports in July 1993, we said that the welfare state had to change because the world had changed; in this final report, our argument is broader. Britain needs to change if it is to find its place in a changed world; changing the welfare state – its conception, its structure, its functions – must play its part in changing Britain.

In the next chapter, we explain three options open to us. The cynics say we should deregulate further, the fatalists say we should level down, and the optimists say we should invest our way to economic renewal and social reform. Who is right?

Notes

1. Nigel Lawson *The View from Number 11* (London: Corgi, 1993)
2. See for example John Gray *Beyond the New Right* (London: Routledge, 1993) and *The Undoing of Conservatism* (London: Social Market Foundation, 1994)
3. 'The case for central planning' in *The Economist*, 12 September 1992
4. Gosta Esping-Andersen *The Three Worlds of Welfare Capitalism* (Princeton, New Jersey: Princeton University Press, 1990)
5. Fritz Scharpf, unpublished paper presented to a seminar organised by the Socialist International, March 1994
6. Giles Atkinson and Richard Dubourg 'Green Approaches'in *New Economy*, 1, 2 (Summer 1994)
7. World Bank *The East Asian Miracle* (Oxford: Oxford University Press, 1993)

8. Centre for Economic and Business Research *US and Japanese Investment in the UK* (London: CBI, 1993)

9. The North American Free Trade Agreement (NAFTA) represents the first major trade agreement that secures rights, albeit minimal ones, for workers

10. British Telecom have cut 6,000 middle management jobs during their restructuring.

11. John Hills/LSE Welfare State Programme *The Future of Welfare – A guide to the debate* (York: Joseph Rowntree Foundation, 1993)

12. Will Hutton *The Moral Economy* forthcoming

13. Ibid

14. James Womack, Daniel Jones and Daniel Roos *The Machine that Changed the World: The Story of Lean Production* (New York: Harper Perennial 1991)

15. Frederick Winslow Taylor developed the principle of 'scientific management', relentlessly sub-dividing work tasks into their smallest constituent units.

16. Duncan Gallie and Michael White *Employee Commitment and the Skills Revolution* (London: Policy Studies Institute, 1993)

17. Jeffrey Pfeffer *Competitive Advantage Through People* (Cambridge, Massachusetts Harvard Business School Press, 1994)

18. Patricia Hewitt *About Time* (London: Rivers Oram/IPPR, 1993)

19. *Social Trends 1994* (London: HMSO, 1994)

20. *Social Trends 1993* (London: HMSO, 1993)

21. Quoted in the *Guardian*, 26 July 1994

22. Susan McRae *Cohabiting Mothers* (London: PSI, 1993)

23. Louie Burghes *Lone parenthood and family disruption* (London: Family Policy Studies Centre, 1994)

24. Jane Millar and Caroline Glendinning, Introduction to Millar and Glendinning (eds) *Women and Poverty in Britain* (London: Harvester Wheatsheaf, 1992)

25. Hewitt op cit

26. See Anthony Giddens *Beyond Left and Right* (Cambridge: Polity Press, 1994)

27. Interview in *The Times* quoted by Hilary Land in 'Money Isn't Everything', submission to the Commission, 1993

28. Michael Bell, Eamonn Butler, David Marsland, and Madsen Pirie *The End of the Welfare State* (London: Adam Smith Institute, 1994)

29. Tariq Modood *Racial Equality: Colour, Culture and Justice* Commission on Social Justice Issue Paper 5 (London: IPPR, 1994)

30. *Financial Times*, 8 March 1994

31. Hills op cit
32. Frank Field 'Don't Sell Granny Short: The Role of Care Pensions' First Annual Pegasus Lecture, Royal College of Medicine, 27 October 1993
33. Melanie Henwood, presentation to the Commission, 1993
34. Peter Drucker *Post-Capitalist Society* (Oxford: Butterworth Heinemann, 1993)
35. David Osborne and Ted Gaebler *Reinventing Government* (New York: Addison-Wesley, 1992)
36. Howard Glennerster *Paying For Welfare* (London: Harvester Wheatsheaf, 1992)
37. Social and Community Planning Research *British Social Attitudes Cumulative Sourcebook: The first six surveys* (Aldershot: Gower, 1992)
38. London Weekend Television *Breadline Britain 1990* (1991)
39. J.K. Galbraith *The Culture of Contentment* (London: Sinclair Stevenson, 1992)

3

PRESCRIPTION: A TALE OF
THREE FUTURES

'We need to invent a national mission – we need to invent a future.'

Chris Webb, Principal of Handsworth
College, Birmingham

● ● ●

The founding premise of this report is that we do have a say in our future. We have choices – economic, social and political – about our fate as individuals and as a society. Government is not simply a matter of who is most competent to run the system; it is a question of who has the vision and the ideas, as well as the competence, to set the country on a new course.

It is possible to make out three rival strategies on offer, presented by the Investors (our preference), the Deregulators, and the Levellers. The Investors combine an ethical commitment to equality of opportunity (and all it entails), a vision of the good society, and a compelling analysis of how modern capitalism works – as well as how it can be changed. They are the heirs of the UK's reforming tradition, but have learnt the lessons, positive and negative, of the social market in Germany and Scandinanvia, active states in Japan and the Pacific Rim, and entrepreneurial capitalism in the United States. The Deregulators are the neo-liberal free-marketeers of the New Right who have dominated British and American thinking for the last two decades. Their recipe is 'more of the same'. The Levellers' main concern is with a fair distribution of whatever wealth is created, rather than with the relationship between distribution and pro-duction, and their main focus is on the role and level of social security benefits.

The pen-portraits we present of the Investors, Deregulators and Levellers are inevitably simplifications. They do, though, provide an indication of the broad approaches open to us.

Future 1: Investors' Britain.

The Investors believe we can combine the ethics of community with the dynamics of a market economy. At the heart of the Investors' strategy is a belief that the extension of economic opportunity is not only the source of economic prosperity but also the basis of social justice. The competitive requirement for constant innovation and higher quality demands opportunities for every individual – and not just an élite – to contribute to national economic renewal; this in turn demands strong social institutions, strong families and strong communities, which enable people and companies to grow, adapt and succeed. Unlike the Deregulators, who would use insecurity as the spur to change, the Investors insist on security as the foundation of change; but unlike the Levellers, the Investors achieve security by redistributing opportunities rather than just redistributing income.

Future 2: Deregulators' Britain.

The Deregulators' dream of a future in which dynamic entrepre-neurs, unshackled by employment laws or social responsibilities, create new businesses and open up new markets; in which there is no limit to how high earnings at the top will rise – and no limit to how low wages at the bottom will fall; in which the market widens and deepens its influence; and in which, in the graphic phrase of the American economist Robert Kuttner, 'every busi-ness relationship is a one night stand'.[1] It is a future of extremes where the rich get richer and the poor get poorer, and where the rewards for success are matched only by the risks of failure. Eco-nomically it depends upon the unceasing drive for competitive-ness through the ever-cheaper production of what we already produce; socially, it relies upon the reduction of public services and public spending. Politically, it is built on a logic of centralisation and exclusivity, destroying publicly accountable institutions that stand between law-making government and individual decision-making in the marketplace.

Future 3: Levellers' Britain.

The Levellers are concerned with the distribution of wealth to the neglect of its production; they develop policies for social justice independent of the economy. Their strategy is founded on the idea that we cannot use economic renewal and paid employment as the basis for a socially just future. The Levellers share many of the aspirations of the Investors, but they have different strategies to achieve these ambitions. Theirs is a strategy for social justice based primarily on redistributing wealth and incomes, rather than trying to increase opportunities and compete in world markets. The Levellers believe that we should try to achieve social justice through the benefits system, rather than through a new combination of active welfare state, reformed labour market, and strong community.

Investment: The High Road

The search for a solution to Britain's decline ultimately depends on our ability – the ability of individuals, families, companies, communities and government – not just passively to respond to social and economic change, but actively to shape it. This is not something that social policy, still less tax and benefit policy, can do alone. Britain's problems – whether under-investment in pre-school education, long-term unemployment or pensioner poverty – are not amenable to *ad hoc* solutions; they are rooted in connected issues of social, economic and political structures, and they must be addressed together.

Investment is important because it is the seedcorn of economic prosperity and social renewal; it generates both wealth and welfare. Investment – by the public and private sectors, and by a partnership of the two – increases the future productivity of the economy. Yet for a long time we have failed to invest enough in ourselves – in the life-chances of all children, in our skills, in our industry and infrastructure, and in our communities. In the last fifteen years, consumption has boomed – with private and government consumption together reaching 87 per cent of gross domestic product, compared with an EU average of 80 per cent. But our industry is weak, our public services neglected, our infrastructure underfunded and our nation divided.

The central argument of the Investors – and of the Commission on Social Justice – is that it is through investment that economic and social policy are inextricably linked; they are two sides of the same coin. An economic high road of growth and productivity must also be a social high road of opportunity and security. That is why this report constantly makes links between work and welfare, between labour market and family policy, between paid and unpaid work, between the production of wealth and the distribution of wealth, between economic and social regeneration, and between the structure of markets and the organisation of politics. To say that economic and social policy cannot be separated means far more than that we cannot afford social justice unless we have economic growth.[2]

There are at least four ways in which economic and social policy are linked. First, social inequality – low educational levels, unemployment, poor health, high crime – holds back economic growth.[3] It does so directly through the costs to government (higher spending on benefits, low revenue from taxes) and also to business (higher spending on security, and on training workers in basic English and arithmetic). It does so indirectly by deterring investors from whole parts of our cities and regions, depressing the demand for goods and services.

Second, where social justice is pursued primarily through investment in opportunities (rather than simply supporting the non-employed on benefits), it contributes directly to economic growth. In a global economy where the most important resource is human capital, investment in people simultaneously contributes both to social justice and to national economic strength.

Third, businesses thrive in supportive social environments, where there are flourishing networks of banks and financial institutions, community organisations, training organisations, technology transfer centres, schools, adult education colleges and universities, cultural and sports facilities.[4] The rich social fabric that allows people to live well enables businesses to do well too: 'social capital' is as important to economic performance as human, financial and physical capital.

Finally, markets (for labour, for finance, for goods and services) are not created by natural or divine forces: they are the product of the values, institutions, regulations and political decisions that govern them.[5] Markets are political – their structure determines their outcome. A minimum wage, for instance, raises the costs of the lowest-paying employers (which is why the Deregulators oppose it) as well as raising the incomes of the lowest-paid employees (which is why the Levellers generally support it); but it also gives employers a powerful incentive to increase their productivity in order to justify the wages (which is one of the reasons why Investors support it). In the same way, environmental taxes and regulations can impose new costs on business (which is why the Deregulators so often oppose them) as well as cutting pollution (which is why environmentalists support them): but their most important effect (and the reason why Investors back them) is to ensure that business finds the most efficient way of producing with less pollution. Intelligent regulation breaks out of the sterile debate of more versus less market power by generating markets that work better.

This is precisely the point of the Social Chapter of the EU's Maastricht Treaty, from which the UK Government negotiated an opt-out clause. The Social Chapter is not a legislative straitjacket: rather, it is designed to promote the investment in people that is at the heart of the Investors' strategy. The priority is to increase job opportunities, improve working conditions, promote dialogue between managers and workers and investment in training, and attack discrimination. The best companies already do these things; the Social Chapter seeks to make the practice of the best the assumption of the average. That is why Investors support it.

Future 1: Fair and Prosperous Britain

Investors, like Deregulators, believe that our economic future depends on successful international trade in goods and services. The difference is that Investors are convinced that, in the new world economy, success is increasingly based on raising the quality of what we produce, rather than on trying to cut the cost. Like Levellers, Investors seek to narrow, rather than widen, the gap between richest and poorest, and to ensure a fair and adequate benefits system. But while Levellers seek primarily to redistribute income, Investors believe that the original distribution of life-chances is as important as secondary redistribution of income; they therefore first seek to redistribute opportunities – to earn, to save and to own.

The Investors' strategy recognises both the social consequences of economic policies, and the economic consequences of social change and social division. Investors argue that anyone who is serious about reforming inequalities of income, power and opportunity must be interested in production as well as distribution. Social justice in the new economic world is above all concerned with economic opportunity, with wealth creation as well as wealth redistribution, and the primary mechanism by which it achieves this is paid work, backed up by the organisation of unpaid caring. Investors seek a redistribution of paid and unpaid work, as well as an end to injustice in employment.

In the past, countries have prospered on the basis of their natural endowment of raw materials. These are still important: the physical raw material of North Sea oil and the cultural raw material of the English language are major assets for the British economy. But they cannot be the basis of competitive strength on their own. Oil and every other natural resource are freely available in global markets: the companies and countries that prosper are those that can add value to the raw materials by combining them with skilled workers and the latest technology. (Japan, the world's most successful steel exporter, has none of the natural resources needed for steel.) The huge potential advantage that the English language gives the UK in the cultural industries – books, films, videos, educational materials – will be realised only

Figure 3.1 – The Link between Investment and Productivity

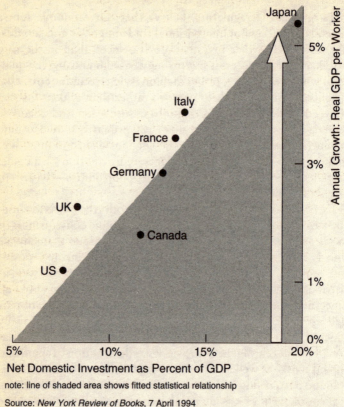

Net Domestic Investment as Percent of GDP

note: line of shaded area shows fitted statistical relationship

Source: *New York Review of Books*, 7 April 1994

if we produce literate, creative, imaginative people who can make the most of this cultural resource.

The chief argument of the free-marketeers is that low costs – low wages and low social protection – must be the basis of competitive strength for the UK, just as they are for some countries that are rapidly industrialising. It is absurd to think that we could cut our wages to the levels of Taiwan or Poland. But unless we raise our productivity very substantially indeed, wages will certainly fall. When he spoke to President Clinton's economic summit in December 1992, John Sculley, then President of Apple

Computers, summed up the strategic choice facing policy-makers: 'Do we want high skills, or low wages?' [6]

The issue facing the UK and other European countries is not how to *cut* our living standards, but how to *earn* them. To do this a programme must be developed to sell goods and services at the cutting edge of high value-added, knowledge-intensive industries. The strategy of constantly upgrading people's skills, the technology with which they work, the organisation of their work, and the goods and services they produce, is precisely that followed in the 1980s by the fastest-growing economies in the developed world. These were the countries which put a premium on social inclusion and opportunity.

A recent World Bank Report showed that in the High Performing Asian Economies (HPAEs), growth had been secured in a way that increased equity – through investment in people and infrastructure. Taken together, the eight leading HPAEs averaged growth rates between 1965 and 1990 of 5.5 per cent, compared with 2.4 per cent across the OECD as a whole; investment accounted for more than 20 per cent of GDP in the thirty years to 1990, and the World Bank attributes more than two-thirds of the growth to the high rates of investment.[7] The link between investment and productivity is starkly obvious: Figure 3.1 shows the power of investment to fuel growth.

While Deregulators and free-marketeers have always been attacked for the *social* consequences of their policies, the *economic* consequences of free-market economics are too often ignored. In reality, it is as true today as it was for Keynes fifty years ago that markets, left to themselves, do not generate satisfactory, let alone optimal, economic outcomes. The reality is that just as the freewheeling capitalism of the 1920s was unsustainable and required Keynesian intervention, so successful modern capitalist economies depend on precisely the social institutions and norms that free markets destroy. For example, the 'hire-and-fire' culture of casino capitalism destroys employee loyalty. The search for a fast buck destroys the trust that is the basis for successful co-operation between firms – in research and development or export marketing, for example.[8] The commitment to short-term dividends for shareholders rather than long-term investment for all stakeholders – employees, consumers and suppliers as well as shareholders – undermines the stability on which growing market share is built.[9]

The high-road strategy for Britain's economic future is based on six fundamental principles:

First, unregulated markets cannot by themselves deliver a satisfactory combination of economic growth and social cohesion; in fact, they deliver the worst of all worlds – low growth and high inequality. The alternative to free market economics is not the command economy; markets need to be shaped and regulated in the social and economic interest, not abolished.

Second, the concept of efficiency has to be supplemented as a measure of success by the idea of 'value-added'.[10] In the future, people are going to be paid for the value they add to the raw materials of a product, and they will be most handsomely rewarded for what they add through the application of brainpower. Efficiency is necessary to win markets, but it is not in itself sufficient; innovation is the key ingredient. What we make is as important as how cheaply we make it – selling semiconductor chips is more lucrative than selling potato chips.

Third, labour should be seen not as a cost but as a resource. Business leaders throughout the world stress that the key to success today is the quality of the people they employ. The failure to employ people as productively as possible and, above all, the failure to employ people at all is economic madness. In a dynamic and complex economic system, redundancy and unemployment will always occur; the challenge is to ensure that it does not last. Frictional unemployment is inevitable, but long-term unemployment is an evil which must be defeated.

Fourth, high wages are essential to give workers as consumers the ability to buy a wide range of goods and services – not merely the cheapest – and to generate the high demand that is essential to expanding employment in the growth areas of personal and leisure services. The primary aim must be to create as many high-paying jobs as possible, but we must also create opportunities for mobility, because low-status jobs are not going to disappear; education, training and benefit reform are the keys to both these ambitions.

Fifth, economic strategy cannot ignore its social consequences, because just as social cohesion has economic value, so social division has economic cost. This is the boomerang effect of modern economics.

Sixth, high investment – in skills, research, technology, childcare and community development – is the last and first step in this virtuous circle of sustainable growth; investment is at the heart of a decision about how to use the fruits of growth, whether we use growth for consumption today, or invest for our own future tomorrow. If we invest, and invest in all our people, then technological advance and human ingenuity can support economic prosperity for future generations.

These strategies for economic prosperity do not only generate the wealth on which social justice depends; in themselves they constitute essential elements in any plan for social justice. In the post-war years the central challenge was to sustain demand at a level commensurate with full employment (for men); the national insurance system was crucial not just to Beveridge's crusade against want, but to Keynes's attempt to save capitalism from the instability of its own business cycle. By boosting demand in times of economic downturn through, for example, unemployment benefit, Keynes and Beveridge ensured that economic and social policy could work hand in hand. Today, however, while demand management remains a fundamental issue at the European level, it is under-investment – and our capacity to export – rather than under-consumption that is the foremost economic problem. This is a major challenge to the existing conception of the welfare state, which must be turned from a safety net cushioning economic failure into a trampoline for economic success. A new sort of welfare state is required to match an investment-led economic strategy.

In the twenty-first century, the demands of a flexible pattern of life, a fast-changing and insecure labour market, and changes in family structure and family life will require the welfare state to play a more ambitious and empowering role. (We return to this in chapter 6.) To match the six principles of economic strategy outlined above, six principles of welfare strategy which are also needed:

First, freedom from poverty for all is at the heart of social justice; and the quickest way out of poverty, for those in a position to take up paid work, is a good job at a fair wage. The welfare state must be designed to promote personal independence, above all by helping people balance work, family and leisure across the life-cycle.

Second, to achieve social justice, we must increase national wealth as well as distribute it more equitably. A higher social security budget is a sign of economic failure, not social success; central to good social policy is an effective economic policy.

Third, social security comes from the confidence and ability to manage social and economic change at the personal level, and it is the job of the welfare state to help provide that confidence and capability. The new universalism is not based primarily on the provision of benefits when things go wrong, but on the investment in services to make sure they go right; not an ambulance service for unwanted contingencies, but a fitness centre to make possible the extension of life-chances. In the new welfare state, services – from childcare to training to eldercare – are as important to opportunity and security as cash.

Fourth, central to any social strategy is a strategy for families – building strong families, whatever form they may take. The economic and social value of good-quality parenting has been neglected for too long. At the heart of a secure family is the unpaid work of parents and other carers which needs to be recognised in family-friendly policies at the workplace and in the organisation of the welfare state.

Fifth, a fundamental ambition of social policy, not just through the benefits system but through its services as well, must be to promote personal autonomy and choice, for example for elderly people seeking care in the community, and for women no longer willing to be economically dependent on men.

Sixth, the categories of the Beveridge welfare state – employed or unemployed, young or old, married or unmarried – have become less rigid. Today, people are also non-employed, 'young elderly', and, in much larger numbers, divorced, cohabiting or remarried. The modern welfare state must therefore be based not on an outdated model of the 'typical' person; no such person exists. It must be personal and flexible rather than monolithic and

Investors' Britain: Economic and Social Principles

Economic Principles

1. Markets should be the servants and not the masters of the public interest.
2. Innovation wins markets; 'value-added' creates wealth.
3. Labour is the key resource; long-term unemployment is a costly waste.
4. The key to a good standard of living is to be found in high real wages and high employment; high productivity and high mobility should go together.
5. The economy is not a self-regulating system: economic policy has social effects, and social inequality rapidly produces high economic costs.
6. Under-investment not under-consumption is our central problem; investment in skills, research, childcare and community development is the precondition of future prosperity.

Social Principles

1. Freedom from poverty is the basis of social justice; and the quickest route out of poverty is a good job at a fair wage.
2. We must help the economy grow as well as distribute wealth more fairly; central to a good social policy is an effective economic policy.
3. Insecurity comes from risk, security from the ability to manage change; in the new welfare state, services are as central as cash to helping people negotiate social and economic change.
4. Strong families are vital social institutions. The unpaid work of parents and other carers must be supported, as much by the workplace as by the welfare state.
5. Social policy exists to promote autonomy and choice for individuals and families.
6. The modern welfare state must be tailored to the changing shape of people's lives.

bureaucratic, geared to the changing and complex life-cycles of the majority of people today.

The Investors' vision is ambitious and idealistic. It envisages the UK as a society marked by prosperous communities, strong families and social mobility, where we can all make a difference to the course of our own lives, and those of our families and our nation. Its wide-ranging strategies for reform, and their implications, are the concerns of the chapters which follow. But, first, a look at the alternatives.

Future 2: Harsher Britain, but Richer?

Powerful sections of the United Kingdom's political and business communities believe that the only way to grapple with global economic competition is to deepen the processes of deregulation, privatisation and opting-out that have governed the UK for fifteen years. The apostles of a deregulated Britain – some of them in the present government – *do* have a vision for this country. It is a vision of a strong economy in which inequality and injustice are the price we pay for an economic system – free market capitalism – that generates levels of prosperity unimaginable, they suppose, under any other system of economic organisation.

The Deregulators argue that Britain has only a few industries and services (mainly services) that can compete in the world economy on the basis of quality. The City of London is one example, at the forefront of a growing international trade in financial services. Companies in these fields must be free to pay their employees as much as they want to – not just in salaries, but in bonuses, share options, 'golden hellos' and 'golden handshakes'. By these means, they believe, entrepreneurs are encouraged, investment is promoted and risk rewarded. For the same reasons, taxes need to be as low as possible. The government's job is to stay out of the way, only providing regulation where it is absolutely necessary, and relying on self-regulation wherever possible. Michael Portillo summed up this view when he said, 'you cannot increase the role of the State without diminishing the scope for the individual'.[11]

In the rest of our industries and services, the Deregulators believe that the only way to compete with the Pacific Rim is to cut costs, in order to make Britain attractive to foreign investment, to compete with imports and to make our products cheaper abroad. That means *lower* wages for workers, less job security (because giving employees rights might discourage employers from creating jobs) and lower benefits (to keep taxes low and to give people incentives to take low-paid jobs).

In this vision, the UK's position in the EU and in the global economy depends upon a small minority of highly paid people earning high profits in high-value goods and services, and a somewhat larger group of people – many of them low-paid – who produce low-cost exports. The exporting sector will enable us to pay for the imports we want from abroad, and provide a stream of profits from foreign investment. On this basis we can stimulate business and domestic services that will provide a growing proportion of jobs: everything from the lawyers and designers to the security guards and sandwich-makers required for business, and everything from leisure and entertainment services to nannies, cleaners, gardeners and restaurants to improve the lifestyles of those with high incomes. Many of these service-sector jobs will be part-time or short-term and, in the Deregulators' plans, low-paid and insecure: but at least more people will have jobs.

Conservative optimists believe that lower taxes at the top and lower wages at the bottom will deliver prosperity for everybody. Conservative realists do not go so far, and say that economic inequality must be ameliorated through sturdy welfare provision.[12] In following this programme, the UK may end up with less equality, but at least it will have a stronger economy. And because the economy will be stronger, the poorest may be better off in absolute terms, even though the gap between them and the richest will be wider than ever. People at the top will do very well, and while people in the middle will struggle to keep up, they will be able to afford some of the cheap services on offer. But people in the bottom half of the population will do very badly indeed – plagued by job insecurity, stagnant or falling incomes, and limited opportunities to improve their situation.

Leaving to one side the morality of the extremes of poverty and wealth, of good services for those who can pay and shoddy provision for those who cannot, this strategy has serious problems. Its central economic proposition – that the spoils of economic combat go to the cheapest producer – is misguided. As Professor Jeffrey Pfeffer puts it:

> Cutting wages, benefits and employment levels can scarcely be a basis for sustained success over time because there is nothing particularly innovative or unique about these strategies – they can be readily imitated by others.[13]

The social consequences of deregulation and a minimal welfare state also have an economic cost that will hobble economic growth. And so an unfair society turns out to be burdened with a weak economy as well. The Deregulators have refused to learn the lessons of other, more successful market economies not only in Europe, but on the Pacific Rim and, most recently, in Latin America: economic growth depends on all citizens; the more productive each individual becomes, the more productive the overall economy; and lifting people out of poverty and sharing wealth more evenly improves a country's overall economic performance.[14]

The Deregulators' strategy has, after all, been tested. For the last fifteen years, the British government has sacrificed fairness, supposedly in order to create a healthier economy. Everything the Deregulators wanted – lower wages, lower rates of direct income tax, fewer employment rights and dramatically reduced trade union power – has been delivered. The result is certainly an unfair society. Yet we now also know that the Deregulators' recipe has not produced the growth miracle that it promised. Between 1979 and 1993, the British economy grew by only 1.7 per cent a year – compared with 2 per cent between 1974 and 1979.[15] As Bill Jordan, President of the Amalgamated Engineering and Electrical Union put it: 'If I could have had one wish, it would be that Mrs Thatcher had been the daughter of a manufacturer, not of a grocer.'[16]

Compared with most other European Union and Scandinavian countries, Britain has *both* a weaker economy *and* a less fair society. Total taxation – both direct and indirect – has risen, not fallen.

Dependency on state benefits has increased rather than the reverse. Crime has soared and disorder is more widespread. The direct costs of unemployment alone are £9,000 in benefits and lost taxes per unemployed person per year. Today, 30 per cent of public expenditure (not including debt interest) goes on social security transfer payments, compared to 8 per cent twenty-five years ago; and this despite the fact that benefits are less generous as a proportion of average earnings than they were then. Rather like the old Communists, who complained that the Soviet Union had never tried 'real socialism', the Deregulators ignore the evidence of failure and instead of questioning their prescription urge its ever more rigorous application.

If the UK did indeed go further along the Deregulators' road, what would be the consequences? In the 1980s, the bottom 10 per cent of the population saw an absolute fall in their level of income; over the next decade, the cancer of falling income will spread to the bottom 20 per cent, just as it has done in the USA. In the 1980s, the word 'ghetto' was used to describe the poorest inner city areas; in the next decade, 'ghetto' will describe middle-class areas policed by private security firms. In the 1980s, the deregulation and privatisation of public transport put mobility beyond the grasp of the poorest; in the next decade, clogged roads will impede the mobility of the richest. Since 1979, the tax burden has been forced up to pay the price of economic failure; in the next decade, it will be forced ever higher to pay the costs of social division, wasted human potential and continued economic failure.

The problem is not simply that the UK will become a less and less pleasant place in which to live. It is not only that an increasing proportion of government spending will be devoted to reacting to economic failure and social division: it will be spent on crime and policing and prisons, on unemployment and related benefits, on supplements to low pay, on homelessness and the health costs of poor housing. Nor is the problem just that lower taxes and lower social protection mean less money for government to invest; schools, hospitals and other services have to be squeezed back, and more people bribed or bullied to pay for these essentials in the private sector, setting in train a vicious circle of weaker and weaker collective services on which we all depend.

The real issue is that the economic strategy of low-cost production and the social strategy of a minimal welfare state completely fail to meet the demands of social and economic change. Only innovation, not cost-cutting, will win markets. The welfare state needs actively to facilitate change and reduce rigidity by promoting opportunities and life-chances across the life-cycle for all citizens.

In other words, deregulation does not address the sources of British underperformance that we diagnosed in Chapter 2. To deregulate further would deepen the economic and social problems we already have. As Professor Stephen Cohen, a leading economist at the University of California, has put it:

> Before Europe, in some futile quest for lower costs, sets out to dismantle its social protection system, it would be well advised to study the ironies of America's "cost savings" in such critical areas as child care, health, and social stability. These complement education and, like education and telecommunications, should be seen in the context of a realistic image of a modern production system.[17]

Future 3: Kinder, Poorer Britain?

In 1981, at the height of the first Conservative recession, Mrs Thatcher coined the expression 'There is no alternative'. She was mocked at the time, even though it was true that the Right were then making the intellectual running. The Deregulators' claim to have reversed British decline is now in shreds; but the claim that theirs is the only option on offer has gained force, partly because the logic of deregulation, short-termism and cost-cutting has become so embedded in our economic and social culture. The question now is whether it is too late to reverse the cycle of decline. Some people believe it is: they are the Levellers, who believe that the job of social reformers is to get the best available deal for the poorest in a system that leaves them vulnerable and excluded.

It is possible that the British economy will grow somewhat faster – at more than 2 per cent a year – for the next few years than it has for the last decade. But the weakness of our industrial and trading base suggests that, on present policies, reasonable growth levels are unlikely to be sustained. Some people would argue that the best we can do is take poor economic performance for granted: the job of a Commission on Social Justice should be to focus on the distribution of the welfare losses that follow from economic decline. If the economic cake cannot be expanded, government's responsibility is to share it out more fairly.

There are good reasons to believe that the external environment is likely to make it difficult for Europe to achieve growth rates on the levels of the 'long boom' of 1945 to 1973. The sharpening of world competition means that gains from trade are distributed between more countries, and the biggest gainers are going to be the Pacific Tigers, China and possibly India. Environmental pressure will put an important constraint on world growth rates, and the greatest burden will have to be borne by the wealthier countries. The growth of unemployment and social division throughout the industrialised world in the 1980s will not be lightly overcome. The social exclusion of anything between a tenth and a third of citizens will impose long term 'clean-up' costs on all the countries that have neglected the growth of inequality.

On top of the general problems facing Europe, the United Kingdom has specific economic problems of its own. At the height of recession, we are still unable to pay our way in world markets; our chronic current account weakness shows that we are unable to export enough goods and services to finance the imports we require. We are on the geographical edge of Europe, with a comparatively poorly educated and trained workforce, and with management practice and work organisation below world standards. Our infrastructure – technical, physical, social – is crumbling.

The Levellers are pessimists, and they have plenty of evidence on their side. The Levellers would, therefore, leave business to get on with producing as much as it could (although within a tighter framework of employees' rights), while the job of government would be to concentrate on redistribution through the tax and benefit system. This strategy is coherent, and it has moral force: whether or not the economy grows, its fruits should be more fairly shared.

At the heart of the Levellers' argument is the view that given current economic trends, redistribution through taxes and benefits must be the basis of social justice, and that we cannot rely on paid work to haul the poor out of poverty. Mass unemployment and underemployment are here to stay, partly because of technological change, partly because of increasing global competition, and partly because the unemployed lack the skills to get jobs in an economy where, according to some estimates, 40 per cent of jobs are going to require an undergraduate degree or better qualification by the year 2000.[18] Even amongst those who do get some employment, a large number will never be able to command a living wage. Either way, substantial resources will have to be redistributed to prevent a large minority of people being completely excluded from social participation.

Levellers' Britain would be committed to reducing extremes. A growing public revulsion against greed, together with redistributive tax policies and, perhaps, some form of incomes policy would mean fewer, if any, people earning vast salaries; while more generous benefits, improved social housing and better public services would prevent youngsters and homeless adults sleeping on the streets. Government would mobilise community groups, churches and volunteers to support the public services and build a new ethic of social responsibility. Higher benefits would cut poverty amongst those out of work; higher expenditure on public services would provide better jobs and an improved quality of life.

However, restraints on top incomes, coupled with high tax rates, would send some – perhaps a large number – of the top earners and businesses abroad. As the economy would grow only slowly, tax rates would have to rise to finance benefits and services – and the practical limits to tax increases would in practice mean that both benefits and services would be cut. If those in work responded by trying to raise their earnings to make up for tax rises, inflation and unemployment could rise again. In practice, there is a fine line between the pursuit of a kinder, poorer Britain and the reality of a harsher, poorer Britain.

Although the pessimists are right about many of the UK's economic weaknesses, they ignore both our continuing potential and the public sense that now is the time to realise it. In two of the four areas identified by the European Commission for future economic growth – tourism and cultural industries – Britain has real advantages of language, cultural heritage and creativity. It is possible that our very early (and painfully over-rapid) shift from industry to services will make for competitive advantage as international trade in services grows. We have companies and institutions – from Marks and Spencer to the BBC – that are the envy of other countries. And above all we have the resource of our people, whose talent is seen in the achievement of thousands who make it to the top, but whose potential is neglected in the millions who do not fulfil their talents.

Conclusion

Like the Deregulators, the Levellers misunderstand the nature of modern capitalism. Both remain trapped by the traditional and self-defeating framework of policy debate in Britain – a framework in which we are forced to choose between collective action and market dynamism, instead of creating a more productive relationship between the two. The reality in the twenty-first century will be interdependence between public and private sectors, between state and market; one cannot exist without the other.

The lessons of the three futures should therefore be clear. To move from the low road of relative economic decline to the high road of secure prosperity, we need to break our economic and social logjam. A project of national renewal cannot afford to leave sections of the population behind. To succeed in the world economy as it is today, and to bind up the social wounds that cost us so much, we have to mobilise the talents of all individuals and the energies of all communities; as the Commission was told in Manchester, there is no social justice without hope, and there is no hope without economic opportunity.

But economic and social modernisation are not easy: the countries that have managed it in the last 100 years – Germany, Japan, and now the countries of the Pacific Rim – have all combined simultaneous reform of the financial system, investment in education and training, and reform of the state machine, to produce a credible strategy for national renewal. In the UK, we need to make a virtue of the democratic impulse that should be at the heart of any change. That is why the Investors' strategy is bottom-up as well as top-down. But the Investors do not offer a magic solution to the UK's problems. The strategy is honest and hard-nosed.

In the policy chapters that follow, we move forward from the description of Chapter 1, the diagnosis of Chapter 2, and the strategies of this chapter. We show how the values of the Investors – opportunity, security, responsibility – can be combined with new policy ideas to tackle the underlying problems facing this country. Together, they constitute a formidable challenge; but our vision is not a mirage, and there is no time to lose in setting out to achieve it.

Notes

1. Robert Kuttner 'Labor Policy' in Mark Green (ed) *Changing America – Blueprints for the New Administration* (New York: Newmarket Press, 1992)

2. This was the argument made by Secretary of State for Social Security Peter Lilley in his Mais Lecture 'Benefits and Costs: Securing the future of social security' 23 June 1993

3. See Andrew Glyn and David Miliband (eds) *Paying for Inequality: The Economic Costs of Social Injustice* (London: Rivers Oram Press, 1994)

4. See for example Robert Puttnam *Making Democracy Work: Civic Traditions in Modern Italy*, Michael Porter *The Competitive Advantage of Nations* (London: Macmillan, 1991) and Wolfgang Streeck and Egon Matzner (eds) *Beyond Keynesianism* (Brookfield, Vermont: Elgar, 1991)

5. See Colin Crouch and David Marquand (eds) *Ethics and Markets* (Oxford: Blackwell, 1993) and Amitai Etzioni *The Moral*

Dimension: Towards a New Socioeconomics (New York: Free Press, 1988)

6. *President Clinton's New Beginning: The Clinton-Gore Economic Conference* (New York: Donald Fine, 1992)

7. World Bank *The East Asian Miracle* (Oxford: OUP, 1993)

8. See Wolfgang Streeck *The Social Institutions of Economic Performance* (London: Sage, 1992)

9. In the UK in the 1980s, dividends rose by an average of 12 per cent per year, profits by 6 per cent and investment by only 2 per cent. And significantly, some of the most important technological advances in the post-war period in the UK have been achieved by companies sheltered from the demands of the stock market for quick profit – for example Pilkington's float glass process, and Reuter's dealing systems.

10. John Kay *The Foundations of Corporate Success* (Oxford: OUP, 1993)

11. Michael Portillo *The Blue Horizon* (London: Centre for Policy Studies, 1993)

12. This was the argument put by Chancellor of the Exchequer Kenneth Clarke in his Mais Lecture 'The Changing World of Work in the 1990s', 4 May 1994

13. Jeffrey Pfeffer *Competitive Advantage Through People* (Boston: Harvard Business School Press, 1994)

14. John Naisbitt *Global Paradox* (London: Nicholas Brealey, 1994)

15. GDP at factor cost; *UK National Accounts 1993* Table 1.1 and *UK Economic Accounts 1994* Table A(i) (London:HMSO 1993, 1994)

16. Quoted in David Bowen, 'Building a world-class workforce', the *Independent,* 13 October 1993

17. Stephen Cohen 'Geo-Economics and America's Mistakes' in Martin Cornoy *et al* (eds) *The New Global Information Age* (Philadelphia: Penn State Press, 1993)

18. David Grayson and John Wybrew 'Work in Society', *RSA Journal* (London: RSA, April 1994)

PART THREE

STRATEGIES FOR THE FUTURE

4

INVESTMENT: ADDING VALUE
THROUGH LIFELONG LEARNING

'Education is the most important thing of all. With it you
can get a job and move up the social ladder.'

*Nadia, a sixth-former at Mulberry School
in London's East End.*

● ● ●

We are inspired by a vision of national renewal, where everybody
is engaged in creating a better society and a dynamic economy. At
the heart of that vision is the extension of opportunity: the opportunity for us all to learn, to earn and to care for our families.

Equality of opportunity is often dismissed as a weak aspiration. But if every child and every adult is to fulfil his or her potential, we need a social and economic revolution. We have to create
an economy that generates new jobs and businesses faster than
old ones are destroyed. Instead of an inefficient and divided
labour market, we need fairness and flexibility to allow men and
women to combine employment, family, education and leisure in
different ways at different stages of their lives. In place of the old
conflict between better protection for working people and lower
profits for employers, we need new social standards designed to
raise the contribution which workers can make to the productivity of their organisations. Above all, we will have to transform
our old education system, designed to serve an academic élite and
to fail the rest, into a means for lifelong learning.

Deregulators argue that the less government does, the more
opportunities there are for individuals. But opportunity does not
depend only on individual effort. That is why Investors argue for
collective action and above all collective investment – whether it

is public, private, voluntary or a partnership of all three – to promote individual opportunity. The first and most important task for government is to set in place the opportunities for children and adults to learn to their personal best. By investing in skills, we raise people's capacity to add value to the economy, to take charge of their own lives, and to contribute to their families and communities. 'Thinking for a living' is not a choice but an imperative.[1]

Thinking for a living

Lifelong learning is at the heart of our vision of a better country. A good education is the most effective way to overcome inequalities of birth and status, to enable people to create and seize new opportunities, and to promote social improvement and mobility. As new technologies transform what is possible, a high level of skills, constantly updated, will increasingly be the passport to satisfying leisure as well as to a decent job. 'Empowerment' is a politician's word: but it is absolutely real to the women we met at Handsworth College in Birmingham, whose vision of what they could do with their lives had been transformed by a 'women-into-management' course.

The social benefits of learning have been central to civic life since the Ancient Greeks. The *economic* centrality of education and training is also now widely accepted.[2] It is absurd to believe that economic success can buy us the 'luxury' of lifelong learning. Only lifelong learning can win us the prize of economic success.[3]

The mass-production economy did not need a well-educated mass of workers. All that was required of most employees was that they obediently followed the orders of the small group of planners and supervisors who did the thinking for everyone. But new high-performance organisations – with flat hierarchies and team working – depend upon a high level of skill and creativity throughout their workforce. Management layers disappear as front-line workers become responsible for many of the tasks – from quality control to production scheduling – that their 'superiors' used to do.

For individuals as well as companies and countries, education and training are the foundations of economic security. Already, the OECD estimates that one in ten jobs in the industrialised world will disappear every year.[4] People starting work now can expect to change jobs and employers half a dozen times or more during their working lives, with the risk that every change could mean a move down and not up. As one 38-year-old software designer in Norwich told us : 'I'm already out of date, compared with the kids coming up behind me.' According to the USA's Labor Department, half of the skills acquired today will be out of date within three to five years. Yet only two decades ago, the average worker's skills lasted between seven and fourteen years.[5] Education and training alone cannot solve the problem of unemployment, although the bankers Kleinwort Benson have gone as far as to estimate that there would be 1 million fewer people unemployed in the UK if our standards matched the best in the OECD.[6] In the modern economy, individual security no longer stems from a job for life, but from skills that last throughout life.

Education and training are already undergoing enormous change in the UK. Some reforms are widely accepted as beneficial: the National Curriculum was long overdue, though its details are very controversial. The delegation of some financial power to schools makes sense. But some of the changes have made things worse, rather than better, notably the creeping return to selection at eleven years old, and the accumulation by central government, in the person of the Secretary of State for Education, of hundreds of new powers since 1979. Although this country is a market leader in the development of distance learning, largely thanks to the Open University, the present government has not begun to grasp the extraordinary possibility offered by modern technology – that we will be able to learn almost anything, anywhere, at any time. Assumptions about who learns, when and where need to be fundamentally rethought. Mobility between and flexibility within institutions of learning will become the rule, rather than the exception.

Of course, 'learning' is not the same as 'schooling'. Provision beyond the school or workplace is crucial to the success of education and/or training within it. That is why Professor Tim Brighouse, Chief Education Officer of Birmingham City Council, has talked of his vision of a 'University of the First Age', coordinating beyond-school opportunities and devoted to 'transforming the expectations and the speed of learning of youngsters', while offering second and third chances for all pupils.[7]

Successful schools are the basis of an educated population. However, the internal organisation of the school system does not fall within our remit. But to revitalise our education system on the basis of high standards and high performance, there are six priorities that need to be highlighted:

- A universal system of pre-school education for 3- and 4-year olds and new investment in childcare
- An attack on the problem of inadequate basic skills
- An end to the divide between education and training for 14-19-year-olds, in order to promote high achievement
- A minimum training investment by all employers
- Expansion of higher education, with a new and fairer system of funding
- A 'Learning Bank' to extend to every adult the opportunity of learning throughout life

Deregulators see investment in education and training as a burden on government coffers like any other; Investors see it as an investment in people unlike any other.

First Goal: Universal Nursery Education and a New Investment in Childcare

We learn more and develop faster in our first five years than at any other time in our lives. If we want to be serious about investing in people, we must start at the beginning. But the investment we make in babies and young children is wholly inadequate.

- Parents' entitlement to time at home with young babies is less than in almost any other European Union country: there is no statutory paternity leave, a shorter period of paid maternity leave, no parental leave, and no subsequent family leave available to either parent in emergencies.[8]

- Investment in education for under-fives in the UK is 4 per cent of the education budget compared to 11 per cent in Norway and 10 per cent in France.[9]
- Childcare services are scarce, fragmented and inequitable. Although 47 per cent of UK mothers of children under five go out to work, there are publicly funded daycare places for less than 1 per cent of under-fives.[10] Eighty-six per cent of childcare services in the UK get no funding from the public purse.[11]

This country urgently needs a coherent, comprehensive approach to the needs of under-fives and young schoolchildren. 'Daycare' has traditionally been separated from 'pre-school education', the former the responsibility of social services departments and the latter of local education authorities. The 1989 Children Act requires local authorities to review all their provisions for children under eight every three years, but there is no requirement to provide pre-school education and they are only required to provide daycare services for children 'in need'. This produces nursery schooling which ignores children's needs for care; publicly-funded care services limited to deprived families and communities; and the development of separate and thereby often stigmatised services for children with working and non-working parents, instead of an integrated approach to the needs of children, their families and others who look after them.

A national strategy for the under fives

The UK needs a new strategy that simultaneously meets the needs of growing children and extends their parents' choices[12]: under-fives provision is good for children, good for parents and good for the economy and society. Although government should take the lead in developing this new strategy, it is not and cannot be the job of government to provide every service itself. Government should set targets for a wide extension of high-quality pre-school education and childcare services, and create a clear national framework of objectives and responsibilities, better training, and publicity for best practice. The UK must not go the way of the USA, where a recent large-scale study has found that more than half of under-threes are being cared for in ways that damage their development and educational potential.[13]

Because babies and very young children need continuous, individual care, consistently given by adults whom they know, the first element in any strategy must be time for parents who wish to care for children themselves. But whatever changes are made to working patterns, many parents need and will continue to need part-time or full-time childcare provision, for infants as well as older children. Some parents may need collective childcare starting immediately after maternity leave, while others may prefer to have children cared for individually, in their own home or in that of the carer. Such private arrangements should not exclude children and their carers from community resources; as well as effective registration and inspection procedures, all local authorities should be encouraged to do what the best already do in offering support to childminders and other carers. Good-quality nursery education, with extended care where it is needed, should be offered to 3- and 4-year-olds; we should also aim to extend out-of-school and holiday care for under-elevens. Collective provision of care and education should not be seen as a substitute for parenting, but as a support for it and an enrichment of children's lives.

The second step should be to build upon the review of services to under-eights which local authorities already have to make, by requiring social services and education departments to work together and with parents, community organisations, businesses and schools to draw up an effective local strategy. As a start, every local authority should be expected to develop a comprehensive information and advice service. North Tyneside Council already offers parents and employers such a service through its 'childcare shop'. Local authorities should be encouraged to develop integrated services brought together in centres that make the full range of services flexibly available to all children and carers. Manchester City Council's children's centres, for example, provide part-time and full-time day nursery care, informal parent-and-toddler sessions and out-of-school care for older children, but the council bears the £12 million cost on its own, with no help from central government.

Universal pre-school education

Following a succession of reports from the House of Commons Select Committee on Education, Science and Arts, the Royal Society of Arts and the National Commission on Education, the support for universal education for three- and four-year-olds is overwhelming.[14] Studies in several countries, including a recent one from the Republic of Ireland, have shown that early-years education has positive effects that last well beyond the primary school years and affects much more than children's academic performance.[15] At sixteen-plus, young people who have had pre-school education are more likely to undertake further education or training than those who have not, *irrespective of their measured success in school.*

In the 'HighScope' study, the most detailed of its kind, American researchers monitored and costed the effect of pre-school education on the fortunes of children from poor African-American families in Ypsilanti, Michigan, tracking them through to twenty-nine years of age. Children who had pre-school education were considerably more likely to complete high-school or further education, three times more likely to own their own homes, four times more likely to earn a good income and five times less likely to have been in repeated trouble with the law. Every $1 invested in nursery education produced a payoff of over $7 – partly because of the savings on police, prisons and probation services, partly because of the taxes paid by those former nursery schoolchildren when they became adult earners.[16]

We endorse the target of the National Commission on Education (NCE) that the UK should aim to provide 85 per cent of 3-year-olds and 95 per cent of 4-year-olds with pre-school education. If we can achieve the target by the year 2000, as opposed to the target of 2005 set by the National Commission on Education, so much the better. Nursery education must, however, be first rate. Although 26 per cent of three-and four-year-olds are in nursery schools and classes, a further 19 per cent are in infants' school reception classes designed for the rising-fives, with one teacher responsible for twenty children or more. Such classes do not and cannot meet the needs of younger children.[17] Instead, education for 3- and 4-year-olds needs to be provided in small, tailor-made groups, whether in pre-school playgroups, nursery classes attached to infants' schools, purpose-built nursery schools or children's centres, with proper adult input.[18]

Teaching young children is now recognised as at least as important, and difficult, as teaching 18-year-olds. Government should set training standards for all those working with young children. A recent survey of 2,000 early-years establishments found that only a quarter of the teachers had been appropriately trained.[19] One step forward would be to make child development a core component of all teacher training. We see no place for cost-saving measures within the teaching profession such as a 'mum's army'. But not every adult working with children needs to be a fully qualified teacher. Classroom assistants, often recruited from among parents, already provide substantial help to teachers, and some will themselves move on to obtain teaching qualifications.[20] As we expand services for children, we should also mobilise the group in the community whose energy and skills remain all too often untapped: the 'Third Age' of fit and active people in their 50s, 60s and even 70s. Some training should, of course, be offered, and some payment should be made. But these volunteer 'social grandparents' would complement, not replace, trained teachers and play-leaders, and would not require the same level of either training or salary.

Paying for childcare and nursery education

Good-quality care and education does not come cheap. The costs of near-universal provision are estimated by the National Commission on Education at £860 million; the Department for Education put the figure for doubling take-up in England among 3- and 4-year-olds to 90 per cent at over £1 billion per year.[22] In either case, it will take several years to achieve universal provision. So great is the importance of this investment, however, that we would make it one of the highest priorities for government investment over the next decade. One option, put forward by the National Commission on Education, is to transfer money within the education budget, broadly from higher education (through an income-related student loans scheme). These resources may, however, be needed to expand the higher education system itself. One alternative possibility for funding nursery education is discussed in Chapter 7.

Nursery education, like statutory schooling, should be free to parents. It is simply not feasible, however, to aim to provide all child*care* facilities, including additional care for children in nursery and primary education, free at the point of use. Where a child is being cared for outside the family, whether privately or in publicly-funded facilities, charges for that care should continue for those parents who can afford them. In Australia a federal government system of daycare fee relief applies to private and community, as well as public, daycare services and has led to a rapid expansion in the number of high-quality places available. Since much UK provision is private, we should consider applying a common system to all registered services, including child-minders and playgroups provided they meet nationally agreed standards. The aim would be to enable service providers to raise standards while the service remains affordable to all. Playgroups, for example, could increase the number of sessions available to each child to five per week, and offer extended days to those requiring them.

Some local authorities have already developed a sliding scale of charges, so that parents on low incomes pay nothing while those who can afford it pay a full fee. While means-testing traditionally causes poverty traps for people on low incomes, this problem can be overcome if the charges start for people earning a reasonable wage. In order to avoid the problem of very different charges in different parts of the country, national government should establish an advisory fee-relief system for local authorities' use.

In developing early-years services, local authorities will also need to establish public/private funding partnerships designed to tap new resources, including subsidies from employers towards childcare places for their employees.[23] Local partnerships will also be able to apply for and receive European Union structural funds, particularly in areas of industrial decline and in deprived rural communities. In some areas, the capital costs of developing a new nursery or children's centre could be partly or wholly met by 'planning gain' (where planning permission for a new development includes the building of social facilities). National government itself should also aim to increase public funding for childcare services, for instance by earmarking a budget available for local programmes which can provide models of best practice. Investment in childcare services can also provide a return to government, as well as families and children. For instance, the Government's own costings for the £40 disregard (for the purposes of calculating Family Credit) for childcare costs announced in the 1993 Budget, suggest that £220 million of £250 million per year expenditure is recouped in savings on other benefits and increased tax revenue as women enter the workforce.[24] In addition, local authorities should be given powers to seek voters' support for raising local revenue for specified purposes, including childcare facilities (see Chapter 7).

Second Goal: Basic Skills for Every Child

There is much to admire in our education system. In classrooms up and down the country, we have seen enormous commitment and high performance from teachers and pupils alike. The number of students staying on at school has risen, partly as a result of the recent recession but also because of the positive effects of new methods of teaching and learning at GCSE level and beyond. We need organisations designed to bring out the best in every individual. The crude testing of individuals initiated by the Government has given attempts to assess school effectiveness a bad name, but more sensitive, 'value-added', school-based measures – designed to measure the progress pupils make – can help schools focus on their own performance, and their own success in adding value. Greater choice for parents is meaningless if there are not enough good schools, and those which are oversubscribed end up choosing which children they want to admit.

We know from detailed academic research what makes a good school: strong leadership from the Head, continuous staff and curriculum review, parental involvement, and a culture of high expectations, among other things.[25] An effective, successful, local school, which increases the knowledge and skills of all pupils, should be the birthright of all children. At the end of the twentieth century it is intolerable that an advanced country should have citizens with problems of basic literacy and numeracy. Yet in the UK one in five 21-year-olds has problems with basic maths, one in seven has problems with basic reading and writing,[26] and reading standards among 11- and 15-year-olds have not significantly improved since 1945.[27]

Illiteracy and innumeracy are an economic disaster: young men and women with poor basic skills are more than twice as likely to be unemployed as the average, and on average they are out of work for five times longer than those who communicate well.[28] Men without basic skills suffer particularly from unemployment; they are twice as likely to be unemployed as women with the same problems.[29] Traditionally, girls have shown earlier aptitude for reading, writing and verbal communication; partly because of highly stereotyped assumptions about the proper role of women, they have also been powerfully encouraged to develop their personal skills. There is now disturbing evidence that boys are falling even further behind in schools, with six boys to every girl in special units for children with behavioural or discipline problems.[30]

Basic skills should be learnt young, when they are most easily acquired. Given adequate educational opportunity and investment, almost all children can learn to read fluently by the age of seven and it is essential that they should do so. Because children who cannot read find it hard to learn anything else, they are more likely to be bored, disruptive or to play truant. Government and local education authorities should therefore commit themselves to the target of ensuring that every seven-year-old can read. Achieving the target will require a proper 'reading recovery' programme for pupils who are having difficulty with reading in Years 2 or 3 of primary education. There are various pilot projects in Britain and abroad from which schools can learn. Professor Marie Clay's programme of one-to-one tuition for half an hour a day for sixteen weeks is a popular and promising model. In June 1994 twenty-six LEAs had set up the scheme. An investment of this kind would after a time save money by reducing the number of pupils unable to cope later on.[31] A Literacy Guarantee should be matched by a 'Numeracy Guarantee' at the same age. In both cases, intensive tuition for 6- and 7-year-olds needs to be followed up by careful monitoring, and perhaps further guarantees, at eleven and fourteen, to prevent pupils slipping behind again, and to ensure that they start secondary education with the essential skills.

As in under-fives services, volunteers can support the work of professional teachers. Three quarters of the pupils at Winton Primary School in the London Borough of Islington speak English as their second language, and two-thirds qualify for free school meals. The Headmistress, Mrs Jane Fulford, has enthusiastically involved not only parents, but Community Service Volunteers and volunteers from local banks and other businesses to offer one-to-one help with reading, to improve the play area, and to coach football. 'I've no doubt that the volunteers have helped us improve standards,' she told us. 'We're having to put more difficult books into the classrooms, which is a pretty good indication that our children are learning to read better.'

We also need to tackle the problem of missing basic skills amongst adults. A good starting point would be programmes targeted at those of the long-term unemployed with basic skills problems; it would be part of the process of reconnecting this group with the labour market. It is also essential that we build on the work being done by the Adult Literacy and Basic Skills Unit in the area of family literacy: educating mothers not only enhances their life-chances, it improves the skills of their children.

In Rathcoole, Belfast, the Commission saw 'Bytes for Belfast', an innovative project housed in a youth centre and supported by the Belfast Action Team. Modelled on a similar and highly successful programme in Harlem, New York, the scheme offers disaffected young people the opportunity to apply their aptitude for video games to a wide range of sophisticated information technology programmes. In the process, they gain the skills and self-confidence they so desperately lack.

Third Goal: High Achievement for Every Young Person

An education system appropriate to the demands of the twenty-first century must be designed to establish a foundation of knowledge and skill for all children and to nurture the particular talents of each child.[32] But that is exactly what our system is failing to do. Only just over one in four English students attains two or more A-levels, with about 10 per cent achieving the vocational equivalent,[33] while the French government is on target to get 80 per cent of school-leavers to *baccalauréat* standard by the year 2000. Although participation rates among 16-year-olds are improving rapidly, the qualifications system blocks progression. Beyond the age of 17, less than half our young people are in full-time education. The talent is there, the demand is there, but both run up against the buffers of a system designed to select an élite rather than educate a majority.

The twin tracks of the English and Welsh education and training systems – academic A levels on the one hand and vocational training on the other – are both flawed. While A levels are too narrow and force early specialisation, the vocational track lacks intellectual rigour and economic status. In the past, graduates from the government's Youth Training Scheme have had a lower chance of getting a job than those with no qualifications at all.[34] The Government introduced General National Vocational Qualifications (GNVQs), with strong general education components, in an attempt to bring vocational training up to A-level status; but this is more a practical recognition of the problem than a remedy for it.

The division between education and training is damaging because it polarises knowledge and skill into separate courses rather than combining them to promote understanding; it splits theory and practice when the demand from the economy and from society is that they be combined; it reduces the motivation of the majority of young people because it condemns them to a 'silver' and 'bronze' level vocational education while the minority are allowed onto the prestigious academic track; and it forces a false choice between general and vocational education when it is a combination that we all need as preparation for a life of change and continuous learning. The requirement is to discover and develop the talent of every young person and deliver to them all a balance of intellectual and practical study.

The traditional approach to reform is to argue that the top third of pupils should take five subjects at A-level standard rather than two or three, and that the quality of the vocational alternative must be improved. Both steps would be helpful. But we agree with the National Commission on Education that a far more radical approach is needed. We must start where the problem starts, with the division between education and training. We must develop a unified qualifications system, broadening the A-level and vocational experience, and incorporating and replacing today's divided pattern. Its components should be organised as modular units, tailored to the pace at which individual students can learn, encouraging them to forge ahead where they are strong and consolidate in areas of weakness. Although students would be based at school or college, they could also study some work-based options.

The present system of qualifications drives our education system towards selecting a few and failing the rest. Reform of qualifications is needed to drive an integrated education and training system towards participation and progression for everyone. The details of a unified system obviously need to be worked out, though models already exist.[35] The aim must be to allow the diversity of talent that already exists to flourish. The basic principles we support for this country are:

- The creation in the long term of a single qualification to be awarded on graduation from secondary education – a 'British Baccalauréat' – broadening the A level experience and providing general educational rigour for those currently in specialised vocational options.
- The development of a credit-based system of learning, so that students have wide choice of courses.
- A review of the status of the GCSE examination at 16-plus – England and Wales are now the only industrialised countries except Russia with a 'school-leaving' exam at 16.

- A combination of continuing assessment of coursework with final assessment through exams.
- A commitment to high-status and high-quality work-based learning.

Youth training

However rewarding the new programme of learning options, some young people will still decide to leave education. There are currently 270,000 16- and 17-year olds on Youth Training and a further 80,000 who are neither in work nor in education nor on youth training. Some of them are homeless, all of them are vulnerable to long-term unemployment and low-paid, insecure work. Raising the school-leaving age is not the way to deal with young adults sick of school.

The Government has announced a 'modern apprenticeship' scheme to provide in-work training up to NVQ Level 3 for 150,000 16- and 17-year-olds. Although new apprenticeships may have a place, especially in the short-term, courses and qualifications should be integrated with mainstream education and training.

Some young adults leave school for a job. But too often their employers fail to train them in the 'learning to learn' skills that are the basis of future employment security.[36] We strongly agree with the CBI's Taskforce on Vocational Education and Training, which emphasised that employers should not be allowed to dodge their responsibility to provide training for young workers.[37] Part-time training, at a standard equivalent to A levels, should therefore be compulsory for all 16- and 17-year-old employees. Employers who do not provide the training themselves should fund it at a further education college. Training and Enterprise Councils (TECs) and, in Scotland, Local Enterprise Councils could provide advice, organise some training themselves and monitor employers. Because of the costs to employers, they should be allowed to pay 16- and 17-year-olds a 'Training Wage' at a lower rate than our proposed national minimum wage (see page 206).

Maintenance allowances

There remains the question of financial support for students beyond school-leaving age. It is unfair and wasteful that 16-19 year-olds sometimes have to give up study in order to support parents or siblings, or simply to get enough money to participate in teenage social life. At present the only financial support for this age group – after the abolition of their right to Income Support – is Child Benefit, paid to a parent.

Some people argue that government should offer educational maintenance allowances (EMAs) or study grants to all 16- and 17-year-olds. However, about three-quarters of 16-year-olds already stay on in education; we have to ask whether an EMA would persuade the minority who currently leave at sixteen to stay on, and whether payments of this kind would be a cost-effective way to raise standards of achievement. An EMA of £30 a week to every 16- and 17-year-old currently in education would cost about £1.5 billion a year; a payment of £50 would cost about £2.5 billion. We do not believe that this is a sensible use of resources. However, the financial pressure on young people from poor homes to leave school and find work (or get a Youth Training place, which pays £29.50 per week for 16-year-olds) should not be underestimated. That is why, despite the problems of means-testing, there is a strong case for a national income-related grant to support the poorest 16- and 17-year-olds who stay on in full-time education and training.

Fourth Goal: Training for Every Employee

This country can only achieve the productivity improvements it needs to create a high-skill, high-pay economy if employers invest in workers' skills and their ability to add value to the company. Although business spends an estimated £25 billion a year on training, according to CBI Director-General Howard Davies, our record is not impressive.[38] Nearly two-thirds of UK employers invest less than 2 per cent of payroll costs in training; three-quarters of French employers invest more than that level.[39]

Under-investment in training is one of the major weaknesses of the Deregulators' neo-liberal economics. Companies are reluctant to train, fearing that staff in whom they have invested will be poached by competitors. The most successful market economies have taken a simple step to cure this market failure by setting minimum standards for all employers. In Germany, businesses contribute nearly 3.5 per cent of payroll towards training, employment and unemployment programmes. In France, the minimum training investment, initially 1 per cent of payroll, is now moving to 2.5 per cent. In Singapore, employers contribute 1 per cent of payroll to a national skills development fund, and Japanese companies invest the same proportion into a national employment insurance fund which provides training as well as unemployment compensation.

The last attempt by the government to tackle this problem – through a training 'levy-grant' system – was, however, bureaucratic and widely evaded, and therefore resented by the employers who did follow the rules. All firms had to pay the levy, and those carrying out satsifactory training gained rebates. Instead of this system, all but the smallest organisations should be required to invest a minimum proportion of each employee's earnings in training, and only required to pay into common funds if their training investment does not reach the specified level. The initial figure could be set at 1 per cent or 1.5 per cent of payroll, moving up gradually to at least 2 per cent. Employers unable to provide that level of training themselves would be required to put the difference towards training, either through collective provision at TEC level, or through the Individual Learning Accounts of their employees set up via the Learning Bank, described below.

Training opportunities are unequally divided within firms and between them. The Institute for Fiscal Studies argues that the growth in skills differentials is primarily due to a polarisation between high-pay jobs in skill-intensive plants and relatively low-pay jobs in low-skilled plants.[40] Compulsory payments into Individual Learning Accounts by firms who do not provide training will allow people to move from low-skill workplaces to high-skill ones much more easily.

Some of the UK's most far-sighted companies are investing

much more than our proposed minimum in creating a learning culture at the workplace. As part of its strategy to overtake the Japanese, Rover invests £200 per employee through a separate company, Rover Learning plc, allowing employees to take up almost any course, from metalwork to French to computer science. But Rover and other employers who make the same investment are only allowed to offset the costs of *job-related* training against tax. A small but important reform would be to allow businesses to deduct all the costs of helping their employees to learn. Rover, Ford and other companies that have given employees new rights to education and training have been astonished by the take-up. We need to think of the skills of a company's workforce as an asset like any other and – as the OECD suggests – reform acccountancy practice so that human capital is a recordable asset which can be considered by investors.[41] People want to learn, our country needs them to learn, and government must help provide the opportunities for them to do so.

Fifth Goal: Expand Higher Education through a Fair Funding System

British universities have always provided a world-class education for a small number of students. But the challenge for the twenty-first century is to extend these high standards to far more people. The growing number of people taking degrees is good news; the proportion of 18 to 19 year olds entering higher education rose from one in eight in 1979 to one in four in 1992. It now stands at three in ten. Many more mature students are also entering degree courses. But the present structure and funding of universities simply cannot cope. Staff are overwhelmed by a bureaucratic paperchase caused by the introduction of an internal market; they lack the critical mass of support necessary to a thriving research base; and support staff, libraries and laboratories are being squeezed. Unless we make fundamental changes, the expansion of our system will be a botched job.

The present government, which wants to see one in three 18 to 19-year-olds entering higher education by the end of the century,

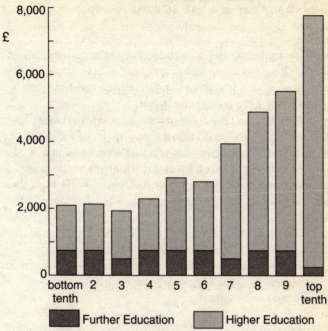

Figure 4.1 Rich Pickings

Expenditure on Further and Higher Education by decile of annualised lifetime net income

Source: Nick Barr, Jane Falkingham and Howard Glennerster
Funding Higher Education (London: BP/LSE, 1994)

is rationing resources through a freeze on tuition fees in order to hold down numbers. This is economic madness. The CBI, among others, argues for a target of 40 per cent by the year 2000.[42] But if standards are to be maintained, more students must mean more resources.

But the present funding system is not only inadequate; it is grossly unfair.

• Because higher education is still dominated by students from well-off families, student grants and tuition fees for students living away from home are worth ten times as much to the richest 20 per cent of families as they are to the poorest 20

137

per cent.[43] Financed in the main by taxpayers who never went to university and whose children do not do so either, student funding is neither fair nor efficient. As Figure 4.1 makes clear, there is a link between education and lifetime income.

- Part-time students – who include many mature students and many of those from poorer backgrounds – have no right to the free tuition which is given automatically to full-time students in higher (but not further) education.
- Because many courses – from professional law to dance – only qualify students for discretionary awards from local authorities, geography may determine whether someone can afford to learn. Across the country, local-government spending on discretionary awards was 8 per cent lower in 1993/4 than three years previously, and in Inner London fell by more than a third.[44]
- Many full-time students are extremely poor. The current combination of student loans and a grant frozen in real terms does not provide an adequate income. The removal of benefits for vacations and reduced temporary employment prospects have exacerbated the problems.

A new funding system must be created to finance the necessary expansion of higher education, maintain high standards, end student poverty and treat people fairly – and all this without breaking the bank. Like the National Commission on Education, we believe that the way forward is to ask graduates themselves to contribute towards the cost of their higher education once they have graduated and entered the labour market. Both retrospectively (in their family background), and prospectively (in terms of their potential earnings), higher education graduates are better off than the average. Like the National Commission on Education, we support a new system of higher education contributions, sensitive to the need to ensure that people can participate in higher education on the basis of their ability to learn, not their ability to pay. By asking the graduates who benefit from higher earnings to make a contribution to the cost of the investment made in them, we can offer high standards of higher education to far more people.

There are, of course, real worries that anything other than free tuition and full grants will discourage students from poor backgrounds. A fair system of student contributions would, however, increase the number of places and therefore allow far more of the people who are now excluded to enjoy higher education. In Australia, a sensitively designed Higher Education Contribution Scheme appears to have had no impact on university entry rates of less affluent students.[45] The real barrier to the expansion of higher education in this country at the moment is not the cost of entry but the supply of places, and raising money from students once they have graduated from university into employment could help cure this.

Once the principle of a student higher education contribution has been accepted, two more detailed questions must be settled. The first is whether the contribution should relate to maintenance, tuition fees or both. The current obsession with maintenance support for full-time students in higher education is in various ways misplaced: it is on the funding of tuition that most of the money – four-fifths – is spent, and from which the greatest inequity, between full-time university students and the rest, stems. The present Government's policy is to ignore the inequities in tuition funding, while weaning students off maintenance support and on to loans. But the funding of maintenance is itself a product of the peculiar assumption in this country, much less true in Scotland, that universities should continue the boarding tradition of public schools. And as more and more mature and part-time students enter the system, the proportion dependent on the full maintenance grant will fall.

The burden of expansion in higher education will have to be borne by people who do best out of the current system – above all full-time university students living away from home. Maintenance support should be increased to take students out of poverty, but turned entirely into a payment repayable on an income-related basis. In order to raise sufficient funds to expand the system, we also support the proposal of the National Commission on Education that a proportion of tuition fees – they recommended 20 per cent – should also be paid back on an income-related basis. Decisions in this area must also take account of developments elsewhere in Europe.

The second question is how graduates should pay back the maintenance payment and share of tuition fees. Since the new system must not compromise the commitment to participation based on ability to benefit rather than ability to pay, graduate contributions should be based on post-graduation income. In any of the three schemes outlined below, the higher education contribution would only last until repayment had been made; this is not a proposal for a graduate tax. There are three main options:

1. A monthly payment by all who reach a certain income (under the Government's current scheme for maintenance, 85 per cent of the average income). The problem with this 'mortgage-style' loan is that repayments are high in the early years, when graduates have the least income, and smaller later when they can probably pay more.
2. A surcharge on National Insurance, until the repayment has been made. While this would mean the government recouped a higher proportion of the support given out, it would also mean graduates started to repay money while their earnings were as low as £57 per week – the level at which National Insurance is first paid.
3. A rising surcharge on National Insurance which only applies to those who reach a certain earnings level, for instance starting at or above average earnings. This would remove the burden from people on below-average earnings, but would bring in less money.

The National Commission on Education estimated that once higher education contributions for maintenance and 20 per cent of tuition were fully in place, the savings to government would amount to about £1.5 billion a year. The levels of saving, impact on individuals, and overall levels of repayment will depend on which of the different repayment schemes is adopted. Piloting, modelling and costings would be necessary before deciding on the specific repayment method. Once the principle of student contibutions is accepted, detailed studies and public consultation will be required to settle the most efficient and fair option.

Sixth Goal: A Learning Bank for Lifelong Learning

Expansion of higher education and new opportunities for adult training (goals 5 and 4) are essential to our future. But reforms in these areas fall into the conventional mode of reforming education and training separately. Instead of starting from where we want to end up, they start from where we are now. To make a reality of the rhetoric of lifelong learning, the long term goal must be radically to transform the funding structure of post-compulsory learning: higher education, further education and vocational training.

The key to this expansion of lifelong learning is the creation of a unified system of funding for adult education and training. Our vision is of a national *Learning Bank* which enables everybody to have access to lifelong learning. Expanding higher education is important – but lifelong learning is much broader and includes adult further education, currently the Cinderella of education and training policy. In the 20th century, a minority have always been confident that compulsory schooling would be followed by A levels and three years' higher education.[46] In the 21st century, we must make the entitlement to extended education across the life-cycle the expectation of everyone – regardless of whether or not they choose the traditional route of A levels followed by an undergraduate degree.

Our aspiration is nothing less than the creation of a learning society: and the Learning Bank would provide a framework for funding it. At the moment the Learning Bank exists only as a concept. Its organisation, and the details of its funding, structure and other matters, need to be developed more fully. But the main features of the Bank would be:

- Funding adult learning on an equitable basis, with no discrimination between different types of learning.

Figure 4.2 – The Learning Bank

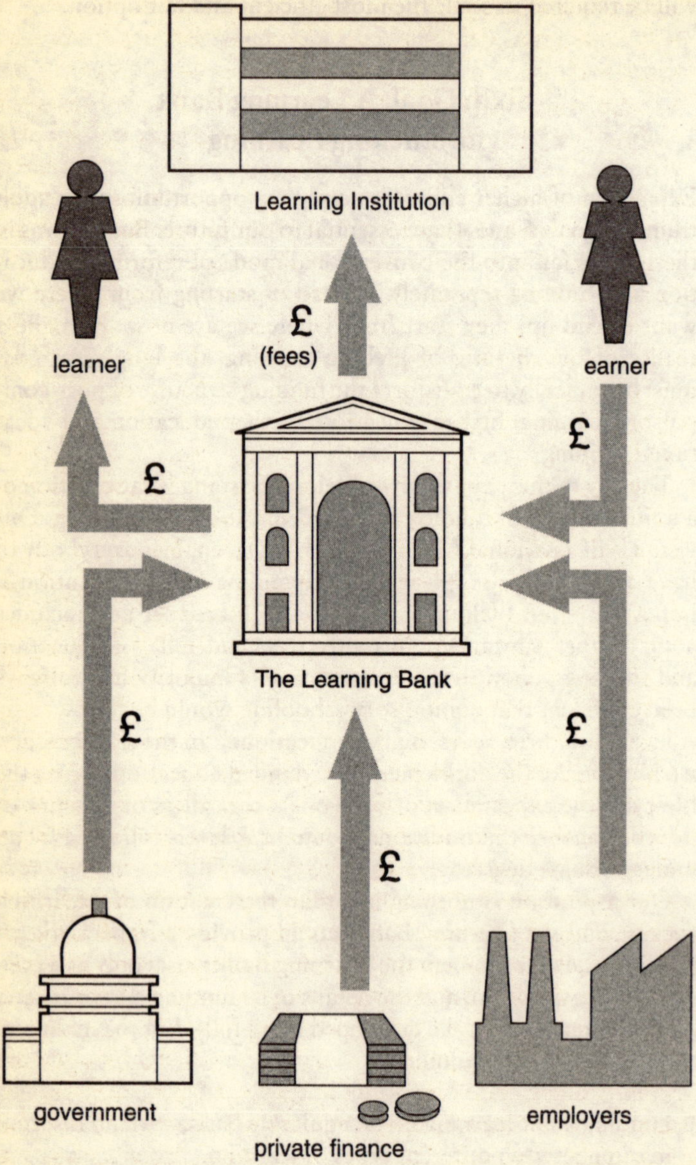

Learning Institution

learner

£
(fees)

earner

The Learning Bank

£

£

£

£

£

government

private finance

employers

- Building on a credit-based system of learning, allowing mobility and choice.
- Providing the flexibility of Individual Learning Accounts to fund education and training.
- Promoting partnership in the funding of learning, between the state (including the 'leveraging' of private finance), employers and individuals.

Figure 4.2 illustrates the basic concepts of the Learning Bank.

Equity

Instead of the traditional emphasis on young academic students, the Learning Bank would be available to people throughout their lives. Instead of the present discrimination in favour of full-time education, the Learning Bank would equally help people studying part-time. Instead of favouring higher over further education and vocational training, the Learning Bank would fund them all on the same basis. This would allow individuals to learn *when* appropriate to them, and in the *form* appropriate to them, without the current discrimination between a 35-year old part-time and a 19-year old full-time student, and without the enormous division between funded 'academic' learning and unfunded 'vocational' training.

Building on credits

The precondition for a new flexible funding system is a shift in the organisation of learning to a modular system of credits. Courses would be broken down into units and a credit framework established to cover all institutions where recognised learning takes place. The accumulation of credits by students would drive the system. The credits would form the building blocks of lifelong learning, shifting the focus from teachers to learners, from a national curriculum to an individual's curriculum. For example, a classroom assistant could gain a credit from a combination of in-work training and home study, adding to that through part-time study at the local FE college or a distance-learning course, and building up to a degree in primary education. Already, 80 per cent of universities and higher education colleges have introduced or are committed to developing credit-based courses.

These credits would create what David Robertson, Professor of Continuing Education at Liverpool John Moores University, and author of a new report for the Higher Education Quality Council, calls a 'ladder of progression' through further education, higher education and vocational learning.[47] A credit-based achievement structure of this kind would be the basis for the funding structure of the Learning Bank. Funding would be based on the individual rather than the institution, allowing people more choice in the subject and place of study.

Individual Learning Accounts

Everyone should have an Individual Learning Account (ILA) at the Learning Bank, to which government, individuals and employers could all contribute. This idea has been developed by, among others, Sir Geoffrey Holland, Vice-Chancellor of Exeter University and former Permanent Secretary at the Department of Education.[48] Some TECs and, in Scotland, LECs are already experimenting with ILAs and credits for Training for Work. ILAs would provide enormous flexibility, by giving people control over their entitlement to learning.

The other strength of ILAs is that they would overcome the current impasse between employers, government and individuals over who should finance training, and provide a mechanism for sharing the cost between them. Investment in the national learning effort is simply too important to be left to any single party.

Partners in funding

Government clearly has a lead role in funding education and training. But there is no reason why government should be the only source of investment in adult learning, even if the public purse has to be 'guarantor of last resort'. The Learning Bank, while wholly accountable to government, would therefore be set up separately from the Treasury, both to attract private finance as well as to ring-fence contributions from individuals and employers.

The Learning Bank would build on and extend the principles for funding higher education outlined in the previous section, with individual learners who go on to be successful earners putting something back into the system from which they have benefited. For those living at home, or studying part-time while in employment, or supported by their parents or a partner, maintenance may not be a problem. But adequate maintenance must be available so that people could choose to move from full-time employment to full-time education or training.

Public money could lever private money into investing in learning. In a study of income-contingent loans for higher education, Dr Nicholas Barr of the London School of Economics estimated that the overall payback from graduates would be about 80 per cent.[49] If this level of payback was realised for payments made by the Learning Bank, the Bank could – in theory – raise £1 billion of private sector money for every £200 million provided by the public sector, although in the early stages the Treasury would need to underwrite a higher proportion of the risk.

Of course, interest would have to be paid to investors. And the balance between affordability for students and attractiveness to private capital is a fine one. It would take detailed studies to produce reliable costings, but we are clear that the Treasury has a role – through the Learning Bank – in bridging the gap between fair interest rates for graduates and sufficiently attractive rates for investors. The use of the National Insurance system and, if possible, other EU social security systems, to collect contributions would add to the Bank's financial credibility and keep its administrative costs down (fewer than 2 per cent of employees default on National Insurance).

Where employers were unable to provide the minimum training investment we proposed earlier, the balance would also be paid into the employee's Individual Learning Account. Once the Bank was established, employers could also offer payments into an employee's Individual Learning Account as part of their remuneration package, over and above general employer-provided training. An employee might choose this over membership of a private medical scheme or a company car and, unlike other perks, support for government-accredited learning could attract full tax relief.

Setting up the system

It would clearly be impossible to offer the whole existing adult population immediate rights to the equivalent of three full-time years of education and training, even with the partial repayment system described. The new system would have to begin for a generation which turns 18 in its first year of operation. It would, however, be desirable to extend the Learning Bank to priority groups of adults, starting with people who have been out of employment for a long time and moving on to employees without educational qualifications. One of the strengths of the Learning Bank is that it would enable government to target specific groups with entitlements to training and education.

There are a number of practical issues to be resolved in relation to the Learning Bank, in particular, the treatment of longer courses, such as Scottish or medical degrees; whether – in the long run – all post-16 education should be covered by the Bank, including sixth form study; what courses should be eligible for

---

Emma and the Learning Bank

Emma leaves school at 18, disillusioned, having failed all but one A level. She finds manual work in a pea-canning factory which offers no training. Her employer therefore has to put a proportion of Emma's payroll into her ILA at the Learning Bank, which she can later use to fund her studies. After three years, she decides to take an access course for a Higher Education Diploma in tourism studies. The access course is full-time for one year. Her parents provide some support, but she also draws out £1,000 from her ILA to help with maintenance. She opts to do the diploma itself part-time over four years, so that she can support herself by working. The Learning Bank pays the fees. When she qualifies, she gets a senior job as a travel consultant, and depending on the income-related funding system, begins to pay back her share of the fees and her maintenance costs to the Bank.

---

funding; how postgraduate study should be funded; and what controls on numbers would be required. [50]

However, the idea behind the Learning Bank is both sound and exciting. Once fully functional, it would allow individuals, government and employers to fund lifelong learning in a way which attracts private capital, allows individual choice and flexibility, and promotes equity of access. There are of course many issues which still need to be worked out. But in the future, the Learning Bank could be sponsoring new opportunities for millions of people. The prize of a learning society would be in view.

Conclusion

If an education system were improved by the number of reports written about it, British education would be the best in the world. Since the Royal Commissions of the mid-19th century, august bodies have repeatedly bemoaned the failings of our education system. There are more than enough policy ideas in the education field; and some teachers and parents are sick of reforms and just want a period of stability. But the desire for continuity in children's learning should not become an excuse for condoning underperformance; and underperformance, relative to potential, marks our system today. There is no more important investment than that in our own education.

Educational improvement is a social and economic mission central to our vision of a more inclusive, productive and cohesive society. In this chapter, we have been keen to add to and build on what exists, rather than subtract and tear down. We have sought at all stages ways of lowering the barriers to high achievement, and improving the incentives for high performance. Out of the current muddle, we have sought coherence and clarity. These reforms could not be implemented overnight, but in time they would reshape our system around fundamental goals – high standards at the beginning, choice in the middle, and investment throughout. They are central to our vision of national renewal.

Notes

1. Ray Marshall and Marc Tucker *Thinking for a Living: Education and the Wealth of Nations* (New York: Basic Books, 1992)

2. The German *Technische Hochschule* – Technical High Schools – were created over 100 years ago

3. For a recent review of the literature, see Roland Sturm *How do Education and Training Affect a Country's Economic Performance?* (Santa Monica, CA: Rand Corporation, 1994)

4. OECD *Employment Outlook* (Paris: OECD, 1994)

5. US Department of Labor *Labor Market Problems of Older Workers* (Washington, DC: Department of Labor, 1989)

6. Kleinwort Benson Securities *Economic Comment,* August 1991

7. Tim Brighouse 'Secondary Schools within the University of the First Age', CLEA Conference, July 1994

8. Bronwen Cohen and Neil Fraser *Childcare in a Modern Welfare System* (London: IPPR, 1991)

9. Report in the *Independent*, 9 December 1993

10. Cohen and Fraser *Childcare* op cit

11. Peter Moss 'Daycare and pre-school education in England: an overview' Thomas Coram Research Unit (presented to Institute of Education Conference, 'Daycare for Under-8s in England: The Children Act', 23 November 1993)

12. A recent study showed the particular problems faced by shiftworkers – from broadcasters to factory workers – in juggling family and work responsibilities. See Marion Kozak *Not Just Nine to Five* (London: Daycare Trust, 1994)

13. Carnegie Corporation of New York 1994. *Starting Points: Meeting the Needs of Children* (April 1994)

14. Select Committee on Education, Science and Arts *Education Provision for Under-Fives* (London: HMSO, 1989), Sir Christopher Ball *Start Right: The Importance of Early Learning* (London: RSA, 1994), National Commission on Education *Learning to Succeed* (London: Heinemann, 1993)

15. T. Kellaghan and B.J. Greaney 'The education and development of students following participation in a pre-school programme in a disadvantaged area in Dublin' (Bernard van Leer Foundation, Studies and Evaluation Paper No 12, 1993)

16. L. Schweinhart and D.Weikart *Significant Benefits: The High/Scope Perry Preschool Study Through Age 27* (Michigan: High/Scope Press, 1993)

17. Penelope Leach *Children First* (London: Michael Joseph, 1994)
18. The National Children's Bureau suggests a ratio of one teacher to six three-year-old children, and one to eight four-year-olds: Gillian Pugh *Investing in Young Children: costing an education and daycare service* (London: National Childrens' Bureau with the Association of Metropolitan Authorities and the Association of County Councils, 1992)
19. Ibid
20. Michael Barber and Tim Brighouse *Partners in Change* (London: IPPR, 1992)
21. See National Commission on Education *Learning to Succeed* op cit
22. Department of Education *The Government Expenditure Plans 1993-4, 1994-5, 1995-6* (London: HMSO, 1993)
23. Many models exist and are summarised in Gillian Pugh *Investing* op cit
24. Parliamentary Written Answer 15 July 1994
25. See Tim Brighouse and John Tomlinson *Successful Schools* (London: IPPR, 1991)
26. Adult Literacy and Basic Skills Unit *The Basic Skills of Young Adults* (London: ALBSU, 1993)
27. Derek Foxman, Tom Gorman and Greg Brooks 'Standards of literacy and numeracy' in National Commission on Education *Briefings* (London: Heinemann, 1994)
28. ALBSU *Basic Skills* op cit
29. Ibid
30. Charles Hymas and Julie Cohen 'The Trouble with Boys' *Sunday Times*, 19 June 1994
31. An evaluation of Reading Recovery in the US appears in Philip Dyer 'Reading Recovery: A Cost-Effectiveness and Educational Outcomes Analysis' in *ERS Spectrum* 10, 1 (Winter 1992)
32. England and Wales have a similar system of secondary education. Scotland has a different – and more successful – system, while in Northern Ireland, the 11-plus remains in place. Although our proposals focus on the situation in England and Wales, the principles apply throughout the UK
33. Andy Green and Hilary Steedman *Educational provision, educational attainment and the needs of industry: a research review for Germany, France, Japan, the USA and Britain* (London: National Institute for Economic and Social Research, 1993)
34. Unemployment Unit *Working Brief* Issue 42 (February/March 1993)
35. See David Finegold *et al A British Baccalauréat: Ending the Division betwen Education and Training* (London: IPPR, 1990), The Royal

Society *Beyond GCSE* (London: Royal Society, 1991), National Commission on Education *Learning to Succeed* op cit

36. Gill Courtney and Ian McAleese England and Wales Youth Cohort Survey: Cohort 4: Young People 17-18 years old in 1990. Report on Sweep 2 (London: Employment Department, 1994)

37. Confederation of British Industry *Towards a Skills Revolution* (London: CBI, 1989)

38. Howard Davies *A Social Market for Training* (London: Social Market Foundation, 1993)

39. Confederation of British Industry *Competing with the World's Best* (London: CBI, 1989)

40. Lucy Chennels and John van Reenan *The Rising Price of Skill: Investigating British skill premia in the 1980s using Complementary Datasets* (London: Institute for Fiscal Studies, forthcoming)

41. OECD *Jobs Study* (Paris: OECD, 1994)

42. Confederation of British Industry *Thinking Ahead: Ensuring the Expansion of Higher Education into the 21st Century* (London: CBI, 1994)

43. Maria Evandrou *et al* 'Welfare benefits in kind and income distribution' in *Fiscal Studies* (February 1993)

44. National Foundation for Educational Research survey reported in the *Guardian*, 7 June 1994

45. H. Tracey *Financing of Higher education in Transition* (Canberra: Department of Education and Training, 1992)

46. Scottish degree courses are in general four years in length

47. David Robertson *Choosing to Change* (London: Higher Education Quality Council, 1994). In Professor Robertson's system, 30 credits are broadly the equivalent of one year's full-time study from A level/NVQ Level 3 upwards. 150 credits would therefore take a student through a sixth-form/further education college, into university and through to an undergraduate degree

48. Sir Geoffrey Holland 'The Challenge: Making it Happen' at 'University for Industry' conference, 16 June 1994

49. Nicholas Barr and Jane Falkingham *Paying for Learning* (London: LSE Welfare State Programme Paper 94, 1993)

50. IPPR is establishing a research project to work through the details of the Learning Bank

5

OPPORTUNITY: WORKING FOR A LIVING

'If you don't think work matters, ask someone who hasn't got it.'

Joseph, 19, unemployed, Birmingham

● ● ●

Work is central to our lives. Paid or unpaid, it is the way in which we meet needs, create wealth and distribute resources. It is a source of personal identity and individual fulfilment, social status and relationships. It is the heart of wealth and welfare.

For us, employment is inseparable from individual opportunity. This is not because paid work is the only form of productive work, nor because we want to create a nation of workaholics. Our society and our economy would not function without the unpaid work which millions of people do in their families and communities and which must in future be recognised within employment policy and a new social security system.[1] But paid work remains the best pathway out of poverty, as well as the only way in which most people can hope to achieve a decent standard of living. Professor Howard Glennerster has said: 'Work is part of welfare, not its antithesis.'[2] He is right: without jobs, there can be no justice.

When we asked a group of schoolchildren in Norfolk to name the biggest problem facing the country, they said, unanimously, 'Unemployment.' But the headline unemployment figure tells only part of the story. In the last decade, the method of measuring unemployment has been repeatedly changed, in almost every case reducing the total. Some unemployed people, especially married women, are not counted because they are not entitled to claim Unemployment Benefit or Income Support. Others are on government training schemes. Taking these groups into account would push the unemployment count to some 4 million.

But even that is not all. Many of the one-third of a million men between the ages of 55 and 65 who are now living on Income Support, early retirement pensions or other benefits would like a job. Most of the 1 million lone-parents now dependent on Income Support would prefer employment now or in the future if only they could find childcare and an appropriate job. Seventy per cent of the estimated two million disabled people of working age are not in work.[3] None of these groups is counted in the statistics.

The level of unemployment and economic inactivity (people of working age not in employment and not in the unemployment count), set out in Table 5.1, depends upon the relationship between the demand for labour and its supply. But supply is not static. Instead of looking at unemployment figures alone, we need to look at the total proportion of people of 'working age' who are actually in employment, and the corresponding proportion out of employment, including those involved in unpaid work. Even amongst men aged between twenty-five and fifty-four (in other words, excluding students and trainees at one end, and those who have chosen or been forced into early retirement at the other), the proportion of men who are employed fell from more than nine in ten in 1973 to about eight in ten in 1992. In other words, one in five men of prime working age is not employed. Amongst women of the same age, however, the proportion employed has risen from below six in ten to more than seven in ten.[4] The Equal Opportunities Commission predicts that there will be an extra 1 million part-time jobs and 700,000 more women in employment by the year 2000, bringing the total to nearly eight out of ten women of prime working age.[5] The gap between levels of labour-force entry between men and women is set to fall to 7 per cent by 2006.[6]

Overall levels of employment and non-employment are not the whole story either. There has been an increasing concentration of both employment and unemployment in recent years – and it is not the traditional North/South divide that is at issue. The con-

Table 5.1: UK Employment Trends by Sex: Percentage of population aged 25–54 years

		1973	1979	1990	1992
Men:	Employed	93.5	91.8	86.3	81.3
	Unemployed	2.1	3.8	6.3	11.5
	Inactive	4.4	4.4	6.3	7.2
Women:	Employed	58.3	62.0	71.0	70.2
	Unemployed	0.3	1.3	2.0	3.2
	Inactive	41.7	36.7	27.0	26.6

Source: World Economic and Social Survey 1994, Table VI.6 (New York: United Nations, 1994)

centration of *employment* has arisen because full-time employees, particularly men, are working longer hours; because of a growth in the number of dual-earner ('work-rich') couples alongside no-earner couples ('work-poor'); and because of the way family responsibilities affect employment opportunities. *Un*employment has also become more concentrated – by family and by geography (for example in particular wards within cities). The distribution of both employment and unemployment is therefore essential to full employment today.

Full Employment in a Modern Economy

As a country, we cannot afford to give up on employment, nor on the commitment, set out in the 1944 White Paper *Employment Policy*, that government should accept responsibility for the maintenance of high and stable levels of employment. It is simply not good enough to treat people's lives as if they were just property or plant, to be written off when no longer required. The Director of the National Institute of Economic and Social Research has rightly said that economists should be 'most reluctant to abandon the objective of full employment, because it points beyond economics to a goal which is not just increasing individual utility but also the cohesion of society as a whole'.[7] The work ethic remains strong in the UK; in a recent survey a majority of employees said that they would continue to work even if they no longer needed to earn a living.[8] We start from the proposition that William Beveridge's definition of full employment – 'a state of affairs in which the number of unfilled vacancies is not appreciably below the number of unemployed persons, so that unemployment at any time is due to the normal lag between a person losing one job and finding another' – is as valid today as it ever was. But translating this definition into reality is not straightforward.

Full employment in a modern economy must recognise that, for both men and women, the world of work has changed fundamentally. In the 1950s, full employment involved full-time, life-time employment for men; in the 1990s and beyond, it will involve for both men and women frequent changes of occupation, part-time as well as full-time work, self-employment as well as employment, time spent caring for children or elderly relatives (as well as or instead of employment) and periods spent in further education and training. Forty years ago the typical worker was a man working full-time in industry; today the typical worker is increasingly likely to be a woman working part-time in a service job. Already, there are more people in Britain employed as child-care-workers than as carworkers.

In a world where skills, products, jobs and companies all change rapidly, full employment depends not only on generating new opportunities for fairly paid work, but also on individuals' own abilities to cope with change. In a paper to the Commission, the labour market expert, Hilary Metcalf, argued that 'the increasingly competitive market has raised issues of shifting from *job* security to *employability* as the source of employment security'. And in Newcastle the Commission was told: 'Unemployment is not about why you lost your last job: it's about why you don't get a new one.'

A summary of the 1944 White Paper, presented to Prime Minister Winston Churchill under the title 'EMPLOYMENT POLICY: Gist of Draft White Paper', was a list of eight points on one side of paper. It set out four conditions for the achievement of high and stable levels of employment, and noted problems facing a 'transitional period', along with requirements for change in the machinery of government. We need the same clarity today. Below is a summary of what would be in our White Paper today:

Full Employment in a Modern Economy

Government must accept its responsibility to secure full employment in a modern economy, a situation in which the number of job vacancies is at least equal to the number of unemployed. Today, this requires the reduction and eventual elimination of long term unemployment (initially defined as twelve months' unemployment) as well as action to increase levels of employment among men and women. There are a number of conditions which must be fulfilled if, in a rapidly changing world, this goal is to be achieved.

1. *The first condition* is a high and sustainable growth rate in overall demand, requiring action at international, European and national level.

2. *The second condition* is the maintenance of low inflation and, in particular, an understanding by government, company directors, employers and unions that average money earnings should rise in line with productivity increases across the whole economy.

3. *The third condition* is a tradeable sector which is sufficiently large and competitive, to ensure that a full employment level of demand can be sustained in the UK.

4. *The fourth condition* is that we achieve greater intensity of employment (so that increases in output are effectively translated into higher employment). This will require:

   Expansion of non-tradeable, labour-intensive sectors, such as personal services.

   Matching the total hours of employment as far as possible to the hours which individuals want to work at different stages in their lives.

---

5. *The fifth condition* is a reintegration of the long-term unemployed into one labour market. This will require:

High quality help with education, training, and personal development through a re-employment service

Wage subsidies, to reconnect the long-term unemployed to the labour market

Help with childcare (especially for lone parents)

Development of intermediate labour markets designed to provide training and employment for the long-term unemployed, as well as subsequent access to regular employment

Sponsorship of small-scale entrepreneurs

Sustainable economic and social regeneration in the most disadvantaged areas.

6. *The sixth condition* is the development of tax and benefits systems which provide incentives, not disincentives, to employment. This will require:

A flexible benefits system to match the increasingly flexible labour market

A reduction in reliance on means-tested benefits, which have inevitable disincentive effects on both claimant and partner

Help for low-income owner-occupiers (to parallel help for low-income tenants)

Gradual reduction in taxes on employment, particularly for less-skilled and lower-paid jobs.

7. *The seventh condition* is a new balance between employment and family across people's life-cycles, in ways which promote greater individual choice and improve the quality of social and economic life. This will require:

> Opportunities for employment breaks to meet family needs, for both men and women
>
> Opportunities for employment breaks to permit further education and training
>
> Flexible retirement patterns, with appropriate pension structures

In this report, we address in detail many of the conditions required for full employment. We are not, however, a commission of economists and if we were we would certainly disagree with each other. Although Deregulators argue that government intervention is the only cause of unemployment and lower wages the only cure, and some on the Left believe that the only problem is an overvalued currency, we do not believe that there is a single or simple answer to modern economies' employment problems. As the OECD put it in its recent *Jobs Study*:

> The appearance of widespread unemployment in Europe ... on the one hand, and of poor quality jobs as well as unemployment in the United States on the other, have thus both stemmed from the same root cause: the failure to adapt to change.[9]

The nature of employment problems varies: the European Union worries about how to create more jobs, the United States about how to create better jobs. We have both these aims for the United Kingdom, but would add an equally important third, concerning the distribution of employment, in other words who gets, or does not get, the jobs on offer. There are three goals which should be pursued simultaneously:

- To increase employment: the labour market should be enlarged by increasing the demand for labour.
- To ensure a fairer distribution of employment and unemployment, especially for those at the greatest disadvantage in the labour market, so that greater employment does lead to more work for those without jobs (and not just longer hours for those in employment).

- To achieve better employment: there must be fair rewards and good conditions for labour.

Deregulation: No Magic Cure

The Deregulators offer one simple solution to the complex problems of unfairness and inefficiency in the labour market. The stumbling-block, they believe, is not a shortage of jobs, but the array of obstacles to the free functioning of the labour market – obstacles like employee rights, wage agreements and trade unions. If only we let the market price everybody into jobs – by removing the regulations which protect jobs and workers – unemployment would disappear. For the Deregulators, regulation costs jobs: 'flexibility' creates them.

In support of their case, the Deregulators point to the USA, where the number of jobs has doubled since 1960, compared with an increase of only 10 per cent in the European Union over the same period. The unemployment rate in the US is 7 per cent; in the EU, it is 12 per cent. Whereas more than 40 per cent of the EU's unemployed have been out of the labour force for more than a year, the equivalent figure for the US is 11 per cent.[10] Follow the USA, say the Deregulators: deregulate the European labour markets and unemployment will disappear.

But the Americans have not solved their employment problems any more than we have. In fact, the Clinton administration wants to take on the best of European experience to *improve* the operation of their labour market. In the USA, just as in this country, official unemployment figures only tell part of the story. Among American men between the ages of twenty-five and fifty-four, more than one in eight is out of work, although fewer than half of them are officially unemployed. That is no better than the position in Germany – the Deregulators' nightmare, with its extensively protected labour market. Amongst younger American men, particularly in the cities, an even higher proportion are completely detached from regular employment, many of them dealing in drugs, involved in other crime and working – if at all – only for cash.[11]

Second, although employment has risen in the USA, wages are stagnant or falling. For the bottom tenth of workers, earnings have dropped by one-third in real terms since 1970,[12] while the average hourly wage of private sector, non-agricultural and non-supervisory workers (some 80 per cent of the total) is *lower* in real terms than it was in 1973.[13] After taking inflation into account, the minimum wage is 30 per cent lower than it was in 1968, and at $4.25 an hour is now worth just a third of average earnings. In 1993, the US Secretary of Labor, Robert Reich, told a European Union employment conference: 'Most working Americans are on a downward escalator in terms of their earnings .... If you are out of work, chances are your next job won't be as good as the one you had before.' The dark side of the American situation is that poverty, destitution and inequality have grown alongside an unprecedented increase in employment.

Third, cutting wages, derecognising trade unions and imposing harsh hours and conditions of work on employees is bad long-run economics. Although the short-term savings to business seem obvious, the costs to business are even more important. Employers have little incentive to train workers who won't stay long; workers who know their job tenure is likely to be brief are not going to be highly motivated. The short-termism of the Anglo-Saxon economies is reflected in the shorter period which the average worker spends in a job: 3 years in the USA and 4.4 years in the UK, compared with 7 to 8 years in Germany and Japan.[14] Michael Frye, former Chairman of the Royal Society for the Arts (RSA) and Chief Executive of Elliott plc, argues forcefully that the most effective way of reducing production costs is to raise productivity rather than cut wages: 'Lowest costs mean lower rejects, zero defects, higher quality and faster service.'[15] Instead of the Deregulators' crude equation of value with price, businessmen like Michael Frye know that low quality is the most costly form of production.

Fourth, a 'flexible' labour market means different things to different people. To the Deregulators, labour-market flexibility means no minimum wages, few – or, better still, no – employment rights, low payroll taxes and short durations of unemployment benefit. Their definition of flexible is Darwinian: let the fittest survive. To the Investors, however, flexibility means the opportunity for people to develop new skills, take on new responsibilities and raise productivity. It means adaptability. It means a wide choice of working hours without the penalties now attached to part-time working. Instead of inhibiting flexibility, regulation can actively promote it, not least by tackling the barriers which keep highly educated women and well-qualified people from many ethnic minority groups out of too many well-paid jobs. There will always be some conflict between the flexibility which working people want and the flexibility which suits employers. But as organisations' success increasingly comes to depend upon the quality of their people, the fair flexibility which enables employees to give of their best will also deliver the productivity which employers demand. In Norfolk, for example, we visited Listawood, a small but rapidly-growing company producing pocket games and fridge magnets. Their success largely depends upon the commitment of a highly adaptable workforce, most of them women working school hours. When we asked several of them (in the absence of the managers) what the disadvantages were, they couldn't think of any: 'We've got the best of both worlds really.'

There is no doubt, on the other hand, that it is possible to *over*-regulate a labour market. In Spain, regulations on hiring and firing are so tight that more than a third of the workforce are now on temporary contracts, and 21 per cent of the workforce are unemployed. The accepted wisdom is that Spanish employers are anxious about the costs of firing and are therefore reluctant to hire. (At the same time, however, Portugal – which, like Spain, has extensive labour-market regulation – has far lower levels of unemployment.) As Figure 5.1 shows, the amount of regulation is not correlated with economic performance: it is the nature of the regulation, its purpose and structure, that counts.

Some outdated restrictions that still apply in parts of continental Europe, for instance on shopping hours, part-time employment and and self-employment, should probably be removed. But these are not relevant to the United Kingdom, and most

---

Deregulation: Not the Answer

Deregulation is put forward as a panacea for the UK's labour-market ills. Given the condition of our economy today, however, it is not the answer:

- The USA has a lower official unemployment rate than many EU countries, but 'disguised unemployment' or 'non-employment' – anyone from the involuntarily early retired to homeless beggars – is higher
- Deregulation is associated with a cycle of low investment and low wages; the working poor are the price of a deregulated economy
- Deregulation increases costs of turnover, low morale and low productivity: it is bad long-run economics
- The best flexibility comes from extending people's choices – through training, childcare, flexible working arrangements and anti-discrimination provision
- Deregulation is a sterile slogan; what matters is not more or less regulation, but intelligent regulation

---

European businessmen who argue for the removal of unnecessary regulation in their own countries would be appalled by the complete absence of protection for millions of British workers. In striking contrast to the UK Government's rejection of the European Social Chapter on the grounds that it would destroy jobs, the OECD concludes in its mid-1994 *Employment Outlook* that 'cross-country differences in regulations and arrangements on labour standards do not alter supply and demand forces in a fundamental way'.[16] A labour market in which employers are required to do too much will fail to create enough jobs, but a labour market which encourages competitive austerity between firms – a process of constantly driving down wages and conditions in order to survive – would be a disaster for the economy and society alike. Economists and governments learnt a long time ago that bad money must not be allowed to drive out the good; so we cannot afford to let bad employers drive out the good.

Robert Bischof, Chairman of Jungheinrich (GB), sums up the problem with deregulation: 'Boom and bust are the twin brothers of hire and fire.'

Labour-market regulation is not just a mark of a civilised society, although it is certainly that. Intelligent regulation is an essential tool in the industrialised world's search for individual employability and business success. Deregulation does not match up to the nature and complexity of the UK's labour market problems. Frank Field MP, the Chairman of the House of Commons Select Committee on Social Security, argues that 'advocating deregulation as the beginning and end of labour-market policy ... fails to identify the genuine obstacles preventing the smooth operation of the market for labour'.[17]

The Demand for Labour: More Employment

It has become fashionable to believe that increasing demand in the economy will no longer produce more jobs, in other words that 'jobless growth' is here to stay. The view may be fashionable, but it is wrong. The OECD report on employment and unemployment states that: 'worries about a new era of "jobless growth" appear unfounded: the current upswing in the US and a number of other countries has brought job growth in its train, and broadly in line with the past relationship between growth and employment.'[18] Demand remains the motor for employment, investment and innovation. In this country, when the economy grew by 25 per cent between 1983 and 1990 (an average of 3.4 per cent per year), employment grew by more than 2 million.[19] Australia, the Netherlands and Spain had a similar experience over the same period. In the USA, in 1993 alone, the economy grew by 2.8 per cent, with more than a million new jobs being created in the private sector. And despite the problems facing unskilled male workers, faster growth meant lower unemployment for them too.

The level of demand matters a great deal to employment. But demand management is increasingly an international, rather than a national, issue. And no level of demand is sustainable unless it is matched by the right quantity and quality of supply – goods and services made in the UK and sold here and across the world.

Figure 5.1 – Regulation and Prosperity Can go Together

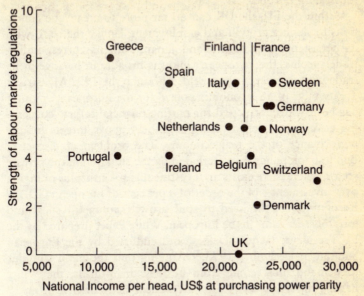

Source: Independent on Sunday, 24 July 1994, from *OECD
Employment outlook*, No 54, December 1993 (Paris: OECD, 1994)

The economic framework

At the international level, where the United Kingdom is a member not only of the European Union and the OECD but also of the G7 (the world's largest developed market economies), the British government should work with other countries to try to create a new, more stable system of international finance and trade, designed to move the global economy out of its present depressed and unstable state. To establish some sort of substitute for the expansionary framework set in place at Bretton Woods in 1946 is no small matter: the agreement would have to be multilateral (rather than just led by the US) and achieve currency stability in the face of an unstable speculative environment. But the UK should be adding its weight to international calls for low real-interest rates, increased global credit and a serious recovery plan for Eastern Europe.

Within the EU, the UK can do far more to create the conditions for higher growth and employment. Unlike the USA, with its persistent trade deficit, and Japan, with its corresponding trade surplus, the European Union is broadly in balance in its trade with the rest of the world. Although the 1992 Maastricht Treaty talks of an 'economic policy' for the European Union, it has been widely criticised for putting financial targets concerning government deficits and public debt above targets for the performance of the real economy. The problem of restrictive Bundesbank policy is exacerbated by the situation in the private sector, where there exists an investment gap – a surplus of saving over investment – of the order of 6 per cent of European GDP. [20] Recognition of the need to spur growth, competitiveness and jobs *together* came in the European White Paper prepared by the EU President, Jacques Delors, and endorsed by the European Summit in December 1993.[21] Arguing that the main stimulus to demand must come from business investment, the White Paper proposed a shift in the investment share of GDP from 19 per cent to 23 or 24 per cent. The creation of new European financial instruments – capitalising on the EU's AAA credit rating within the world's financial markets – could play an important role in funding not only the transport and telecommunications infrastructure envisaged by M. Delors, but also education programmes of the kind we propose with the Learning Bank. The British government must form close alliances with member countries, including Austria and the other new entrants, to turn the vision of a European economic and jobs strategy into reality.

The need for new international and European approaches does not, however, mean that the UK government can do nothing by itself. In this country too, the boost to demand must come through investment rather than consumption. The instability of consumption-led booms followed by correcting slumps is bad enough in itself, but the underlying neglect of investment also damages our future productive strength. There is considerable scope for increasing investment within this country. The relationship between financial institutions and industry needs to be reformed to redress the bias against short-term distribution of dividends, rather than longer-term investment, and government should take the lead in creating imaginative new public-private partnerships to fund projects as diverse as high-speed railways and individual traineeships. Construction projects in particular, from homes to an 'information super highway', will rapidly help generate employment.

Public investment not only funds the common goods that individual firms have no incentive to invest in themselves (because they cannot capture the gains from the investment). Because such investment in public infrastructure (transport, energy efficiency, telecommunications) has low import content, it can increase demand in the economy without exacerbating balance of trade problems. It is also job-intensive: two-thirds of general government non-military spending is directly on employment and many jobs, for instance in the construction industry, can be created for precisely those sections of the population, the less qualified, who have been worst affected by unemployment. Public investment can lead to technological advance: investment in energy efficiency and other environmental goods, for example, offers potentially high returns.

Although large-scale investment will mean more people employed, it is also designed to help our industries and services become more competitive in the global economy – by improving productivity and adding more value to products and processes. But if we improve productivity and narrow the gap between productivity growth and output growth, will we create *fewer* jobs? Could we even find, as France did in the 1980s, that by raising productivity faster than output generally – thus making ourselves increasingly competitive in world markets – we have turned the economy into what French economist and businessman Michel Albert calls 'a machine for unemployment'?

Tradeables and Non-Tradeables

The answer to the apparent conflict between productivity and employment lies in understanding that different parts of the economy operate in different ways. We need to run the economy at a higher level of demand, which in turn can only be done if we build competitive strength in the tradeable sector. But we then must find ways to transmit the wealth earned in competitive markets to job creation in the rest of the economy, through further infrastructure development (including housing and education), personal services (like community care) and leisure services. Employment in the non-tradeable sectors must not, however, mean second-class employment: if employment is divided between very highly-paid jobs for some, and very low-paid jobs for others, the problems of social division and exclusion will only be intensified. It thus becomes vital to set minimum standards for employment and to provide pathways from lower-paid into better-paid jobs.

In Japan, although the manufacturing sector is one-third more productive than ours, the retail and distributive sector is half as productive, and that is where the jobs come from. Far from making a fetish of productivity, the Japanese economy, taken as a whole, is *less* productive than that of the UK – but their productivity is highest where it matters most. Deregulators see only the high prices and apparent over-staffing of Japanese shops, restaurants and other services: in reality, the Japanese use employment as a highly effective means of social integration, because they know nothing is more expensive than social disintegration. Edward Luttwak, author of *The Endangered American Dream*, vividly illustrates the difference between the Japanese and the Anglo-Saxon approach:

> When I drive into a petrol station in Japan, four clearly under-employed young men leap into action to wash and wipe the headlights and windows as well as the windscreen, and check tyre pressures as well as the oils, in addition to dispensing the fuel. With government-regulated petrol prices being high and uniform, that is how the local oil companies compete. In exchange for the excellent service, I have to pay a higher price for the petrol than a free market would charge. But when I fill my own tank so much more cheaply from a self-service pump back in the United States, there too

four young men await – sometimes even in person but certainly by implication. I do not have to pay their wages through high petrol prices, because they are not employed by the oil company, or by anybody else for that matter. But in reality I still have to pay for the young men, by way of higher insurance rates caused by their vandalism and thefts, by way of my taxes that cover police, court and prison costs, even a little by way of welfare benefits. ... the American free-market is thus expensively cheap, as compared to Japan's employment-generating, cheaply expensive petrol.[22]

In the tradeable sectors of the economy, where international competition will continue to become ever more intense, higher output will not necessarily mean more jobs. The tradeable sector – above all manufacturing but some services too – remains an engine for wealth creation, but not necessarily an engine for employment. In engineering, for example, it is estimated that between the end of 1993 and 1995 total output will rise by 3 per cent while total employment will fall, also by 3 per cent.[23] Although very substantial increases in manufacturing output can also mean higher employment, the crucial aim, as far as this sector is concerned, is to raise productivity and value-added as rapidly as possible, making ourselves more competitive in world markets and creating the wealth we need to sustain and improve our quality of life.

However, global competition does not reach everywhere. We cannot get our children cared for and educated in Bombay (even though children and adults will increasingly use distance learning as part of their education). We cannot send our elderly people to Taiwan to be nursed and cared for (even though the health service will increasingly use international telecommunications for long-distance diagnosis by world medical experts). If we want bus conductors, train guards, park attendants and more police officers on the beat, we must employ them here. Developing and caring for people and for public places is labour-intensive work; it needs to be done and its social value should be reflected in our willingness to pay for it.

In the last twenty years, employment growth in the industrialised world has been concentrated in various parts of the service

Figure 5.2 – Work and Wealth Creation

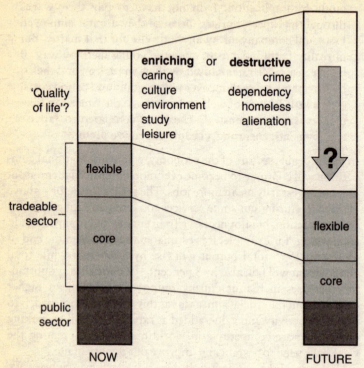

Source: Shell (UK) Ltd

sector. In Sweden, more than 80 per cent of total net job growth since the 1970s has taken place in the social services, with most of the new jobs going to women. Meanwhile the American job 'miracle' has occurred almost exclusively in private services, with little or no productivity growth, and much of the employment low-paid, non-unionised and unprotected ('McJobs'). The private service sector, which is far less developed in most of the European Union, will in future have to provide more of the job growth that is needed. Although business services often provide a route into well-paid professional and managerial jobs, many of the new private service jobs will be low-skilled and low-paid. Employment policy should be designed not to prevent the emergence of such jobs, but instead to prevent gross exploitation and to promote job mobility, preventing people becoming stuck at the bottom of the labour market for most of their lives. McDonald's recently announced that it plans to double its UK workforce over the next ten years. But half of the McDonald's workforce are under the age of 20.[24] Lifelong learning is the key to transforming what could be dead-end jobs into stepping-stones to better opportunity.

Public service provision also involves a lot of relatively low-status work. Care workers need tremendous commitment and a willingness to accept a high level of responsibility, but not necessarily a high level of technical expertise, although a more imaginative view of their role would enable them to offer even more. Park-keepers, guards and bus conductors make public services safe and inviting, but the value they add through their work is not visible to accountants. Traditionally, much of this work has been done in the public sector, financed through taxation. But this is precisely where the Conservatives' obsession with the ideology of 'public bad/private good' has driven through cuts in budgets and employment, and where productivity has been judged solely in terms of costs, not in the quality of service provided.

There is a clear market failure here. Although there were real inefficiencies in the old ways of delivering many services, today too many of the jobs are not done at all. There are goods which we all want and need – clean public spaces, efficient transport and safe streets – but the common, public nature of these goods makes it impossible for a 'free' market to translate collective needs into measurable economic demand – in other words, to fix a price. It is up to government to articulate these needs and provide mechanisms for their satisfaction, whether through taxes, charges, partnerships or other means. Imaginative new strategies, going well beyond the old public/private divide, will be particularly necessary to transform the prospects of those who have been out of employment for longest. It is crucial that we do so if employment is to maintain its function as a mechanism of social integration.

Figure 5.2, prepared by Shell UK for Business in the Community's 'Work and Society' enquiry, provides one way of thinking about the relationship between employment and wealth creation over the next thirty years. Even in an optimistic scenario, in which the UK improves its trading performance, the tradeable sector is likely to employ fewer rather than more people, and fewer of those employed are likely to have full-time, permanent jobs. Will the wealth created in a dynamic tradeable sector be used to employ other people in services which enrich the quality of all our lives, and to support breaks in employment which can be devoted to family, study and leisure – or will a growing number of people be excluded from social participation as well as from employment? There is a fine line between a virtuous circle of social inclusion and improving quality of life, and a vicious circle of exclusion and division, in which the costs of inequality spoil things for everyone.

The Distribution of Unemployment: A Fair Chance for the Long Term Unemployed

When demand increases, it is crucial that we have efficient and equitable ways of distributing the employment that is generated. Unfortunately, in the UK the distribution of unemployment as well as employment currently deepens social injustice and holds back economic prosperity. While two-thirds of the people who become unemployed find another job within six months, the rest risk slipping into long term unemployment. Over the last twenty years, long term unemployment has increased markedly: in June 1994, one in three unemployed people in the United Kingdom (and one in two in Northern Ireland) – more than one million people in all – had been unemployed for more than a year. In the upturn from recession between April 1993 and April 1994, when unemployment across the population as a whole fell by 9 per cent, very long-term unemployment – more than two years – among people older than 25 rose by 50 per cent.[25] The concentration of joblessness is rising as it affects the same people for longer periods, rather than being spread evenly across more people.[26]

A 10 per cent unemployment rate where no-one is out of work for more than three months is clearly better than a 5 per cent rate consisting entirely of people out of work for several years.[27]

While short-term, 'frictional' unemployment is inevitable in a dynamic market economy, and may even increase as jobs come and go faster than before, long term unemployment is a plague which can and must be prevented.

Men without employment and little chance of getting it are twice as likely to see their marriages break up, to suffer ill-health or to die prematurely.[28] The poverty in which thousands of lone mothers live, largely excluded from employment, is reflected in the poorer educational results which lone parents' children, on average, achieve.[29] Meanwhile, not only does unemployment cost the Exchequer substantial sums in benefits and lost taxes, but long term unemployment has a 'scarring' effect on the unemployed themselves. Skills are depleted, work habits eroded, morale and self-confidence dissipated – and the chances of securing a job fall because employers view the long term unemployed with suspicion. Indeed, the likelihood of someone being unemployed in a particular year is more influenced by an experience of unemployment in the previous year than all other factors put together.[30] As savings disappear and debts build up, the risks associated with a move into employment also increase: for too many people, particularly those with children, the stability of income support and 'passported' benefits becomes a necessary evil compared with the insecurity of a low-paid or casual job. Together, these factors mean that the longer a person is out of work, the harder it is for him or her to get back in: on average, someone who has already been unemployed for twelve months will remain unemployed for another twenty.[31]

A carefully designed and sustained strategy is needed to ensure that those who have been unemployed for longest have a fair chance of acquiring the jobs that are going. One-third of those unemployed for more than twelve months have A level qualifications or equivalent, but need some job-specific training or assistance with job search.[32] Others suffer from low skills and inadequate recent work experience; and a third group, who have health and other personal problems and may have completely lost work habits, need intensive support and training before employment becomes a realistic option.

Jobs, education and training: a new strategy

The centrepiece of a new strategy to help the long-term unemployed earn their way out of poverty should be a Jobs, Education and Training (JET) programme. Although its first purpose would be to ensure that everyone who has been registered as unemployed for more than twelve months gets a job, it should not be confined to them but should also help lone parents and others outside employment to move into employment. (Obviously, not everyone receiving benefit can move into employment; those who cannot, including some who are severely disabled and others with long-term full-time caring responsibilities, must not have their benefits jeopardised and should also be able to rely upon an efficient and sensitive service from the Benefits Agency.)

Australia has pioneered a JET programme for lone parents which has, over the last five years, reached nearly half of that group, significantly raising levels of training, employment and earnings amongst its clients. Savings have consistently outstripped targets and are now close to the overall programme costs.[33] Indeed, the programme has been so successful that the Australian government is now considering extending it to the registered long-term unemployed.

A JET programme for this country should have six goals:

- First, it should create a comprehensive re-employment service.
- Second, it should use training investment as a lever to improve people's employability.
- Third, it should sponsor 'micro-entrepreneurs' who have the talent to move from unemployment to self-employment.
- Fourth, it should offer lone parents additional help with finding good childcare facilities.
- Fifth, it should encourage the development of Intermediate Labour Markets – half-way houses to the formal labour market – in areas of greatest economic hardship.
- Sixth, it should use wage subsidies to reconnect the registered long-term unemployed to the labour market.

The First Goal: An Active Re-Employment Service

Information is a vital weapon in the armoury of someone seeking employment. An active labour market policy (concerted attempts to match employee aspirations with employment opportunities through guidance, training and counselling) is central to a well-functioning economy. Unfortunately, the government has given priority to policing the unemployed, through ever more strict eligibility criteria, rather than enabling them to become employed. The Unemployment Unit recently reported that the Employment Service has been asked to try out a new approach to unemployed claimants, who will now be offered particularly hard-to-fill vacancies in order to test their job-seeking activities.[34] Instead of attempting to find vacancies for which unemployed people are qualified, or helping them gain the skills for which there are vacancies, the Employment Service is in danger of looking for the least suitable vacancy in order to justify withdrawing the claimant's unemployment benefit. The imbalance between 'passive' and 'active' support for the unemployed is dramatic: for every £10 spent on unemployment benefit, the Government spends £1 helping the unemployed become employed.[35]

The JET Programme should transform the Employment Service into a 'one-stop re-employment shop' to advise the long-term unemployed about education and training services, career possibilities, job openings and childcare facilities, as well as help in moving from out-of-work to in-work benefits. The Re-Employment Service will need a high level of well-trained staff, including some transferred from the Benefits Agency, as well as the support of sophisticated information systems, so that it can provide a first-rate service to those who otherwise risk social and economic exclusion. In the United States, the Clinton administration is setting up a National Labour Market Information System under the Workforce Security and Re-Employment Act to emulate the best of European, and especially Scandinavian, practice. Pilot projects are bringing together detailed information about the current state of the local labour market and prospects for future job and business growth, as well as the success of different local education and training courses in leading their students to qualifications and jobs. Work in Sheffield on TAPs (Training Access Points) has shown the power of on-line information for finding training courses across the country; this approach is desperately needed for jobs and education too.

In April 1996, the Government intends to replace the present National Insurance Unemployment Benefit with a new Job Seeker's Allowance, lasting for only six months. By limiting its duration and requiring all claiming the new allowance to draw up and sign a personal job-seeking plan, the Government risks wasting staff time on a large number of people who would have found jobs in any case. We agree with Pam Meadows, previously a senior officer in the Department of Employment and now director of the Policy Studies Institute, who has argued that Employment Service resources should be shifted from the short-term unemployed to those in danger of staying out of work for a long time. People unemployed for less than twenty-six weeks should simply be signed on, while advisers concentrate on helping those already unemployed for twelve months or more to find employment, and making sure that claimants who reach six months' unemployment do not reach twelve. The Re-Employment Service should monitor closely the quality as well as the quantity of the jobs they find for their clients: in assessing success, we need to know what level of qualifications previously unemployed people have obtained, what qualifications are required in their new job, how much they are earning and whether they are still employed twelve months later.

A dilemma which applies to a number of active labour-market measures, but especially to training and job-search assistance, arises from the distinction between the flow into long-term unemployment and the existing stock of the long-term unemployed. Policies to prevent the former and to tackle the latter might, in some instances, be in conflict. Training the long-term unemployed succeeds in part at the expense of the short-term unemployed, although the problem is less severe if total demand for labour is growing. As studies of Restart in the UK and a similar scheme in France have shown[36], helping the long-term unemployed look for jobs more effectively can also displace people who have been unemployed for a shorter period. Because long-term unemployment is the greatest waste of resources and talent, however, its abolition must take priority even if that means living with some trade-off between short- and long-term unemployment.

The Second Goal: Improving employability

As one poor-quality scheme has replaced another, it is hardly surprising that unemployed people have become increasingly cynical about the value of training and work-experience programmes. It is, none the less, absolutely essential to help adults without basic skills or qualifications to acquire them, to help people whose skills are out of date to update them, and to raise the confidence of anyone whose morale has been undermined by a long period away from employment. People without skills are five times more likely to become unemployed than those with higher education level qualifications; in the end employment goes to the employable.[37] There is good evidence that high-quality training for the unemployed helps people to find work. Skills Training – now abolished – increased an unemployed man's chance of getting a job by at least 25 per cent.[38]

Training is more effective when targeted on specific needs, such as basic skills: because the needs of unemployed people are so diverse, generic training rarely works. Good training does not come cheap, but in the face of rising unemployment, the Government has chosen to cut spending on training by more than a third in real terms since 1987, from £4.3 billion to £2.6 billion in 1992/3.[39] This resulted in a 30 per cent cut in Employment Training (ET) funding and an 11 per cent cut in Youth Training funding. Cuts in training, which are reflected in the quality of provision, are a short-sighted saving. Comparisons of government and voluntary-sector training schemes for the long-term unemployed find higher costs per person in the voluntary sector, but *lower* costs per successful outcome.[40] Money spent on poor-quality training is almost completely wasted.

There are four related problems with the current provision of training for the unemployed through Training for Work and its predecessor, ET. First, it is too rigid, and neglects the diverse needs of unemployed people. Second, its separation from mainstream education and training stigmatises the schemes and lowers standards. It is not good enough that only 30 per cent of people referred to ET left with a qualification, and that only 30 per cent (not necessarily the same people) left ET for a job.[41] Third, it assumes that all training for the unemployed can be provided within the same framework, which seriously limits flexibility. And fourth, because ET was limited to registered claimants, it excluded many of the people who want to return to employment, including many people with disabilities as well as women who have been at home caring for children. The result is a complicated and confusing structure, where access to training depends upon someone's social security status instead of their ability to profit from a course.

Instead, we propose an integrated strategy to extend education and training to the long-term unemployed. As with the Re-Employment Service, the new education approach would cover lone parents and women in families dependent upon Income Support as well as registered claimants. Within this broad group, our aim should eventually be to ensure that anyone with qualifications below A level or NVQ Level 3 reaches that standard, gradually replacing Training for Work and Youth Training with Learning Bank credits, as described in the previous chapter. An approach which concentrated resources on fewer people at a time would be controversial – but queues are tolerable if they lead somewhere. Instead of being actively encouraged to acquire new qualifications, Income Support claimants are currently barred from studying for more than twenty-one hours a week, a rule which should be abolished for long-term unemployed claimants.

Training and Enterprise Councils (TECs) provide the basis for the integrated local labour market organisations which Germany has long benefited from and which the UK previously lacked. They should be strengthened by extending their membership to represent a wider range of local interests; and they should be given clearer goals and more stable funding. A shift towards a demand-driven system may also alter the role of TECs from the present emphasis on provision of training towards advising trainees, monitoring standards and promoting the development of new training facilities.

The Third Goal: Backing micro-entrepreneurs

Leaving unemployment does not necessarily mean becoming an employee: self-employment is growing. Although many self-employed people work extremely long hours for very little reward, helping to finance their ambition and ideas makes far better sense than handing out benefits for unemployment. We have been much impressed by the work of the Prince's Youth Business Trust, which provides financial backing to young unemployed people who wish to set up in business. Most of the people the Trust supports (20,000 people since the start of the programme) are in their 20s and have been unemployed for more than a year. In East London we met two dynamic, able, hard-working young men who ran businesses – one an art shop and the other a catering company with forty-five people on the payroll. Both had been able to get started only because of the ongoing support of the Trust. Nationally, two-thirds of these businesses are still going three years later. This is a better survival rate than for businesses supported by the high street banks, an impressive achievement given that the Prince's Trust only supports young people who have been refused a bank loan. The key to the Trust's success is the management as well as financial support it gives to young businessmen and women, persuading larger companies to provide 'mentors' to advise and guide the businesses. It is an approach which backs up the view of employment experts Professor Richard Layard and Dr John Philpott, of the Employment Policy Institute: 'there is nothing to promote self-help more than a little well-judged help from others'.[42]

There is a lesson here which government is ignoring as it moves public money away from supporting self-employment for the previously unemployed. The replacement of the Enterprise Allowance scheme with the Business Start-up Allowance, along with the accompanying changes in eligibility criteria, has caused a large drop in the number of unemployed people receiving support, despite the welcome removal of the rule that required people to have £1,000 of their own capital before qualifying for a grant.

In 1984, more than one in four people receiving the Enterprise Allowance had been out of work for more than a year; in the first year of Business Start-up only one in ten successful applicants had been long-term unemployed. Surveys of TECs show that only 10 per cent of them see Business Start-up as a measure for helping the unemployed.[43] In part this is because funding allocation has shifted from 'new starts' to long-term survivors, so TECs are inclined to pick what they see as 'winners' – i.e. not the unemployed. It is ironic that, in fact, survival rates for businesses set up under the old scheme were comparable to those today. Instead of squeezing out the long-term unemployed, TECs should set targets for the number of long-term unemployed (including lone parents) to be helped through Business Start-up, and the funding assessment should be shifted back towards new starts.

The Fourth Goal: Helping parents with childcare

A major reason for the success of the Australian JET programme is the help that it offers with childcare. Not only do lone parents who are training or employed receive priority in publicly funded childcare services, but the JET programme itself can finance a temporary extra childcare place where one of its clients continues to experience problems finding suitable help.

If a JET programme is established in the UK, re-employment advisers should be able to help all clients with access to childcare. Lone parents find it far more difficult to get the informal childcare help on which most employed mothers continue to rely. Although lone parents will benefit, along with others, from the general expansion of childcare facilities which we propose earlier, funding for the JET programme should also include an amount to help lone parents if no other childcare facility is available.

The Fifth Goal: Intermediate Labour Markets

Attachment to the labour market – even if it is only for a short time in the initial stage – is the key to breaking the vicious cycle of long-term unemployment and social exclusion. The long-term unemployed very often live in the same places, even the same homes, as each other. In the travel-to-work area with the highest registered unemployment in the country, the chances of being unemployed are six times higher than in the area with the lowest unemployment; but the chances of being long-term unemployed are twenty-three times as high.[44] While this can mean that there is more social support available, the overall effect is that the individual problems of long-term unemployment are enormously exacerbated by the collective ones of a declining local economic base, poor services, high crime levels and a poor community reputation.

Enhancing the quality of life, reputation and confidence of people in these areas is a vital condition for increasing employment opportunities; to this end, we propose in Chapter 7 new community development strategies. But government also needs to encourage 'intermediate labour markets' (ILMs) – a combination of training and employment which moves people off Income Support and into employment – to help the people who have been out of work for longest in the areas with the fewest jobs. The Commission saw the principle put into practice in Glasgow when we visited the Wise Group, a non-profit-distributing company which employs and trains previously unemployed people on insulation projects, landscaping local estates and general environmental work. The 450 Wise Group trainees are on benefit for the first eight weeks, and are then paid a proper wage for the rest of their twelve months' employment. Working for wages rather than benefit is a crucial feature of the Group's success: 55 per cent of people move into jobs in the formal labour market, compared with 35 per cent for the government schemes Employment Training (now Training for Work) and Youth Training.

'Social economy' organisations like the Wise Group, funded from a wide variety of sources, can provide local services and overcome a real market failure where the private sector cannot translate needs into economic demand or where potential customers simply cannot afford to pay for private services. There is enormous potential for the creation of *new* markets in which social economy organisations are the main participants: examples are environmental improvements, energy-conservation measures such as insulation, and so on. In Germany, a market niche was identified in the repair of bicycles – and *Soziale Betrieb* (social economy organisations) filled it very successfully. Many of these 'new' markets are very employment-intensive; for example, energy efficiency work creates 40 per cent more employment than energy supply.[45] Consultants Peter Welch and Malcolm Coles argue that local authorities could extend their support of social economy ILMs by considering them as potential recipients of tenders for service provision, subject to the same quality controls as typical private-sector bidders.[46]

Government could also encourage social economy organisations to develop ILMs by allowing them to keep part or all of the Income Support which would otherwise continue to be paid to someone who has been unemployed for twelve months. EU funds must also be mobilised in the areas of greatest deprivation in this country: at the moment, the UK receives less than it could from the EU, mostly because of the UK government's reluctance to provide 'matching' funds.[47]

The Sixth Goal: Wage subsidies to support employment, not unemployment

Direct wage subsidies have a useful part to play in reconnecting long-term unemployed people to the labour market. Wage subsidies should not be designed merely to give someone temporary work experience for as long as the subsidy lasts; the aim should instead be to use the period of subsidised employment to raise the worker's productivity and therefore the chance of remaining in non-subsidised employment. This is a very different approach from that of the Government, which is committed to a long-term strategy of cutting wages at the bottom of the labour market and offering a permanent subsidy to low wages through an extended system of means-tested Family Credit. Instead, we propose to use direct wage subsidies as part of a concentrated effort to bring back into employment those people who now have little hope of a job.

During the 1970s, the subsidy paid to small firms in high-unemployment areas helped to increase employment.[48] In the USA, the New Jobs Tax Credit of 1978 was estimated to have created up to 400,000 extra jobs.[49] A new report to the French Senate has recommended wage subsidies as part of a comprehensive strategy for reducing unemployment.[50] Most studies find, however, that more than half the programme costs are absorbed in 'deadweight' – helping people who would have got jobs anyway. In Spain, wage subsidies had to be cut back because employers became dependent on subsidised staff on temporary contracts.

The UK Government has launched a pilot programme, called Workstart, which gives employers a subsidy worth £2,300 for taking on someone from the pool of long-term unemployed. Results are mixed, mostly because of poor programme design: the scheme is limited to 1,000 people per pilot area, bureaucratic obstacles make the matching of the unemployed with employers difficult, and most importantly there is no effective mechanism for preventing employers substituting subsidised workers for other employees.

People who have been unemployed for a long time face such extensive discrimination in the labour market, however, that it makes sense to tip the scales in their favour. Properly designed wage subsidies should therefore be used on a much larger scale to help reintegrate the long-term unemployed into the labour market. The following examples illustrate the various mechanisms available:

- Employers could be entitled to offer a 'job trial' of, say, one month to a long-term unemployed person. For that period, benefit would continue to be paid instead of wages. If a longer-term job was then offered and accepted, the employer would get a further month's free labour, with benefits continuing to be paid while Family Credit and Housing Benefit were processed. A 'back to work' grant might also be necessary to help with the immediate costs of taking up employment, such as buying essential tools.

- An employer who takes on a long-term unemployed person could be exempted from paying National Insurance Contributions for that person for, say, a year. In effect, part of the benefit that would have been paid had the person not got a job becomes a wage subsidy given directly to the employer.

- Government could create a benefit transfer programme, which allows the long-term unemployed to transfer part or all of their individual Income Support and/or Unemployment entitlement to an employer in return for a job. The employee would be paid the wage for the job: the employer would receive the benefit. Professor Dennis Snower, an economist who has proposed such programmes, argues that allowing people to convert their benefit into a wage subsidy would cost government nothing, and might even save money.[51]

Wage subsidies must, however, be linked to training, either by being made conditional upon the provision of training, or by offering a higher subsidy to firms who use the whole of the subsidy for training.[52] Any scheme must also contain safeguards to prevent unscrupulous employers sacking an existing employee, dipping into the pool of long-term unemployed, taking on a subsidised employee for twelve months, and then throwing him or her back in the pool in order to take out another subsidised employee – although this is less likely to happen if the employee has been helped to become fully productive.

Workfare?

Wage subsidies are necessary to close the gap between an acceptable wage and the value of the employee to the employer. An alternative is to force people to work for less than the minimum wage – 'workfare'. In America, workfare is a requirement that 'employable public assistance recipients receive benefits only if they work off their grants in unpaid jobs'.[53] Few US states operate a pure workfare scheme. Many have voluntary work schemes for the unemployed, without the sanction of loss of benefits if someone chooses not to participate. Professor Robert Walker argues that popular 'logic and emotion call for individuals to work for wages, rather than for benefit', and one of the reasons why workfare proper has not been widespread in the US is that policy-makers and programme managers recognise that people need opportunities, not sanctions, in order to work.[54] The condemnation by Frank Field MP of compulsory training is equally applicable to workfare schemes: 'trying to force people into a scheme by threatening to reduce their benefits is counter-productive, since [it] simply becomes a very expensive system of monitoring.'[55] There is a real danger, too, that if young people are offered the choice between workfare or inadequate training and the loss of their benefits, they will reject both workfare and benefits and choose a third way – the cash-and-crime economy.[56]

Supporters of greater compulsion often point to Sweden as an example. But the Swedish system is better described as a social insurance approach because the jobs which unemployed people are required to take, on pain of forfeiting their benefit, are paid at the rate for the job. Workfare, by contrast, tries to make unemployment disappear by converting it into public works programmes paid at benefit plus a weekly top-up. But the long-term unemployed, like everyone else, want to work for wages, not for benefit or benefit-plus. As Alan Sinclair, founder of the Wise Group, stressed to us: 'We have to get people *out* of "Giroland".'

The benefits system has always required unemployed claimants to demonstrate that they are available for work; this must, of course, remain the case, with the changes we recommend later (see page 239). Some people, however, continue to argue for tougher rules for the long-term unemployed, often linked to a 'job guarantee' from the public sector if they do not find work or training elsewhere. Professor Layard and Dr Philpott, for instance, argue in favour of the 'employment principle', that the state has a duty to offer work or training to the long-term unemployed, and that claimants have a duty to accept it.[57] Peter Ashby of Full Employment UK argues for a job guarantee at eighteen months. He describes his 'opportunity guarantee' – a choice of training or work in return for benefit plus a supplement – as a work-based safety-net.[58]

There is a real danger, however, that a new job guarantee would be regarded by both the unemployed and employers as just another attempt to fiddle the unemployment figures, and that participation in such a scheme would reduce rather than enhance an individual's chances of getting a job in the formal labour market. The labour-market analyst Anne Costello emphasises that provided new jobs are created, 'public money on wage subsidies goes further than it does in public sector job creation. Instead of the state paying 100 per cent of the wage, it pays between around 10 per cent and 50 per cent'.[59] There is also the problem that someone who knows that they can rely upon a job guarantee after twelve months' unemployment may have less incentive to look for a job in the few months before that – which is why, if public-sector job guarantees are to be used at all, they should be restricted to the minority of very long-term unemployed people within each local area, for whom a temporary job in the public sector may be the only way to reconnect them to employment. (In some areas, there are few people who have been unemployed for more than two or even three years; in places where unemployment is most severe, however, five or six years might be the appropriate definition of very long-term unemployment.) It would be essential for any such job-guarantee programme to include high-quality training leading to appropriate qualifications, and to work closely with local private employers to ensure that it gained a reputation as a real stepping-stone back into employment.

The Distribution of Employment

Creating opportunities for people who have spent years out of work is itself an enormous challenge. But we also need to improve the way in which the labour market works for people who are in employment, so that it offers choice and promotes mobility. Crucial to achieving this goal is an understanding not just of the changes going on in the labour market, but the changes going on in people's lives and families. The problems confronting us are:

- Growth in employment is absorbed in significant part by those already in work, rather than spreading to those wanting work.
- Employment opportunities are drastically reduced for women with family responsibilities, largely because of the unequal distribution of unpaid work between men and women.
- Employment is unequally distributed between work-rich and work-poor households; women married to unemployed men are only about one-third as likely to be in employment as women whose partners are in work.[60]
- Discrimination against people from minority groups is inefficient as well as unfair.

Men's work, women's work

The Sex Discrimination Act was introduced in 1975 to help bring down the barriers which kept women out of men's jobs. Although women's employment opportunities are increasing even faster than men's are shrinking, women are still concentrated in lower-paid, lower-skilled employment and form the majority of low-paid employees. The 'glass ceiling' which keeps too many women out of senior jobs, especially in management, is not only unjust to women: it is a waste of educated abilities that the country simply cannot afford. Furthermore, it is madness that so many well-educated women are employed in lower-level administrative and clerical jobs which could be done just as well by less qualified people who are now out of work. In the collision between employment and family, it is women who lose out.

Despite two decades of equal opportunities legislation, the UK labour market is heavily segregated: two-thirds of the workforce are in a job where more than two-thirds of their colleagues are of the same sex. Women predominate in the retail, public and service sectors, men in manufacturing industry and construction. As traditionally male employment declines, a new problem is arising – many men cannot obtain or are reluctant to accept what have traditionally been seen as 'women's jobs'. But it is this sector of the labour market that is growing.

The disadvantages faced in the labour markets of modern economies by men with low educational qualifications are extremely serious not only for them and their families, but for society as a whole. For generations, the essence of masculinity has been defined by the man's ability to support his family. His personal esteem and place in the family and wider community depended upon reasonably stable and decently paid employment, and the type of employment mattered too. Ian Spence of the GMB general union in Cardiff told us about his growing concern for young working-class men who, in the old days, would have got an apprenticeship or joined the Army:

We knew that the men who were made redundant from the mines and the steelworks in their 50s wouldn't ever work again. But we thought that their sons might be all right. It hasn't worked out like that. These lads want a proper job – and a proper job means something tough, something dirty even, like working down the mines, or in a foundry or steelworks, or in a construction gang, something that you can boast about to your mates. They're not going to go and ice cakes in the local hotel.

Policy-makers should not accept stereotyped notions of what men can do, any more than they now accept stereotyped views of women's abilities. Many of the men who worked in the mines or heavy industry hoped that education would offer a route to something better for their sons, as indeed it often did. But nor should policy-makers under-estimate the dislocation in men's lives created by the rundown of great industries. The difficulties involved in opening up the full range of work to men are at least as great as those involved in bringing women into traditionally male employment.

Unemployment itself is beginning to change the distribution of work within families. In Easterhouse, we met Willie pushing his youngest child in a pram. He told us how he had worked for years as a master baker and then, after he was made redundant, as a building worker. 'I used to travel all over the country – wherever there was a job to do, I went. But once we started having kids, it just got too much. I never saw the wife and children, and with five kids she couldn't manage on her own. Round here, there's just no work for me to do. But she's got a job now, part-time in an office, so we get Family Credit and I stay home to look after the weans.' An economy which has no use for Willie's skills is manifestly inefficient. But he takes pride in his new role and is relieved that someone in the family has a job.

As men start to apply for conventionally female jobs, they encounter many of the same obstacles as women trying to enter male-dominated employment. Nearly half of the complaints that the Equal Opportunities Commission receives about employment discrimination now come from men.[61] The problem is often not openly discriminatory rules but stereotyped assumptions about men's capabilities on the part of employers and, sometimes, men themselves. One businessman who runs a food factory put his finger on the problem:

> Twenty years ago, almost all the manual workers in my operation were men and a lot of the work consisted of humping sacks of potatoes around. Today, it's all fiddly work putting sauce on the bits of chicken for Marks and Sparks, and the assembly line is 90 per cent women. Mostly men don't apply for it – it's part-time and they see it as women's work.

There are other reasons why men find it particularly hard to consider the part-time jobs which form a growing proportion of all jobs, and an even higher proportion of vacancies on offer. While most women who are employed part-time have partners in a full-time job, very few unemployed men have partners who are employed at all, let alone full-time. There is therefore no foundation of earnings within the family upon which the unemployed man could build by taking a part-time job. Even if it were practicable in other ways, the prospect of the woman working full-time and the man part-time may be unacceptable because it challenges the traditional distribution of both paid and unpaid work within the family.

Concern about male unemployment should not lead to romantic notions about the re-creation of the male breadwinner earning a family wage. The old jobs which offered a reasonable wage to men without a good education will not return, and nor will women's entry to education and employment be reversed. For a two-parent family, the most secure route to a decent standard of living is to have two earners, not necessarily both full-time. But if the men who are now unemployed are to have a fair chance of employment in future, we will need as vigorous an effort to pull down the barriers which keep men out of 'women's jobs', as that embarked upon two decades ago to open up 'men's jobs' to women. Women engineers, airline pilots and chief executives are no longer seen as oddities; we need equally to transform attitudes towards male secretaries, childcare workers, nurses and home helps, as well as to fathers remaining at home to care for their children. In the 1970s, 'wider opportunities for women' courses succeeded in encouraging many women to train for non-traditional employment; in the 1990s, our JET training programme needs to do the same for men.

Family-friendly employment

Unequal opportunities in the workplace are partly a reflection of unequal responsibilities in the home. Crudely put, the time men spend at work determines how much time they have left over for their families; but the time women spend caring for their families determines how much time they have available for employment. Equal pay and sex-discrimination laws have gone some way towards giving women a better chance in traditionally male-dominated jobs. But equal opportunities policies will continue to produce disappointing results unless employers and politicians abandon the idea that the only real job is a full-time job, and that a successful career demands a full-time, life-time commitment and the sacrifice of everything else.

Full-time employment by both parents, or by a lone parent, leaves a gap at home, which may be filled by partners juggling their hours of work, by other relatives, or by various forms of childcare. For the one in five children in the UK that the Kids Club Network calls 'latchkey' children, it is a gap left unfilled.[62] But the 'male' model of full-time employment is not the only way to organise production; and in the modern economy, it is increasingly not the most efficient way either. In a world where women want to fulfil their economic potential, where society recognises their right to do so and where the economy needs them to do so, meeting the needs of children requires different options for the employment of parents. As the economy moves away from a pattern of full-time employment which both depended upon and shaped traditional family structures, we have a strategic opportunity to create new forms of employment that will be both family-friendly and contribute to efficient production.

It is not for government to dictate employment or family patterns, but it can encourage wider choice. At the moment, about one in four of the women who want to stay at home after having a baby ends up in employment, in order to maintain the family income, while the same proportion of those who do stay at home would prefer to be in a job.[63] In the absence of public standards, some organisations will in their own interests offer career breaks, maternity leave and help with childcare to at least some of their women employees; very few will understand the need to offer the equivalent to fathers as well. Some employers will demand hours of work which are not only damaging to health and safety, but disastrous for family life: British men already work the longest average hours in Europe.[64] Thus, government must set new minimum standards, encourage employers to do better and – by pooling many of the costs – ensure that those employers who have a 'bulge' of employees of childbearing age do not end up bearing a disproportionate share of the cost of family-friendly employment.

Now that the British Government has reluctantly complied with a new EU Directive, women who have been employed for at least six months with the same firm have the right to eighteen weeks' paid maternity leave, which they can begin to take up to eleven weeks before the baby is born. They also have the right to return to their previous job within twenty-nine weeks of the baby's birth or adoption. Other EU countries, however, are still far more generous than the United Kingdom in requiring employers to give their employees paid or unpaid time off from work. Such working practices can *save* employers money by improving recruitment and retention rates and by reducing skills shortages. Midland Bank has calculated that while it costs £18,000 to replace an assistant manager with 11 to 15 years' experience, a subsidy towards a nursery place costs £2,500 a year, so that the bank saves at least £8,000 over four years by retaining these managers.

Employment breaks are valuable in themselves, as an investment in families, and will produce economic rewards as they help women keep employment which fits their skills. But they also generate new employment opportunities. A maternity leave replacement may only be a temporary post, but it can give an incomer a foothold in the organisation, with the possibility – given normal turnover rates – of obtaining a more permanent job later, as well as valuable work experience to offer in applying for other jobs.

The state of the British economy, however, means that it will take time before we can expect all employers to reach the standards of the best. In the long-term, our aspiration should be to make it possible for either parent to choose to take leave (or both parents to share it between them) for at least twelve months after paid maternity leave ends. This could be funded through the new social insurance programme described in the next chapter, which is designed precisely to provide the sort of choice needed to match social and economic change. There are various intermediate steps that could be implemented in a phased and sensible way over the medium term to start the march towards the long-term goal. Different people will have different priorities, but in principle the following measures all have much to commend them, though they could not be introduced overnight or all at once.

A statutory right to two weeks' paid paternity leave on the birth or adoption of a child would be a simple and cheap measure which would none the less symbolise the importance society wants to attach to fatherhood. Similarly, the extension by six months to either parent of the right to reinstatement, now enjoyed by women on maternity leave, would expand choice and promote a sensible balance between work and family. Parents returning after maternity or parental leave should, wherever possible, be entitled to move if they wish into part-time employment in the same job or at the same level as before.

There is also the issue of time off work for family emergencies – most obviously sick children. Professionals who control their own time are in a position to take a morning or day off as necessary, and make it up later; other workers may face the sack if they put their children first. Ideally, everybody should be able to take occasional short-term paid family leave in an emergency. In Sweden, where this provision is already available, the average emergency leave taken is about two days, although the maximum allowed is higher. Good employers, of course, already make this sort of formal or informal provision. As a long-term target, we should aim to spread this best practice through a new right for all employees. Of course, however the entitlement is phased in, it could not offer unlimited leave, and the eventual maximum of ten days a year seems sensible.

Family-Friendly Employment

- A national childcare and education strategy for the under-fives
- More individual choice of working hours
- Sign European Directive on Working Hours
- Extension of care services for before and after school
- New leave arrangements for parents and other carers
- Equal rights for part-time workers (above 8 hours per week)

In the long term, the establishment for informal carers of older people of the equivalent of maternity and parental leave would iron out an anomaly in treatment. One of the USA's leading insurance companies, Travellers Inc, on finding that more of its employees were responsible for older family members than for children, extended its 'family policy' to support employees who are also carers, helping to ensure that the company did not lose experienced workers because of a family crisis.

Shorter working hours

The UK is alone in the EU in having no regulations on working hours. Everywhere else, working hours are controlled by law or collective bargaining. We do not wish to see this country moving towards a nationally imposed standard working week of the continental kind; that would remove the real benefits to both employers and employees which greater choice over working time can offer. Indeed, Germany and other EU countries have recognised the need to relax their controls on working and trading hours.

None the less, the UK situation is unsatisfactory. Because there are no upper limits on working hours, too many employees are forced to work dangerously long hours. Studies in several countries have provided substantial evidence about the damage done by long working hours and some shift systems, particularly those involving night work or a frequent change between night and day shifts. The ill-effects can extend beyond workers to members of the public: the official enquiry into the Clapham Junction railway disaster in 1988, which killed thirty-five people, found that the senior technician responsible for the faulty wiring which caused the accident had been working a seven-day week for the previous thirteen weeks.

Between the 1860s and the 1970s, men's working hours fell fairly steadily throughout the industrialised world. In the United Kingdom, for instance, the average weekly hours of male manual workers fell from 57 hours in 1860 to below 39 hours by the end of the 1970s. In the rest of the European Union, this trend continued through the 1980s. But in the UK, largely thanks to increased overtime, the hours worked by full-time male manual workers started to rise again in the mid-1980s. The hours of non-manual workers, however, have been rising steadily, with the proportion of men working over 45 hours a week rising from 16 per cent in 1975 to 26 per cent in 1988. Nearly four in ten of Britain's full-time male workers put in more than 46 hours a week, compared with an average of only one in seven in other EU countries.[65] It is sometimes argued that shorter hours will not create more jobs because the difference will simply be made up in productivity gains. Studies consistently show substantial cuts in work performance as hours of work lengthen.[66] Even allowing for productivity gains, however, Dr Paul Gregg of the National Institute for Economic and Social Research has estimated that if working hours had continued to decline throughout the 1980s at their previous rate, an additional 1 million people would now be employed.[67] The Trade Union Research Unit estimates that if working hours were to fall, the gain could be as high as 1.5 million.[68]

Different European countries with similar levels of output and productivity succeed in employing very different proportions of their workforce. There is a clear contrast between countries which employ fewer people working longer hours and those which employ more people working shorter hours. Both Denmark and the Netherlands, for example, employ a high proportion of their population, with short average hours for full-time employees and a high proportion of part-time workers. In contrast, in Belgium and Italy, where levels of productivity and income per head are similar to those in the Netherlands, average working hours are much longer and a smaller proportion of the population is employed. If Belgians worked the same hours as the Dutch, and productivity remained the same, 15 per cent more people could be in work.[69]

It is not possible to solve the unemployment problem by compulsory reductions in working hours. In the rest of the European Union, however, there is growing interest in the possibility of translating voluntary shorter working hours into lower unemployment. In 1993, when the German company Volkswagen was faced with the need to reduce production and costs, management and workforce agreed to cut the working week from five days to four, with a corresponding reduction in pay, in order to prevent redundancies. A year later, when the company needed to increase output and wanted to enlarge its workforce again, it found that many of its employees no longer wanted to return to full-time working. All vacancies in the German government sector are now open to those wishing to work part-time or to share a job, as well as to full-time workers.[70]

Voluntary working-time reductions are much easier to achieve when earnings are as high as at Volkswagen. But there are comparable examples in this country too. Early in 1993, British Airways offered ground staff at Heathrow Airport the option of voluntarily reducing their working hours while staying in the same job, on the same hourly rate of pay (with pension rights for people over fifty continuing to be calculated on full-time, not part-time earnings). Not only did BA meet its targets for reducing the workforce, without adding anybody to the dole queue, but it also saved on redundancy payments. The Inland Revenue Staff Federation has a longstanding agreement which allows full-time Inland Revenue staff to apply to reduce their working hours. More than 7,000 people in a workforce of 60,000 have taken advantage of an arrangement that suits management (which needs more flexible staffing to meet variable workloads) as well as employees.

Too many manual workers in the UK are forced by inadequate basic wages into long hours of overtime in order to maintain a decent income. At the same time, there is a significant minority of full-time workers who would prefer to work shorter hours even at the price of lower earnings – sometimes because they need time for their families more than they need money, sometimes because with their children grown up and mortgages paid off they would prefer extra leisure for themselves.[71] Although government cannot force employers to give workers more choice over their working hours, it should certainly take the lead by offering a greater choice of part-time employment throughout the Civil Service and Next Steps agencies. Redundancy laws, which already require employers to consult with employees in advance of large-scale redundancies, could be amended to require employers contemplating redundancies to start by offering voluntary cuts in working hours. Given the costs of redundancy payments, such a move would cost employers nothing and could even offer them substantial savings.

Other EU countries have accepted the European Directive on Working Time which sets the objective of a maximum 48-hour average working week. In place of the cumbersome and partial opt-out negotiated by the Government, the United Kingdom should fully endorse the Directive. Far from imposing shorter hours regardless of business needs, it recognises the need for business to go beyond this limit in particular sectors such as oil drilling, or when there is an unexpected increase in workload. It exempts professional and managerial workers completely, recognising that they have considerable control over their working hours. But by requiring proper protection for health and safety for those who have no choice over working long hours or on shifts, and by encouraging employers to enter into collective agreements where working patterns outside the Directive are needed, it strikes a sensible balance between the needs of employers and those of employees.

Combating discrimination

Despite their longing for a truly 'flexible' labour market, the Deregulators never seem to be greatly concerned about the rigidities created by discrimination against people because of their race, sex or disability. But discrimination is not only immoral; it is bad economics, preventing companies from using the human capital of our population effectively. A glance at any job advertisement today suggests that the equal-opportunities employer has arrived, and there is no doubt that real progress has been made over the last twenty years in tackling both race and sex discrimination in education, training and employment. But discrimination, both through action and omission, has proved striking in its resilience and adaptability. Economic and budgetary pressures on employers have been used as an explanation for pushing equal opportunity measures to the back of the queue – 'extras' rather than 'basics'. Good employers understand the need to make the best possible use of all the potential available to them, although even they have been helped by equal opportunities laws to understand the effects of some apparently neutral working practices. For the rest, intervention by government is essential to create genuinely open access to employment and efficient use of our most important resource – people.

The USA has demonstrated the potential of contract compliance procedures to deliver maximum effect for minimum intervention: public sector contracts are awarded only to employers meeting basic standards of good practice. They offer the capacity to harness the huge purchasing power of the public sector through central and local government in order to accelerate the effect of anti-discrimination and positive equality measures in recruitment, promotion and access to training. Contract specifications can ensure that good practice in terms of racial equality, gender and disability becomes the norm. Those who fail to demonstrate their ability to meet such standards will be the losers when contracts are allocated. We would therefore like to see government supplement anti-discrimination laws with contract compliance throughout the public sector. A single government unit should be responsible for monitoring contract compliance and advising government departments, Next Steps agencies and local authorities.

Although the Sex Discrimination, Equal Pay and Race Relations Acts have all proved their worth, they need to be strengthened. We regret that the Government has rejected the detailed practical proposals made by the Commission for Racial Equality (CRE) for improving enforcement of the laws and closing various loopholes, and would like to see their amendments, and those proposed by the Equal Opportunities Commission, implemented in future.[72] In particular, anti-discrimination laws should be made consistent throughout the United Kingdom.

Other groups are now arguing powerfully for new anti-discrimination laws. Disabled people routinely face personal discrimination, when for instance an employer refuses to consider a properly-qualified person for a job, simply because of their disability, or when companies refuse to provide services without any justification. But they also face structural discrimination – the unintended consequences of buildings and facilities designed without any thought for disabled people.[73] Although it will take considerable time to overcome all these problems, legislation against the pervasive discrimination faced by disabled people is clearly required. Although the Government rejected a Private Member's Bill to outlaw such discrimination, it has accepted the case in principle and announced its own plans for a weaker law. Groups representing lesbians and gay men have also argued that discrimination on grounds of sexual orientation should be outlawed. Rather than trying to develop a series of separate anti-discrmination laws, government should consider the case for a single law prohibiting unjustified discrimination in employment, education and access to goods and services. (For instance, a job applicant could not be rejected on grounds unrelated to the job.) Detailed regulations and guidance would then deal with discrimination against different groups of people. This omnibus approach would provide a legal framework which is both straightforward and flexible.

A comprehensive anti-discrimination law could be enforced and promoted by a single Human Rights Commission, allowing anyone who felt they had been discriminated against to turn to one source of help, although different strategies and separate divisions would still be needed to deal with different kinds of discrimination. Whereas both the EOC and the CRE have long experience of enforcing anti-discrimination laws and promoting equal opportunities, there is no tradition of effective action to counter discrimination against disabled people. None the less, a single Commission, able to respond to changing needs, would avoid the bureaucracy and cost of establishing a new agency for every group to whom the protection of anti-discrimination laws is in future extended.

A comprehensive anti-discrimination law would certainly help to fight the growing problem of age discrimination, which not only unfairly curtails individual opportunity, but is becoming increasingly economically wasteful as older people capable of contributing to production are forced into early retirement. Inaccurate assumptions about the productivity and learning capacity of older people are reinforced by many organisations' pay and pension structures which make it financially more attractive to replace older with younger workers, and create a disincentive to older people to reduce their hours before retiring fully. The extension of employment protection laws up to the age of seventy would help to encourage more flexible retirement, while a law against age discrimination, which has existed in the USA since 1967, would challenge the widespread use of 'age bars' in recruitment as well as the often automatic selection of older workers for compulsory redundancy.

Rewarding Employment

Paid work is – or should be – a route to an adequate income, social networks and personal fulfilment. Too often it is none of these things. The negative effects of global changes in the nature of employment and, particularly, of the falling demand for unskilled labour have been exacerbated by Conservative policy in the last fifteen years. The curtailment of employment protection laws, combined with the declining influence of trade unions, has added enormously to the insecurity caused by economic restructuring. It is typical of the Deregulators to see laws against unfair dismissal, for instance, purely as a cost unnecessarily imposed upon employers, instead of understanding how employment laws can help to shape workplace organisation for the better.

Investors understand that exploitation is not just morally undesirable, it is bad business strategy. The Chief Executive Officer of the hamburger chain Wendy's realised that his company would never become the first choice of customers unless it also became

Table 5.2: The Decline of Collective Bargaining

	Percent of Private Sector Employees Covered (Manufacturing and Services)					
Extent and nature of collective bargaining (c.b)	1950	1960	1970	1980	1984	1990
Pay not fixed by c.b.	20	25	30	30	40	50
Pay fixed by c.b.	80	75	70	70	60	50
c.b. is multi-employer (industry, regional etc)	60	45	35	30	20	10
c.b. is single-employer (company, factory etc)	20	30	35	40	40	40

Source: Professor William Brown *The Scope for an Incomes Policy for Britain in the 1990s* (submission to the Commission on Social Justice, 1994)

the first choice of employees. He put in place a package including improved benefits, perks, a quarterly bonus, and employee stock options. The result was clear: 'Our turnover rate for general managers fell to 20 per cent in 1991 from 38 per cent in 1989, while turnover among company and assistant managers dropped to 37 per cent from 60 per cent – among the lowest in the business. With a stable – and able – workforce, sales began to pick up as well.'[74] Labour is an asset, and should be treated as such.

Setting wages and salaries

The UK hardly has a 'system' of wage bargaining. It would be more accurate to describe it as a patchwork quilt of custom, informal agreements and decentralised power struggles. We are as far as anyone could imagine from the ordered pay round of the 'corporatist' countries, where employers, government and trade unions hammer out a deal at a national level that is then implemented across the country. In the absence of a coordinated wage-bargaining system, the danger is that measures to increase growth and employment may simply generate an inflation spiral, as 'insiders' push up wages at the expense of 'outsiders'. In a paper presented to the Commission, Professor James Meade argued that 'Keynesian full-employment policy ... collapsed simply and solely because a high level of money expenditures came to lead not to a high level of output and employment but to a high rate of inflation of money wages, costs and prices in spite of growing unemployment.'

Even with 3 million unemployed in the 1980s, wages for those in work rose at up to twice the level of inflation. The reality is that unemployment is not an effective brake on inflation, partly because a growing proportion of the unemployed have been out of work for so long that they cannot compete effectively for jobs and are therefore not a moderating force on wage rises. It is also the case that pay is now driven as much by the state of product markets – the ability of firms to sell the goods and services they produce – as by the state of the labour market.[75]

Throughout the post-war period, pay policy has foundered on the inability of employers' and workers' organisations to deliver the sort of wage discipline that is common on the Continent. In a submission to the Commission, Professor William Brown argued that the most effective attempt at national pay coordination was the first, in 1948-50, when a few national, industry-wide agreements delivered pay restraint to the Attlee government. Today, as Table 5.2 suggests, this sort of national deal is scarcely feasible, although it should be noted that in Ireland a significant wages accord has been developed despite decentralised bargaining structures.

Pay is increasingly product-specific and single-employer, a trend which is unlikely to change. It will certainly not be changed by the imposition of statutory pay control, however desirable that may seem to modellers of the UK economy. More effective investment in education and training, coupled with other measures to bring those now excluded from employment into the labour market, will, however, reduce the skill shortages which helped to push up earnings in the 1980s and increase the number of 'insiders' competing for jobs where earnings are now growing most rapidly.

No one should under-estimate the danger posed to employment by earnings inflation. Political leaders need to help the country understand that unemployment *and* inflation can be kept down only if the average increase in money earnings is no higher than the average increase in productivity in the economy as a whole. If, however, high productivity growth in one sector is matched by substantial pay rises, a 'going rate' will be set for *all* employees which is well beyond what the lower-productivity sectors can justify. Even if most hold back, some employers and employees will choose to 'free ride' by awarding themselves higher pay rises. The result will be familiar: either higher inflation or higher unemployment. While the Deregulators' answer is to weaken or eliminate trade unions and abolish all minimum wage protection, Investors want to enable employers and employees to create the collective institutional framework which is necessary to achieve both low inflation and low unemployment. The United Kingdom is in a worse condition than virtually any other European country in this respect; but government could make a start by establishing a consultative body of employers and trade unions, whose first responsibility would be to address the question of earnings. If, for instance, pay bargaining were to be synchronised so as to avoid 'leap-frogging' during the pay round, government would also have an opportunity to reinforce its message to company directors, managers and employees about what the economy as a whole can afford. In the longer term, the only sustainable strategy for improving earnings without accelerating inflation is to raise the productive potential of the economy, which is precisely what the Investors' strategy is designed to achieve.

A national minimum wage

Earnings inequality is now greater than at any time since 1886.[76] Between 1980 and 1993, the pay of the bottom quarter of the wage-earning population fell in comparison to the median by between 6 and 10 percentage points, while that of the upper quarter and upper 10 per cent rose by between 11 and 23 points.[77] The last wage-protection bodies in the UK – the Wages Councils, which covered 4.5 million workers – were abolished in 1993/4, with the exception of the Agricultural Wages Board, which was given a temporary reprieve after pleas from both employees and employers.

The UK is now almost alone in the developed world in having virtually no minimum wage system at all: even the US has had a minimum wage since the 1930s, albeit at a relatively low level. In order to combat low pay in a coherent and effective manner, many policy-makers have suggested a national minimum wage, which should be well-advertised and well-enforced. We agree with them.

There are four main arguments in favour of this approach. First, it is wrong in principle that adult workers should be forced to work for as little as £1 or £2 an hour. Deregulators claim that minimum wages interfere with individuals' freedom to price themselves into work. But power is not evenly distributed between employers and employees, especially at a time of high unemployment. Many employers seeking labour at the bottom end of the labour market exercise 'monopsony' power: as the only employers offering jobs to people with few skills, they can drive wages down *below* the level which would operate in a properly functioning labour market where employees had some choice of employers. A modern, still wealthy country should outlaw the worst forms of exploitation.

Second, it is essential to social security benefits reform to set a wages floor at the bottom of the labour market. The Exchequer cannot afford to subsidise exploitation pay. We must allow people to combine partial benefits with low and/or part-time earnings and, in some cases, subsidise low wages either directly or through Family Credit (see Chapter 6). But if that is done in the absence of a minimum wage, employers will have an immediate incentive to drop wages lower and lower, relying on the taxpayer to make up the difference. In the nineteenth-century 'Speenhamland' system of outdoor relief, it was precisely this problem that took local parishes into bankruptcy. Studies suggest that government finances could *benefit* from the introduction of a minimum wage, as a result of contributions and taxes paid on higher earnings, and savings on in-work benefits such as Family Credit. Today, a minimum hourly wage of £3.50 for employees aged eighteen and over would increase government revenues (taking benefit savings into account) by between £1.3 and £1.6 billion.[78]

Third, low pay often reflects an under-valuation of employees' skills. Studies of residential and nursing care, for example, suggest that workers are paid more than 15 per cent below the marginal value of their labour.[79] The most notable casualties are women, who form the majority of the low-paid. Equal-pay legislation has had a limited impact on this injustice against them; a minimum wage would have a direct effect.

Fourth, and at least as important, low pay damages our economic prospects. Because low pay produces a high turnover of staff when job prospects improve, it further weakens employer investment in training, and thus in the quality of goods and services produced. Furthermore, encouraging employers to compete by holding down wages provides a way for inefficient producers and obsolete technologies to survive. The futility of low pay as a long-term competitive strategy is strikingly apparent in the UK's clothing and textile industries. Since the early 1960s, wages in the clothing industry have fallen from over 90 per cent of average male manufacturing earnings to around 80 per cent. At the same time, employment has declined by almost two-thirds and imports, which used to be in balance with exports, now exceed them by more than £4.5 billion.[80] By contrast, Germany has successfully shifted its clothing industry upmarket, improving design and marketing, and thus producing a high-value-added sector capable of sustaining relatively high wages. Smart work, not low wages, is the source of competitive strength.

What are the arguments against a minimum wage? First, that a minimum wage would do little to reduce family poverty since many of the low-paid are women living with relatively well-paid men, while most poor families do not have anyone in employment at all. In fact, out of the 13.9 million living on an income below half the average, as many as 4.6 million people live in a household with an earner.[81] Moreover, it was estimated that the introduction in 1991 of a minimum wage of £3.40 an hour would have made some four million families better off, even though 40 per cent of them contained no one in employment. The minimum wage would have made it worthwhile for at least one person in the family to take up a low-paid job.[82] Although a minimum wage cannot be justified solely on grounds of preventing poverty, it would certainly help to reduce working poverty. Particularly when coupled with a reformed system of welfare benefits, it would further increase the incentive to women in couples to seek employment. A minimum wage would particularly help women in families where the man's earnings are not fairly shared; more generally, increasing women's command over an independent income is important to reducing women's poverty.

The second and most important argument made against a national minimum wage is the effect it might have on jobs. Opponents claim that a minimum wage would cause massive job loss: rather than lifting people out of poverty, it would condemn people to dependency. Supporters argue that a minimum wage need not reduce employment and may indeed stimulate job creation. Which of these conflicting views is right?

Clearly, a minimum wage which is set too high will produce job losses. But a minimum wage also gives employers an incentive to raise productivity through increased investment in training and equipment and improved work practices, as a result of which the cost of production may actually fall. The OECD in their recent *Jobs Study* recognised that different countries needed different minimum wages to fit their economic circumstances. In order to understand the effects of a minimum wage and decide how an appropriate rate should be set, we need to look at the empirical evidence as well as at economic theory. A report for the Ministry of Agriculture, Fisheries and Food concluded that 'minimum wages in agriculture have not harmed the performance of the agricultural labour market. They have maintained the wages of what are low-paid workers with no obvious adverse effects on employment.'[83] A 1991 survey of employers found that one in two large firms said that a minimum wage would not affect their wage costs at all, and two-thirds said that employment would not change. The effects of a minimum wage would be greatest in retail, hotels and catering, cleaning and security services, and clothing.

The evidence from other countries with longstanding minimum wage laws is also reassuring. A study of the minimum wage in France concluded that: 'We have not been able to establish satisfactorily that increases in real youth labour costs have had a negative impact on youth employment ... even though we believe this to be the case. The adult employment elasticity with respect to the minimum wage appears to be zero.'[84] In New Jersey, which increased its minimum wage in 1992 to the highest in the USA –

$5.05 per hour (about £3.35 at $1.50 to the pound, or £3.68 adjusted for local purchasing power by the OECD Index) – employment in fast-food restaurants actually increased.[85]

This apparently paradoxical result arises from the fact that labour markets for low-paid workers simply do not work in the way that economics textbooks would like them to. Instead of a competitive labour market with a market-determined wage, there is great variety in pay and working conditions, with would-be employees unsure about what different employers offer. Employers who can make extra profits by paying below-market wages to their employees may, however, find themselves unable to expand: advertising for new workers at the market rate would mean a pay rise for *all* their employees. Imposing a minimum wage for all employees may reduce profits (depending on whether the increased wage bill is compensated for by higher productivity, higher prices or a combination of both); at the same time, however, the minimum wage makes it easier for employers to hire more people, expand output and therefore raise their profits again.[86]

A third fear is that a minimum wage would serve only to push up earnings generally, as higher-paid workers reasserted differentials. A study of 120 pay agreements which gave higher awards to lower-paid than to higher-paid employees found no evidence, however, that raising the pay of the lowest-paid workers led to moves to restore differentials.[87]

We firmly believe that a national minimum hourly wage is essential. Our purpose is straightforward: it is to banish exploitation in the labour market, encourage employers to invest in people and prevent taxpayers paying a large part of an employer's production costs. But we are mindful that a minimum wage really deals with the symptoms of low pay rather than the causes: low skills, low investment, short-termism, low productivity, and gender segregation and inequality. As Chris Pond, Director of the Low Pay Unit, stressed in his evidence to us: 'A minimum wage is not a panacea.' Our strategy is therefore designed to maximise the potential benefits of a minimum wage, while minimising the potential costs.

There are good reasons for setting the initial rate of the minimum wage with some caution. The state of the labour market has deteriorated substantially in the last few years. There are more low-paid workers and more businesses struggling to survive. Rather than risk highly publicised job losses or threats to small businesses, it would be better to start at a level which government can be confident will not have an adverse effect on employment. Furthermore, a *national* minimum wage has to take account of the difference in wages and cost of living across the country. Government should set the minimum wage in relation to the state of the labour market. Research for the Commission, conducted at the London School of Economics and based on detailed studies of the labour-market effects of the Wages Councils, concluded that in today's conditions, a minimum hourly wage of up to £3.50 would have no adverse effect on overall employment.

Nationally, at least one in ten employees earns below £3.50 an hour and one in five below £4 an hour, with 30 per cent of women part-time workers earning less than £3.50.[88] In some

---

A National Minimum Wage

A National Minimum Wage, set with care, can be a force for social justice and economic efficiency in the UK. A minimum wage should be designed to banish exploitation in the labour market, encourage employers to invest in people and prevent taxpayers paying a large part of employers' production costs.

- In a rich country like ours, no adult workers should be expected to work for £1.50 or £2 an hour
- Without a minimum wage, the taxpayer ends up subsidising low-paying employers through the social security system
- Labour-market research shows that at the bottom of the labour market, where employers are most powerful, low pay undervalues the skills of workers
- Low pay is a symptom of a cycle of low investment, high turnover and low-quality production, which needs to be reversed

---

parts of the country, such as Northern Ireland, the concentration of low pay is even greater. Although very low pay is far more common in the private than the public sector, within the NHS and local government, 78,000 people earn below £3.50 an hour and 700,000 below £4 an hour.[89] Contracting-out has also reduced the pay of many of those who were previously employed within the public services.

We have considered the case for regional variations in the minimum wage, including the possibility of a 'London weighting'. On balance, the advantages of simplicity seem to us to outweigh the arguments for variations. The information required to set different levels is difficult to acquire and it would be hard to justify a regional variation while rejecting others, such as a sectoral weighting. Moreover, regional weighting may institutionalise geographic inequalities in an undesirable way. Because the tax and social security systems (with the exception of Housing Benefit) have no regional variations, a regional minimum wage would set up different relationships between the labour market and the social security system in different parts of the country, making it even harder for unemployed people to assess the effects of moving into low-paid work.

A government committed to a national minimum wage should consult widely with employers, including small businesses, and trade unions before settling on the appropriate rate. Young workers, aged sixteen and seventeen, should be designated as trainees and paid a trainee wage, at say two-thirds the level of the minimum wage. The minimum wage itself should be uprated regularly, preferably annually, so that it does not become eroded over time, as has happened in the USA; the impact on jobs and businesses should, of course, be monitored closely and taken into account when the minimum wage is uprated.

The minimum wage obviously has important consequences for pay in the public sector; whether or not it has an official incomes policy, government must have a view on public-sector wages. Over the last fifteen years, pay in different parts of the public sector has swung from the relatively generous settlement of the Clegg Commission in 1980 to the punitive cost-cutting promoted by some contracting-out. The minimum wage would set a floor on public-sector pay, in the same way as it would for the private sector.

There is also across the country genuine and justifiable outrage at huge pay rises at the top of the income scale. Some have argued that Britain needs a maximum as well as a minimum wage. It would, however, be impractical for one country to try to set a legal limit to the amount people could earn: high-earners would simply move to other European Union countries, or further afield, possibly taking their companies – and jobs – with them. Within the private sector, however, shareholders should be given far tougher powers – and should take far greater initiative – to control the pay of directors and senior managers, while government should set its own guidelines for the top management of public-sector institutions such as NHS Trusts.

Minimum legal rights for employees

Regulation of the labour market should encourage employers not only to treat employees fairly but also to build close and productive relationships with their workforce. Far from praising the hire-and-fire culture of the USA, the business leaders who participated in the Commission on the Skills of the American Workforce – investors all – looked with admiration at the example of 'other countries [which] are driven to pursue high productivity work because public laws make it difficult to pay low wages and lay off workers'.[90]

In this country, employees are not generally protected against unfair dismissal and redundancy until they have been continuously employed by the same organisation for two years. This is too long; the earlier qualifying period of six months would be more appropriate. The existing law fails to protect one in four full-time workers and more than half of all part-time employees.[91] In an increasingly mobile labour market, two years is considerably longer than is needed to demonstrate commitment to a company or to assess an employee's suitability. In mid-1994, the British courts decided that, under European law, pregnant women were protected from the first day of employment against being dismissed on grounds of their pregnancy. Although it would be possible to extend all legal protection to all employees regardless of their length of service, a qualifying period is generally reasonable in principle, and its complete abolition would create substantial practical problems for already over-burdened industrial tribunals.

As non-standard employment contracts become more common, we are particularly concerned about the use of 'zero-hours contracts' which require an employee to be on constant standby without payment or any guarantee that work will actually be offered. USDAW emphasises that 'an employee may go for several days without the offer of work, but cannot take up a second job elsewhere as they are contractually obliged to be available for work at all times'. Such contracts, which are quite different from the voluntary rosters of casual workers that many employers keep for times of high demand, leave workers completely unprotected as employers throw on to them all the risks of unpredictable demand for the goods and services they produce. They should therefore be outlawed.

The treatment of the growing number of part-time workers also needs to be addressed. Flexibility need not be bought at the expense of fairness: the two can – and should – go together. Part-time employees should have the same rights as full-timers, on a pro rata basis, with regard to hourly pay, employee benefits, training, leave and other conditions of employment. The ruling of the House of Lords in March 1994, that a part-time employee working between eight and sixteen hours a week should qualify for redundancy pay and protection against unfair dismissal after two rather than five years' continuous employment, is a welcome step along this path.[92]

We therefore support the European Union proposal that employment rights should apply on the same basis to all employees working on average at least eight hours a week. Although some would argue for the abolition of any minimum threshold, the administrative problems associated with trying to extend legal protection to people employed for only an hour or two a week would outweigh the potential benefits. An eight-hours rule would cover nearly nine out of ten part-time workers; its impact should, however, be carefully monitored in case employers seek to reduce part-time employees' hours below even this threshold.[93]

Partnership at the workplace

Many of the rewards of employment are intangible – a sense of worth, status, of contributing to a collective effort, and of being part of a worthwhile enterprise. But they interact with the material benefits. Effective forms of employee representation and involvement – of which trade unions are the most important – have a vital role to play in our project for a more socially just and economically prosperous society. Collective forms of representation are not optional extras; they are necessary for efficiency, democracy and regulation. By building trust and

---

The Work Story

1. We can and must create more jobs by expanding demand at an EU and international level – this is the EU jobs challenge

2. And we can and must ensure that jobs are better rewarded in the name of efficiency as well as equity – this is the US employment challenge

3. These are not enough on their own: we also need to think about who gets the work. The distribution of paid – and therefore by definition unpaid – work across the life-cycle, and between families, regions, races and sexes, is critical – this is the UK work challenge

4. Markets – as well as governments – can create rigidities. Intelligent intervention by government can overcome rigidities by matching people to jobs more effectively

5. Tackling long-term unemployment, implementing the working-hours directive, abolishing the benefits barrier, overcoming discrimination, regenerating communities and investing in employability are vital to a new prescription for full employment. We have to redistribute both the pain of unemployment and the gain of paid and unpaid work

---

allowing communication between workers, effective forms of representation can improve the efficiency of companies. In modern technological and market conditions, managers have to trust workers if they are to delegate decisions to them, and workers have to trust management not to exclude them from the benefits of their efforts.

The tradition of social partnership is reflected in the European Union's Social Chapter, which sets out the principles of a basic core of workers' rights and entrenches partnership in political and industrial governance. The Social Chapter's objective of improved communication and consultation between employers and their staff should be welcomed and not rejected. But giving workers a say in their workplace is not simply a mechanism for productively integrating capital and labour; it is also a democratic imperative. 'Industrial democracy' – empowering workers – is often neglected in the preoccupation with 'governmental democracy'. But the firm is an important polity in itself. Turnout in elections to Works Councils in Germany regularly tops 90 per cent. The right to a say in the running of an enterprise to which a worker contributes seems to us to be essential.

It is paradoxical that at a time when job insecurity has never been higher, business leaders are increasingly concerned about the need for partnership in work. The 'Tomorrow's Company' enquiry, established by the RSA under the leadership of Sir Anthony Cleaver, Chairman of IBM (UK), argues that successful companies require long-term, reciprocal relationships with *all* their stakeholders – employees, customers, suppliers and the community as well as shareholders.[94] Most European and Scandinavian countries benefit from well-established partnerships between unions and management. Conflict is not eliminated, but whether at national, regional or local level, representatives of Chambers of Commerce and trade unions are closely involved in the development and enforcement of policy on matters as diverse as pension provision, training and technology transfer. Trade unions and other collective bodies act as important supplements to government inspectorates in regulating employee rights and conditions. As 'on the ground enforcement agencies' they are better placed to guard rights from encroachment.

The role of trade unions

For more than 100 years, trade unions have been the most important and powerful mechanism for the protection of workers' interests. Mass organisation of workers grew rapidly from the end of the nineteenth century, in response to a legal and economic onslaught on the position of working men and women. Collective organisation was therefore born to defend interests, rather than advance them, but over the years, as the power of unions increased, unions became a central part of the reforming coalition that achieved economic and social change in this country through the course of the twentieth century.

The nature of trade unionism in the UK was in some ways defined by its early struggles. Above all, unlike in many other countries, unions were craft-based rather than industry-based, and there were therefore literally hundreds of unions. Furthermore, individual unions were strongest defending their own patch; the Trades Union Congress (TUC) has never had the power in this country of the trade union confederations on the Continent. It has taken more than a decade of change to set in train a process of amalgamation and reorganisation that will ultimately alter the trade union structure for ever, with fewer unions, more broadly organised, dominating the scene. This has forced the TUC into a re-evaluation of its role, and the new initiatives being developed promise an enhanced and positive contribution by the TUC to national life.

Trade union membership has fallen dramatically in the last fifteen years. The number of people in trade unions was a third higher in 1979 than today. Nine million people – 31 per cent of the workforce – are members of trade unions, a drop of 4.2 million since 1979 and the lowest level of membership since 1946.[95] The proportion of workplaces with a recognised trade union fell from 52 per cent in 1984 to 40 per cent in 1990. The collapse of employment in industries with a strong union tradition, coupled with the growth in unemployment and low-paid and casual work, all help to account for falling union membership. But the decline in both membership and influence is also in part the result of hostile legislation, designed to extend 'management's right to manage', weaken individual employees' rights and denude trade unions of power and authority. As it has become harder for trade unions to get recognition, it has become harder to persuade employees that it is worth joining. Employers have been able to 'derecognise' trade unions more easily (something virtually unheard of previously): 9 per cent of companies with twenty-five or more employees did so between 1984 and 1990. New legislation on the collection of membership subscriptions aims to weaken unions' financial position further, by requiring every member to sign a fresh subscription mandate every three years – something which has never been contemplated for the millions of organisations which collect subscriptions or regular bills through direct debits.

Trade unions remain the most effective source of protection for employees. Employees in workplaces without unions are two and a half times as likely to face dismissal or compulsory redundancies as those in unionised workplaces. Trade unions have a vital and constructive role to play in empowering workers and improving the performance of companies. Surveys of public opinion regularly find that a majority support the principle of trade unionism. Many trade unions have begun to rise to the challenge of constant economic change and, as in many other European countries, assert their position in a coalition for broad social change and civil rights.

Because the right to join a trade union should be recognised in any democracy, the laws which undermine this should clearly be repealed. The 1992 Trade Union and Labour Relations Act, which allows employers to discriminate against trade unionists, and is designed to discourage people from joining unions, has been recognised across the political spectrum as iniquitous. The defence of the rights of employees, and the advance of their interests, must, however, be pursued in the new context of a changed labour force, new international conditions and change at the workplace. Many trade unionists are critical of their past failure to adapt to change: 'Unions have remained stuck in a historic posture of reacting sceptically to all management initiatives rather than setting our own agenda. 'We have rarely looked beyond the next pay round,' says a GMB/UCW discussion paper.[96] Many trade unions clearly see their role as helping to create success within a workplace, rather than fighting rearguard actions against decline: thriving companies need the co-operative employee relations which unions can help to achieve.[97] The TUC's study of 'human resource management', presented to its Congress in 1994, suggested that – despite the anti-union policy of some employers – union officials, shop stewards and members have been involved by other employers in a constructive process of reorganising work and raising productivity. Just one example of successful change was provided by Paul Gates, Union Director of Bury/Bolton TEC, who told the TUC Conference on Full Employment in July 1994 of the support given to a local company, Halbro Sportswear, when business was flagging. The establishment of an internal training school helped trade union members move to multi-skilling; the level of rejects was cut to below 10 per cent; unit costs and labour turnover both fell; and as orders picked up, the business took on more employees. As job change becomes more frequent, trade unions are also ideally placed to offer a new source of security to their members, through advice and access to good-quality education and training, pensions provision, legal and other services.

Developing Works Councils

The decline in trade union membership over the last decade has not been offset by any increase in other forms of representation of non-managerial employees' interests.[98] Strategies to reduce the 'democratic deficit' in the workplace are imperative. Many other European countries have well-developed systems of Works Councils, sometimes described as a 'second channel' of industrial relations.[99] They are workplace or company-based institutions of worker representation and labour-management communication. Their status and functions are distinct from, though not necessarily in competition with, trade unions. As one trade unionist put it to us: 'If we can't win seats on Works Councils, we don't deserve to represent people!' In Germany, it is a source of pride for the largest union federation, DGB, that it regularly wins 80 per cent of the Works Council seats nationwide.

Because of the UK Government's opt-out from the European Social Chapter, the Works Council Directive will only affect about 90 UK-based multinational companies. In the rest of the

EU, the Directive requires companies with more than 1,000 employees to establish democratic procedures for discussions between workforce and management at least once a year. Many British employers are hostile to the Directive, fearing that it will slow down decision-making and cost money. But many European companies, such as Philips in the Netherlands, have come to value a structure for negotiating with employees.[100] Studies of Works Councils have shown that by contributing to 'industrial citizenship', encouraging better communication and building trust and loyalty, they help to *improve* efficiency rather than impose new costs on companies. We therefore wish to see the Directive implemented in this country.

Employee ownership and co-operatives

A different approach to industrial democracy is to enable employees to take a financial stake in the company they work for. The stake can range from modest individual shareholdings promoted by a variety of tax concessions to complete collective ownership of companies (the John Lewis Partnership and the Scott Bader Commonwealth are good examples of the latter). In addition to different kinds of co-operatives, an increasing number of companies now have Employee Share Ownership Plans (ESOPs) or Trusts, in which employees hold anything from a small proportion to the entire equity of the company. Trade unionists are increasingly interested in forms of ownership which give them a say, as well as a stake, in their company. 'My members want ownership,' said Gavin Laird, General Secretary of the AEEU and chair of Greater Manchester Buses North (an employee buyout organised by TGWU members who were faced with the threat of privatisation). The TGWU members who are also owners of Southampton Cargo Handling (see page 76) were enthusiastic in their praise of the new system. Unlike traditional forms of public ownership which transfer property rights to the state, employee ownership diffuses both rights and responsibilities.

Ownership is one important ingredient in changing attitudes to the relations between companies and their employees. It is not a magic solution and needs to be accompanied by the sort of changes promoted by the Involvement and Partnership Association, chaired by Sir Bryan Nicholson and supported by, among others, John Edmonds, General Secretary of the GMB general workers' union. It promotes employees' involvement and participation, which it defines as 'any activity which helps to release the full potential of work'. Its slogan, 'Towards a common purpose at work', sums up the cultural shift towards the greater partnership required in UK companies. One example of partnership at work can be found at Manchester Airport, where the development of employee skills at all levels, as part of a Europe-wide programme, has produced higher productivity, better labour relations, and more satisfied staff and employers: what people there call a 'win-win' situation.

ESOPs are still on a relatively small scale in the UK, though there have been important developments in the bus industry and in local government. In the USA, where ESOPs have been encouraged by extensive tax reliefs, there is now a large number of companies with such plans, including several substantial companies that are wholly owned by the workforce, such as the Avis car-hire firm. Jeffrey Gates, one of the principal architects of the tax concessions in the US, told the Commission that ESOPs are designed to create 'social institutions that enable people to become good citizens by creating conditions that support them in this goal... government must be involved in the evolution of new financing techniques designed to foster widespread economic empowerment.' We welcome the development in this country of the statutory ESOPs and the recent changes in the 1994 Finance Act concerning Employee Benefit Trusts, which should make the earlier tax concessions much more attractive to owners contemplating a sale to their employees.

Worker ownership through co-operatives has a much longer history than the recently developed ESOPs, though in the UK it has never achieved the scale of the consumer co-operative movement. Most worker co-ops are small and together amount to around 10,000 members. They are most effective in areas and sectors which are not attractive to conventional companies, and which can play an important part, along with housing co-operatives and credit unions, in local regeneration strategies. They have been sustained by the Industrial Common Ownership movement, local Co-operative Development Agencies, the Co-operative Bank, Unity Trust and other bodies. While it is unlikely that large numbers of new co-operatives will be established or that many existing companies will convert to the co-operative form, it is becoming increasingly clear that their methods of working set an important example, and one to which the DTI is rightly drawing attention.[101]

Notes

1. For example, the opportunity of paid maternity leave for a new mother is at least as important as the opportunity to return to employment later
2. Howard Glennerster *Paying for Welfare* (London: Harvester, 1992)
3. Bert Massie *Disabled People and Social Justice* (London: IPPR, 1994)
4. *World Economic and Social Survey 1994* Table VI.6 (New York: United Nations, 1994)
5. Robert Lindley (ed) *Labour Market Structures and Prospects for Women* (Manchester: Equal Opportunities Commission, 1993)
6. Employment Department *Employment Gazette* (London: HMSO, May 1994)
7. Andrew Britton *Full Employment in a Market Economy* paper for the TUC/Employment Policy Institute Conference, July 1994
8. Duncan Gallie, paper given to the Employment Department Conference, Rotherham, 22-24 November 1993
9. *The OECD Jobs Study: Evidence and Explanations* (Paris: OECD, 1994)
10. Ibid
11. Edward Balls 'Danger: Men Not at Work' in Edward Balls and Paul Gregg *Work and Welfare* (London: IPPR, 1993)
12. Ibid
13. USA Bureau of Labor Statistics
14. *World Economic and Social Survey 1994* Table VI.4 (New York: United Nations, 1994)
15. Michael Frye 'Who walked among the stones of fire?', inaugural lecture of the Chairman of the RSA. *RSA Journal,* December 1991
16. OECD *1994 Employment Outlook* (Paris: OECD, 1994)
17. Frank Field *et al Europe Isn't Working* (London: Institute for Community Studies, 1994)

18. OECD *Jobs Study* op cit
19. OECD *Economic Outlook 54* December (Paris: OECD, 1993)
20. The European Socialist Party *Statement on Employment in Europe* (Brussels: ESP 1994)
21. Commission of the European Community *Growth, Competitiveness, Employment* (Brussels: CEC, 1993)
22. Edward Luttwak 'The poor get poorer' *The Times Literary Supplement*, 10 June 1994
23. *Engineering Economic Trends* Spring 1994
24. *The Times*, 27 April 1994
25. Unemployment Unit and Youthaid *Working Brief* June 1994
26. Paul Gregg 'Jobs and Justice' in Balls and Gregg op cit
27. Richard Freeman 'Jobs in the USA' *New Economy* 1, 1. As he points out, a 10 per cent unemployment rate could require everyone to be jobless for two weeks a year, or one in ten workers to be jobless indefinitely
28. Richard Lampard 'An examination of the relationship between marital dissolution and unemployment' in Duncan Gallie, Catherine Marsh and Carolyn Vogler *Social Change and the Experience of Unemployment* (Oxford: OUP, 1993)
29. Elsa Ferri *Growing up in a one-parent family* (London: National Foundation for Educational Research, 1976)
30. Jonathan Gershuny and Catherine Marsh 'Unemployment in work Histories' in Duncan Gallie, Catherine Marsh and Caroline Vogler *Social Change* op cit
31. Richard Layard and John Philpott *Stopping Unemployment* (London: Employment Policy Institute, 1992)
32. John Philpott 'The Incidence and Cost of Unemployment' in Andrew Glyn and David Miliband (eds) *Paying for Inequality* (London: IPPR/Rivers Oram, 1994)
33. Family Programs Division, Department of Social Security *Jobs, Education and Training (JET) Facts Sheet* (Canberra: Department of Social Security, 1993)
34. Unemployment Unit and Youthaid, *Working Brief*, July 1994
35. OECD *Employment Outlook 1993* (Paris: OECD, 1993)
36. Ibid
37. Philpott 'Incidence and Cost of Unemployment' op cit
38. OECD *Employment Outlook 1993* op cit
39. *Financial Times*, 11 July 1994. Figures in 1993 prices
40. National Council for Voluntary Organisations *Compromising on Quality* (London: NCVO, 1993)

41. 'Evaluating Training and Employment Measures for the Unemployed' *Labour Market Quarterly Review*, May 1993 (London: Employment Department, 1993)

42. Layard and Philpott *Unemployment* op cit

43. Unemployment Unit and Youthaid *Working Brief* May 1994

44. Anne Green and David Owen 'The Changing Structure of the Unemployed and Economically Inactive and their Spatial Segregation in Great Britain' (University of Warwick, unpublished paper forthcoming)

45. Chris Smith MP *Energy efficiency for the environment and the economy* (London: Labour Party, 1993)

46. Peter Welch and Malcolm Coles *Towards a Social Economy* Fabian Pamphlet 564 (London: Fabian Society, 1993)

47. Greg Clark *The Single Regeneration Budget and European Union Fund* (London: NCVO, 1993).

48. Richard Layard, Stephen Nickell and Richard Jackman *Unemployment: micro-economic performance and the labour market* (Oxford: OUP, 1992).

49. Daniel Hamermesh *Labour Demand* (Princeton: Princeton University Press, 1993)

50. OFCE International Expert Group *Report* (Paris: OFCE, 1994)

51. Dennis Snower *Converting Unemployment Benefits into Employment Subsidies* Discussion Paper No 930 (London: Centre for Economic Policy Research, 1994)

52. Dennis Snower, *Financial Times*, 19 May 1993

53. Robert Walker *Workfare in America* (London: HMSO, 1992)

54. Ibid

55. Ibid

56. Balls, 'Danger' in Balls and Gregg op cit

57. Layard and Philpott *Unemployment* op cit

58. Full Employment UK submission to the Commission on Social Justice 1993

59. Anne Costello *Workfare in Britain?* (London: Unemployment Unit, 1994)

60. Gregg 'Jobs' in Balls and Gregg op cit

61. Equal Opportunities Commission *Annual Report* (Manchester: EOC, 1993)

62. *The contribution of out of school playcare to social justice* Kids Club Network submission to the Commission on Social Justice 1994

63. Susan McRae 'Returning to work after childbirth: opportunities and inequalities' *European Sociological Review* 9, 2, 1993

64. Catherine Marsh *Hours of Work of Women and Men in Britain* Equal Opportunities Commission (London: HMSO, 1991)

65. *Labour Force Survey* (London: Eurostat, 1994); *New Earnings Survey* (London: HMSO, 1993)

66. Michael White *Working Hours* (Geneva: International Labour Organisation, 1987)

67. Paul Gregg 'Share and share alike' *New Economy*, 1, 1, (Spring 1994)

68. USDAW submission to the Commission on Social Justice, 1994

69. Commmission of the European Communities *Employment in Europe 1993* (Brussels: CEC, 1993)

70. Paul Ormerod 'Why Western employment policy is going around in circles'*Demos Journal* 2/1994 (London: Demos, 1994)

71. Patricia Hewitt *About Time* (London: IPPR/Rivers Oram, 1993)

72. Commission for Racial Equality, submission to the Commission on Social Justice, 1994

73. Massie *Disabled People* op cit

74. Quoted in Jeffrey Pfeffer *Competitive Advantage through People* (Boston: Harvard Business School Press, 1994)

75. William Brown *The Scope for an Incomes Policy for Britain in the 1990s'* submission to the Commission on Social Justice, 1994

76. *British Labour Statistics Historical Abstract: 1886–1968* (London: HMSO, 1971) and *New Earnings Surveys 1970–1991* (London: HMSO)

77. Brown *Scope* op cit

78. Calculations by Steven Webb for the Commission

79. Paul Gregg, Stephen Machin and Alan Manning 'High Pay, Low Pay and Labour Market Efficiency' in Andrew Glyn and David Miliband (eds) *Paying* op cit

80. Peter Lowman, National Union of Knitwear, Footwear and Apparel Trades, personal communication

81. Department of Social Security *Households Below Average Income 1979–1991/2* (London: HMSO, 1994)

82. Holly Sutherland *The Immediate Impact of a Minimum Wage on Family Incomes* (London: LSE, 1991)

83. Richard Dickens *et al The Effect of a Minimum Wage on UK Agriculture* LSE Working Paper No. 514(London:LSE , 1994)

84. Stephen Bazen and Philip Martin 'The Impact of the Minimum Wage on Earnings and Employment in France' in *Economic Studies* Spring (Paris: OECD, 1991)

85. David Card and Alan Krueger *Minimum Wages and Employment: A Case Study of the Fast Food Industry in New Jersey and*

Pennsylvania (Cambridge, Mass: National Bureau of Economic Research, 1993)

86. Edward Balls 'US findings defy logic that minimum wage costs jobs' the *Guardian*, 2 May 1994

87. Institute of Public Management *Minimum Wage Fixing in Britain and the Prospects of a Statutory Minimum Wage* (Warwick: University of Warwick, 1991)

88. Because these figures are drawn from the *New Earnings Survey*, which excludes a substantial minority of part-time employees, the position is in fact even worse

89. Measured in full-time equivalents. Calculations by UNISON for the Commission

90. Report of the Commission on the Skills of the American Workforce *America's Choice: high skills or low wages!* (New York: National Center on Education and the Economy, 1990)

91. Linda Dickens *Whose Flexibility? Discrimination and Equality Issues in Atypical Work* (London: Institute for Employment Rights, 1992)

92. *Equal Opportunities Commission and another against the Secretary of State for Employment* [1994] 1 All ER 910

93. *Hansard* 28 April 1994

94. Royal Society of Arts *Tomorrow's Company* (London: RSA, 1994)

95. Department of Employment *Employment Gazette* (London: HMSO, June 1994)

96. GMB and UCW *A New Agenda for Prosperity* (London: GMB/UCW, 1993)

97. Phillip Bassett and Alan Cave *All for one: the future of the unions*, Fabian Pamphlet 559 (London: Fabian Society, 1993)

98. Neil Millward *The New Industrial Relations?* (London: Policy Studies Institute, 1994)

99. See Joel Rogers and Wolfgang Streeck 'Workplace Representation Overseas: The Works Councils Story' in Richard Freeman (ed) *Working and Earning under Different Rules* (Chicago: NBER and University of Chicago Press, 1993)

100. *Financial Times*, 20 April 1994

101. *Network*, Issue 4, November 1993, UK Cooperative Council

6

SECURITY: BUILDING AN INTELLIGENT WELFARE STATE

'The main feature of the Plan for Social Security is a scheme of social insurance against interruption and destruction of earning power and for special expenditure arising at marriage, birth or death.'

Sir William Beveridge,
Social Insurance and Allied Services, 1942

● ● ●

As he looked back at the 1930s and forward to the 1950s, William Beveridge saw the need for a welfare state that would protect working people against the predictable crises of their lives. His plan offered a guaranteed income when illness, disability, unemployment, old age or death deprived a family of the breadwinner's wages. Embracing a National Health Service and family allowances as well as the National Insurance scheme, the 1945 Labour Government's welfare state was designed to provide security 'from the cradle to the grave'.

The post-war welfare state assumed that wages would support earners, that most earners would be men, and that most men would earn an adequate family wage. As far as social security was concerned, the welfare state was *passive* when people were economically *active* – either earning a living themselves or relying upon the family breadwinner while they brought up children. It became active only when people were passive, unable for one reason or another to participate in employment. Work and income security were assumed to go together; lack of work meant lack of security.[1] As a result, the resources of the welfare state were concentrated on the earliest and the last years of life, and on unemployment and sickness in between.

This model of welfare is clearly not adequate today. Too many people are not in employment, and work for too many no longer guarantees income security. Because the conditions that gave birth to the post-war welfare state no longer exist, the post-war assumptions about the role of the welfare state must also change. Professor Gosta Esping-Andersen, author of *The Three Worlds of Welfare Capitalism*, makes the point vividly:

> The Fordist welfare state [the welfare state developed to match the economics and risks of mass-production capitalism] slices up the life-cycle and ignores the active adult part on the assumption that a Fordist economy guarantees decent pay and secure employment. The post-industrial economy is less likely to provide such guarantees; indeed, the average worker's life-cycle risks will increase substantially.[2]

Far from making the welfare state redundant, social and economic change creates a new and even more vital need for the security which the welfare state was designed to provide. Frightened people cannot welcome change; they can only resist it or be defeated by it. It takes secure people – secure in their abilities, their finances and their communities – to cope with change at the workplace or in the home. If the welfare state is to deliver on its promise of social security for all, it must be transformed to meet people's changing lives and changing demands.

These 'life-cycle risks', the new sources of insecurity, include the changing demands of family life – separation, divorce, elderly dependents – as well as the prospect of continual change in the workplace, with its attendant threats of unemployment and low pay. These risks are less predictable and more probable than were those of the 1950s. They will not be resolved by cash benefits alone; they require good-quality services – from training to child-care to eldercare – to help people escape and stay out of poverty. They cut across divisions of class, though of course the most underprivileged have fewest resources to cope with problems.

Instead of a welfare state designed for old risks, old industries and old family structures, there is a need for an intelligent welfare state that will be active throughout our lives, helping people to negotiate unpredictable change at work and home. Instead of a safety net to relieve poverty, we need a social security system that can help to prevent poverty. Instead of a health service designed primarily to treat illness, we need a health policy whose priority is to promote better health. In other words, the welfare state

---

The Intelligent Welfare State

An intelligent welfare state works with rather than against the grain of change:

- Wealth creation and wealth distribution are two sides of the same coin; wealth pays for welfare, but equity is effcient
- Social justice cannot be achieved through the social security system alone; employment, education and housing are at least as important as tax and benefit policy in promoting financial independence
- Labour-market and family policy go together; the social revolution in women's life chances demands a reappraisal of the role of men as workers and fathers as well as that of women as employees and mothers
- Paid work for a fair wage is the most secure route out of poverty. Welfare must be reformed to make work pay; if 80 per cent tax rates are wrong at the top, they are wrong at the bottom too
- The intelligent welfare state prevents poverty as well as relieving it, above all through public services which enable people to learn, earn and care
- The welfare state must be shaped by the changing nature of people's lives, rather than people's lives being shaped to fit in with the welfare state; the welfare state must be personalised and flexible, designed to promote individual choice and personal autonomy

---

must not only look after people when they cannot look after themselves, it must also enable them to achieve self-improvement and self-support. The welfare state must offer a hand-up rather than a handout.

It is the social security system above all that traps people between old assumptions and new realities. Faced with an increasingly flexible labour market where the majority of vacancies are part-time or temporary, the benefits system has become increasingly inflexible. When most couples rely on two jobs for a decent standard of living, the benefits system clings to its assumption that families only need one earner. In place of a benefits system which helps to keep poor people poor, we need a revolution in welfare to enable people to earn their way out of poverty.

Earning and Caring: Financial Security for Working People

The social security system, whether through National Insurance, means-tested or other benefits, is still a crucial source of financial security for most people – but it is not the only one. We live in a mixed economy of welfare where private pensions and other forms of savings are increasingly important, and where tax allowances and reliefs provide a 'middle-class welfare state' at substantial public expense. Both public and private provision have their strengths and their weaknesses. Dogmatic assumptions about 'private good, public bad' – or the reverse – make it impossible to find the best ways of enabling people to achieve the financial security they seek. Instead, we need to be clear about our objectives and then find the fairest and most efficient way of meeting them.

The system of benefits, tax allowances and private provision, taken together, should serve six main objectives:

1. To prevent poverty where possible and relieve it where necessary.
2. To protect people against risks, especially those that arise in the labour market and from family change.

3. To redistribute resources from richer to poorer members of society.
4. To redistribute resources of time and money over people's life-cycles.
5. To encourage personal independence.
6. To help promote social cohesion.

In our proposals, we have not tried to examine every aspect of the benefits system, the rules of which run to thousands of pages. Instead, we focus on the structure that government should aim to build in the future, and suggest practical steps that could be taken to construct an intelligent welfare state. We have not recommended short-term increases in particular benefits; that is not our job. It is, however, astonishing that social security benefit levels in 1994 are derived from a notion of physical subsistence which was developed in 1899. Research at the University of York has estimated that families with young children living on Income Support receive up to £35 a week less than the cost of a minimum standard of living based on the standards of the general population.

One way of measuring the effectiveness of a range of government policies designed to relieve poverty would be to establish a *minimum income standard* as a benchmark for social security and employment policy. Unlike the USA, government in the United Kingdom does not set a minimum income standard as an official indication of the lowest income required for people to be able to stay out of poverty and take part in ordinary social life. A minimum income standard does not mean that the government guarantees to top up everybody's income to that level; instead, it is a goal to aim for, a standard against which people's earnings, pensions and other benefits can be judged.

The European Commission has urged all European governments to set minimum income standards at a level 'considered sufficient to cover essential needs with regard to respect for human dignity'. We endorse this recommendation. The British government should commit itself to the principle of a minimum income standard, commission the necessary research and, in the light of the findings, review benefit levels.[3]

From welfare to work

Our goal is to ensure that people can earn enough to meet their needs without relying on means-tested benefits. That will take a long time, and considerable investment in raising skills, productivity and wages: the solution certainly cannot be found within the social security system alone. But the benefits system must be designed to help individuals capable of work – whether they are living alone or in a family – to move from unemployment into employment, and it must enable 'work-poor' families to become 'work-rich'. At the same time, it must provide adequate support for those who cannot move into paid work.

We agree with the Child Poverty Action Group, which told us:

It is helpful to differentiate between – on the one hand – investing in strategies that can have a positive effect on both economic growth and individual prospects and – on the other – public expenditure which seeks simply to compensate individuals for their lack of opportunities or to ameliorate the worst effects of the market. The former approach has some chance of becoming self-financing in the longer term and has the added advantage of providing public goods, both now and later. The latter approach might be essential in the short term but is inefficient compared with preventative measures to tackle at source the barriers to opportunity and adequate income. Compensation policies also lock both the Exchequer and individuals into the kind of cycles and spirals of 'dependency' and expenditure that prevail at present – as shown, for instance, in the high rates of spending on unemployment benefits rather than on employment and training strategies.[4]

Instead of being part of the solution, the present benefits system is all too often part of the problem. People who are unemployed and living on means-tested Income Support find that every pound they earn means a pound less in benefit. Moving into low-paid work, topped up by Family Credit, is risky and insecure. In a two-parent family, where one partner manages none the less to take a low-paid job topped up by Family Credit, every additional after-tax pound which either partner earns means 70p less in benefit; as a result, there is little point in pursuing the best route to a decent standard of living, which is to have two (not necessarily full-time) earners.

In essence, Income Support and Family Credit, both dependent upon a family means-test, are preventing no-job families from becoming one-job families and one-job families from becoming two-job families. An effective 'welfare to work' strategy requires structural changes to the benefits system. Changes designed to help people earn their way out of poverty will return a high economic and social dividend.

Relatively small changes to means-tested benefits could help more no-job families become one-job families (pages 245–258). A short-term strategy of topping up low wages through the benefits system must, however, be underpinned by a minimum wage to prevent unscrupulous employers from driving down wages while the taxpayer takes the strain. But far more radical reforms are needed to help no-job families become two-job families. Women as well as men need individual benefits in return for individual contributions, so that one partner's benefit does not affect the other partner's employment. The benefits system itself must be designed for the non-standard employment which is rapidly becoming the norm, and it must recognise and value the unpaid work of parents and carers. A new social insurance scheme should be the foundation of long-term reform; although we may never eradicate means-tested benefits completely, the reforms we propose will help restore them to the purpose Beveridge always intended – a last resort in time of trouble.

The new Social Insurance system

William Beveridge inspired the British people with his vision of a comprehensive national insurance system. Today, however, several million part-time, self-employed and low-earning workers fall through the gaps of a national insurance scheme designed for full-time employees. For instance, more than three million employees, two-thirds of them women, earn too little to pay contributions.[5] A total of 850,000 self-employed people pay no contributions at all, while the contributions of another 2.3 million

The Approach to Social Security: Deregulators v Investors

Deregulators and Investors have different goals:

The Deregulators want to tackle unemployment and poverty by encouraging people to take low-paid jobs, topped up by means-tested benefits.

The Investors want to tackle unemployment and poverty by enabling individuals and families to earn their way to a decent standard of living.

Deregulators and Investors have different strategies:

1. Deregulators fail to understand the connection between economic and social policy. Economically, they believe low wages are the answer to unemployment. Socially, they believe the benefits system can solve the problems created by a deregulated economy

   Investors want economic and social policy to work together, so that social security reform is part of a coherent strategy for improving competitiveness, employment, skills and earnings

2. Deregulators want to pursue a long-term strategy of reducing pay at the bottom of the labour market, abolishing any minimum level for wages while topping up low wages with means-tested benefits. Such a strategy gives employers a perverse incentive to transfer more of their production costs to the taxpayer

   Investors would use a minimum wage, carefully set to prevent job losses, to prevent unscrupulous employers abusing the benefits system

3. Deregulators pretend that family change has no implications for the benefits system. Instead of recognising that most two-parent families are also two-earner families, they cling to a system of means-tests designed for one-earner families

> Investors recognise that, although means-tested benefits should be improved, the goal must be individual benefits in return for individual contributions, to promote financial independence and prevent one partner's benefit entitlement from damaging the other partner's employment prospects

self-employed people do not earn them any protection for unemployment or family responsibilities. More than a million temporary and seasonal workers pay only irregular contributions, with the result that they are unlikely to qualify for benefit when they later need it.

In place of the limited and cumbersome benefits system which we know today, government should start to build a modern system of social insurance tailored to changing employment risks and family needs. Like the old National Insurance system, the new Social Insurance Programme will help to protect people against the risk of unemployment; but it will also be part of a strategy to enable people to acquire new skills and new jobs. Like the old system, the new social insurance scheme will help to protect people who are sick or disabled; but it should also provide for people looking after very young children or caring for disabled adults. Beyond the welfare state's traditional redistribution of earnings from employment to unemployment, sickness and retirement, social insurance should act as a 'time bank' which enables people to invest resources they earn during some parts of their lives, and draw on them to finance time off work for family responsibilities and education at others. There are four strong arguments in favour of building the social security system upon a modernised social insurance scheme.

1. Social insurance can protect people against unemployment and sickness more cheaply, efficiently and fairly than any scheme of private insurance

Deregulators argue that government no longer has a role in providing social insurance. Insurance should come from the private market, with means-tested benefits to pick up those who fall through the private insurance net. In particular, they say, employees should be required to insure themselves against unemployment, thus relieving the state of the burden.

Supporters of private insurance often talk as though it cost nothing. They argue that taxpayers will benefit by paying lower taxes or National Insurance Contributions. Yet no mention is made of the private insurance premiums that will take their place. However it is provided, security has to be paid for. Sweeping a problem off the government's balance sheet may count as success for the Treasury, but the problem does not go away for the rest of us. In any case, the idea that private insurance can simply replace social insurance has serious defects in principle and practice.

Some of the largest private insurance companies in the United Kingdom have made it quite clear to us that no insurer can offer an adequate scheme of unemployment insurance. Although they are able to predict the risk of burglary, fire or death fairly accurately, and calculate premiums accordingly, unemployment depends heavily on the economic cycle: the recession of 1991 (the depth of which few forecasters predicted) would have wiped out insurance companies who had set their premiums only the previous year. Furthermore, just as insurance companies use investigators and loss adjustors to rule out arson or check the value of a claim, so they would have to maintain their own unemployment investigators to ensure people were genuinely unemployed. Administration, advertising and sales commissions would all add further to the costs of insurance, as would ensuing litigation when insurance companies deemed people 'voluntarily unemployed'.

Above all, the people who are most at risk of unemployment and least able to afford contributions – those with low levels of education and skill – would be charged the highest premiums. Government would still have to take responsibility for the 'bad risks', without the ability to share the costs amongst all contributors. Exactly the same problem arises with proposals for private insurance against sickness and disability. Such schemes are important for the self-employed and those with high earnings;

but if social insurance did not exist, anyone with a history of earlier illness would be faced with unaffordable premiums or denied insurance altogether.

These arguments do not apply, however, to protection against risks for which employers are themselves responsible. If employers were required to insure themselves against the costs of industrial injuries and diseases, in order to refund the benefits paid out in such cases, they would face a powerful incentive to improve their health and safety precautions – or face high insurance premiums. At the moment, taxpayers are subsidising dangerous and irresponsible employers, to the sum of £655 million per year.[6] Employers themselves should be required to take out insurance to meet at least part of these costs, although a compensation scheme would still be necessary for employees of firms which went out of business. (This is a different argument from that made by the Government when it required employers to carry more of the costs of statutory sick pay, increasing the risk that employers would discriminate against people with disabilities or previous ill-health.)

2. Social insurance rewards personal effort

Unlike means-tested benefits, which are based on the family or household, social insurance benefits belong to the individual. Thus, if the man loses his job and claims insurance, there is nothing to stop his partner remaining in her job, extending her hours, or taking up employment if she was not previously employed: indeed there is every incentive for her to do so. Whereas means-tested benefits penalise people who have saved, insurance benefits can be combined with savings and other sources of help to tide people over until new employment has been found. Some means-tested benefits will always be needed, to help with housing costs, for instance, but they should not be the centrepiece.

3. Social insurance balances rights with responsibilities

Social insurance is a contract between individuals and society. When we are earning, we accept the responsibility of paying in; when we are not, we have the right to draw out. Where means-tested benefits divide society into two classes – those who need to

231

claim and those who are forced to pay – social insurance is based on an ethic of mutuality which is essential if we are to create a better community.

Because of this balancing of rights and responsibilities, National Insurance Contributions are more popular than income tax. They are seen as 'something for something' rather than just another levy. The TUC stressed to us that social insurance has a broad base in history and in international custom: it is 'an expression of common citizenship'. By creating a modern social insurance system, as we propose, the United Kingdom would be moving into line with the systems which operate in virtually every other European Union country. This would be a real advantage as more people spend part of their working lives in other parts of the EU.

4. Social insurance has a unique role in helping people distribute income across their increasingly varied life-cycles.

The welfare state has always achieved two kinds of redistribution: from rich to poor, and across people's life-cycles. A recent study showed that, when education and health are taken into account along with financial benefits, life-cycle redistribution is considerably more important than the 'Robin Hood' function of redistribution from rich to poor. [7]

The conditions for which Beveridge designed national insurance – unemployment, sickness, disability, retirement and widowhood – are no longer the only reasons why earnings cease. Breaks from employment are also essential, part-time or full-time, when people have small children or other relatives to care for, or when they need to update their education and skills. Modern social insurance has a unique potential to help people distribute earnings across the life-cycle to meet these new needs. Private insurance cannot begin to cover these eventualities. Indeed, it has always refused cover for maternity, which it regards as a self-inflicted injury.

Personal savings, on the other hand, have an extremely important part to play in helping people allocate income from one part of their lives to another. But many people, even when they are in a job, simply cannot afford to save; and, of course, if they are told to rely on means-tested benefits when an interruption to work becomes inevitable, the little they may have managed to save will count against them in the calculation of entitlement.

Furthermore, the pattern of people's lives does not necessarily fit the savings cycle: the private savings market will not lend the cost of parental leave to the young couple in return for a contribution from their later earnings. Yet that, in effect, is exactly what social insurance can do. Just as social insurance can pool risks more comprehensively than private insurers, so it can spread income in ways which private savings cannot manage.

Membership of the Social Insurance System

A new social insurance system must fit new patterns of employment, embracing people who work for part of the week or the year as well as those in permanent full-time jobs. One way of starting to fill in the gaps would be to extend social insurance membership to people employed for an average of at least eight hours a week – the threshold suggested by the European Commission which we also propose to apply to employment laws.[8] Although it would be possible to include people employed for even fewer hours, the benefits they would gain are unlikely to outweigh the practical problems and costs of doing so. Since part-time employees earning below the contributions threshold (currently £57 a week) could not afford to pay full contributions, it might also be possible to follow the example of Ireland, where social insurance members with very low earnings are exempt from payment. Contribution credits should, of course, continue to be available for unemployed people and others receiving social insurance benefits, as well as those who qualify for home responsibilities protection; 'starting' credits should also be restored to school-leavers. The eventual goal should be to bring parents and others providing family care fully within the social insurance system.

As self-employment becomes increasingly important, the exclusion of the self-employed from full membership of the national insurance system is indefensible. Thousands of people who have unsuccessfully tried to set up businesses after being made redundant have found that, despite years of paying contributions as an employee, they have no entitlement to unemployment benefit. Although private insurance is available for accidents, sickness and permanent disability, no scheme offers reasonably priced cover for short-term sickness, while insurance against unemployment is hardly available at all.[9] In the United Kingdom, more than half of agricultural workers and more than 10 per cent of industrial and service-sector workers are now self-employed. We need to follow the example of two other European Union countries – Denmark and Luxembourg – which have gradually extended their social insurance schemes to the self-employed, for instance by including them in unemployment insurance.[10]

Modern social insurance could also give its members the option of paying higher contributions in return for higher benefits. National Insurance contributors can already earn a higher pension by delaying their retirement (a full five-year deferral increases the pension by 37 per cent). The principle could be extended, perhaps by allowing someone who has paid additional contributions for a specified period to receive extra benefit for maternity or parental leave.

Social Insurance against unemployment

Although some system of unemployment benefit will always be needed, it should play a diminishing role in people's lives and in the national budget. There is already much government can do to strengthen job creation within the economy and to help the unemployed get the new jobs. In the longer term, anything more than a brief period of unemployment between jobs should be replaced by time invested in education and training; eventually every member should be able to draw on social insurance to help finance a 'sabbatical' during his or her working life.

In the more immediate future, unemployment insurance should be redesigned to fit the modern labour market. The Child Poverty Action Group, for instance, is fiercely critical of the way in which the 'insurance principle' – which it supports – is translated into practice in this country. The United Kingdom now has some of the most demanding qualification conditions in the EU, which merely serve to exclude many contributors from receiving benefit. Instead of imposing complex contribution conditions, the system should aim to make unemployment insurance available to anyone who has been an employed or self-employed member of the social insurance system for a specified recent period. The rules concerning involuntary unemployment would remain in place, and benefit claimants would, of course, be required to be available and looking for work. The rules should also encourage unemployed people to take the risk of casual work, by allowing them to link different employment periods in order to qualify for unemployment insurance.

Unlike unemployment benefit, which is now paid for up to twelve months, the new Job Seeker's Allowance will last for only six. Young people under the age of twenty-five will get a lower allowance, even if they have a full contribution record. These changes would not only put the United Kingdom out of line with the rest of the European Union, but also ignore reforms in the USA, where unemployment insurance is being extended to protect the workers hardest hit by structural economic change. The new time limit on the Job Seeker's Allowance will force thousands more families to run down their modest savings and claim means-tested benefits, with all the barriers to employment these benefits create, while many married women will find themselves ineligible for any benefit at all. More families would be forced to spend more time relying on benefits rather than being helped into employment, with the result that spending on benefits would increase rather than decline, as the Government intends. Instead, unemployment insurance benefit should last for up to at least twelve months. People who have contributed for longer than the minimum needed to qualify could also be entitled to a longer-lasting benefit, an innovation which would be particularly helpful to people in their fifties, who now find themselves pushed on to means-tested benefits and forced to run down their savings, despite paying full contributions during years of steady employment.

Modern social insurance should also take a different approach to families. The present national insurance system offers additional benefits for a claimant's partner, but nothing for the children – the reverse of what is required by a 'welfare to work' strategy. Extra benefits for a spouse reduce the incentive for him or her (usually her) to keep or take a job, while the withdrawal of child additions is yet another reason why most unemployed people are forced to claim means-tested benefits, compounding work disincentives for the partner. Because the most effective pathway out of poverty for two-parent families is to have two earners, we do not see a role in future for the partner's addition, which the Government proposes to abolish in any case when job seeker's allowance is introduced. Restoring child additions, however, would help to encourage the partners of unemployed claimants to take up and stay in work. As in Ireland, each partner in a two-parent family should be able to claim half the child additions. Compared with the present system, this structural reform would save money.

Unemployment insurance also needs to take account of people who are part-time unemployed. The part-time worker who is made redundant needs unemployment insurance just as much as a full-time employee, yet few part-time workers now qualify for benefit. Although it is perfectly reasonable to expect people without caring responsibilities to be available for full-time employment, the benefit rules should also respect the fact that many people with dependents to care for will actively choose part-time employment; unemployed workers with family responsibilities should therefore be allowed to look for a part-time job without losing their benefit.

Although eight out of ten women working part-time do so because they do not want a full-time job, six out of ten men in part-time employment still want full-time work.[11] In all, about three-quarters of a million part-time workers should be recognised as part-time unemployed. Several other European countries have begun to create part-time benefit systems; the United Kingdom, which has one of the highest rates of part-time employment in the EU, needs to do the same, giving people who have lost full-time jobs an incentive to take up one of the growing numbers of part-time jobs if there is no full-time alternative.

The costs of part-time unemployment insurance will depend upon the detailed approach chosen and will be substantially

Creating a part-time unemployment benefit

Option 1 Unemployment benefit is assumed to cover a full-time job of, say, 35 hours a week. (The present single-person's benefit of £45.45 a week would be equal to about £1.30 an hour.) An unemployed person's previous hours of work (averaged over, say, six months) would determine whether benefit was paid in full or in part. Someone receiving full benefit who then took up a part-time job could continue to claim part-benefit. If, for instance, the new job averaged 10 hours a week, 25 hours' benefit would be paid; if it averaged 20 hours a week, 15 hours' benefit would be paid. There would be an earnings limit so that benefit was not paid to people with high part-time earnings, and a time-limit on the payment of part-benefit

Option 2 Unemployment benefit would be paid in full to any unemployed person, regardless of previous hours of work, subject to a maximum percentage (say, 80 per cent) of previous net earnings. (That rule would be necessary to prevent someone whose part-time earnings had been *below* benefit level from receiving more when unemployed.) An unemployed person who moved into a part-time job would be allowed to keep their benefit for a specified period, again with a limit on the total of benefit-plus-earnings

Option 3 Unemployment benefit would be paid on the basis of the individual's *present* availability for work, rather than past employment record. Anyone seeking full-time work would therefore receive full benefit (subject again to a maximum percentage of previous earnings), while someone looking for part-time work would be entitled to part-benefit. The system would distinguish between 'willing' part-time workers (who would not get any extra benefit) and 'unwilling' part-time workers, who would receive part-benefit while they continued to look for full-time work. There would be an overall earnings limit, to prevent the well-paid part-time worker also claiming part-benefit

The Welfare-to-Work Strategy I

Geoff works full-time as a sales rep, Irene works part-time in a local shop. They have a son of fourteen and a daughter of eight. What happens when Geoff is made redundant?

Present system Geoff qualifies for Unemployment Benefit, but has to claim Income Support as well because the family cannot live on his Unemployment Benefit and Irene's part-time earnings. Because Irene's earnings reduce their Income Support, there is no longer any point in her working, and she gives up her job. The family now has no one in employment.

Social justice strategy Geoff qualifies for Unemployment Benefit and an additional sum for the children. Higher Child Benefit (see Chapter 7) helps keep the family off Income Support, and Housing Benefit helps with the rent (as it does under the present system). Irene stays in work and manages to increase her hours while Geoff looks for another job. Unable to get full-time work, he takes a part-time sales job, but keeps part of his Unemployment Benefit as a top-up.

The family is better off than they are under the present system – and so is government which saves all the Income Support it is now paying for a family of four (currently £56 on top of Unemployment and Child Benefit).

If 250,000 families like Geoff and Irene moved off Income Support, one year's benefit savings could total £725 million.

offset by savings on means-tested benefits. A government committed to the goal of part-time unemployment insurance should consult widely with employees and their unions, employers and others, learn from the experience of other EU countries, and analyse the costs in more detail before settling on its approach. There are various different approaches which could work in practice.[12]

Testing availability for work

The Conservative Government has introduced a series of increasingly rigid 'actively seeking work' rules for unemployed people, which it proposes to make even more demanding with the introduction of the Job Seeker's Allowance. Claimants are required to attend Job Clubs, produce evidence that they have applied for so many jobs each week and so on. But a detailed analysis of the new rules found that they had only a limited impact on the way in which people looked for work, and no impact on their chances of finding a job. The new rules have reinforced some employers' suspicions about the motivation of the long term unemployed, making them reluctant to recruit people they perceive as unwilling conscripts.[13] The evidence shows that unemployed people do want a job, that they do not 'price themselves out of work' by demanding excessive wages, and that they are highly flexible in what they will take. Of course, someone who unreasonably turns down a job or training offer cannot expect to continue claiming full benefit. Indeed, that rule should also apply to the partners of unemployed men who, in practice, are allowed and even encouraged by the present system to give up their own jobs.

The long-term aim should be to bring more parents within the 'availability for work' rules. At present, although men with children and working-age adults without children are required to be available for employment before they can claim benefit, lone parents are not required to be available for work until their youngest child reaches the age of sixteen. The same is true for partners in families with children receiving Income Support or Family Credit. Although the rules are not sex-discriminatory in theory, in practice it is almost always the mother to whom benefit is paid without any requirement that she be available for employment.

The rules appear to be a generous recognition of family responsibilities, but assumption that women should be at home until their children have left school does them no favours at all. By helping to lock mothers out of the employment which most of them want, it not only condemns them and their families to poverty for many years, but blights their future employment and pension prospects as well. Most women who try to return to employment

239

after a very long period on inadequate benefits find it extremely difficult to obtain well-paid, skilled work, while the loss of possible occupational pension rights can never be made up.

Once our comprehensive strategy is in place to offer parents the help they need in returning to employment – including, most important of all, good childcare facilities – it would be both appropriate and desirable to expect parents of older children to register as available for at least part-time employment if they or their partners wished to claim means-tested benefits. A careful judgment will need to be made about the circumstances in which this new requirement would apply. Although many mothers of pre-school children choose to return to employment, the benefits system should not require them to do so; indeed, all parents should have a wider choice about how they look after their young children. An availability-for-work rule could, however, be applied when the youngest child reaches the age of five and goes to school, or at a somewhat later age. A parent caring for a disabled child of any age should continue to be exempt, and no parent should be expected to take a job if the working hours would combine with inadequate childcare alternatives to risk leaving a child unsupervised outside school. Because of the very disruptive effects which separation, divorce or widowhood can have on children of any age, someone who has become a lone parent when her children are older should still be able to claim benefit if necessary for at least a year without being available for employment. With these extremely important qualifications, however, the extension of the availability-for-work rule would follow naturally from the successful establishment of our JET programme.

Social insurance for family responsibilities

A modern social insurance system needs to recognise the family responsibilities which occur during most people's working lives. Although the United Kingdom Government has recently – and reluctantly – brought maternity leave into line with minimum European requirements, we still lag behind in many respects.

During the 1980s, several Western governments began to extend maternity leave into other forms of paid leave for early childrearing.[14] Sweden's provision is the most extensive, with eighteen months' parental leave (since mid-1994, two months is paid at 90 per cent of previous salary, ten months at 80 per cent, three months at a lower rate and the final three unpaid). Although most of the leave can be taken by either parent, in June 1994 the Swedish parliament made one of the 90 per cent months available only to fathers (although lone parents can continue to take the full leave themselves).[15] Current trends in Western societies suggest that childrearing benefits are likely to play an increasingly important role.

We have already argued that the reinstatement right available to mothers for up to twenty-nine weeks after the child's birth or adoption should be gradually extended to at least twelve months, with the additional period available to either parent. The development of parental-leave insurance would be a desirable step forward, but different schemes would have different effects on families. The experience of both Germany and Denmark – where only a handful of fathers take up their childrearing entitlements – suggests that flat-rate payments reinforce the usual division of responsibilities at home, because fathers generally stand to lose so much more of their earnings if they take leave. One way round this, although inevitably more expensive, would be to build in an earnings-related element, although more effective anti-discrimination and equal pay laws are also required to close the pay gap. Parental-leave insurance could not be afforded immediately, but it would do so much to improve the quality of children's and parents' lives that it should be accepted in principle and introduced gradually. As more part-time employees are brought within the new Social Insurance system, Statutory Maternity Pay and National Insurance Maternity Allowance could also be extended to them.

Caring for small children is not, of course, the only family responsibility that affects people's ability to earn a living. Nearly seven million people are involved in caring for a chronically ill or disabled relative or neighbour, one million of them providing 35 hours or more of care each week. Many of these carers are themselves over pension age. For those who have to give up their job or cut their hours in order to provide care, Invalid Care

Allowance (ICA) goes a little way towards replacing the earnings they sacrifice. It is sometimes suggested that these resources should go to the person who is ill or disabled, allowing him or her to 'purchase' the care needed, whether from a family member or from outside. Recipients of care should certainly have far more control over their lives, but this should not be achieved at the expense of the many carers who, in meeting the needs of their families, are also saving taxpayers an enormous amount of money. Disabled people, however, should be entitled to receive community care funding directly from local authorities if they wish to control their own care packages, while direct support should continue to be provided through ICA to family carers.

As a non-contributory benefit, ICA is paid at lower rates than National Insurance benefits (currently it is £11 less than Unemployment Benefit and £23 less than Invalidity Benefit). Entitlement is tied to the receipt of other benefits by the person receiving care. Once the reforms we propose to contribution tests and credits are in place, it would be logical for the present non-contributory benefits (Severe Disability Allowance as well as ICA) to be brought within the social insurance scheme and paid at the same rate as other contributory benefits.[16] People who gave up or reduced their employment in order to look after someone else could then receive full or partial carers' insurance to help replace their earnings, maintain their connection with the labour market and safeguard their future pension and unemployment insurance rights; their entitlement to benefit would no longer depend upon the benefits status of the person for whom they were caring. As

The Social Justice strategy for disabled people and carers

- Outlaw discrimination against disabled people (Chapter 5)
- Reform disability and carers' benefits (Chapter 6)
- Long-term care insurance (Chapter 6)
- Extend family friendly working hours, giving carers more choice (Chapter 5)
- Leave for carers (Chapter 5)

an interim measure, government could begin the process of reform by gradually raising Invalid Care Allowance to the same rate as Unemployment Benefit. A first step towards making eligibility for carers' benefit independent of the benefit received by the person being cared for would be to extend ICA to people caring for someone in receipt of the lowest rate of Disablement Living Allowance. Particularly as the need for long-term care increases, it will make good economic, as well as social, sense to acknowledge the value of carers' work within the social-security system rather than trying to meet the full costs of professional care.

Protection for sickness and disability

In 1983, National Insurance Sickness Benefit was replaced for most employees by Statutory Sick Pay (SSP) administered by employers. For many employees, the system works efficiently and is often combined with more generous employers' arrangements. The Government has, however, abolished the refund system under which most SSP costs were shared by all employers (although small firms will get full reimbursement after someone has been ill for four weeks). The changes risk encouraging employers to discriminate against people with poor health records, and against disabled people – though as a matter of fact disabled people are no more likely to be absentees than other employees. The previous system of sharing costs should therefore be restored.

A recent report from the National Audit Office reveals considerable problems with the administration of SSP.[17] Some employers have simply dismissed people who became ill, rather than pay benefit, while other employees have been unable to get the information they need to claim National Insurance benefit if they cannot qualify for SSP. Furthermore, up to one in three SSP payments checked by government inspectors turns out to be wrongly calculated. The Auditor-General, who is responsible for ensuring proper controls on public expenditure, found that the information collected on SSP was so inadequate that it was impossible to estimate either the scale of employer error or the extent to which employees are failing to receive sick pay. His recommendations should improve the situation, but the abuse of SSP by unscrupulous employers reinforces the need to extend protection against unfair dismissal to employees with less than two years' employment.

In the longer term, there may be lessons to learn from the more radical approach pioneered in Sweden, where government is increasingly concerned about the waste of money and human resources caused by unhealthy working conditions. There, the 'Health at Work' service is responsible not only for granting paid sick leave but also for preventing occupational ill-health and rehabilitating sick or injured employees.

Although many disabled people have jobs, usually very low-paid, it is estimated that 70 per cent of working-age disabled people are not employed.[18] Social security benefits are therefore more important to disabled people's finances than they are to other adults. Within the present system, the Disability Living Allowance recognises that disabled people have higher living costs. Existing benefit levels, however, are too low to pay for care services and other extra costs such as higher heating and laundry bills.

The Government has now decided to merge National Insurance Sickness and Invalidity Benefit into a new Incapacity Benefit, which will be taxed and based on tougher medical criteria. But the effect of a disability depends upon social as well as medical conditions, and the proposed medical criteria need to be balanced against a wider recognition that two people with the same medical condition may have very different employment prospects, depending partly on their age, partly on where they live and their present or possible skills. Whereas a blind person aged fifty-five is unlikely to get an appropriate job if they have already been out of employment for many years, a similarly disabled person aged twenty may well gain employment if given good training and support. Older people whose age and disability combine to make employment highly improbable should be able to claim Incapacity Benefit without a regular review; for people unlikely ever to recover from a disability, such reviews are unnecessary and wasteful.

For the last 25 years, disability organisations have campaigned for a comprehensive disability income designed to create greater equity between disabled and non-disabled people, and to treat people with different degrees of disability fairly. A comprehensive disability income should fulfil two functions. First, it should compensate disabled people for the additional expense of being disabled by offering tax-free benefit, based on up-to-date evidence of living costs. Second, because disabled people are much more likely than others to be unemployed or only partially employed, it should offer some compensation, through a taxable benefit, for the loss of earning potential. Although the objectives are clear, there is no consensus on how to introduce such a reform. The financial needs of disabled people must be addressed by any government committed to social justice, but further debate is needed about how best to do so.

Reforming means-tested benefits

'The Chinese water torture is meant to kill you drop by drop. That's what being on benefit is like. It destroys your soul.'
    Susan, unemployed, mother of two children, Lancashire.

In our view, a modern social security system should be built upon the foundation of social insurance. It is often argued, however, that a simpler and cheaper solution to the problems of the welfare state would be to means-test all benefits so that they go only to the people who 'really need them'. This is the Deregulators' approach and the essence of the Government's strategy. The increase in the number of people claiming means-tested benefits over the last fifteen years is no accident, but the intended result of a policy of raising means-tested benefit levels faster than other benefits while reducing the scope of National Insurance. Although this approach reduces the role of the welfare state to a residual attempt to relieve poverty among the poorest people, it has the virtue of being based on an apparently simple and attractive idea. But the strategy is fatally flawed.

A significant proportion of the people who are entitled to means-tested benefits fail to claim them. By contrast, virtually everyone who is entitled to claim non-means-tested Child Benefit or the National Insurance retirement pension does so. Despite extensive publicity campaigns, Family Credit – the centrepiece of the Government's strategy for subsidising low wages – according

Figure 6.1 – No Better Off on £10,000 a Year

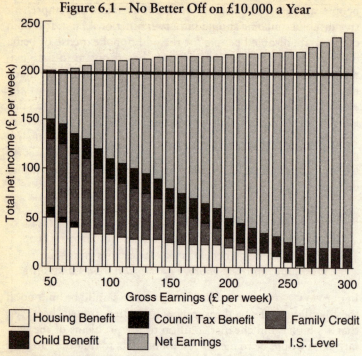

note: Figures for couple with two children. Line shows level of Income Support, with free school meals.
1994 tax and benefit rates.

Source: Robert Walker 'Springing The Poverty Trap' *New Economy* Vol 1 Issue 3 (London: IPPR/The Dryden Press)

to the most recent figures, is not claimed by nearly two out of every five people who should benefit from it, at an average loss to them of £22.25 per week and a total under-payment of some £200 million. One-fifth of those entitled to Income Support do not claim it – more than a million people; amongst elderly people alone, it is estimated that 570,000 do not claim their Income Support.[19] Means-tested benefits, which cannot prevent poverty, are also remarkably inefficient at relieving it.

Moreover, these benefits are extremely expensive to administer. For every £1 paid in Income Support, 11p is spent on administration, while every £1 paid from the Social Fund costs 45p to

---

Trapped in Poverty

I am a married man with three sons and one daughter and I currently work for the Benefits Agency. The very poor salary offered causes me to have to claim state benefit in the form of Family Credit. The totally inescapable position I find myself in is that I am far, far worse off for going to work.

Working		Income Support	
£114.00	Take-home salary	£135.95	IS
£85.00	Family Credit	£34.30	Child Benefit
£34.30	Child Benefit		

£233.30		£170.25	

Less rent £35, council tax £11 approx, no school meals	No rent, no council tax, free school meals, clothing grant etc

£188 to manage on each week for six people – ie food, clothes, gas, electric, water etc.

So for less than £20 I am working and still feel a failure to my family. *Please* do not use my name, since I cannot risk upsetting my employers.

Letter to the Commission on Social Justice, April 1994

---

administer. In striking contrast, £1 in Child Benefit costs 2p to administer, and £1 in retirement pension only just over 1p.[20]

Means-testing also encourages dependence on benefits, rather than independence. Not only does Income Support penalise extra earnings, but as people move back into employment, the combination of National Insurance Contributions, income tax and the withdrawal of means-tested benefits means that half a million of the poorest people are effectively paying marginal tax rates of 70 per cent or even higher, creating a very long 'poverty plateau' where families can remain on low incomes for a very long time.

As Figure 6.1 illustrates, at 1994 tax and benefit rates, a family with two young children and a weekly rent of £60 would be hardly any better off if they earned £10,000 a year than if they claimed Income Support; their annual earnings would have to reach £14,000 before they were completely clear of means-tested benefits. The disincentive effects of means-testing are compounded by the fact that homebuyers who lose their jobs find that help with mortgages is available only if they stay out of work and claim Income Support.

A further disadvantage of means-testing is that it penalises savings. Anyone who has saved £8,000 or more cannot claim Income Support or Family Credit at all, no matter how low their income. As many elderly people know to their cost, the earnings put away for retirement may leave them just as badly off as if they had never saved at all. Instead of preventing poverty, means-tested benefits help people only after they have largely exhausted assets which they really need to help supplement inadequate benefit and to save as protection against future needs, such as those arising from severe disablement. As younger people observe the effects of asset-testing, they may well decide that it is not worth saving after all.

These traditional arguments against means-testing are now familiar. But changes in the structure of families and the economy make means-testing increasingly short-sighted and anachronistic. Even though most women now expect to be employed (part-time or full-time) for most of their working lives, means-tested benefits, based on total family income, rarely make it worthwhile for the claimant's partner to keep or take a job. Married women's decisions about whether or not to take a job or to increase hours of work are clearly affected by the benefits system.[21] The disastrous effect of means-testing is vividly illustrated by a story told to us by the late John Smith MP. On election day 1992, he met a woman who told him in tears that her husband had been made redundant and that her family were now pressing her to give up her part-time job. She did not earn enough to keep them all and unless she too became unemployed, her family would be denied the help they needed. To extend a system which is already splitting families would be madness.

248

Although the tax system has recognised married women as individuals since the late 1980s, means-tested benefits are based on the income of the couple, not the individual. It is hard to see how they could be otherwise, without either undermining the purpose of means-testing or introducing unacceptably intrusive questioning about income-sharing between partners. As more people live together without marrying, however, means-testing requires increasingly complicated cohabitation rules, which are particularly difficult to enforce where the partners sometimes live together and sometimes separately. And by giving higher benefits to two adults who live separately than to a couple, the present means-tested benefits system has the perverse effect of penalising partners and parents who live together. Paradoxically, the more the benefits system recognises women as individuals, the more it will encourage partners to stay together, as well as tackle poverty and increase personal autonomy.

Instead of providing a predictable and stable financial base from which people can deal with change, means-tested benefits create further insecurity. For example, a woman who knows she is guaranteed her Child Benefit, whatever else happens, is more likely to take the risk of an insecure job or to move herself and her children away from a violent and abusive partner than if she has no money she can count on. Means-tested benefits for people in work continue to assume stable earnings from employment, in defiance of a labour market which frequently offers insecure, unpredictable and fluctuating earnings. As the shopworkers' union, USDAW, emphasised to us: 'Flexibility of hours means that no planning can be made based on weekly income because it may be infinitely variable.'

Finally, if means-tested benefits are intended to provide a residual safety-net for those who cannot afford private savings and private insurance, then they will deepen the problem of social exclusion. There is ample evidence that systems with benefits paid to the majority are considerably more popular as well as more efficient than those which reserve benefits solely for the poor. In the USA, 'social security' – insurance for old age – is powerfully defended, while 'welfare' – means-tested help for lone parents – is generally regarded as a disaster. We are not prepared to condemn the most vulnerable people in our community to an inadequate existence on benefits which can never offer them dignity, security or independence.

In this country, 'targeting' is always taken to refer to means-testing: people having to prove their poverty before receiving benefit. Benefits can of course be targeted on a particular group without any means-testing (as is the case with Child Benefit and One Parent Benefit), or their value to better-off people can be restricted, as in some other European countries. In Australia, all benefits are 'means-tested', not in the sense of being 'for the poor' but meaning 'not for the rich'. Thus, family allowances and retirement pensions are withdrawn from the very well-off, instead of being confined to the very poor – an 'affluence' rather than a 'means' test. It is essential to bear this distinction in mind when 'targeting' is debated.

Our aim is to reduce dependence on means-tested benefits to the absolute minimum, in the longer term replacing both Income Support and Family Credit with a single, genuinely residual means-tested benefit designed mainly to help a small number of people with unusually high costs (such as housing or a large number of children). Our employment strategies, together with the creation of a modern Social Insurance system and a higher Child Benefit, will make an important contribution towards reducing means-testing to a minimum. These strategies will, however, require time to take effect and many people will depend on means-tested benefits for some time to come. For them, reform of means-tested benefits is essential.

The administration of all benefits must respect people's basic rights. Too many claimants find themselves frustrated and depressed by lengthy delays in having their applications dealt with, and by the physical conditions in which they have to wait and Benefits Agency staff have to work. Staff themselves may be bewildered by the sheer complexity of the present system: workers at the Norwich Citizens' Advice Bureau told us that claimants were sometimes referred to them by officials. People from minority ethnic communities, however, are particularly likely to suffer from inadequate service, often because no facilities are offered to those for whom English is their second language. The Benefits Agency has begun to take a more positive approach towards equal opportunities by introducing improved complaints procedures and a Code of Practice on discrimination and racial harassment. This process needs to be developed further and the links between social security and immigration laws, which undermine the rights of some minority ethnic claimants reviewed.

Reforming Income Support

The most important means-tested benefit is Income Support, on which some ten million people now rely. The benefits they receive are too low to allow people to feed and clothe themselves adequately, let alone participate in the broader life of the community; as we proposed earlier, benefit levels should be reviewed. Although increasing the level of Income Support would improve the situation, it could also increase the numbers of people who depend on it. Our emphasis is therefore on the development of a modern social insurance system and other measures which will help people living on benefits to move into paid employment.

As part of the strategy to help claimants earn a living, it would make good sense to allow people receiving Income Support to 'roll up' over a much longer period the earnings they are now allowed to receive without penalty. The present level, £5 a week, is not much use to anyone: but even £260 a year would allow claimants to earn the occasional lump sum without jeopardising their Income Support. A higher-level disregard of, say, £260 every three months would do even more to encourage people to take the casual jobs which are increasingly on offer, and would help them to meet one-off costs, such as children's clothes, which now cause such anxiety and distress. From October 1994, lone parents claiming Family Credit will have up to £40 of their weekly childcare costs disregarded. An even greater incentive to take employment would be provided if childcare costs were disregarded in full, together with part of any maintenance payment from an absent partner.

Sixteen- and seventeen-year-olds are no longer entitled to claim Income Support. Everyone of that age should, of course, be in full-time education and training, or combining education with employment. But the scandal of young homeless people is in large

The Social Justice strategy for lone parent families

Research from the UK and abroad shows that the most effective way of helping lone-parent families is through measures which help all families – above all measures to help parents earn a living.

- National strategy for under-fives, including nursery education and childcare (Chapter 4)
- Jobs, Education and Training Programme (Chapter 5)
- Family-friendly employment policies (Chapter 5)
- Income Support disregard on childcare expenses (Chapter 6)
- Reform of Child Benefit (Chapter 7)
- Reform of the Child Support Act (Chapter 7)

part a direct result of the withdrawal of benefits. Many of those who end up on the streets have suffered from family conflict or abuse; others have just left local authority care. Income Support is a last resort, but it should once again be available to this desperately vulnerable group.

Perhaps the most soul-destroying aspect of Income Support is the Social Fund, which provides additional help (much of it in the form of loans) with one-off costs – a new cooker, a replacement coat, bedding or essential furniture – which cannot be met out of a weekly income which is already too low for regular needs. According to the latest figures, 11 per cent of Income Support claimants, some 643,000 people, are having to repay Social Fund loans through deductions from already inadequate benefits, while the very poorest families find that because they have no hope of paying anything back they are denied the loans they desperately need.[22] In the past the Social Security Advisory Committee has suggested, and we would support, a three-tiered system to replace the single discretionary payments and loans which now exist. Regular one-off payments should be made to claimants, including one at Christmas, to provide help with larger costs. Special payments should be available for defined crises, such as a cooker or washing-machine breaking down completely. And officials should have a wider discretion than at present to help meet special needs.

Reforming Family Credit

Income Support ceases to be paid once anyone in the family is employed for sixteen hours a week or more. At that point, another means-tested benefit, Family Credit, becomes available to low-paid workers with children. Family Credit is central to the Government's policy of encouraging the unemployed to take low-paid jobs, topped up by benefit. Both the European Union and the OECD have expressed support for the principle of in-work benefits, while the Clinton Administration plans to extend the Earned Income Tax Credit (EITC) which is the USA's equivalent of Family Credit. But Family Credit has too many defects to be the centrepiece of an effective 'welfare to work' strategy.

Quite apart from its low take-up (which is still below two-thirds, despite extensive publicity campaigns), Family Credit is modelled on the old assumption of a single breadwinner earning a family wage. For lone parents, of course, this is not a problem, there being no other breadwinner in the home. But a recent study of Family Credit showed how far antiquated thinking has a debilitating effect on two-parent families: 'Among couples on Family Credit, only 12 per cent had a second earner [compared with 60 per cent of all couples where the man is employed]. While Family Credit might encourage lone parents to go out to work, it encourages married mothers to stay at home and look after their children.'[23] In effect, Family Credit provides a child-rearing benefit to the parent at home in a low-income, two-parent, one-job family. For some, it is a temporary cushion until the children are older and the woman can get a job offering full-time or long part-time hours. At that point, Family Credit will end and the family, now supported by two wages, will move out of poverty. For others, the subsidy to the man's wages offered by Family Credit can lock the mother *out* of employment for so long that she finds it impossible to get a job at all or one which is worth taking. Most couples receiving Family Credit on the basis of the man's wages assume (sometimes wrongly) that if the woman also takes a job, Family Credit will end. These families remain on Family Credit for a long time, trapped in low incomes and with the woman losing not only potential earnings but future pension entitlements as well.

Trapped in Poverty

I am a lone mother with two school-age children. Ever since my youngest started school I've been looking for a job. Three years and many failed interviews later, I've been offered and accepted a 25-hour a week job at about £3.50 an hour with the local health centre. That was two weeks ago and I'm due to start on Monday. I was so happy until this week when I went round to the dole. Since then, my life has become a nightmare. I can't sleep and several times a day I find myself fighting for breath because I've been overcome with panic.

I thought the Government wanted people like me to get a job, but I just can't see how I'm going to manage. The job pays monthly and I'm not allowed to cash this week's (fortnightly) giro because it would overlap with the start of the job. That might sound fair enough, but it means that for the first ten days or so I will have only my Child Benefit to live on. How can I feed and heat myself and the children on £18.10 a week? I'm being 'fast-tracked' for Family Credit, so I *should* get that after ten to fourteen days and that'll be about £60 a week, which will get me up to £78.10 for the next few weeks. But what if the Family Credit doesn't come as fast as they say? My Housing Benefit also has to be stopped and started again and I can't work out whether all or just some of my rent will be paid by my new HB so I'm not sure whether I'll owe rent when my FC and finally my wage come through. I can't get help from my ex-husband because he's unemployed. I can't get help from my own family because they're struggling already. I just want to give up.

Letter to the Commission on Social Justice from a lone parent in Belfast

---

In the longer term, we would like to see Family Credit relegated to a residual role, while the other measures we suggest will reduce the number of people who depend upon it. Nevertheless, Family Credit will continue to provide substantial help to thousands of families for some time to come. It should therefore be made to work better, particularly by reforms which ease the transition from Income Support. Most low-income families do not know how Family Credit is calculated and cannot predict with any accuracy what their income would actually be. Moving into a low-paid job means abandoning the relative security of Income Support and waiting up to six weeks until a Family Credit claim is processed. In the meantime, the family still has to eat. Once Family Credit is assessed, it cannot be changed for six months, with disastrous results if earnings drop in the meantime. There is, of course, also the risk that the worker will be made redundant again and that it will be several more weeks before Income Support is received once more. Many of the jobs at the bottom end of the labour market are casual; they may involve 'own account' work where the only wages are commissions; and cowboy employers may not pay regularly, on time, or at all. There is now ample research to confirm that it is security, not money, that can make Income Support preferable to low-paid employment, and trap people on benefits.[24]

Although the problem can never be fully resolved while Income Support and Family Credit remain separate systems, some shorter-term changes would help. Far more publicity needs to be given to the 'fast-track' procedure for Family Credit applicants referred from the Employment Service. More significantly, Income Support should continue to be paid while Family Credit is calculated, a reform that is unlikely to cost more than £20 million per annum and may well save money as more people move into employment, while alleviating real distress among a small group of families. Subject to the rules about voluntary unemployment and misconduct, someone who has moved from Income Support to Family Credit should be guaranteed an immediate re-entitlement to Income Support if the job ends within a specified period (perhaps six months). The United Kingdom should also follow the example of proposed benefit reforms in Ireland, which will allow

The Welfare-to-Work Strategy II

Betty and Bert have a son of three and a daughter of five. They live in a council flat, neither of them has a job and they depend upon Income Support.

Under the present system

Bert has been out of work for nearly a year and has little hope of ever getting regular work again. He has thought about taking casual work as a builder, but the family can't risk giving up Income Support and waiting for Family Credit to come through. In any case, his earnings would go up and down while Family Credit stayed the same and Betty is worried that some weeks they wouldn't be able to put food on the table or pay the rent.

Social justice strategy

Income Support claimants are now allowed to earn up to £260 every three months, instead of just £5 a week. Bert takes on a small building job and uses the cash to buy some desperately needed clothes for the children and to pay off the most pressing bills.

Through the people he has met on his casual job, Bert is then offered and accepts six months' work – Income Support will be paid until his Family Credit claim is processed, and the child at school will continue to receive free school meals for another year.

Meanwhile, Betty has registered with the Re-Employment Service which hopes to find her a training course during school hours, with a crèche for her youngest child, so that she can look for a part-time job once both children are at school.

The family is better off – and government is paying less in Family Credit than they would have continued to pay in Income Support.

unemployed people moving into employment or self-employment to keep the equivalent of passported benefits (including free school meals) for up to two years. All these steps would make it easier for people in the poorest families to take up the part-time and casual jobs that make up the majority of vacancies today. More ambitiously, help needs to be given to low-paid home-buyers through reformed Housing Benefits.

Reforming Housing Benefit

The challenge of providing help with housing costs other than through means-tested benefits defeated even William Beveridge and has vexed reformers ever since. More than three million households now receive means-tested Housing Benefit to cover part or all of their rent and, for those on Income Support, inter-est payments on mortgages up to £125,000. Although the Gov-ernment has made the scheme much less generous over the years, the Housing Benefit bill has ballooned from £5.1 billion in 1988/9 to more than £9.3 billion in 1992/93.[25] This is partly the result of increased unemployment and lone parenthood, partly the result of a deliberate policy of subsidising households rather than homes, which has pushed up local authority and housing association rents.

Although Housing Benefit consumes more than 10 per cent of the Government's social security budget and is central to its hous-ing policy, the system is a mess. Housing Benefit, reduced by 65p for every extra pound earned after tax and contributions, is one of the main causes of the 'poverty plateau' which keeps poor families poor. In addition, there is the gulf between tenants (who can receive Housing Benefit while in low-paid work) and home-buyers (who can get help with the mortgage only if they stay unemployed).

It is time to restore a better balance between subsidising fami-lies and subsidising bricks and mortar. That will require substan-tial changes to the housing market (see Chapter 7). But short-term reform is also needed as part of an effective 'welfare to work' strategy. The aim should be to continue protecting the poorest tenants, ease the poverty plateau through a lower benefit withdrawal rate, help unemployed homebuyers to move back into employment and reduce the incentives for people to move into more costly housing at public expense.

One way of achieving these goals has been proposed by John Hills, the Director of the Rowntree Foundation's Enquiry into Income and Wealth.[26] Under his suggested two-tier Housing Benefit, tenants who now receive full Housing Benefit would continue to have their entire rent paid, but benefit would be withdrawn at a reduced rate of 60 per cent (instead of the present 65 per cent) as their net incomes rose. Tenants now receiving partial benefit would in future have their Housing Benefit calculated on only 60 per cent of their rent, but with a much more gradual withdrawal rate of, say, 20 per cent. There would therefore be a greater incentive for people to increase their earnings, but no incentive to find more expensive accommodation.

Low-paid homebuyers also need help with mortgage costs, if those now trapped on Income Support are to be encouraged to move into employment.[27] Again, the system needs to be designed in a way that prevents taxpayers financing the purchase of more expensive homes. Low-income households could be eligible for full help with mortgage costs up to a specified limit (for example, the average repayment cost of a new mortgage was £70 a week in 1991), with benefit then declining gradually until it disappeared completely. Although such a scheme would help some people with mortgages who are already in low-paid work, it could produce substantial savings by helping unemployed families to take up employment.

Tax benefit integration and Negative Income Tax

Integrating the income tax and social security system is the Holy Grail of benefits policy – constantly sought and never found. One approach to tax benefit integration is the introduction of Negative Income Tax (NIT), under which everybody's income would be assessed and benefits paid out or taxes collected accordingly. In effect, NIT would extend means-testing to every family and every benefit.

An expert study of tax benefit integration, carried out specially for the Commission, concluded that there were enormous

The Welfare-to-Work Strategy III

Joe and Maria have three children under the age of ten. They are buying their home on a large mortgage. Joe works as an electrical engineer, Maria has a part-time job as a care assistant. What happens when Joe loses his job?

Under the present system

The only way Joe and Maria can ensure the mortgage is paid while he looks for another job is to claim Income Support. Because Maria's job is twenty hours a week, they could claim Family Credit but this doesn't help with the mortgage. Even with Family Credit, her earnings aren't enough to keep the family and pay the mortgage, so she gives up her job too. Joe goes on looking for a full-time job which will pay enough for the mortgage, but there aren't any available.

Social justice strategy

Because Housing Benefit now extends to mortgages, Joe and Maria can avoid claiming Income Support; they are also helped by the fact that Child Benefit has been raised. Maria stays in her job and takes the first opportunity to increase her hours. With at least one of them still working, they have a better chance of hearing about any full-time jobs which might be available.

Joe and Maria are much better off than if Maria had been forced to give up her job – and government has saved money too. The cost of Family Credit and Housing Benefit (for the mortgage) is much less than that of Income Support plus mortgage help. In fact, government might save as much as £60 per week.

If 250,000 home-buying families like Joe and Maria are moved off Income Support, government saves itself around £750 million. Even allowing for some displacement (someone else may stay unemployed for longer because Maria has remained in her job), the savings will still be more than sufficient to fund the extension of Housing Benefit to low-paid homebuyers already in work.

problems with NIT.[28] First, the income tax and benefits systems each serve a group of 'high-contact' clients whose complex circumstances demand considerable administrative resources: for income tax, these are higher-rate taxpayers and the self-employed; for benefit claimants, these are unemployed and others claiming Income Support. There is very little overlap between these two client groups. In between them are the majority of people, for whom PAYE tax and benefits such as Child Benefit or the retirement pension are easy and cheap to administer. The National Audit Office reports that only 15 per cent of all taxpayers receive an income tax assessment in any one year; they would hardly welcome more frequent contact.[29] Using Tax-Benefit Integration to try to solve the problems of the minority caught between taxation and means-tested benefits would be like using a sledgehammer to crack a nut.

The second problem is that income tax and means-tested benefits operate on quite different timescales. Although income tax is assessed on income received in a tax year, Family Credit is assessed over six weeks' earnings and paid for six months, while Income Support can be assessed weekly for families whose circumstances change frequently. A supposedly 'integrated' system would, in practice, have to retain two quite different systems.

An integrated system would also have to decide whether taxes and benefits were assessed for the individual or the family. If the individual were chosen, government would find itself paying negative income tax to a woman who had no income of her own but who was married to a wealthy company director. On the other hand, using the family as the basis of NIT would mean reversing the commitment to independent taxation of married women.

Finally, despite claims that NIT would produce administrative savings, it would in fact require a huge reorganisation of government, involving thousands of civil servants and new information systems. The change would affect almost every household in the UK and administrative costs could run into millions of pounds over several years before any savings might be achieved.

Citizen's Income

An alternative view is put forward by those who argue for a Citizen's (or Basic) Income. Funded by general taxes, Citizen's Income would be paid unconditionally to every resident (although, given the Single Market, even the definition of who exactly qualified might pose some problems). Citizen's Income would replace all existing National Insurance benefits, personal tax allowances and as many means-tested benefits as possible. Ideally, it would offer enough for people to survive on, a basic income to be supplemented by earnings. As a new form of security in an increasingly insecure world, it has been urged by many authoritative writers of various political outlooks.

The case for Citizen's Income is partly moral and partly economic. The moral case rests on the principle of social citizenship – the principle that, in order to make democratic self-government a reality, civil and political rights must go hand in hand with economic and social rights. And just as civil and political rights belong unconditionally to all citizens as individuals, irrespective of need or desert, so all citizens have a right to a share in the social and national product sufficient to make it possible for them to participate fully in the common life of society.

In theory, this principle could be realised in other ways. Indeed the Beveridge Revolution and the post-war welfare state were themselves inspired by the ideal of social citizenship. The social benefits that Beveridge envisaged were to be entitlements, guaranteed equally to all citizens, not charitable doles subject to the test of need. Yet the welfare state of today is far removed from the Beveridge principle of equal entitlement for all citizens. Rather, it is a jungle of partial benefits, often subject to arbitrary tests of need, and penetrated by a latter-day version of the Victorian distinction between the deserving and the undeserving poor. At the heart of the moral case for a Citizen's Income lies the belief that this distinction, no matter how expert those who make it, is improper. In other words, the state is no more entitled to say which citizens have a right to a sufficient share in the common stock to participate fully in the life of the society than to say which citizens have a right to vote or to a fair trial. And in modern conditions that principle can be realised more simply and more completely by a Citizen's Income than by any other mechanism.

The economic case rests upon the falling demand for unskilled labour. As we have already argued, a large part of the solution to this problem is to invest heavily in human capital, so that those currently without skills can be equipped to find decently paid jobs. But although everyone is agreed on the need for much higher investment in skills and training, some people believe that this strategy, even coupled with the other measures suggested in this report, is unlikely to solve the problem. And if it remains unsolved, our hopes for social justice will still be mocked by a pool of unskilled, jobless and alienated fellow citizens, effectively excluded from full membership of society. The economic case for a Citizen's Income is that it offers the simplest way to drain that pool, enabling even those without saleable skills to take low-paid or casual jobs of some kind, while at the same time receiving an income large enough to enfranchise them, without the stigma of a means test.

In present circumstances, however, there are severe difficulties with any fully fledged Citizen's Income. A change of this magnitude would have to be backed by a broad-based consensus, of which there is, as yet, no sign. In a society with a strong work ethic many people would oppose, as giving 'something for nothing', a scheme deliberately designed to offer unconditional benefits to all. Citizen's Income does not require any *act* of citizenship; it would be paid regardless of whether someone was in a job or looking for one, caring for children or other dependents, engaged in voluntary work or not.

Second, although Citizen's Income is intended to be a means of social inclusion, it could just as easily become a means of social exclusion. In Belgium, an unconditional benefit for young people was introduced some years ago. Detailed monitoring has since suggested that, instead of providing a foundation for education or employment, levels of participation in education and training may have actually fallen.[30] Disturbed by these results, the Belgian Government has now imposed new conditions before the benefit can be paid.

A third problem with Citizen's Income lies in the tax rates that would be required for funding, and their possible effects. For instance, a Citizen's Income of £40 a week could be funded by raising the standard income tax rate to 38 per cent, the present higher rate to 55 per cent, and introducing a new top rate of 66 per cent. An alternative approach to funding Citizens Income, suggested by Professor Meghnad Desai of the London School of Economics, is to abolish all tax allowances and reliefs, as well as most non-means tested benefits such as Child Benefit and Unemployment Benefit, and some means-tested benefits such as Family Credit. These measures could pay for an adult Citizens Income of £50 a week without changing the existing income tax rates. The problem with this approach is the distributional effect: over half the people in the poorest tenth of the population would be worse off, many of them becoming taxpayers for the first time, while many better-off people would gain.[31] Work carried out by the Institute for Fiscal Studies for the Equal Opportunities Commission suggests, however, that the combined effect of offering an unconditional benefit and raising tax rates would cause many married women to leave employment, risking future insecurity and poverty.[32] Men's employment is less directly affected by taxes and benefits, but the effect might still be further discouragement for those at the bottom of the labour market to try to gain skills and a job. If, instead, Citizen's Income were funded by higher VAT and an extension of VAT to currently exempt goods, the poor would lose out by considerably more than they would gain.

We believe that in present conditions our new social insurance scheme is more likely to win popular support and to provide an effective foundation on which people can build through their own earnings and savings. It would be unwise, however, to rule out a move towards Citizen's Income in future: if it turns out to be the case that earnings simply cannot provide a stable income for a growing proportion of people, then the notion of some guaranteed income, outside the labour market, could become increasingly attractive. Work incentives might matter less and those who happened to be in employment, knowing that they probably would not remain so throughout their 'working' lives, might be more willing to finance an unconditional payment. Our measures would not preclude a move to Citizen's Income in the future.

Participation income

The Citizen's Income is typically seen as an alternative to social insurance. Yet there have been proposals, notably by Hermione Parker of the Basic Income Research Group, for a partial Basic Income which would replace tax allowances but keep the existing structure of National Insurance (whose benefits would be reduced by the amount of the partial Basic Income). This approach may be developed into an alternative conception of the Citizen's Income, one which sees its role as reducing dependence on means-tested benefits, and as complementing rather than reducing social insurance.

This alternative approach would preserve the principles of a Citizen's Income which avoids means-testing and is paid on an individual basis. At the same time, for the reasons set out earlier, it would not be paid unconditionally. Instead, it would be a Participation Income: there would be a condition of active citizenship. It would thus not be vulnerable to the criticism that people were getting 'something for nothing'. The definition of such a condition would need detailed consideration, but those qualifying would probably include all UK residents in employment or self-employment, those unable to work because of sickness, injury or disability, those unemployed but available for work, those in approved education or training, and those caring for young, elderly or disabled dependants. As the last cases make clear, the condition of participation would be a wider definition of social contribution than just paid work, and would therefore be similar to the comprehensive system of credits and benefits which we see as the eventual goal of our modern social insurance scheme.

The Participation Income could be introduced at a modest level in a way that had no revenue cost, being financed by the abolition of tax allowances and the reduction in national insurance benefits by the equivalent amount. It would thus overcome the present unfairness that people whose income is too low to be taxable cannot make any use of their tax allowances and it would

---

The Social Justice strategy for older people

- A Minimum Pension Guarantee
- Universal second pensions
- Age-discrimination legislation (Chapter 5)
- Long-term care insurance

---

reduce the number dependent on means-tested benefits. But because a revenue-neutral Participation Income would in effect share the present value of tax allowances with many people who are currently neither income-tax payers nor national insurance benefit claimants, it would mean somewhat higher tax bills for those already paying income tax. Conversely, introducing a Participation Income at the same value as present tax allowances would require extra expenditure. If it could be afforded, particularly at a higher level than that available through abolishing tax allowances, it could go a long way towards eliminating means-testing, recognising the value of parents' and carers' unpaid work and encouraging people to take up employment, education or training.

Security for Retirement and Older Age

The most pressing and immediate problem facing any government concerned about security in old age is the extent of poverty amongst people who have already retired. For them, no new savings schemes are possible: the issue is how much extra income we are willing, as a society, to give them, and how it should be distributed.

Since government ministers regularly stress the rise in pensioners' living standards over the last decade, this emphasis on poverty may seem surprising. But (as with the population of working age) the rise in elderly people's *average* incomes conceals the fact that those at the top have done very well, those at the bottom very badly. Since 1979, the top two-fifths of pensioners have seen their income grow by two-thirds in real terms. The income of the bottom fifth grew by only 10 per cent over the same period. Instead of looking at misleading averages, we need to understand that, of today's pensioners, only one-third are

---

'Pay As You Go' and 'Funding': Definitions

Pay-as-you-go (PAYG) pension schemes require today's contributors to support today's pensioners. Today's working people accept the responsibility of paying for the previous generation's pensions, in the expectation that future contributors will in turn pay for their pensions. This is how the basic retirement pension, the State Earnings Related Pension (SERPS) and some occupational pensions are financed in this country, and how virtually all pensions are financed in other European countries. A funded pension scheme, on the other hand, invests today's contributions, earning interest to build up a fund from which future pensions will be paid.

Once pensions are actually being paid, the difference between PAYG and funding has no particular economic significance. All pensions come out of the country's total wealth at the time, regardless of whether they come from taxes or from interest payments; PAYG and funding simply represent different ways in which retired people express their claims on national resources. But the difference may matter in other ways. Some economists argue that private funding helps to increase the level of savings and can therefore help raise investment (although Germany, which does not fund its pensions, has higher investment and a stronger economy than the UK with extensive private funded schemes). People in work may be more willing to put aside more of their earnings if they can see it going into a fund for their own retirement.

Both PAYG and funding operate in this country and both will continue to be needed. In particular, PAYG is the only way to improve the position of those already retired.

---

income-tax payers, one-third live at or below the poverty line, and the remaining third fall in between.[33]

The gap between Income Support and the start of income tax is narrow. (Income Support today provides £64 plus housing costs for a single person aged between sixty and seventy-five; someone of the same age starts paying income tax at £80 a week.) Many of those paying small amounts of income tax, and all those in between income tax and Income Support, are living on very modest incomes indeed. But it is the bottom third about whom we must be most concerned in the first instance, and whom our *pension guarantee* is particularly designed to help. They include the 1.4 million single people and a further 230,000 elderly couples over the age of 60 who in 1992 were receiving Income Support.[34] But they also include the 570,000 older people who are officially estimated to be eligible for Income Support, but are not claiming it.

There is no simple cure for the problems of poverty, insecurity and inequity among older people today and in the future. We must begin by recognising that we are not, as a nation, investing enough in retirement and old age. Whether we pay for pensions through taxes and national insurance, through contributions to occupational and personal pension schemes, or through a mixture of both, we will need to invest more.

The basic pension and the new pension guarantee

The first tier of pension provision is the basic state retirement pension, earned through retired people's previous National Insurance Contributions. Since 1980, however, Parliament has required the basic pension to rise only in line with prices, rather than with earnings. As a result, its value has dropped from 20 per cent of male average earnings in 1977/8 to about 15 per cent by the early 1990s. If this policy continues, by the year 2020 the value of the state pension will have dropped to less than 9 per cent of earnings, and by 2040 to 6 per cent of earnings (assuming real earnings growth of 2 per cent a year).[35] If the single person's pension had been linked to prices and not earnings since it was introduced after the war, it would now be worth a mere £23.[36]

Michael Portillo, among others, has recently suggested that this first-tier pension should be abolished completely for the under-40s and replaced by occupational schemes or personal pension plans. We disagree. Only half of today's workers belong to occupational pension schemes and the decline in life-time employment within large organisations suggests that this proportion may well fall. Many personal pension schemes have been revealed as expensive and risky, and as every reputable life insurance company confirms, they are wholly unsuitable for the 2 million men and 6 million women earning less than £8,000 – £10,000 a year.[37]

Furthermore, the Portillo proposal would impose an unaccept-ably high double burden upon people under the age of forty when it was introduced. In addition to paying sufficient contributions to finance their own pensions, they would have to go on paying towards the pension rights already earned by older people. It is this transitional problem which, above all, rules out any proposals for trying to fund the basic pension. Furthermore, the growing inse-curity of the labour market, and the risk that more people will spend at least part of their lives in low-paid employment, makes the foundation of a basic PAYG pension essential.

Despite its important role, however, the national insurance retirement pension does not fulfil Beveridge's objectives of meet-ing the basic needs of elderly people. Currently paid at the rate of £57.60 to a single person and £92 to a married couple, the basic pension is anything up to £15 lower than Income Support levels (the gap being widest for people aged eighty or over, whose Income Support entitlements are higher). The difficulty facing any government is that an across-the-board increase in the basic pension is expensive (raising it to £80 for each pensioner would cost about £9 billion a year, even allowing for other savings). It would substantially help the poorest pensioners who fail to claim the Income Support for which they are eligible. But those claim-ing Income Support would benefit only if Income Support rates rose by the same amount, leaving the same number of elderly people dependent on means-tested benefits. If means-tested ben-efits were not increased, the increase in the basic pension would simply be deducted from Income Support, leaving 1.6 million poor pensioner households no better off, while wealthy pensioners enjoyed the benefit of the increase (minus the tax they paid on it). Under this proposal, a third of the total expenditure would go to elderly income-tax payers who, although generally not rich, are clearly not those most in need of help.

The Government's response to the dilemma has been to widen the gap between the basic pension and Income Support even further. But leaving more pensioners to depend upon means-tested benefit has two insuperable problems: many fail or refuse to claim it and are thus trapped in deepening poverty, as the relative value of the basic pension falls; and pensioners with modest savings find that they are no better off for having made the effort to save than those who were unable or unwilling to do so.

The best way of resolving this is to create a new *pension guarantee*, set at a level which is not only higher than today's basic pension but also above the present Income Support level. This proposal has been made by the Independent Pensions Research Group, amongst others. The aim is to ensure that every elderly person receives at least this guaranteed level of income, without the stigma and inefficiency of means-tests.

Under the guarantee, those reaching pension age after it was introduced would claim it automatically along with their basic retirement pension (and any other state pension entitlements, such as SERPS). Those who have already retired would have their guarantee entitlement calculated on the basis of the information already known to the Department of Social Security and the Inland Revenue, with a minimum of additional information required from a minority. The costs of the pension guarantee would depend upon the level at which it was set. Such a decision can only be made by government in the light of overall resources and other priorities; but we hope that the principle will commend itself.

Once established, the pension guarantee would need to rise faster than prices to prevent it from losing its relative value, as the basic pension has done. Pensions are often described as a percentage of 'average male earnings' which, in a workforce already nearly half women, is an inappropriate basis for comparison. The best way of ensuring that elderly people share in the rising living standards of the community would be to link the pension guarantee level with average net (after-tax) earnings. Within that framework, government would have the discretion each year to decide how rapidly the basic pension should rise, and could balance the extra costs of raising the basic pension by more than inflation against the benefits which doing so would offer to those just above the guarantee level.

The new pension guarantee could be developed in two different ways, each of which has its strengths and weaknesses. In the first approach, an individual or couple's *pensions* income – basic retirement pension, SERPS, occupational, personal and widow's pensions – would be added together and, if necessary, brought up to the guarantee level. If the total were already the same as or higher than the guarantee, they would receive no top-up, although their basic retirement and other state pensions would, of course, be paid in full. To deal with the problem that some people – including MPs and judges – can remain in well-paid employment beyond pension age, earnings above a certain level would also be taken into account when calculating any guarantee entitlement. (For example, £5,000 of earnings over a year could be ignored, allowing elderly people to supplement their pension with part-time or occasional work.)

In many cases, the guarantee payment could be adjusted automatically, along with upratings in the basic pension. Where no occupational or personal pension was payable, that fact would be included in the initial claim for the retirement pension; if a widow's occupational pension subsequently became payable, that too would be noted along with the claim for a widow's social insurance pension. Closer liaison with the Inland Revenue, leading to a complete integration of the social security and tax files for elderly taxpayers, would enable those with higher incomes to make a single return.

A pension guarantee implemented in this way would mean an end to means-testing for pensioners. There would be no test of assets or income other than pensions and earnings, and all those people now failing to claim Income Support would be substantially better off. There might, however, be a sense of unfairness between people whose occupational or personal pension scheme took them above the guarantee level, and those who were in no such pension scheme but had saved for their retirement through, say, a building society, and therefore received the guarantee payment as well. It could, however, be argued that people with an occupational or personal pension had already received substantial benefits from tax relief, which were not available to people who had saved through a building society. Although it is also possible that younger people would switch their money out of pension schemes into other forms of savings which would leave them free to claim the guarantee top-up as well, the problem could be minimised by ensuring that all working people contribute to a pension scheme.

A different approach to the pensions guarantee would take into account income not just from pension schemes but from all

---

The Pension Guarantee

The Problem: the basic retirement pension is lower than means-tested Income Support. Thousands of elderly people do not claim the Income Support to which they are entitled. An across-the-board increase in the basic pension, however, is extremely expensive and would not help the people who are claiming Income Support.

The Social Justice Strategy: a new pension guarantee.
Everyone reaching pension age would claim the retirement pension in the usual way. All their pensions – the basic pension, SERPS and any occupational or personal pension – would be added together, and if necessary an extra amount would be added to their basic pension to bring them up to the level of the pension guarantee. Unlike Income Support, where earnings above a small limit produce an immediate reduction in benefit, the pension guarantee would only take account of substantial earnings (say £5,000 a year). Unlike Income Support, which cannot be claimed by anyone with assets of £8,000 or more and which assumes quite unrealistic returns on capital, the pension guarantee would ignore assets although it could take account of actual savings income above a certain level.

---

savings and assets. As before, those whose pensions and other income fell below the guarantee level would receive a top-up payment; those above would not. Only the investment income actually received would be taken into account (unlike the Income Support system which assumes a notional, and wildly unrealistic, income from people's assets). The administration of the guarantee could still be streamlined, although more declarations would be needed as, for instance, a pensioner's rental or savings income rose or fell. Although treatment of assets would differ from the present Income Support rules, this approach might be seen as being closer to traditional means-testing, with the risk that some people who have already retired would continue not to claim.

In practice, however, the difference between these two approaches is unlikely to be as great as it seems. Among today's retired people, one-third have no income at all from investments or savings; one-third receive less than £8 a week; and only a third have weekly income of £8 or more.[38] If savings income up to, say, £500 a year were ignored, the guarantee payment in the second scheme would be calculated in exactly the same way as under the first scheme for the majority of elderly people; but the possible problem of giving a guarantee payment to a well-off pensioner with high investment income, but no occupational or personal pension, would be avoided.

Both the basic pension and the pension guarantee should remain in place for future generations of retired people. But they should be a foundation of pension provision, rather than the whole edifice, as people become entitled to second-tier pensions from occupational pension schemes, personal pensions or the State Earnings Related Pension Scheme (SERPS). It is essential to ensure that all these schemes provide good benefits for as many people as possible.

Second pensions for all

In theory, everyone now at work is contributing to a second pension, either through SERPS (introduced in 1975 by Barbara Castle when she was Secretary of State for Social Services) or through an occupational scheme or approved personal pension plan. In practice, millions of people are not doing so, including many of the self-employed who are excluded from SERPS and not required to join any other scheme, as well as people earning too little to pay National Insurance Contributions. Although people who are unemployed, sick, receiving Invalid Care Allowance or staying at home to care for children receive contribution credits to protect their basic retirement pension, they are not credited with SERPS contributions and 'home responsibilities' protection for SERPS will not begin until 2000.

Only about half the workforce is covered by occupational pension schemes, which declined during the 1980s as the public sector and large companies – the traditional bastions of occupational schemes – have shrunk. Schemes which calculate pensions on the basis of final salary penalise early leavers in the interests of those who stay until retirement. They effectively redistribute money from the lower-paid to the higher-paid and from women to men. Pensions for widows are not always adequate, those for widowers usually non-existent, and divorce can destroy the accumulated rights of a married woman to a pension on her husband's death. Employees who joined such schemes in the 1960s and 1970s, and have stayed in membership ever since, will benefit considerably when they come to retire; but they are a minority and, given the employment patterns that are emerging, occupational pension schemes seem likely to decline.

The personal pension schemes that formed the centrepiece of Conservative government policy have proved, in many cases, disastrous. As the Securities and Investments Board revealed, up to half a million people may have been wrongly advised by insurance company sales representatives to leave occupational pension schemes for personal pensions which, in virtually every case, attracted no employer's contributions and were marred by high commissions and administrative charges. Personal pensions can work well for young people who are likely to earn well and to move often. But many of those who have taken out personal pensions are earning below about £8,000 a year – with the result that most, and sometimes all, of their contributions in the early years (when many policies are surrendered) will be absorbed in the costs of selling and running the scheme. Add to that the risk that the insurance company's investments may underperform, and that annuity rates may be highly unfavourable when the personal-pension holder retires, and it becomes easy to see that future generations of retired people will include many who have been cheated out of the expectations they were offered. This entirely foreseeable disaster has, furthermore, been subsidised by taxpayers through rebates costing over £8 billion in 1993/4 designed to attract people out of SERPS and into personal pensions.[39]

Neither occupational nor personal pension schemes can guarantee people's living standards after they retire. Contracted-out occupational schemes are currently required to increase pensions in line with prices, up to a maximum of 3 per cent. Personal pensions offer no such guarantee. (After 1997 the situation will improve a little, with the whole of any deferred salary-related pension accrued after that date having to be revalued with prices up to 5 per cent). The chances of an occupational or personal pension being increased in line with *earnings* are remote. Thus a second pension which is reasonable at the age of sixty or sixty-five may be inadequate by the age of eight-five or ninety. For people in this situation (as well as for those with little or no second pension at all), the continuation of the basic pension and the introduction of a pensions guarantee are vital.

Our objective is to overcome these problems and ensure a second pension for all citizens. The main features of our proposals are:

- Every employee or self-employed person will belong to a properly regulated second pension scheme of their choice. Personal pension plans, in particular, will be required to meet higher standards.
- Working people and their employers will make a minimum second pension contribution; additional optional contributions will also be encouraged.
- Contributions will be paid or credited to people who are unemployed or caring for people at home.
- Every year, contributors will receive a statement of the total pension they have earned so far and the target pension they could expect to reach.

There are two ways in which this aim could be achieved. The first approach is to improve the present combination of occupational, personal and SERPS pensions, particularly by improving and extending SERPS. The second is to ensure that everyone in work saves towards retirement through a fund where members' contributions are invested for the future, with government making additional contributions for people who are unemployed, ill or caring for children or other dependents. In either case, it is essential that government tackles the scandal of inadequately regulated personal pensions, and improves the regulation of occupational pension schemes. As with our proposed pension guarantee, much wider debate is needed before a new government carries out any proposals, but the objective itself should be firmly accepted.

Option 1: Improving SERPS

There are several ways in which SERPS could be strengthened in order to help achieve our aim of a universal second pension. First, the self-employed should be allowed to join. Indeed, as with social insurance, the aim should be to bring all self-employed people into a second pension scheme.

Second, home-responsibilities protection could be introduced before the year 2000 and extended to people involved in caring for only part of the year (instead of being restricted to those with home responsibilities for a full tax year, as now proposed). Third, SERPS could be made more generous. SERPS pensions are based on earnings on which National Insurance Contributions are paid (in today's terms, between £57 and £430 a week). The original plan was that pensions should eventually be 25 per cent of the contributor's earnings averaged out over their best twenty years – a formula designed particularly to help women with broken employment records. In 1986, however, the Government changed the formula for people retiring after 2000, so that SERPS will now only provide 20 per cent of earnings averaged across the whole working lifetime. In effect, this reduced by more than half the amounts it would provide. Restoring the '20 best years' rule would be an important but expensive step towards providing decent second pensions for the people who are most vulnerable to poverty in retirement. The SERPS formula could also be made more favourable to low-paid workers by including earnings below the national insurance threshold in the pension calculation.

Assessments of this option depend upon one's view of SERPS. There are many arguments to be made in its favour. It provides a second pension for part-time employees and low-paid workers, who are usually outside occupational pension schemes and whose earnings are so low that the administrative costs of a personal pension could eat up most of their contributions. (In 1991/2, half of the 4.2 million women who are now members of SERPS earned below £3,700 a year, and half of the 3.4 million men below £7,400). Seventy per cent of all SERPS members were earning below £10,000 a year.[40]

SERPS is also particularly good for women, who are more likely to be poor in old age than men, and, unlike personal pension plans where retirement income depends entirely on investment performance and interest rates, SERPS offers a guaranteed pension based on earlier earnings. Furthermore, because contributors can remain in it no matter how often they change jobs, it is ideally suited to an increasingly mobile labour market. SERPS is consistent with the approach taken in most other European Union countries, where earnings-related pensions (generally far more generous than in the British state scheme) are provided on a pay-as-you-go basis. Finally, SERPS provides the basis for regulating occupational pension schemes, which are generally required at least to match its benefits. For these reasons, some members of the Commission favour this approach and would reject Option 2, which proposes a funded scheme.

Several arguments can, however, be made against option 1. SERPS offers today's workers higher pensions than are paid to today's retired people. Because it is a pay-as-you-go scheme, it requires future workers to pay higher contributions than today's workers: the more generous the formula, the greater the contributions required in future. Where both the population and real income levels are growing, each new generation of workers can afford to pay a higher pension to each new generation of pensioners. In the UK, however, these conditions are no longer met and are unlikely to be so in future.[41] As a Pay-As-You-Go

(PAYG) scheme, therefore, SERPS suffers from political risks: even if a new government were to introduce a more generous formula, a change of government could reduce it again and future taxpayers might resist the increased contributions that would be needed to finance the increased benefits. Although other countries have long-established PAYG pension schemes – Germany's, for instance, has survived nearly a century of political upheaval – this country has failed to create a sustained consensus about pension arrangements, and Conservative support for SERPS in 1974 proved short-lived.

The second problem is that running SERPS alongside funded private schemes requires complicated contribution rebates so that people in the different systems are treated fairly. The more government tries to make the system fair to people of different ages, the more complicated it becomes.

A third difficulty is that the present combination of SERPS and a basic pension linked to prices will in the longer term *reduce* government expenditure on pensions for people with very low earnings or who have suffered long periods of unemployment, while increasing it for the higher-paid. Our proposed pension guarantee would, however, help deal with this problem.

Option 2: Funded second pensions

A different way of creating a universal second pension would be to ensure that every earner saves for retirement through a funded scheme which invests contributions to finance future pensions. Additional contributions, paid by government out of current resources, would help people maintain pension contributions if they are unemployed, sick, or caring for someone at home.

Under this option, every employee and self-employed person would make a minimum contribution to a funded pension scheme of their choice, with a matching contribution for employees from their employers. They would be able to choose between occupational pension schemes, properly regulated personal pension plans, the new 'industry schemes' which trade unions are beginning to set up, and a new National Savings Pension Scheme. Older working people (those over the age of forty-five or fifty), whose contributions could not be invested long enough to earn a reasonable return would remain in SERPS. For everyone else, SERPS would be wound up in its present, pay-as-you-go form, although entitlements earned to date would, of course, be preserved.

A careful judgment would need to be made about the level of the minimum second pension contribution. At the moment, people contracting out of SERPS receive a rebate of 4.8 per cent (divided between employer and employee), with an additional 1 per cent 'incentive' rebate to people over thirty moving into personal pension schemes. If, however, every member of SERPS were to contract out at this level, the National Insurance fund would be short of the money it needs to pay today's pensions. One way to overcome this problem would be to estimate the rebate which could be made available if every contributor were to opt out of SERPS, without requiring any increase in National Insurance Contributions to finance present benefits.[42] This rebate would then become the minimum contribution (divided between employers and employees) to the funded second pension, which would apply from the same level of earnings (currently £56 a week) as National Insurance Contributions. People receiving a social insurance benefit (because they are unemployed or on maternity or parental leave, for instance) should also have their pension rights protected through the payment of the minimum pension contribution into their pension scheme.

As with Option 1, second pensions would be extended to all self-employed people. Given the growth of self-employment – and the risk that unscrupulous employers will try to save on pension contributions by turning employees into self-employed subcontractors – the self-employed should be expected to make the same minimum contribution, and those to whom they sell their services (effectively, their employers) should do the same.

A minimum contribution based on the present rebates would be well below the 15–20 per cent joint contribution which is paid into most occupational pension schemes, although properly invested it would produce a *higher* pension for someone now below the age of forty than SERPS will do following the present Government's changes. The National Association of Pension Funds estimates that someone aged thirty who wants to retire at

278

sixty with a second pension of 50 per cent of their earnings needs to invest 15 per cent of their annual pay. It is clearly impossible for many workers and their employers to approach anything of this order, which in any case does not take account of the basic pension. Instead, the minimum pension contribution should start low, with additional voluntary contributions permitted and indeed encouraged by the continuation of tax relief on them. As people's earnings rise in future years, however, it is vital that some of the increase be earmarked for a higher investment in pensions.

The first argument in favour of this option is that it asks today's working people to accept the responsibility of saving towards higher pensions in their own retirement, rather than promising ourselves higher pensions on the assumption that future generations will pay. The cost of pension provision therefore becomes more obvious. Second, funded pensions create individual ownership rights, making it much harder for a future government to undermine people's pension entitlements in the way that the present government has done with SERPS. Although funded pension schemes involve financial risks, a 'mixed economy' of a pay-as-you-go first tier and a properly regulated, funded second tier can create a sensible balance of political and financial risks.

Higher pensions for future pensioners have to be paid for, one way or another, and higher contributions are more likely to be acceptable when they take the form of personal savings rather than higher taxes. Funded schemes can offer a high degree of flexibility – individual choice of retirement age, higher benefits in return for higher contributions, and so on – which is difficult to create within a PAYG scheme.

Although most other European Union countries operate extensive PAYG pension schemes, the projected increase in the proportion of elderly people (which is considerably lower in the UK) and the extent of unfunded pension liabilities are beginning to cause serious concern. In Sweden, which has a longstanding, earnings-related PAYG system, a review of pension policy by an all-party group concluded that the combination of an ageing population and sluggish economic growth made the present policy unsustainable. They now propose to combine a new basic pension guarantee with a universal second pension based on the contributions paid by each individual during their working lives, supplemented by additional contributions for people not employed. Australia too has recently introduced national superannuation for all working people, with contributions gradually building up over the next ten years.

Critics of this option, including some members of the Commission, argue, however, that any second-tier pension which requires only a minimum level of contribution but no minimum level of benefit cannot guarantee the level of income people receive in retirement. 'Money purchase' schemes – in which the pension simply depends upon investment performance – leave people completely vulnerable to the ups and downs of the financial markets and the strengths or weaknesses of their particular fund managers. The critics prefer the first option, in which SERPS offers a guaranteed minimum that opted-out pension schemes are required to match. The relative merits of 'defined benefit' and 'defined contribution' schemes are hotly contested by pension experts; although 'defined benefit' schemes (such as the majority of occupational pension schemes, where the pension is linked to final salary) have traditionally been preferred in Britain, recent research suggests that 'defined contribution' schemes would have delivered higher pensions for the majority of occupational pension scheme members over the last few decades.[43] None the less, only a defined benefit scheme can guarantee the pension it offers in relation to previous earnings.

The second problem with funded second pensions is that they are not necessarily any more secure than those based on PAYG. Governments can substantially reduce the value of occupational or personal pensions by changing their tax treatment: altering contribution rebates, for example, or imposing tougher regulations. Furthermore, funded schemes face substantial capital market risks: different schemes will produce completely different investment returns, while the pension acquired when someone retires will depend on the interest rates at the time. Third, as we have seen, personal pension schemes often have extremely high administration charges and sales commissions, which eat up much of the individual's contributions. If personal pensions remained in their present state, moving towards a funded second-tier pension for everyone would be quite unacceptable.

Both options for a universal second pension – improving SERPS and creating new funded schemes – require effective regulation of occupational and personal pensions.

Second pensions: regulation

Occupational pension schemes, obviously, would remain in existence under either of these options, although the legal basis of their operation must be reformed to prevent further scandals. We therefore support, as a necessary but not final step, the various recommendations of the Goode Committee Report *Pension Law Reform*, the key recommendations of which were the establishment of a Pensions Regulator with wide-ranging powers; the appointment by scheme members of at least one-third of the Trustees (with a minimum of two); the enforcement of minimum solvency requirements; restrictions on withdrawal of surplus; and a compensation scheme to cover deficits arising from fraud and theft. We therefore regret that the present Government has stopped short of implementing these recommendations in full, and that the new Regulator has fewer powers than those proposed. We believe, in any case, that the Goode Committee did not go far enough. Because there is still no compensation if an employer goes bankrupt and there is a deficit which is not due to fraud or theft, people will continue to find that their pensions are less well protected than their package holiday. Furthermore, we want to see early leavers – who are the majority of occupational pension scheme members – treated far more equitably than they are at present. The real value of early leavers' accrued rights must either be preserved and increased in line with investment performance or transferred to another fund. Although widows can inherit substantial pensions from their husbands' occupational schemes, these rights are lost to women whose marriages end in divorce. And although some allowance of their value may be made in dividing other assets, the pension rights themselves (which are usually the man's) cannot be divided. In future, the courts should at least be given the power to divide pension rights or, better still, be required to do so.

In Australia, the introduction of national superannuation has been followed by the creation of 'industrial pension schemes', initiated by trade unions and managed by independent companies. The great advantage of these schemes is that they offer complete pensions security as members move from one job to another and, by virtue of their size, can offer very low administrative costs as well as effective protection against fluctuations in the financial markets. In this country many unions (including the GMB, TGWU, UNISON and USDAW) are applying the lessons learned by Australian practice to develop industry schemes for their members.

Good personal pension schemes will also have a place within the range of second pension providers. But they must be properly regulated, with the present system of self-regulation replaced by statutory controls. In particular, they should be required to publish full details of their commissions and administrative charges; and insurance company directors should personally be penalised if the company persists in selling personal pension contracts to those for whom they produce little or no gain. Bad personal pension schemes could also be put out of business by the creation of a low-risk, low-cost, funded pension scheme to take the place of SERPS. This could take the form of a National Savings Pensions Plan, as proposed to us by Joel Joffe, formerly Deputy Chairman of Allied Dunbar and a powerful critic of the present state of personal pension schemes.

The National Savings Pensions Plan (NSPP) would offer a completely secure investment with very low charges for investors, acting as a spur to competitors within the industry. It would be kept as simple as possible, meeting the needs of people on lower incomes and others who do not want the more elaborate products offered by financial service companies. Marketing and publicity for the NSPP would be combined with National Savings, although investment management would be done at arms-length from government. Pension contributions would be invested in index-linked funds, which could include government funds as well as a fund which 'tracked' the FTSE 100 – effectively, investing in the British economy. At retirement, contributors would be able to use their accumulated fund to purchase pensions on the open market if life companies offered better rates than the NSPP.

If universal second pensions are to offer real security, further reforms need to be made to financial institutions. At the moment, the fund available when an occupational or personal pension contributor reaches pension age must be used to purchase an annuity on the day of retirement (except for any lump sum taken). People who have the bad luck to retire on a day when the Stock Market is low will suffer for the rest of their lives from the depressed value of their pension fund. The same applies if annuity rates are unfavourable. One answer is to change the Treasury's pension rules so that the person retiring, if necessary, can use part of their capital to live on for a certain period and purchase an annuity later. Industry schemes and the NSPP offer possibilities for pooling risks in ways which personal pension plans cannot manage; they are, therefore, particularly suited to the needs of lower-paid workers.

Retirement age

At present, the basic pension is paid to men at the age of sixty-five, women at sixty. Although it continues to be called a 'retirement' pension, this is misleading: the abolition of the earnings rule has effectively transformed it into an 'old age' pension. The Government has announced plans to raise women's pension age to sixty-five in gradual stages between 2010 and 2020.

Since women on average live longer than men, their lower pension age has always been hard to justify. It was introduced in the first place to encourage more women into employment and to reflect the fact that women tended to marry men older than themselves. Many people would argue that raising women's pension age now is unfair to women, who have contributed in the expectation of being able to claim at sixty and for whom an earlier pension offers some compensation for their lower average lifetime earnings. There also seems to be a contradiction between raising women's pension age and the steady decline in men's effective retirement age, with 59 per cent of men aged between fifty-five to sixty-four now out of employment, compared to 8 per cent in 1977.[44]

Occupational pension schemes have already been required, under European Community law, to equalise pension ages, and the majority are doing so at the age of sixty-five. Clearly, unequal pension ages within the state system could not be allowed to continue. Reducing men's entitlement age to sixty, however, would cost £3.4 billion a year and would accelerate the trend to early retirement.[45] Although equalising the entitlement age for men and women at 63 would not impose additional costs, it would mean forfeiting the savings which will come in future from a common pension age of sixty-five. But as people live longer and as health improves, further reducing the working lifetime and increasing the retirement period does not make sense, particularly when retirement is enforced and not chosen. Expanding employment and tackling age discrimination should enable more older people to remain in work, in some cases combining part-time earnings with a partial pension. Where people have managed to save enough during their working lives to finance earlier (full-time or part-time) retirement, occupational and personal pensions can offer enormous flexibility in choice of retirement age, and our universal second pension will help to extend this choice more widely.

We do not, however, think that it is a priority for present or future public expenditure to reduce the age at which men can claim the basic pension. Of course, government must protect the rights earned by women who have contributed for a very long time in the expectation of being able to claim their pensions at 60; any change in the pension age, therefore, should not affect women now within fifteen years of pension age. But it is quite reasonable to start phasing in a common pension age of sixty-five in the next century, for both the basic pension and our proposed pension guarantee, provided that the savings are properly used. The Social Security Advisory Committee proposed, for instance, that resources could be invested in an improved SERPS, enhanced home responsibilities protection, the extension of Invalid Care Allowance to women up to the age of 65 and the raising of the ICA and the Severe Disablement Allowance.[46] We would endorse their view that equalisation of the pension age at sixty-five must be linked to plans to use the savings to help the most vulnerable groups, as many of the measures we have ourselves proposed are designed to do.

Health, Care and Social Justice

This country is scarred by health inequalities. The poorest and least powerful members of our society are ill more often and die younger. Along with the gap between rich and poor, the gap between healthy and unhealthy has grown wider in the last decade, a direct result of more unemployment, more poverty, more stress, and greater social inequality itself. The health gap between different social classes, different regions and different communities is not inevitable and is simply unacceptable. In a just society, everyone should be able to enjoy the best possible health and to receive as far as possible the treatment and care they need.

Discussion about health policy in the United Kingdom usually starts and ends with the National Health Service. We have taken a much wider view of the fundamental questions that our society needs to resolve. The first issue we address is how best to promote good health and reduce health inequalities. The second is how inevitably limited resources within the NHS can best be used and allocated. The third is how to meet rapidly growing needs for community care. We have not, however, tackled the complex issues which arise from the present internal reorganisation of the NHS; they would require a commission of their own.

Promoting better health

Improving the health of those who are now most at risk involves far more than just the National Health Service. In the past, the biggest leaps forward in life-expectancy have come just as much from public health measures – such as the introduction of improved sanitary and water facilities in the nineteenth century – as from advances in treatment. Achieving the right balance between policies and investment to cure illness, and those designed to promote health, is a peculiarly difficult challenge: the needs of the ill are immediate, while the possibility of health promotion is longer term. But it is essential that we start with the goal of improving health and reducing health inequalities – in other words, health gain – rather than allowing health policy to be dominated by the treatment of illness.

Our aim is not to eliminate all health differences, for that would be impossible, but rather to reduce or eliminate those that result from factors which are both avoidable and unfair. Sadly, the Government's White Paper on public health, *Health of the Nation*, dismissed health inequalities between rich and poor as 'the result of a complex interplay [of factors which are not] fully understood'. In fact, we have a very good idea of the causes of health inequality and, therefore, of what needs to be done.

There are four factors affecting people's health that can often be influenced by public policy: individual lifestyle; social and community networks; living and working conditions; and general social, economic and environmental circumstances.

People's own lifestyles include activities which directly affect their health, such as smoking, drinking, diet and exercise. Children are also seriously affected by their parents' lifestyle, for instance by passive smoking, and by what parents know about diet and are able to provide in the way of food. Far more could be done by government, beginning with a ban on tobacco advertising and more rigorous food labelling.

But individual lifestyle is not just a matter of individual choice; it is directly affected by broader social and economic conditions. Poor people have less to spend on food and many low-income parents often end up going without food themselves in order to feed their children. Not only is healthy food more expensive generally, but low-income families often live in areas where healthy food is hard to find and all food costs more. In Easterhouse, in Glasgow, we were told that before a food co-op was established, the main source of food was the roving vans, typically charging 20p more for a loaf of bread than in the city's main shopping centres. The stress of unemployment and poverty is one of the main reasons why poorer people are more likely to smoke, helping to create a vicious circle of poorer health.

The quality of social support and networks available to families also contributes to their health. Isolation can compound stress, which itself is a major contributor to mental and physical ill-health. When people with little money live on a badly vandalised estate with no social facilities and no transport they can afford, even good health comes under pressure. Women who have little money and remain home all day to look after small children are particularly vulnerable to depression and other problems of mental health.

The broader conditions in which people live and work are equally influential. Poor people are more likely to work in dangerous conditions, unhealthy environments or in jobs where they have little control over what they do. It is also the people in lower-paid, less skilled and therefore less healthy occupations who are most vulnerable to unemployment and the stress and ill-health which go with it. Equally, poor families are more likely to live in lower-quality housing where there is more damp, more overcrowding, more pollution in areas around the home, more stress associated with nuisance, vandalism and the risk of crime. In many parts of Britain's cities, Asian families live in fear of racist violence which – in addition to its impact on the victims – threatens the normal life of the community and often produces serious mental ill-health.

Even that most basic necessity of healthy living – clean water – is becoming harder for many families to secure. In 1993, more than 12,000 homes in England and Wales had their water supplies cut off for failure to pay the bills. The compulsory introduction of volumetric water meters in new or refurbished homes causes poorer families to reduce consumption and puts hygiene and health at risk. Pay-as-you-go meters, which are starting to be introduced on a trial basis, may cause poorer families effectively to cut off their own supplies, simply because the money has run out. In the interests of good health, government should ban water authorities from disconnecting supplies and end the compulsory introduction of meters.

Finally, the general social, economic and environmental conditions in which we all live profoundly affect our health. In London, for instance, the rapid rise in diagnosed asthma over the last ten years is generally attributed to the rise in levels of pollution. Local and national transport policies can have a direct bearing on the health of adults – particularly the elderly – and, even more so, children.

By analysing the different causes of good and poor health, we can understand why tackling inequalities in health goes well beyond what is conventionally thought of as health policy. The best way to reduce health inequalities is to ensure a more equitable distribution of income; better distributed and better quality jobs; higher standards of education and childcare; a healthier environment with clean and affordable water and better housing, transport and leisure facilities. The economic and social strategies for which we argue throughout this book are not only desirable in themselves, they are the best way to close the health gap in this country.

Setting goals for health gain

It is essential that government sets clear goals for reducing health inequalities (something which the present Government signally failed to do in *Health of the Nation*). For instance, through health, employment and child care programmes, Sweden has succeeded in achieving virtually the same infant mortality rate for every social class. In Merseyside, local health experts have proposed that by the year 2000 infant mortality rates and low birth weight rates in the most disadvantaged local area should be raised to those of the best-off area. Infant mortality rates are an important reflection of broader health inequalities, and we would like to see the British Government commit itself to the goal of steadily cutting infant mortality and morbidity rates in the bottom social classes until the present gap is eliminated. These goals should be accompanied by clear strategies, so that all those responsible for other areas of policy know the contribution which they are expected to make to promoting better health; and progress towards the goals should be monitored and published.

The new emphasis that we want to see on health promotion will require national and local government to take a fundamentally new approach to health. Instead of health being viewed as the concern only of the Department of Health and the regional and local health authorities, it should be integrated into the work of every government department. For instance, relevant initiatives from other departments could include a 'health impact statement'. Locally and regionally, there is no doubt that health policy suffers from the division of responsibilities (except in Northern Ireland) between local authorities (health promotion, social services and community care) and health authorities and hospital trusts (NHS services), although the creation of integrated elected authorities would require further administrative upheaval. Whatever the structures, every area must have a community-health needs assessment to form the basis for health promotion targets, and a programme that actively engages public, private and voluntary organisations, as well as individuals, in meeting them. This reorientation of health policy towards health promotion is central to the policy drawn up by the African National Congress (ANC), with the assistance of the World Health Organisation, for the new South Africa: 'Primary healthcare offers the only viable alternative for sustainable and equitable health developments ... Primary healthcare, with its concern for equity in healthcare, using available appropriate resources, is the best possible form of healthcare for everyone, rich and poor alike, in any society.'

Equal access to health services

Although good health involves so much more than the National Health Service, it is also vital to ensure that the NHS continues to deliver the best possible treatment to those who are ill and that everyone has equal access to that treatment, regardless of their ability to pay.

Despite criticisms, the NHS has been remarkably successful in promoting equal access to healthcare. Although one study found that elderly men with low incomes were less likely to use their GPs than better-off men with otherwise similar needs, the pattern was the reverse for elderly women. Amongst adults suffering from acute or chronic illness, the poorest are more likely to see a GP than the richest. Good primary care can help people transform their lives. In Easterhouse, for instance, we met Carol, who was raped when she was fourteen and whose first baby was taken into local authority care. 'I was on so many drugs for my depression that I didn't know what I was doing,' she told us. 'Then I met my boyfriend – we're now married – and the council threatened to take our new baby into care too. But this new GP got me off the drugs and helped me sort myself out. Both the children are back with us and we're really happy.' At the St Dismas Centre in Southampton, we saw an example of the 'outreach' work which NHS primary care needs to provide; in this case, nurses offer a drop-in facility and immediate treatment for homeless people, almost all of whom are not even registered with a GP, and guide them towards any specialist services they need.

Unfortunately, there is other evidence that people in poorer families and in some minority ethnic groups get less satisfactory treatment. Not only are well-informed, middle-class people often better at getting what they need from the Health Service, but the creation of fundholding GP practices (which are in any case more common in middle-class areas) is already producing a two-tier service which is unjust and unacceptable. A study in the North Thames region found that fundholding practices have more money per patient for both inpatient and outpatient hospital services.[47] Low-income areas – both inner-city and rural – tend to have fewer GPs; and sadly, as the Tomlinson Report study revealed, there are more poor quality GPs in deprived areas.

Cultural and language barriers also stand between the Health Service and some ethnic-minority patients. Some health centres have provided sensitive education for Asian women which has substantially raised the take-up of cervical smear tests. Progress has been made in many hospitals in recognising different needs, for instance by providing a wider variety of food and menus in different languages. Every hospital, residential home, care unit and GP should learn from these and other models of good practice.

Every health authority should be under a statutory duty to reduce inequities in health care provision. Although it is not possible to guarantee equal *outcomes* from health care, it is possible to promote equal access to health treatment. The aim should be to give people in the most deprived communities GP and hospital services which are as good as the best offered by the NHS within that region, although it will take many years to close the gap which now exists. Local people and patients, as well as health experts, must be involved in identifying the most serious inequities and the best ways of reducing them. In particular, ethnic-minority communities must be engaged in ensuring that health services meet their specific needs.

Health rights

The right of equal access to health care should be part of a broader vision of social rights. If citizens are to enjoy a 'right to health', the right to health treatment and care must be seen as fundamental. The right to good health cannot in general be treated as a *legal* right; it is a moral and social right, to be realised through political action.

Fairer treatment within the health service itself, however, can be assisted by giving patients clear and enforceable rights. A choice of doctor, information about treatment, access to second opinions and limits on waiting times are all important. So also are principles of consent and confidentiality. The Patient's Charter has better defined these rights, but only to a limited extent, since it is not law. Generally, people should have a right to the fair distribution of all health and social services, with decision-makers under an explicit duty to treat people equally and consistently, aided by clear rights of access, appeal and complaint.

Funding health

There is clear evidence of underfunding within the NHS: long waiting-lists, closed wards, dilapidated hospitals, underpaid and overworked staff. Funding the NHS raises two questions, both of them difficult. The first is what share of national resources to devote to the NHS, compared with other priorities; the second, how to allocate scarce resources within the NHS.

Since good health is the result of factors that are almost entirely outside the control of the NHS, the goal of improving people's health will be served by spending outside and not only within the NHS, while the balance of NHS resources needs to be shifted further towards prevention rather than treatment. Spending a larger proportion of national income on the treatment of illness does not necessarily improve a nation's health. The USA, which spends the highest proportion of income on health care of all the OECD countries, has shockingly high infant-mortality rates. We undoubtedly need to invest more in our own health, but generally that will be better done through investment in health promotion and in wider social, environmental and economic programmes, than through spending substantially more on the treatment of illness. Preventing heart disease makes more sense than paying for heart transplants.

For that reason, we are extremely sceptical about the proposal for an earmarked 'health tax' which has recently become fashionable. It is argued that such a tax would make NHS costs more obvious and encourage people to pay more towards a better service. (Expressed in terms of income tax, the NHS costs about 14p out of the standard rate of 25p.) The problem is that an NHS tax would in reality be an illness tax, not a better-health tax. Earmarked by the Department of Health, it would inevitably be devoted to the health services rather than to the wider strategies which could do far more to cut child mortality, reduce chronic disease and enable people to lead healthier lives. The immediacy of health treatment needs, combined with a 'health tax', could push up NHS spending very rapidly indeed, without necessarily producing any real health gain. Policies for financing should not reinforce the view that health means treating illness.

Deciding priorities

Since 1973, NHS spending has doubled in real terms, but waiting-lists have grown longer. The increased numbers of very elderly people, together with the fact that NHS costs rise faster than prices generally, help to explain the discrepancy: once these factors are taken into account, NHS resources are in fact about one-third above what they were twenty years ago.[48]

There are good reasons to be sceptical about alarmist fears that the NHS will break the national bank. The costs of an ageing population will add less to the health budget over the next twenty-five years than has already been absorbed over the last ten.[49] While it is true that most countries, as they get richer, spend a higher proportion of their total national income on health services, this may simply reflect people's desire, as they become better off, to invest more in their own health.

Projecting current spending into the future ignores the possibility that demand for health care could change quite fundamentally. It may grow and, clearly, new treatments will continue to become available for illnesses which are now effectively untreatable. But not all new treatments are expensive: one effect of medical technology is to enable people to diagnose some conditions themselves (pregnancy and blood cholesterol tests are now available over the counter, instead of only in the surgery), while much of the surgery now performed expensively in hospital will in future be performed far more efficiently in GP practices, health centres or newly-developed specialist day-care centres. Better investment in health promotion should reduce the demands for some kind of treatments, and this effect of health-gain measures should be carefully monitored.

Whatever level of funding is available for the NHS, however, there will always be hard choices about who gets what treatment. These have existed since the NHS was founded. In the days when people believed that professionals always knew best, the decisions were left to the doctors and not generally exposed to public scrutiny. The creation of an 'internal market' in the NHS, and the purchaser/provider split, have now brought these issues to the surface; the decisions by many health authorities to restrict in vitro fertilisation treatment for infertile couples is one example. The old system was inadequate; the new system, which has transferred many decisions from doctors to accountants and managers, is even worse. But priorities there must be, and we urgently need better ways of deciding them.

There are many different ways of rationing medical treatment, including waiting lists, charges or co-payments, or the substitution of cheaper for more expensive treatments.[50] Providing patients with better information about the possible risks of treatment and the alternatives to drugs or surgery is also a way of reducing demand for expensive interventions. At the most extreme, a particular treatment may simply be withheld. All of these approaches already exist in one form or another within the NHS.

Decisions about priorities can also be made in different ways. They may be made openly or in secret; by doctors, by administrators and accountants, or by involving many other people, including the public. In Oregon, USA, the health authorities conducted a public opinion poll to order health care priorities. Some health economists have proposed the use of QALYs – 'Quality Adjusted Life Years' – which rank treatments on the basis of a cost-benefit analysis. Whoever makes the decisions, and on whatever basis they are made, priorities can only be sensibly settled if far more is known than at present about what forms of treatment and care are effective, and who now gets what. If some forms of treatment (whether surgical or pharmaceutical) are shown to be largely ineffective, or only partly effective and then only at very high price, then there is no good reason for them to be generally available. On the other hand, if some treatments are demonstrably more effective than others, despite being also more expensive, we may wish to see them in general use rather than barring them on cost grounds. It is essential that government and medical research institutes invest in the research which will enable better decisions of this kind to be made.

As better information becomes available, we believe that the best approach to the problem of priorities is to involve not only doctors (who remain the people whom the public most trust), nurses and other professionals, but also the wider public. This does not mean adopting Oregon's populist approach: majority views must not become the arbiter of individual or minority rights. But the preferences of the public – the actual and potential patients, as well as the funders of health services – should certainly be brought into play, not only through qualitative opinion research and 'deliberative polls', but more directly through community consultation at a local level. To combat the risk that this process will simply ignore the needs of people with mental illness or learning disabilities, or those of the poor and inarticulate, it is essential to develop advocates for these groups, through self-help and other voluntary organisations.

One possible outcome of a national debate on priorities would be the creation of a universal healthcare guarantee setting out the treatment which would be available as of right and within a specified time limit throughout the country. The development of such a guarantee would require a substantial process of research and consultation, perhaps through a new Standing Commission on Healthcare. It would, however, begin to transform the moral right to treatment into a legally enforceable right. Treatment and care not included within the healthcare guarantee would either not be offered by the NHS at all (if, for instance, it had been found to have no value), or it could continue to be provided on the present basis. A healthcare guarantee could, however, mean that the NHS budget, like the social security budget, was dictated by levels of demand, rather than by an overall judgment of the resources available. In practice, therefore, any such guarantee would have to depend in part upon what could be afforded, as well as upon what was desirable and effective, although local or regional health authorities might choose to seek additional local revenue to fund further treatments. Despite the difficulties involved, we think the idea of a healthcare guarantee is worth further debate as our society comes to grips with the problem of reconciling healthcare needs and healthcare resources.

There will always be some treatments that are not provided by the NHS (at present, these include tattoo removal and most other cosmetic surgery as well as many forms of 'complementary' medicine), while others may not be available as rapidly as people wish. Some people will always be able to buy private treatment here or abroad, and it is not up to government to forbid this, nor is it practical for government to do so. There is no reason, however, why taxpayers should be asked to subsidise private treatments, as they are with tax relief given to elderly people on medical insurance premiums. This relief, which costs some £85 million a year, should be abolished. But the NHS is also funding the training of most private medical and nursing staff, and there is a good case for requiring private hospitals to reimburse at least some of those costs, for instance by extending VAT to private medical treatment.

The future of community care

If the present state of pensions is unsatisfactory, the condition of community care is a nightmare. Until recently, it could be assumed that government, through the National Health Service, local authority provision or Income Support, would meet people's needs for long-term care. But the rapid growth in the number of people needing long-term care has meant a rapid increase in expenditure, and new demands upon families whose informal care accounts for most long-term care in this country. As an indication of how government expenditure on care has grown, Income Support payments for residential and nursing home fees grew from a mere £10 million in 1979 to £2.5 billion in 1992.

The 1990 NHS and Community Care Act, however, has radically changed the situation. Since April 1993, new residents of old-people's and nursing homes do not receive Income Support to meet their care needs. Instead, local authorities have been given care budgets, set by national government, together with the responsibility for assessing and funding people's needs for care. In theory, local social services workers decide, together with the person needing care and family members, what 'care package' should be provided from the full range of sources – informal family care; local authority, voluntary or private services to people in their own homes; and, where care at home is not possible, residential homes. In practice, because local authorities estimate that their care budgets are at least £200-300 million below what is needed, a care assessment may become a statement of what will be provided rather than what is actually needed. Furthermore, local authorities are discouraged from continuing to run their own residential homes and homecare services, being required to spend 85 per cent of their care budgets outside the public sector. The result is, as with the NHS, the development of a two-tier community care service, with a well-off minority able to buy the domiciliary or residential services they need, and the rest of us vulnerable to the growing pressures on local authority budgets.

It is, of course, impossible to predict what effect changes in medical technology will have on people's life-expectancy, or on the extent to which longer lives will mean healthier lives. But we can be certain that the people who now provide over three-quarters of all the care offered to those with disabilities or chronic illnesses – the informal carers in families and communities – will not be able to keep up with increased need. In 1961, there were slightly more than a million people aged over eighty; today, well over two million have reached that age. In 1900, for every individual over the age of 85, there were twenty-four women in their 50s (the group which provides most informal care). By 2000, the ratio will be one to three. By guaranteeing and supporting breaks in people's working careers, we will make it easier for them to care for elderly relatives. But we should also confront now the need to invest more in our own long-term care in the next century – whether we pay for that through taxes, through social insurance or through private insurance contributions.

Whose responsibility?

It is not at all clear at the moment where responsibility for community care lies. The possibilities include the individual needing care; the immediate family; the local authority social services department; and the local health authority. Despite the Government's intentions, responsibility for services has not been clearly transferred from the NHS (where they would be free at the point of use) to local authorities (who are entitled to charge for them). Although the NHS has for several years been reducing the number of beds for geriatric patients, recent cases call into question whether it can or should continue to refuse services to patients who need continuous or regular nursing care, rather than medical treatment. Increasingly, patients find themselves discharged from hospital either into the care of their own families (who are not necessarily in a position to provide it), or into a private nursing home, which will have to be paid for by the patient, the family or the local authority. In a recent case in Leeds, the Health Service Ombudsman criticised the transfer of a brain-damaged patient from a hospital to a nursing home. [51] Because that case was handled by the Ombudsman, rather than by a court, it does not set a legal precedent; earlier medical cases suggest that the courts would refuse to recognise a 'right' to NHS care if resources were not available to provide it. Nonetheless, every health authority and hospital is having to confront the question of what long-term care services, if any, to provide, and patients and their families can find themselves shunted back and forth between the social services department and the health authorities. New guidelines from the Secretary of State for Health attempt to define the responsibilities of health authorities and GP fundholders for reviewing patients' long-term health care, although it is too early to assess their effect. Until the issues of responsibility are decided, it will be impossible to develop a consistent, comprehensive approach to the provision of long-term care.

As things stand, decisions about residential care are also unnecessarily difficult. The 1990 Act allowed local authorities to finance a place in a nursing as well as a residential home, creating an overlap with the health authorities which may also purchase nursing care. An NHS Trust or health authority may discharge a patient from hospital, shifting responsibility onto the local authority, while a local authority may arrange residential care simply because there are not enough domiciliary services to meet the demand. Given the current organisation of most institutional care, the decision to 'go into a home' implies a radical break with home, family and neighbourhood. More flexibility in the design and organisation of residential care, enabling family members to remain more closely involved, could help to bridge the gap between domiciliary and residential care. In Sheffield, we found that the Family and Community Services department had used the restriction on public sector provision as an opportunity to build much closer links with organisations like the Alzheimer's Disease Society and Help the Aged. But the department stressed to us, as others have done, the need for a level playing -field between public, private and voluntary provision. Good-quality public provision can itself set a standard for other providers, while government itself should set tougher standards and give local authorities more effective powers of inspection and enforcement.

Financing care

How we meet our present and future needs for long-term care is an even bigger challenge than how we provide for pensions. The Institute of Actuaries has estimated that the number of disabled adults could grow from 6.4 million in 1991 to 8.5 million by 2031.[52] Of the total number in 2031, 6.8 million are expected to be over the age of 60, and more than a third – 3.2 million – would need either regular or continuous care. With the proportion of disabled adults in the total population growing from fourteen in every 1,000 to an estimated 26 in every 1000 by 2031, we would need nearly to double the resources devoted to continuous care (per head of the population) simply to maintain the present, imperfect, level of service.

Allocating responsibility is directly relevant to the question of how we finance community care. Although the dividing lines between treatment and care can be difficult to agree, the distinction offers the basis for a clearer approach to funding. Essentially, the difference is between the treatment needed for illness or injury, and the assistance needed in performing the routine tasks of daily living. The need for medical treatment itself should remain a collective responsibility, within the National Health Service. It would therefore continue to be funded through taxation, and could form part of a future healthcare guarantee. This would apply to all categories of community care users.

Given the many demands on resources, however, it is not feasible to extend the founding principle of the NHS – that treatment should be free at the point of use – to the comprehensive provision of care and help with everyday activities. Long-term care in old age is a sufficiently predictable risk to suggest that responsibility should start with individuals. For people already over the age of sixty, or already receiving regular care, however, no new insurance scheme is possible: their needs must be met within the present system, which should be improved as far as possible. The same applies to people who are born disabled or become disabled when younger, a risk which is largely unpredictable.

Where care users have sufficient assets or income to contribute towards the cost of care, it is reasonable that they should do so. The partner of someone who has moved into a nursing-home should not be required to sell their home in order to fund nursing home fees, but in many cases it is inevitable that the next generation's expectation of an inheritance will be disappointed. We cannot expect people's homes to finance all long-term care needs: only 50 per cent of people aged seventy or over own a house and (quite apart from partners' rights) the average sale price of around £65,000 could rapidly disappear in nursing home fees. With the recent growth of home ownership, however, more people will in future have assets on which to draw. Local authorities are required to charge for residential and nursing care, and increasingly do so for other community care services, usually on the basis of a means test. Because both charges and means tests vary so extensively, two people with the same needs may be charged completely different amounts for the same service, simply because of where they live. Since we see no alternative to making some charge for community care services for those who can afford it, it is essential that national government draws up guidelines on means-testing for all local authorities. Rather than risk deepening the poverty in which most disabled people already live, charges should only start well above Income Support levels and should disregard benefits awarded for other purposes (such as meeting extra heating needs).

Meeting care needs in future

Given the predictions that the resources needed for long-term care could double by 2031, now is the time for younger people to consider, individually and collectively, the possibility of insurance against the risk of long-term care. Such insurance would be designed to cover the costs of long-term care needs, whether provided by public, private or voluntary organisations. Insurance could be organised through our proposed new social insurance scheme on a pay as you go basis, or through private insurance, building up a fund in the same way as an occupational pension scheme. Some private insurance companies in the USA and the UK have begun to develop long-term care insurance schemes, sometimes linked to life insurance. A new proposal to combine care insurance with a personal pension (with a lower initial pension being traded against the guarantee of a higher payment should long-term care needs arise) was, however, overturned by the Inland Revenue.

It is not easy for insurance companies to predict long-term care needs and therefore to calculate premium levels, nor is it possible to judge with any certainty how long someone now aged thirty might possibly need intensive domiciliary or residential care in forty, fifty or sixty years' time. For these reasons, long-term insurance in the UK and the USA has so far incorporated reviewable premiums and/or benefits – with the result that it offers far less security to contributors. In New York, the State Government has proposed that someone who has exhausted the benefits from a state-approved private insurance plan should then be eligible for long-term care payments from the state itself, free of means-testing.

An alternative would be to pool the risks of long-term care on the simplest basis possible – social insurance. The German parliament has recently approved a small extension of social insurance, with extra contributions equivalent to one day's pay (financed by one day's less holiday) to finance a new entitlement to community care. Social insurance offers the great advantage of comprehensive coverage, including people on low incomes who could not afford private insurance premiums. In effect, social insurance would redistribute resources from families in the happy position of not needing long-term care for their elderly parents to those who needed such care.

Private long-term care insurance schemes will continue to develop – with the corresponding danger of a new gulf opening up between the well-provided for elderly or disabled care-user and the rest of us. Furthermore, no private insurance scheme will cater for the needs in old age of someone who has had disability or chronic illness since they were young. It would none the less be sensible for the British government to take some modest steps towards encouraging long-term care insurance, by changing the Inland Revenue rules to allow both occupational and personal pension plans to offer such insurance as well. The long-term solution may well lie in providing universal long-term care insurance as an integral part of the universal second pension, or in developing a long-term care guarantee, like the possible health guarantee, financed through higher taxes or social insurance contributions. Since, however, much less is known about how best to finance long-term care, government should establish a far fuller enquiry than we have been able to carry out ourselves, to develop funding options and seek agreement on the best way forward.

Above all, we need to recognise that if those of us who are not in need of extra care now want to be sure that we will be protected should the risk arise, then we will have to find the resources. Whether we pay privately to insurance companies, or publicly through taxes or social insurance contributions, and whether the carers are family members, professionals or volunteers, the resources will have to be found.

Conclusion

The approach we have taken to health – that prevention is better than treatment – reflects our fundamental view of the changes needed within the welfare state. People who are unemployed need more than the grudging provision of income: they need active help with finding another job. Because means-tested benefits lock families into unemployment and low paid work, and penalise older people for their savings, they cannot be the basis for effective reform. Instead, we propose a transformation of social security, centred on a modernised social insurance system, designed to help unemployed people to take employment, and to enable parents and carers to fulfil family responsibilities without risking future security. Our pensions guarantee combined with a universal second-tier pension will offer security and dignity for all elderly people. Instead of desperately trying to patch up a system designed for an old world, as the present government is doing, we propose a welfare state which is tailored to the changing realities of families and work, and which will help people to cope with the insecurities which increasingly derive from both.

Notes

1. Gosta Esping-Andersen 'Equality and Work' in David Miliband (ed) *Reinventing the Left* (Cambridge: IPPR/Polity Press, 1994)
2. Ibid
3. See John Veit Wilson *Dignity not Poverty* (London: IPPR, 1994) for a full discussion of proposals for a minimum income standard
4. Child Poverty Action Group, submission to the Commission on Social Justice, 1994

5. *Hansard*, 9 February 1994, col 292

6. DSS Departmental Report (London: HMSO, 1994)

7. Jane Falkingham *et al William Beveridge versus Robin Hood: Social Security and Redistribution over the Life-Cycle* (London: LSE Welfare State Programme, 1993)

8. 751,000 part-time workers work less than 8 hours a week, of whom 629,000 are employees and 122,000 self-employed. *Hansard* 28 April 1994, col 293

9. L. Luckhaus and L. Dickens 1991 quoted in Joan Brown *Escaping from Dependency* (London: IPPR, 1994)

10. For a detailed discussion of how this might be done, see Joan Brown op cit

11. Department of Employment *Employment Gazette*, July 1993

12. For a fuller discussion, see Brown *Escaping* op cit

13. Alex Bryson and John Jacobs *Policing the Workshy* (Aldershot: Avebury, 1992)

14. Sheila Kamerman and Alfred Kahn (eds) *Child Care, Parental Leave and the Under-3s: Policy Innovation in Europe* (New York: Auburn House, 1993)

15. Germany offers parents a childrearing allowance of DM600 (£240) a month, starting after the end of maternity pay and available to either mother or father. The allowance is paid as of right for six months and tested against income for a further twelve, although government aims eventually to extend the allowance to three years, with parents able to use it either for at-home care or for a pre-school programme. Luxembourg and the Netherlands offer 16 weeks paid leave at 100 per cent of earnings, and Luxembourg also offers a means-tested allowance for families with a child under two years of age

16. The new system would need to protect the position of those who would have been entitled to ICA under present rules, and a small number of young disabled adults would need to be exempted altogether from contribution requirements for Severe Disability Allowance or Invalidity Benefit

17. National Audit Office *Statutory Sick Pay and Statutory Maternity Pay* (London: HMSO, 1993)

18. *Surveys of Disability in Great Britain* (London: OPCS, 1987)

19. Department of Social Security *Income Related Benefits: Estimates of Take-up in 1990 and 1991* (London: HMSO, 1994)

20. *Hansard*, House of Commons, 20 July 1993, col 203

21. See Eithne McLaughlin *Flexibility in Work and Benefits* Commission

on Social Justice Issue Paper 11 (London: IPPR, 1994) for a full review of work incentives and the interaction between the benefits system and the labour market.

22. *Hansard,* 11 July 1994, Cols 399–400

23. Policy Studies Institute 'Families, Work and Benefits' in *DSS Research Yearbook 1992/3* (London: PSI, 1993)

24. Eithne Mclaughlin *Flexibility* op cit

25. Department of Social Security: *Expenditure plans 1994-5 to 1996-7* (London: HMSO, 1994). Figures for Housing Benefit and Community Charge Benefit

26. John Hills *Unravelling Housing Finance: Subsidies, benefits and taxation* (Oxford: Clarendon Press, 1991) and *Thirty-nine Steps to Housing Finance Reform* (York: Joseph Rowntree Foundation, 1991)

27. Steve Webb and Steven Wilcox *Time for Mortgage Benefits* (York: Joseph Rowntree Foundation, 1991)

28. This study was generously carried out for the Commission by Andersen Consulting. The full results are contained in David Clinton, Michael Yates and Dharminder Kang *Integrating Taxes and Benefits?* (London: IPPR, 1994)

29. National Audit Office *Inland Revenue: Getting Tax Right First Time* (London: NAO, 1994)

30. J.Vranken, University of Antwerp, unpublished paper, 1994

31. Holly Sutherland and Moira Wilson, calculations for the Commission. The Expert Working Group on the Integration of the Tax and Social Welfare Systems in Ireland also found that a citizen's income of £35 a week would require an income tax rate of 61%; one of £55 a week, roughly equal to the old-age pension, would require a tax rate of 86% to be self-financing.

32. Alan Duncan, Christopher Giles and Steven Webb *Social Security Reform and Women's Independent Incomes* (Manchester: Equal Opportunities Commission, 1994)

33. Andrew Dilnot *et al Pensions Policy in the UK: an economic analysis* (London: Institute of Fiscal Studies, 1994)

34. Department of Social Security *Statistics 1993*, Commission on Social Justice Issue Paper 7 (London: HMSO, 1993)

35. Paul Johnson *The Pensions Dilemma* (London: IPPR, 1994)

36. John Hills *The Future of Welfare* (York: Joseph Rowntree Foundation, 1993)

37. Bryn Davies *Better Pensions for All* (London: IPPR, 1993)

38. *The Pensions Debate: a report on income and pensioners in retirement* (London: Age Concern, 1994)

39. *Statistical Supplement to Autumn Statement 1993* (London: HMSO, 1993)

40. *UK Treasury Statistics 1994* (London: HMSO, 1994)

41. For a full discussion of this and related issues, see Dilnot *et al Pensions* op cit

42. At present rates, the rebate for all contributors would be around 3.7%. Calculations by Bryn Davies for the Commission

43. Dilnot *et al Pensions* op cit.

44. Paul Gregg 'Jobs and Justice' in Edward Balls and Paul Gregg *Work and Welfare – tackling the jobs deficit*, Commission on Social Justice Issue paper 3 (London: IPPR, 1993)

45. *Options for Equality in State Pension Age* (London: HMSO, 1991)

46. *Options for Equality in Pension Age: A Case for Equalising at 65* (London: Social Security Advisory Committee/HMSO, 1992)

47. 'GP fundholders "get twice as much"' the *Guardian*, 1 July 1994

48. Hills *Welfare* op cit

49. Ibid

50. For a full discussion of these issues, see Stephen Harrison and David Hunter *Rationing Health Care* (London: IPPR, 1994)

51. Health Service Commissioner's Second Report for 1993/94 *Failure to provide long term care for a brain damaged patient* (London: HMSO, 1994)

52. Stephen Nuttall *et al, Financing Long-Term Care in Great Britain* (London: Institute of Actuaries, 1993)

7

RESPONSIBILITY:
MAKING A GOOD SOCIETY

'The people here aren't the problem. They're the solution.'

*Bob Holman, community worker, Family Action
in Rogerfield and Easterhouse, Glasgow.*

●　　●　　●

It is far easier to destroy than to create a sense of community. Building a good society is about far more than the success of its component parts. A good society depends not just on the economic success of 'I', the individual, but the social commitment of 'We', the community.

This is a notion that the Deregulators have scorned for more than a decade. The credo of market individualism reduces relationships to contracts; it turns citizens into buyers and sellers in the marketplace. This is no basis for a stable or thriving society, as the condition of the UK demonstrates. As the Archbishop of Canterbury has put it: 'One-eyed individualism and the privatisation of morality exacts a high price in personal and public dimensions of life alike.'[1] For fifteen years we have been the subject of a more or less clinical experiment in free market economics, and the results are plain for all to see: the social institutions on which a free society rests are in a state of advanced decay. John Gray has written that 'Maoism of the Right ... the paleo-liberal celebration of consumer choice and market freedom as the only undisputed values has become a recipe for *anomie*, social breakdown and ultimately economic failure'.[2]

Investors argue that investment in social institutions is as important as investment in economic infrastructure. At the heart of social justice is not just the idea that we owe something to each other, but the belief that we gain from giving to each other. The pioneering socialist and social scientist R.H. Tawney was already insisting on this fundamental principle in the 1920s:

> No individual can create by his isolated actions a healthy environment, or establish an education system with a wide range of facilities, or organise an industry in such a manner as to diminish economic insecurity...Yet these are the conditions which make the difference between happiness and misery, and sometimes indeed, between life and death. In so far as they exist they are the source of a social income, received in the form not of money, but of increased well-being.

This does not mean that institutions cannot be bureaucratic, inflexible and out of touch with people's needs. That is why in this chapter we stress the need for accountability and democracy within institutions, and for new sorts of institutions, from Springboard programmes, drawing upon volunteer commitment to provide one-to-one tutoring for pupils excluded from school, through credit unions to devolved housing management and a Citizens' Service programme. It shouldn't take riots to draw attention to the poorest parts of our country; early action and early investment must be the aim.

The Meaning and Making of Social Capital

The ideas of reciprocal responsibility and social well-being are at the core of this chapter. The American economist and sociologist Robert D. Putnamm calls this *social capital*, the 'networks, norms and trust that facilitate co-ordination and co-operation for mutual benefit.'[3] Social capital consists of the institutions and relationships of a thriving civil society – from networks of neighbours to extended families, community groups to religious organisations, local businesses to local public services, youth clubs to parent-teacher associations, playgroups to police on the beat. Where you live, who else lives there, and how they live their lives – cooperatively or selfishly, responsibly or destructively – can be as important as personal resources in determining life chances.

During our visits around the country, we saw for ourselves what social capital – and its absence – can mean. Hackney and Tower Hamlets, in North-East London, include some of the most disadvantaged areas in Britain. Over centuries of migration and settlement, thriving communities have built up, often around churches, synagogues and mosques. Conflicts over scarce resources, notably housing, can produce racial resentment and violence. Local businesses and shops are struggling to survive in recession, but they provide a toehold for people trying to make a living, while a flourishing network of voluntary groups and local council projects offers opportunities for training and community development.

Six miles from Glasgow's city centre, Easterhouse suffers similar problems of unemployment and poverty. But the estates built in the 1950s (which now house 40,000 people) are almost bereft of churches, businesses, shops and banks. Nearly one in three Easterhouse men is unemployed, and many more are excluded from the register. Four in ten households live on income support, their money swallowed up by basic essentials; there is no cash left on which business and work can be based. A credit union offers loans at 1 per cent interest as an alternative to local loan sharks, and a food co-op counters the extortionate prices charged by travelling food vans. This is not an underclass, but strong people struggling to build social capital from the bottom up.

The moral and social reconstruction of our society depends on our willingness to invest in social capital. We badly need to mend a social fabric that is so obviously torn apart. Social capital is a good in itself; it makes life possible. But social capital is also essential for economic renewal; the two go together. As Putnamm argues, economic prosperity depends not only on economic but also on social resources. Social capital can encourage new investment as well as making existing investment go further; it is the glue that bonds the benefits of economic and physical capital into marginalised communities.

Communities do not become strong because they are rich; rather, they become rich because they are strong.

Successful schools depend upon involved parents as well as good teachers. Job training is more effective if it is coupled with the broadening of social networks through community organisations. Entrepreneurs are more likely to succeed if they know local people who can help them find funds, advice, supplies and customers. In other words, social capital improves the efficiency with which market economies operate.

Social Capital

- Social capital enhances quality of life, extends social networks and builds institutions to strengthen the reputation – the 'reputational capital' – of an area
- This means that investment in economic and human capital is attracted and retained because stocks of 'community collateral' offer insurance against failure
- This in turn creates conditions for 'bottom-up' job creation through new small businesses, not-for-profit Intermediate Labour Markets (ILMs) and 'micro-entrepreneurs'
- These flowerings of economic activity connect individuals to each other and disadvantaged communities to the outside world; a virtuous circle of investment and prosperity is created and can be maintained

---

One reason for the repeated disappointments of policy initiatives over the last fifteen years is that they have failed to understand the importance of social capital. As a government-sponsored report found, the £10 billion spent on property-led regeneration in inner-city areas during the 1980s has largely been wasted.[4] Instead, the aim must be to build amongst local people the capacities and institutions which enable them to take more responsibility for shaping their own futures. The 'problem' with social capital (or community strength, civic wealth, call it what you will) is that those who have already got it get more of it, and those without it find it hard to build. Some inner-city communities and outer-city housing estates have become almost completely cut off from employment and business opportunities; the result is a vicious circle of economic disinvestment and social exclusion.

Social capital needs to be nurtured by individuals on their own and by the community as a whole. And it is enhanced when used, rather than depleted like other resources. It must be at the heart of people-led regeneration, which gets to the core of what really matters to the success or failure of an area – the confidence and capacities of the people who live there.

Small and local initiatives, based on a partnership of public, private and voluntary sectors, are the essential foundation of lasting empowerment. The involvement of private companies in their local community should be seen in business rather than philanthropic terms. Professor Brian Robson, Pro-Vice-Chancellor of Manchester University and an expert on urban renewal, makes clear the value of small investments in many local communities:

> The argument that Urban Programme funds merely pepper-potted small sums of money in random patterns may have had bureaucratic force, but this is precisely the strength of local volunteers on the ground ... What they need is small, relatively unconstrained sums to tackle problems scattered widely throughout impoverished communities.[5]

Social capital begins at home. The success of families is the foundation of the strength of the world outside. We start, therefore, with the smallest social institution, families, and the way they bring up children.

Children and their Families

Children's well-being is a touchstone of the health and strength of a society. But Britain is not a good place in which to be a child. The financial, emotional and educational impoverishment suffered by millions of our children is not only unjust, it is economic folly.

Families are the first social institutions children know and the means by which they are introduced to all the others. But in a society where people's worth seems increasingly to be measured by how much money they can earn, the unpaid work of parents – especially mothers – is regarded as little more than an impediment to their earning power. If we really want to create a better society, we must value children and the families that nurture them far more highly than we do now.

As a society we demand a great deal of parents but offer them little support. Those who fall below acceptable standards risk personal criticism, institutional intervention and, as a final sanction, the loss of their children. But those who meet high standards of care, even under exceptionally difficult circumstances, get no special recognition because children are widely regarded as just another 'lifestyle choice'.

Children are not a private pleasure or a personal burden; they are 100 per cent of the nation's future. Children who trust themselves and others, who have learned well and want to learn more, who feel themselves respected and therefore have self-respect and respect for others, are likely to grow into responsible and productive members of their communities. Such children will not always behave well, of course, any more than adults do. But the children who become involved in violence, in drug-dealing or in any of the seriously anti-social behaviour that inflicts enormous harm on our communities, are usually children on whom families or communities, whether by commission or omission, have already inflicted enormous harm.

Children's life chances have economic as well as social effects. Economic success increasingly depends on human resources: on us, now, while we are of working age and they are children, but on them when we reach retirement age and they are the workforce. Because the best indicator of the capacity of our economy tomorrow is the quality of our children today, government should create and publish an annual index of childhood well-being, including the proportion of under-fives receiving appropriate pre-school education.

There is a growing gulf in this country between families who are materially well off, and those who are not. But that is not the only injustice we must overcome. All parents, however well off, compete with people who do not have children, or whose children are grown up, spreading their time and energy between working and caring, stretching their incomes to meet their children's needs as well as their own. And mothers, even more than fathers, bear the practical and economic responsibilities of parenthood. If we are to value our children properly, we must start to close the gaps between poorer and richer families, between parents and non-parents, between fathers and mothers.

Family Change

Families are changing fast. Growing concern about the effects of family change on children reflects, in part, the fact that so many children are not growing up healthily and happily. But there is also a lazy stereotyping of some families which distorts the facts, blocks debate and stigmatises those least able to defend themselves – the children involved. At its most extreme, it leads to the offensive moral authoritarianism represented by the 1988 Local Government Act and its ban on the 'teaching' of 'pretended' (gay and lesbian) family relationships.

We are in no doubt that children benefit from spending their childhood with their own natural parents who live together in reasonable harmony, just as they suffer from parental conflict and the separation and divorce which often follow. The problem is what to do when reasonable harmony does not exist. Lone-parent families include families in many different circumstances, which even on average produce very different outcomes for children. But the poverty in which most lone mothers and their children live is, overwhelmingly, the factor which accounts for the children's diminished life chances.[6] The effects of family change on children are complex, and the averages in which statisticians must deal do not tell us about the position of individual children in particular families.

Instead of allowing ourselves to be obsessed with family structures, we need to concentrate on family *functioning*. As research studies reveal, and common sense confirms, children thrive in any kind of family where there is consistent love and nurture, support and discipline, and in no kind of family where those qualities are missing. A government that is serious about children should therefore develop policies for families built around three objectives.

- First, we need to ensure that all our children grow up in surroundings which enable their needs – physical, emotional, intellectual – to be met. A strong community should support its families, rather than expect strong families to make up for the limitations of weak communities.
- Second, we need to empower women to share financial, as well as emotional and practical, responsibility for their children.
- Third, we need to encourage and enable men to share the emotional and practical, as well as the financial, responsibilities of parenthood.

The proposals in this chapter must be seen in the context of strategies which would enable parents locked out of employment to start earning a living, and combine employment and family responsibilities. In Chapter 4, we argued for an expansion of childcare services and nursery education. In Chapter 5, we proposed a Jobs, Education and Training programme for the long-term unemployed and for lone parents, together with the development of family-friendly employment. In Chapter 6, we proposed a new social insurance system which, together with reforms of means-tested benefits, would provide real incentives to parents to take up part-time or full-time employment. In the rest of this section, we look at other ways in which society can support parents both financially, through Child Benefit and a reform of child maintenance, and through a new framework of laws and services.

Money for Children

The best way to help the one in three children growing up in poverty is to help their parents get jobs. But more is needed, not only because too many jobs do not pay a living wage but also because, at any given level of income, parents are at a financial disadvantage compared with people without children.

Giving a child a good start in life takes much more than money, but it cannot be done without money. Professor Jonathan Bradshaw and the Family Budget Unit at the University of York have calculated that a child under five costs about £62 a week to feed, clothe, house and nurture at a 'modest but adequate level'. Every Western country, through its tax or benefits system or both, has always recognised that parents who incur these extra costs cannot be treated in the same way as people with a similar income but no children. In this country, the costs of children used to be acknowledged through child tax allowances. But tax allowances have the enormous disadvantage of being worth much more to higher-rate taxpayers than to standard-rate taxpayers, and offering nothing at all to parents who are too poor to pay income tax. For that reason, they were replaced by Child Benefit.

Child Benefit, however, is frequently attacked as an 'indiscriminate' subsidy which fails to concentrate help on the poorest. But this is to misunderstand its purpose, which is not simply to relieve poverty, but to even things up between parents and nonparents – to establish what economists call 'horizontal equity', as opposed to vertical equity between richer and poorer. Indeed, countries such as West Germany and Denmark, which decided to subject Child Benefit to a means test, partly in order to make it 'fairer', found that better-off parents soon demanded the return of the much less fair child tax allowances.

Child Benefit remains the fairest and most efficient way of recognising the extra responsibilities borne by *all* parents; its take-up is 98 per cent, compared with below two-thirds for Family Credit. It is paid directly to the person with daily responsibility for the child (usually, but not always, the mother) and virtually all of it is spent on the children. In families where the father fails to share his income or where benefit payments are delayed, it can be the mother's only reliable income, and it provides secure income in the case of family break-up.

Child Benefit also plays a crucial role in helping parents move into employment. As we argued in Chapter 6, means-tested benefits often lock people into unemployment – and therefore poverty – because the wages for any available job incur disproportionate loss of benefit. Child Benefit, precisely because it is *not* means-tested, tops up low wages and therefore encourages mothers, as well as fathers, to take employment that can make all the difference between hardship and a reasonable standard of living. In other words, Child Benefit is not only an efficient form of fair redistribution, it is also an effective investment in self-help. For all these reasons we are convinced that Child Benefit should stay. We also believe it should be paid at the same rate for all children; the present higher rate for first children discriminates against larger families which are at greatest risk of poverty.

Child Benefit, now paid at £10 a week to the first child and £8.10 for others, represents only about one-sixth of the direct cost of raising a child at 'modest but adequate' levels. We believe it should be raised, but, given all the other claims on public expenditure, it is unrealistic to seek new funds in the foreseeable future for a substantial increase. There are two ways, however, in which resources could be found within the present tax and benefits system. This is one area in which we match a proposal for benefit reform with a proposal for tax reform.

The tax system has always given a higher personal allowance to married men than to other income-tax payers. Originally intended to recognise the costs of supporting a dependent wife, the Married Man's Tax Allowance (now the Married Couple's Allowance) in reality goes to all couples, even those without children and where both partners are high earners. The present Government, recognising that the allowance is an indiscriminate and anomalous subsidy, has already limited its value to the lower rate of income tax, and will further reduce it to 15 per cent from April 1995.

This process of phasing out the Married Couple's Tax Allowance should be completed for people below the age of 55. (We have chosen the age of 55 rather than the age of retirement because so many people are effectively retired, often on low incomes, in their late fifties or early sixties). The need to invest in families with children is so important that all the savings from this reform should be invested them. There are different ways, however, of achieving that goal. Some Commissioners believe that the resources should be used entirely to increase Child

Benefit, giving direct financial support to children of all ages and offering parents greater choice about whether to care for their children at home or to return to employment and, if necessary, pay for substitute childcare. Removing the married couple's allowance completely would save over £2.5 billion and allow for an increase in Child Benefit of about £5 per week. Others argue that if less than half of these savings were used to fund nursery education, the targets for universal provision we proposed could be achieved, while the balance would still finance a higher Child Benefit.

The second reform concerns making Child Benefit taxable. We have considered and rejected several different taxation options. If, for instance, all mothers were taxed on their Child Benefit, those with very low earnings would suffer (at current figures, a mother with two children would start paying income tax once her weekly earnings reached £47.85). Furthermore, a couple with one child who pay basic-rate tax, would actually be worse off once the abolition of the Married Couple's Allowance was also taken into account. A different possibility would be to tax mothers on their Child Benefit at the standard rate of income tax, but only when their earnings reached a point significantly above the income tax threshold. At the moment, however, so few women with children have earnings near the male average that the additional revenue would scarcely be worth the trouble. (Only about 500,000 mothers earn more than £15,000 a year; taxing them would raise little over £100 million, or the equivalent of a 20p increase in Child Benefit.) In the future, however, this option would be worth considering.

If, on the other hand, fathers were taxed on the benefit paid to the mother, government would no doubt face protests of the kind provoked by the Child Support Agency, together with demands for the restoration of Child Tax Allowance and possibly even the payment of Child Benefit to the father himself. There would also be administrative costs in matching up fathers' tax files with mothers' benefit records, particularly where the   parents were not married. The 'clawback' which operated in the late 1960s was one of the reasons why Family Allowances (the predecessor of Child Benefit) became so unpopular, particularly with fathers.

If, however, government taxed Child Benefit where either father or mother was a higher-rate taxpayer, it could increase popular support for a benefit that fulfils an essential purpose while raising additional revenue. Although tax files would still have to be matched, this should be a manageable task given that there are only just under one million fathers paying tax at the higher rate. At the moment, there are so few mothers who pay higher rate income tax (some 50,000 at most) that taxing them would produce negligible revenues. It would, however, be wrong in principle to tax higher-rate fathers without also taxing higher-rate mothers. Furthermore, in future, as women's earnings continue to rise, the taxation of Child Benefit on higher-rate taxpaying parents will produce an even more progressive benefit. Using the tax system to withdraw 40 per cent (the present higher rate) of Child Benefit from the best-off families – the option we favour – would produce additional resources (at present, about £300 million a year) which should continue to be devoted to the direct support of children through a further increase in Child Benefit.

Reforming Child Maintenance

Child Benefit has always helped mothers whose partners fail to share their income equitably. This problem is not diminishing as women move into employment; indeed there is evidence that some men cut back on housekeeping money and expect their partners to pay for homes and children out of their own earnings, while childcare costs are usually met from the woman's earnings as well. But failure to share income is most common after a divorce or separation: before the introduction of the Child Support Act, only about 30 per cent of maintenance orders and agreements were paid.

The Child Support Act and Agency have replaced an old system of child maintenance which was generally agreed to be inequitable, inaccessible and inefficient. The principle of the Act – that absent parents should accept and share financial responsibility for their children – is clearly right. But the practice has been disastrous. Assessments have left a number of absent parents impoverished and in some cases their ability to be good parents to a second family has therefore been jeopardised; other parents have found their relationship with their first family threatened by the failure of the assessment formula to take into account the costs of travelling to visit their children. Furthermore, a drop in the absent parent's living standards seldom means a rise in the standards enjoyed by his former partner and their mutual children. If the lone-parent is on Income Support, money from maintenance is simply deducted from it, pound for pound. If the maintenance received is sufficient to take the custodial parent off Income Support altogether, the parent and the children may be left worse off as a result of losing passported benefits such as free school meals.

The Child Support Agency has become so unpopular with absent parents, and has disappointed the hopes of so many custodial parents, that there is a real risk of government rushing into further ill-considered changes in response to immediate public pressure. We have not tried to carry out a detailed review of the system ourselves. Government should, however, learn from the lessons of the Australian child-support system which, despite real difficulties, has been significantly more successful than this country's.

Unlike the British child-support scheme, the Australian system was clearly perceived by the public to be part of a broader strategy to improve children's well-being. For instance, the custodial parent is allowed to keep a significant part of the extra maintenance paid before benefit is reduced. At the same time, the British system contains an undesirable feature which is absent from the Australian scheme, requiring the absent parent to contribute directly towards the maintenance of his or her former partner. This element within the present formula should instead be treated as an allowance towards childcare costs and be partly disregarded when means-tested benefits are assessed. The introduction of a maintenance disregard would mean that any sacrifice made by the absent parent whose maintenance is increased would result in a real benefit to his (or her) children. If, for instance, the first £15 of maintenance were ignored for Income Support, as it already is with Family Credit, an estimated quarter of a million lone parent families would benefit, a small number of whom would be floated off Income Support completely.[7] If this change had its desired effect of helping to make child-support more acceptable, and if the Agency became more efficient at collecting maintenance payments, benefit savings need not be reduced and could even increase.

Because the Australian scheme was never made retrospective, it avoided creating the real sense of injustice felt by many British parents who had previously agreed a substantial property settlement in lieu of maintenance payments. Although it might have been preferable to have adopted this approach from the outset, we believe that if government were now to try to remove the retrospective application of the child-support formula, it would represent yet another downgrading of the claims of children and custodial parents, while creating further complexities in an already difficult system. Instead, we believe that an accessible and affordable appeals mechanism is required, together with careful criteria for departing from the formula.

Despite its relative success, the Australian system still does not manage to collect all the maintenance awarded nor deliver it on time to custodial parents. Reforms to the British system should be designed to ensure that maintenance provides a secure income to the custodial parent, in or out of employment. This could be achieved by following the example of Sweden, for instance, where child maintenance is guaranteed by their child-support agency.

Although financial responsibility for children is important, money is not the only thing children need. The loss of all contact with the absent parent, usually the father, is a devastating blow which affects more than half the children of divorce. As far as possible (and with the obvious exception of abusive or violent parents), public policy should encourage all parents to remain actively committed to their children. Measures to ensure that non-custodial fathers accept their share of financial responsibility need to be matched by strategies to encourage all fathers, including those who do not live with their children, to share in their emotional and practical care. It is inevitable that the Child Support Agency will become a lightning-conductor for anger and conflict in divorce. By extending conciliation and mediation services for parents facing separation, divorce or disputes over custody and access, government can help to reduce conflicts over child support and make it easier for children to stay close to both their parents. And parents who are close to their children are more likely to pay child-support readily.

Investing in Families and Children

Children are 100 per cent of the future. Investment in their life-chances is the best social and economic investment we can make. Key reforms include:

- Childcare and nusery education for under-fives (Chapter 4)
- Welfare-to-work strategies for lone-parents (Chapter 5)
- New policies for flexible working (Chapters 5 and 6)
- Tax Child Benefit for high-earning mothers or fathers – and increase it, to help children out of poverty and reduce disincentives to paid employment
- Reform child maintenance
- Strengthen parental responsibility

The responsibilities of parents

As we confront the impact of family change on children and our failure to ensure the best possible opportunities for every child, we need to develop a far stronger acceptance of the importance of parenthood and the responsibilities which go with it. Although the law alone cannot transform people's attitudes, a clear legal statement of parental responsibilities would help to underline a new commitment to children. Almost every other European Union country has a statement of parents' responsibilities; the United Kingdom needs one too.

Traditionally our society has regulated the relationship between parents and children through the laws on marriage. We have come a long way since children were regarded as their fathers' property and 'parental rights' were absolute. Modern thinking, set out universally in the United Nations Convention on the Rights of the Child and nationally in the Children Act, sees children as having rights of their own; parents as having the responsibility to ensure that they are respected; and the state as their final guarantor. Although the UN Convention and the Children Act stress that both parents have equal responsibility for their children's upbringing, English law (like that of most European countries) only clearly recognises this principle in its entirety for married couples. Since more than a third of children born each year in the UK are now born outside marriage (and that proportion is growing), and since more than half those unmarried parents are living together in committed partnerships at the time of the birth, marriage no longer provides an adequate legal framework for defining parents' responsibilities for children or the state's support for and regulation of family life.

In common with the emerging consensus amongst leading family organisations, we believe that family size and structure are a matter for adults' private choice, but that dependent children are entitled to 'good enough parenting' based on a commitment that lasts throughout their childhood, whether parents are living together or apart.[8] 'Once a parent, always a parent' is one of the principles of the Children Act, but although that legislation recognises children's need for continuing contact with both parents after separation or divorce, as well as their right to be heard in legal proceedings affecting them, it fails to set out the responsibilities that being a parent entails, or to address many difficult problems inherent in umarried parenthood. An unmarried father in the UK is legally liable to contribute to a child's maintenance, for example, but the mother has sole parental responsibility in all other respects unless she agrees, or a court decides, that it should be shared with him. Difficult questions follow, for example whether dual parental responsibility automatically applies to cohabiting partners as it does to married couples, and also to sexual partners who share a relationship but not a home.

This country needs a new statement of parents' responsibilities. The development of such a statement should draw on the work of organisations concerned with all aspects and stages of family life, on suggestions such as that made by Lord (Michael)

Young and Professor A.H. Halsey for a 'Family Covenant' to be entered into by parents at the birth of a child,[9] and on the work of the Scottish Law Commission which has proposed and drafted a statutory statement of parental responsibilities.[10] Once agreed, it should be the focus for a wide-ranging effort to raise public consciousness of the importance of children's early experiences and the nature of parents' commitment to them.

Violence within families

Violence within the 'privacy' of the family is not a private matter. The police now respond more actively and effectively to spouse- and child-abuse, and violence against elderly and disabled people is at last being acknowledged as a widespread problem. But many children still suffer, and some die despite the publicity and campaigning. And many adults, mostly women, are trapped in violent families from which they can see no escape.

A recent Audit Commission report argued that Family Centres were an important part of a strategy based on prevention of violence rather than just reaction to it. Twenty-four-hour counselling services should be available for victims of domestic violence (as they already are for victims of rape). But rescue is not enough. Emotional scars do not go away, and victims who do escape can find themselves in poverty or homeless. Refuges need specialist workers with the skills, experience and contacts to smooth the re-entry of people into normal life.

The most important finding of modern research is that domestic violence is both a source and a symptom of violence of other kinds. Family violence, community violence and social violence are a continuum. Where society ignores, tolerates, even rewards violence, it will foster family violence. Conversely, when violence in society is reduced, so family violence can be curbed.

We therefore agree with the American Commission on Youth and Violence that the Government should lead a national strategy to promote non-violent values. A national education campaign should publicly condemn all forms and degrees of inter-personal violence and promote non-violent discipline in homes and schools. Such a campaign would provide an overall context within which community and voluntary initiatives could be co-ordinated at a local level, to suit local needs. The American Commission on Youth and Violence has forcefully presented the issue:

> Everyone who comes into contact with the child – parents, relatives, teachers, daycare providers, health professionals etc – has the potential to contribute to a child's attitudes towards violence and propensity for violent behaviour. Similarly, every institution that touches children's families – schools, mass media, community, religious organisations – can contribute positively to children's sense of safety and to their preference to alternatives to violence.

It is in that preference that a less violent future for the UK must be vested.

Building Strong Communities I: Regeneration from the Bottom Up

The neighbourhood where a family lives directly affects parents' ability to create good lives for their children. Disadvantaged people living in disadvantaged places pay the highest price for economic and social failure. There are parts of the UK where there is virtually no local economy left, following the departure of the most important employers and the process of disinvestment that often results. The loss of public services, as well as shops and banks, has resulted in the outflow of what economic capital was available. The 'landscapes of despair', on the margins of the British economy, identified by Professor David Donnison, are inhabited by people who experience cumulative and concentrated disadvantage.[11] Poor employment prospects, low educational achievements, high levels of crime and vandalism, poor quality housing and little choice in shopping or services too often go together. The concentration of disadvantage fuels the flight of those able to leave and creates no-go areas for prospective residents, future investment and even some of the statutory services. Crime is only one indicator, but it is a good one: the UK's poorest

323

council estates face the highest risk of burglary,[12] and the growth of drug economies has produced fear and violent crime in the most brutalised parts of the UK.

Beatrix Campbell, author of *Goliath: Britain's Dangerous Places*, has described 'the Brazils of Britain', places where debt directs the flow of money and a 'fiscal haemorrhage' is taking place.[13] A recent unpublished study by the Bank of England noted that one in six of the wards in Birmingham, the UK's second city, is no longer serviced by a local bank or building society.[14] One bank outlet remains in Greater Easterhouse in Glasgow, to serve a population of 40,000. At the Birmingham Settlement in the city's Newtown district, we heard of interest rates of between 60 and 500 per cent, of physical brutality against the most vulnerable people, and a cycle of despair that robbed people of hope and dignity. In places like Newtown, money which comes into the area (for example in the form of benefit cheques) only circulates between one or two people before it is exported from the local economy; in middle-class areas, money can go through five or ten pairs of hands before leaving the community. In poorer areas, what money is left to spend cannot be spent locally, because shops have closed and moved.

The problems arising from the downward spiral set in train by economic decline threaten to defeat even the most committed teachers, social workers, employers and police staff. The reaction is 'fire-fighting', responding to problems after they have emerged. But this is inadequate to the challenge at hand. Regeneration strategies that have been established in some communities under the City Challenge programme to revive depressed areas, and attempts to tackle and prevent crime through the Safer Cities initiative, for example, are uneven in their success. Most projects fail to make the most of what money is available because they fail to build a partnership with local people. And the common denominator is the short-term approach to regeneration: problems which have taken decades to develop cannot be solved quickly, and certainly not according to the vagaries of the electoral cycle. It takes political guts to invest in projects whose dividend will only be reaped beyond the term of a parliament or council cycle; but it is necessary none the less.

Community action

In Chapter 5, we mapped out a six-point strategy for the integration of long-term unemployed people into the labour market, with initiatives ranging from the development of Intermediate Labour Markets to the sponsorship of 'micro-enterprise'. But we also stressed that economic regeneration is impossible without social regeneration; investment in human and physical capital depends for its success on investment in social capital. Employability and regeneration go together: in Miles Platting in Manchester, the Development Trust itself was directly responsible for the creation of a relatively small number of jobs (around twenty people in community businesses), but its staff have helped to place more than 150 local residents in mainstream employment through its trusted job search and counselling service. Similarly, Bootstraps, a long-established community enterprise in Hackney, has shifted its focus from establishing small businesses itself to helping local people get 'customised' training organised in conjunction with nearby employers (including a major supermarket chain). One important difference between our proposals and a range of central government initiatives – from Urban Development Corporations to many of the City Challenge schemes – lies in our emphasis on the need to build linkages between the economic, human and social capital investments required to achieve sustainable regeneration.

Investment-in-community capacity is more likely to reverse the trend towards 'twin-speed' cities than investment in property. It requires a higher degree of community participation in the planning stage than the 10 per cent input estimated by the Community Development Foundation (CDF) in the first round of City Challenge bids. Paul Henderson of the CDF in Leeds told us that such a social capital investment strategy is no easy option:

> Community development does not offer a panacea to the deep-rooted social and economic problems of British society. But it can help to bring forward the language and political agenda of communities which are exhausted and suspicious of external agencies. It can be a means of keeping hope alive and kicking.[15]

People-led regeneration does not mean that communities should be left to work on their own. There is no magic about 'community'. It does not replace the need for effective government (nor for that matter the need to reinvent the way governments work). 'Community' may bring about the best of local loyalties; or it may be racist, discriminatory and exclusionary. Collaborative relationships are rarely built without risks being taken or without some failures. Contests over whose projects get funding are inevitable. The aim is to open a public debate rather than to suppress differences.

In the United States, where the history of federal sponsorship of community action is more extensive, President Clinton's new Community Empowerment agenda tries to reflect what has been learnt by focusing government action on five areas: new programmes to provide access to capital, credit and banking services for distressed communities; the extension of small business support to inner city and ethnic minority businesses; new public/private partnerships for economic development; a concentration on the educational capital of an area; and a new infrastructure programme to reconnect distressed communities.

It is difficult to exaggerate the change in thinking and working required of central government and civil servants, away from a top-down approach towards one rooted in the needs and skills of local communities. The Fabian notion, that governments know better than citizens what they need, cannot stand. The future lies in a new partnership, where national and local governments share power with their citizens, enabling local people to use the skills which are now being wasted. Much of the local outreach work of the Belfast Action Teams, for instance, demonstrates how social capital can be nurtured through vital links made between local communities and civil servants seconded to the Teams. The quality of personal contact with the community is a key resource: much depends on engaging people who understand the problems communities face and are open-minded about how to tackle them.

We found on our own visits to Meadowell in Newcastle and to the Miles Platting and Ancoats Development Trust in Manchester that community action has been encouraged by a number of small but tangible projects that have an immediate effect on people's quality of life – from the purchase of a coach for youth outings to the development of play facilities and youth clubs for children and adolescents. But it is the local people who make the investment work: the Outer Belfast Action Team told us, for example, that although the area desperately lacked children's play areas, there was no point building a playground until a local group was able to take responsibility for it. A study of the Mead-owell experience for the Joseph Rowntree Foundation by Dr Tony Gibson, who worked on the estate for five years, concluded that economic and social decline could be reversed, but only by using the untapped skills and potential of local residents.[16] Changing the attitude of people towards themselves is as impor-tant as changing the attitude of others to the estate.

The experience of Meadowell in the initial stage revealed the importance of local people having hands-on experience, and not just a say. The Planning-for-Real exercises which took place there and in other community development projects helped to give local people real power over the planning process. Because of its considerable power for good as well as bad, the planning system must be central to community development. Planning authori-ties, both local and national, have profoundly affected life in Britain over the past fifty years. They decided where the new estates, to replace the slums, should be, and what kind of hous-ing should be built: Easterhouse is just part of the result. They have increasingly determined where workplaces should be, not necessarily close to where people live. They helped to encourage a revolution in shopping which favours car owners and disad-vantages the old and the poor. The planners' intentions were admirable – better housing, more modern factories, cheaper and more attractive shops, efficient motorways. But the results include decrepit housing in estates which are a paradise only for vandals, lengthy and expensive commuting and a weakening of links between workplace and residential communities, a decline of local communities and shops, and growing congestion on the roads. A more democratic and transparent planning process will need a revitalised system of local government. But the public must also be consulted much earlier in planning procedures, with local communities given the power, through the Community

Development Trusts we propose below, to prevent damaging developments.

Deregulators dislike the planning system, which they see as an encumbrance on the free operation of the market. It does indeed give political power to people who lack market power: it is one important way in which economically marginalised people can be given a seat at the bargaining table with powerful economic interests, from supermarket chains to housing developers to multinational companies. Planning gain can help local people get what they actually want, rather than what they are assumed to need; and local communities must also be given the chance to say what they do not want.[17] 'Value-added' comes most obviously in a wider choice of housing. Community approval for local, regional and strategic development plans increases community 'ownership' of development strategies, and builds local trust and commitment. 'Citizens' plans' represent the ultimate step in the development of community expertise and confidence, but people will only make the effort to develop them if they are convinced that it is worthwhile, and that their views will be listened to.

Community Development Trusts

The focus of a new, bottom-up regeneration strategy should be Community Development Trusts, established in the most disadvantaged areas to bring together residents, voluntary organisations, religious and other groups, and local authority councillors and officers. The central role of such a Trust in Meadowell and elsewhere in the country is a model with wide applicability. The establishment of the Development Trusts Association (DTA) in 1993 provides an opportunity to extend the work of the hundred Development Trusts which already exist in the UK. As Paddy Doherty of the Derry Inner City Trust explains:

> Standing in the vacuum between private enterprise, unwilling to become involved because of the lack of profit on the one hand, and government on the other, and harnessing help from both sides, we can fill that vacuum .... The best vehicle to fill the gap is the development trust movement.[18]

Local communities need to be funded to buy in professional advice from lawyers, architects, planners and others to help them draw up a regeneration plan. In effect, communities become the purchaser and developers become the provider. It should not just be the private sector which determines the strategic vision for regenerating communities, and which profits from the investment.

A Community Development Trust should then be established as a registered charity, able to attract a wide variety of funding. One of its first tasks might be to conduct a Skills Audit to help the local community identify the economic and social strengths which could enable it to drive the regeneration plans. In some areas, the need for environmental improvements and better security will be the main concern. Elsewhere, housing opportunities will be the first priority. Each Trust should aim to provide services which can be used by individuals as well as local groups, for instance by establishing premises which should not be seen as the 'property' of any one neighbourhood, group or party and which could house a credit union, a Citizen's Advice Bureau and if possible a community law service. Although the legal system rarely has a high profile in this area of public policy, it posesses enormous power to influence people's lives for the better. Employed on behalf of the community, lawyers can be in a position to bridge the gap between the formal planning process, local government and residents.[19] In any case, a comprehensive review of how the legal and planning systems interact is now needed.

Perhaps the most important principle of all is that the Trusts should integrate their work with existing activities, whether in benefits advice, education and training provision or business start-up support, to expand social capital, improve the quality of life and enhance people's employability. For example, if a group of parents want to launch an after-school club, the Development Trust might co-ordinate training for some of the parents. If other residents wanted to introduce a local minibus service between neighbourhoods on an estate, they should be trained to drive a minibus. We have met community groups who decided to develop childcare centres, security services and local catering groups; these and many other ideas could become the basis of a local 'social economy'. In some cases, the Development Trust could work with the Intermediate Labour Markets we described in Chapter 4 to promote local training and employment. But whether or not community action leads to commercially viable services, the employability of the people involved will have been increased, at the same time as the quality of life for everyone in the community has been improved.

A compelling case was made to us by Dr Brendan Nevin and Philip Shiner of the University of Central England that central government should support the Trusts through a new National Community Regeneration Agency (NCRA), composed of community representatives, local councillors, voluntary sector representatives and community development experts.[20] (In Scotland, the new Parliament would decide how to support community development, while the functions of the Agency could also be devolved to future regional assemblies.) The Agency would monitor and appraise local projects, advise on good practice and on the release of government funding to Trusts which can show they have engaged local people in a regeneration initiative. Funding for community projects must not take place unless a number of conditions have been met. The present system of competitive bidding directs money to those places that anticipate central government's preferences best, rather than to those with the greatest needs. So new conditions should be added to the release of government funding for regeneration, for example incentives for Trusts to build partnerships based on consultation and capacity-building in the initial community development stage. Development Trusts which demonstrate their commitment to listen and to share power should secure further funding.

Our job is not to prescribe detailed activities here. But the Development Trusts could be encouraged to raise further funds from private industry and charitable sources, as well as from the European Union's structural funds. A Trust could act as the financial intermediary for all regeneration funding in an area, and be audited in the same way as any business. It would be a charitable body dedicated to maximising income and service flows within a community, with the aim of establishing itself as an important institution for regeneration activity. The Trusts

People-led Regeneration

The best route to sustainable community regeneration is to connect investment in economic, physical and social capital. The key to this is the involvement of local people. The creation of Community Development Trusts would provide an institutional base for regeneration efforts led by local people.

- A new National Community Regeneration Agency (NCRA) should be set up to support the establishment of local regeneration initiatives and audit the work of local Trusts.

- Once the NCRA is satisfied that communities have demonstrated a willingness and capacity to share responsibility for regeneration, core regeneration funding would be allocated to newly designated Community Development Trusts.

- Local groups and individuals would be able to approach the Trust with ideas for projects to be funded. The Trust would be co-ordinated by a locally-elected board and would be established as a non-profit distributing charity.

- It would be the task of the Trust to develop working links with the local authority, local employers and training agencies and to reflect the local regeneration priorities.

- The Trust's mission would be to develop the social wealth, quality of life and reputation of the area, reconnecting the community to mainstream education, training and job opportunities.

- Trusts should focus on long-term sustainability by developing new funding sources and contracts. Their work could support emerging intermediate labour markets and community development banks.

could therefore incorporate but also extend the mainstream economic development efforts of Regional Development Agencies, TECs and local authorities.

Community safety

The time for adopting a more sophisticated approach to community safety in this country is long overdue. As in other areas, the focus of policy is currently on punishment, picking up the pieces when crimes are committed rather than investing in strategies which aim to prevent crime in the first place. Crime is not just a threat to community safety and an attack on social capital – it is a huge drain on households and the economy. In too many cities, ethnic minority communities are particularly vulnerable to the growing problem of racially motivated violence. A new law on racial violence is overdue, and we support it.

We need to strike a balance between punishment and prevention, recognising that traditional approaches – building more prisons, for example – fail to tackle the symptoms let alone challenge the causes. There are a number of innovative approaches already under way to prevent offending among young people and to prevent re-offending among those who have previous convictions.

Community regeneration must also involve community safety. We have seen many collaborative projects where local authorities, voluntary groups, individuals and employers are sharing the task of crime prevention with the police and the probation services. Crime Concern, for instance, backed by the TSB Foundation, sees family, school and community as the vital links in the crime prevention chain: it supports police, social services departments and other organisations to provide activities for older school-age children during the summer holidays. Local businesses have invested in the projects by offering volunteer supervisors and transport as well as cash. Over two years, almost 20,000 young people and 500 local businesses have taken part. Although it is difficult to measure the effect of the initiative, the police reported 30 per cent fewer complaints about young people's behaviour in some areas.

In response to growing fears about young boys stealing and smashing cars, the National Association for the Care and Resettlement of Offenders (NACRO) and other organisations, including the police, now operate some 200 car-theft diversion schemes in Britain. The aim is not simply to teach repair and maintenance but to develop negotiation skills, the discipline of group rules and an understanding of the consequences of offenders' actions for other people as well as themselves. Cuts in support for youth clubs and sports facilities, and in the youth service, will prove to be a costly step in the wrong direction. This is especially important given the danger of drug economies which have grown by default in some of the poorest and most dangerous communities.

If we are to tackle seriously the rate of re-offending, we need to give priority to those strategies which combine punishment with rehabilitation. Time-intensive as much as resource-intensive initiatives, such as the STOP programme in Mid-Glamorgan,[21] could run in parallel with the wider use of community service orders for many offenders who would otherwise be imprisoned. Recognising that opportunities to earn are the key to preventing ex-offenders becoming re-offenders means that employment and training projects initiated by groups like NACRO (involving employers like British Rail) should be extended.

Community Service Volunteers (CSV) and the Home Office offer up to 300 young offenders the choice of serving the last month of their sentence in prison or becoming voluntary community service workers. At the end of a nineteen-month sentence in a young offenders'institution, after several years of teenage crime, Jonathan volunteered to work in a home for people with disabilities. Still only twenty, he is now employed there full-time as a residential social worker. 'If it wasn't for CSV, I'd be back in prison already,' he told us. 'They ought to get CSV into court before people go to prison. Unless they're really dangerous, give them community service first. If they don't do it, then it's straight off to prison. But they might enjoy it just like I did. It gives you the chance to grow up.'

Funding regeneration

Total expenditure under the new Single Regeneration Budget (SRB) for 1994/95 is £1.44 billion, falling to £1.32 billion in the following year. Yet there are no new uncommitted resources for the current year and no new partnerships to be created. The SRB, which does not release any significant new resources until 1996/97, signals a move away from an urban policy which systematically targets resources on areas which are disproportionately deprived. In England, for example, the fifty-seven Urban Priority Areas have been abolished. In future all English local authorities will be able to bid for SRB resources. Areas of the most entrenched long-term problems should be a priority for public policy.

The existing urban-regeneration budget would go much further if part of it were invested through Community Development Trusts. One approach would be to identify the 250 most disadvantaged areas of the UK for phased release of community regeneration funding over a ten-year period (with the most disadvantaged fifth receiving funding for ten years and the least disadvantaged fifth being funded for three years). There are a number of ways to identify disadvantage, but long-term unemployment and low levels of economic activity should be priority indicators. Populations of around 10,000 (5,000 households) should be targeted for regeneration funding. Our regeneration initiative would then reach 2.5 million people and probably one quarter of the registered unemployed. Each of the Community Development Trusts could be paid £100 for each resident (an annual total of £1 million) provided it met the necessary conditions. The total resources spent in this way would rise from £50 million in year one to £150 million by the fifth year and £250 million in the tenth year (a total investment of £1.6 billion over a decade). There has been extensive debate about how to identify areas for regeneration funding. There is the established approach of targeting resources to communities with the highest concentration of problems such as unemployment. But researchers Stephen Thake and Reiner Staubach have challenged this assumption by arguing that some neighbourhoods may now be 'irretrievable' and that a 'worst-first' strategy denies resources to other areas which might benefit more in the long run.[22] In other words, we should be wary of throwing good money after bad.

Regeneration funding obviously has to be selective, and the regeneration strategy we endorse here is intended for those communities most in distress; we do not believe that the country should allow no-go areas to fester, we must arrest the drift towards American-style ghettos, beyond the reach of mainstream society. There are, however, good reasons for also reforming the basis of calculating local government grants to meet the needs of less acutely disadvantaged areas. One specific reform, supported by the Centre for Local Economic Strategies (CLES), would be to increase the weighting given to unemployment or non-employment in local government grant funding for community projects.

Sustainable regeneration also involves creating the capacity within a community to continue regeneration after central government funding has been reduced and then withdrawn. With an eye on the future, therefore, Development Trusts should negotiate with other agencies to find new funders and contractors for local projects. Sustainability of regeneration is central to the 'exit strategy' of the Waltham Forest Housing Action Trust, which is evolving into an economic development company, with the aim of reinvesting development profits back into the community. Training local people to manage resources and run projects is crucial to effective community regeneration.

Examples of new ways to regenerate communities are not lacking. What is, however, is the political commitment to recognise these ways and extend them. That is why we endorse the conclusion of Stephen Thake and Reiner Staubach in their recent report for the Rowntree Foundation:

> Without a national priority accredited to community regeneration and a framework in place which permits that commitment to be put into practice, multiply-deprived communities will remain at the margins of society.[23]

Community capital

One of the most important problems to be addressed by an effective strategy for community regeneration is the complete absence of capital. The poorest places in the UK are also some of the most expensive to live in. Not only are shops and public transport often more expensive than in other communities, but the cost of credit is high. The closure of banking facilities, amounting to 1,000 branch closures since 1989, leaves those in most need of credit with least choice. But credit unions can provide a community-owned outlet for saving and gaining credit at low rates of interest. By recycling local capital within the community, the 'fiscal haemorrhage' from poor areas can be slowed and eventually reversed. In 1991, more than 50,000 people were members of community-based credit unions in Britain. In Cranhill in Glasgow, we saw a credit union where individuals pay anything from £1 to £5 per week. Investors in the Winson Green Credit Union in Birmingham can borrow up to twice the amount paid in at an interest rate that is a fraction of that charged by private money lenders.

In comparison to Ireland, where one household in four is involved in a credit union, the British credit union tradition remains weak, and in the face of the debt economies in some marginalised communities the contribution of credit unions has, so far, been limited. Nevertheless, we believe they are an essential requirement of any serious strategy for local regeneration; the growth of the credit union movement is a vital part of the reinvestment equation.

We strongly support the expansion of credit union facilities, starting from a base established by Community Development Trusts. Funding for Community Development Trusts should recognise the way in which money flows through low-income communities 'like water through sand', according to Pat Conaty, Development Director of the Aston Commission. Local credit unions could become the 'banks' for regeneration grants, helping to retain and expand capital and improving local people's opportunities to save, to borrow and to reinvest. There is also a strong case to be made for the DSS allowing people to cash their benefit cheques either at a credit union or at a post office.

Credit unions are one part of a wider strategy concerned with widening access to capital and credit, and with trying to staunch the chronic disinvestment from low-income communities. They are in embryo a version of large-scale community banking developed around the world, from Gramene in South India to Chicago in the United States. The South Shore Community Development Bank in Chicago invests in the rehabilitation of property to rent and the finance of small businesses. Ron Grzywinski, Chairman of the Bank, believes the reason for their success is simple: 'We've probably done better because we do banking in the old-fashioned way – we know the neighbourhood and it is the same people.' The South Shore Bank has reduced default rates on loans to tenant co-operatives and small businesses to 1.5 per cent – significantly lower than that achieved by the major banks.

Richard Ferlauto, Public Capital Programme Manager of the Center for Policy Alternatives in Washington, summarises the lessons of his work on the development of community capital as follows. First, micro-economic strategies depend on creating community capital through the regulation of private capital flows (for example through Community Reinvestment Acts), the capitalising of community development financial institutions, and the direction to targeted areas of institutional investments. Second, the non-profit sector must develop community-based alternatives to private sector firms and public bureaucracies for the business of housing and community development.

Instead of giving employment to people who live far beyond an area receiving regeneration funding, the development of locally directed capital allows local communities to reap some of the benefits of the investment in their own future. Instead of money spent *on* people, money should be spent *by* local people *for* the benefit of local people.

In contrast to the UK, the concept of community banking is well developed in the USA. Government initiatives have concentrated on encouraging banks to meet communities' credit needs. The Community Reinvestment Act (CRA), passed in 1977, which aimed to improve community banking and stop the process of 'redlining' that was marginalising poor communities, is being strengthened by the Clinton administration. As a result of the Act, banks are making commitments to low- and moderate-income areas. The Bank of America, for example, is committed to lending $12 billion to low income areas over the next decade. A programme of Economically Targeted Investments (ETIs), designed to strengthen local communities by investment in affordable housing, community development, employment training and environmental improvement, and funded through pension and other large institutional funds, is growing in the US. A total of $20 billion is now invested in ETIs, with 27 out of 53 state retirement systems using them. Meanwhile, the Department of Housing and Urban Development has created a $1.2 billion ETI pool with the AFL-CIO Housing Investment Trust for low income housing development.

In this country, alternative ways of investing in community capital are only now beginning to emerge. The Aston Reinvestment Trust (ART) in Birmingham is being developed to act as a community-based bank with a targeted lending and reinvestment mission. The project begins from the understanding that financial institutions are reluctant to fund economic activity in what are likely to be initially high-risk/low-return communities. The aim is to rebuild a healthy stream of affordable credit provision by recycling people's savings, as part of a much broader set of development opportunities. The ART is establishing two parallel companies, the first with an investment fund (to lend to self-employment, social housing, small businesses and general banking activities) and the second with a development fund (to pay for necessary development costs and to provide a local guarantee fund). It aims to work closely with local credit unions and, significantly, with the mainstream banks: the ART does not see itself in a competitive role but in a supportive one, to close a funding gap where bank branches have closed. A strong credit union movement would provide potential customers, rather than competition, for the formal banking sector.

The longest-established social bank in the UK, Mercury Provident, invests in projects with 'added social value' and offers choice as to which project money is invested in. Reinvestment funding in the future could come to include pension and insurance funds. Such companies have been reluctant to invest in community sector initiatives in this country, although progress in the USA suggests that pension funds could be harnessed to capitalise infrastructure investments (in housing for example) as well as community services like childcare facilities. Reinvestment funding will fully come to fruition only when there are too many good reasons for financial institutions not to invest in low-income neighbourhoods.

There is also scope for Community Development Trusts to support and extend the informal economy and exchange of non-monetary goods and services. The 1990s have witnessed a remarkable growth of informal local barter systems, with almost 200 Local Exchange Trading Systems (LETS) operating throughout the UK. LETS work by encouraging people and organisations to trade skills, services and goods without needing to use the cash economy, although they can be used alongside it. Some of the fastest-growing LETS are in relatively prosperous areas such as Avon and Surrey; but there is an obvious danger that LETS further disconnect marginalised communities from the national economy.

The first formal LETS scheme was established in Canada in 1983 and then spread to Australia and New Zealand. They work by developing a local directory of skills which can be traded in an organised informal sector; use of LETS is 'paid' for by debiting the number of credits in an account. The key to an effective scheme lies in the extent to which credits can be exchanged. An informal economy is not the same as a 'black market', which involves either trade in illegally obtained goods or the evasion of tax through payment in cash, and the social and economic pay-offs of LETS activity can be significant. LETS schemes obviously raise important questions for the Inland Revenue, which is currently turning a blind eye to the benefits received in kind by households involved in LETS schemes; it should continue to do so. As we argued in relation to citizen's income schemes in Chapter 6, our ambition is to make work pay for all citizens; as in that case, however, if the UK does not manage to tackle entrenched problems of structural unemployment, more detailed consideration will have to be given to LETS.

Regeneration is an ongoing process, not a one-off; but our conviction is that we can 'level up' the position of poor communities, rather than allowing their poverty to level-down the whole of our country. Mainstream investments in education, housing, health and transport will all have a major role to play in connecting marginalised economies and communities to the rest of the economy and society. The targeted measures outlined here are a necessary complement to them.

Building Strong Communities II: Housing

It is a disgrace that nearly half a million people are homeless in this country, that more than a million more live in homes which are officially unfit for habitation, and that 800,000 homes are standing empty. Slum clearance – an end to 'squalor' – was an important feature in the Attlee Government's plan for post-war renewal. Housebuilding, to high standards, was the priority. By the early 1950s, Churchill's Conservative Government was over-seeing the building of 300,000 new houses a year. By the 1970s, problems of housing shortage seemed to have been eliminated. But many of the brave new post-war estates have become today's slums. Fewer new homes are being built for rent than at virtually any time since the war. But British families spend more and borrow more on housing than on any other item; and the cycles of boom and slump in the economy are partly the consequence of our skewed systems of housing provision and finance.

The problems with housing in the UK reflect both the way housing is financed (and the balance between private and public investment) and the way it has been governed (including questions of design, allocation and management). Compared with other OECD countries, a higher proportion of the UK's personal wealth is locked into servicing housing costs. On average, a quarter of household incomes is spent on housing and related items.[24] Yet we are close to the bottom of the OECD table of national investment in building and renewing homes. The Rowntree Foundation reports that if the UK had invested the same proportion of GDP in housebuilding during the 1980s as Germany, we would have more than 600,000 additional homes.[25]

In the last fifteen years, government has encouraged the expansion of owner-occupation, most obviously through the sale of council houses, but also through the deregulation of mortgage lending and the widespread growth of the 100 per cent mortgage. It is now the mass tenure in the UK, rather than simply the majority tenure, as in Denmark, or a large sector alongside a large rented sector, as in Germany or the Netherlands. In the European Union, only Spain, Greece and Ireland have larger owner-occupied sectors. For those in relatively well-paid and secure employment, owner-occupation opens doors. But for others, the housing situation is marked by lack of choice. For the large number of homeless people, housing is an aspiration rather than a reality.

The way we finance housing provision is irrational and inefficient. Mortgage interest tax relief is a poorly targeted subsidy for private owners; housing benefit is increasingly narrowly targeted but cannot compensate for failures in the labour market; and the private rented sector is either subsidised in an inappropriate way or not at all. The result over the last decade has been rapid house price inflation, followed by slump, labour-market 'bottlenecks', mortgaging beyond means, and debt, repossessions and unemployment traps. Rent levels in both the council and housing association sectors have increased faster than incomes; almost half of housing association tenants in work are now eligible for Housing Benefit, a proportion which has doubled in only four years.[26] As more tenants become entitled to Housing Benefit, the result is a cost to the Exchequer of £10 billion.

Public support for capital investment in bricks and mortar through the Housing Association Grant and through local authority capital receipts is a more efficient and effective subsidy than that of rents through Housing Benefit, which is costly to administer and fails to improve housing or work opportunities. Despite this, councils are restricted in how much of their sale receipts can be reinvested in rehabilitation and new building. Housing associations are facing reduced grant support from central government: in 1994/95 the average level of grant support will fall from 62 per cent of the cost of a home to 55 per cent.[27] This move threatens the long-term stability of housing associations, and is likely to increase rents still further. For housing associations, the need to attract greater private investment sharpens the dilemma between the needs of their tenants (for small-scale and affordable housing) and their funders (for lower costs per unit). The result is more expensive housing in general, and a trade-off that may favour quantity rather than quality.

Lastly, housing rights have been diminished for some low-income households in particular. The Housing Act of 1980, most famous for introducing the 'right to buy', also introduced a Tenants' Charter, strengthening the rights of local authority tenants. However, new forms of private-sector rented tenancies involve fewer rights for tenants, and new housing associations provide assured tenancies with fewer rights than previously secure tenancies and less security than in the council rented sector. Most striking of all is the proposal that the right to permanent accommodation for homeless people with priority needs be eroded. Security of tenure is again a major housing issue for this country.

Building more homes

If we want to end the scandal of homelessness in all its forms, we need to build and refurbish more homes for rent at affordable rates. This involves changing Treasury restrictions to permit the gradual release of the estimated £6.5 billion which local authorities have received from council house sales, and finding ways for housing associations (which are not subject to the same restrictions on borrowing) to attract more capital themselves. Even on cautious estimates, an annual investment of £650 million – as suggested by Shelter in its 1993 Budget proposals – would create at least 50,000 new and refurbished homes for rent and generate around 45,500 new jobs. Furthermore, these jobs would tap skills which are being wasted, provide new training opportunities and have a low import penetration level. Since it is generally estimated that the shortfall in social rented housing will be about 50-60,000 houses per year over a decade, a target of at least this scale should be set nationally for new and refurbished homes.

We are not, however, simply arguing for a return to council housing. Although the overall share of the council rented sector has declined, it is housing an increasing proportion of the poorest households. In 1991, 65 per cent of the lowest income tenth of households were council tenants, an increase of 5 per cent since 1980. Furthermore, almost one-third of council tenants are now concentrated in that lowest income 10 per cent band (compared with 17 per cent in 1980). The aim should be to reduce, not to intensify, the concentration of the poorest and most vulnerable people in particular forms of housing, including the least desirable council estates.

Effective use of the planning system to achieve the planning gain of mixed housing tenure developments would make a higher level of investment in social rented housing go even further. It should be applied to ensure that we learn from past mistakes. For example, many local authority developments have failed partly because they were too big. The most effective approaches to management and tenant participation appear to occur in developments no larger than 1,000 houses. Local authorities and housing associations should therefore enter into joint management arrangements, and local authorities should obtain nomination rights to housing association developments. In keeping with the approach we have taken towards Community Development Trusts, the people who are to be rehoused in new or refurbished housing should themselves be actively engaged in designing them. Home-building must include more single-person housing, particularly in cities with large numbers of young homeless people; the Foyers which have been developed in London by the Prince's Trust provide one imaginative model of how good quality, affordable housing can be integrated with social facilities and access to training. Accommodation for people with special needs should also be a high priority within the housing renewal programme.

Local Housing Companies

We want to see private, as well as public, capital invested in the renewal of Britain's housing. Local authorities should be given the power to establish Local Housing Companies responsible for developing and managing social rented housing and able to create public/private finance partnerships.[28] (Tenants who want to continue to rent directly from the local authority should, however, be able to do so). Local Housing Companies would be democratic bodies, involving tenant representatives as well as local councillors. Because housing stock conditions vary so widely between local authorities (debt per property for example), it will still be necessary to include provision for debt subsidy for those Housing Companies inheriting the largest debts.

A major source of funding for the new Housing Companies should be a new national Housing Bank, which would provide a capitalised intermediary for social rented housing. By pooling risks across the housing stock of all Housing Companies, the Bank would improve their access to the securities market, offering improved terms for investment funds. Capital receipts could be paid into Housing Companies and used to lever in funding from the Housing Bank.

Housing associations, either separately or as part of local Housing Companies, will also have access to investment capital through the Housing Bank. But they must be able to rely on central government support in order to attract outside funding. That means that Housing Association Grant (HAG) levels should be planned in advance and represent a substantial proportion of costs. (One independent estimate shows a need for government to increase the national average grant rate to 63 per cent, rather than cut it to 55 per cent as is currently being proposed.[29]) This acts as a form of 'free equity', attracting financial-sector investment: in the five years to 1992, private sector investment grew from £8 million to over £1 billion.[30] According to Steven Bell, Chief Economist with Morgan Grenfell: 'The higher the percentage of government grant, the more we want to lend. That is one clear way in which more private money could be brought into the social rented sector.'[31] Financial markets for social housing are weakly developed, and need to be encouraged by government.

The problem of rapidly rising housing association rents must also be addressed. As a start, the Housing Corporation should consider guidelines on rental affordability and adjust its grant allocations to favour schemes working within those guidelines. But more fundamental reforms are needed, to provide the subsidies for bricks and mortar which allow rents to be kept low, in place of the subsidies for people through means-tested Housing Benefit with its inevitable poverty traps.

A flexible housing market

This country's housing system is increasingly at odds with social and economic realities: a rapidly growing proportion of one-person households (partly the result of later marriages and more divorce) and an increasingly insecure labour market. The United Kingdom needs more homes of the right size, in the right place and at the right price, to rent as well as to buy. We need to extend better choices to people of different ages, particularly young people who may be faced with no option other than to buy before they have accumulated savings; we need to make it easier for people to move from one part of the country to another; and we need to enable people to change their housing tenure when their circumstances change, without necessarily changing their home. For low income and jobless households, affordable rents in the local authority and housing association sectors would make them the most appropriate options.[32] Since neither home-buyers nor lenders can rely any longer on the security offered by lifetime jobs, every building society, bank and local council should aim to offer shared-equity schemes, which match the proportion of property ownership to households' changing incomes, reducing the risk that losing a job will mean losing a home as well. The tenant co-operative model developed in Sweden provides one example of how costs and capital gains can be shared and pooled over time. Several British local authorities have co-ordinated 'mortgage to rent' buy-back schemes particularly for ex-council tenants who have difficulties in keeping up mortgage payments. Equity-release schemes, although limited in their potential, may also provide a way to capitalise on the value of housing assets when they may be required to pay for expensive repair and maintenance work.

These reforms have been supported by a number of housing commentators in this country, usually with young and elderly households in mind. Tenure flexibility should, however, become a much more common approach to housing, with wider applicability to households which are likely to move more often than others and for those who work in low-paid or insecure jobs. Such reforms will involve the creation of a far more flexible system of housing finance, provided for instance by Housing Benefit reforms, as well as a greater capacity for local authorities and future Housing Companies to invest in capital programmes and the establishment of a level playing-field in subsidies and the tax treatment of different tenures.

Private renting has an important role to play in making the housing system more flexible, more efficient and more just. Private renting offers quick access, is often popular with young people and could offer more housing choice in areas of job growth. The UK's private rented sector is unusually small (at 7 per cent of the housing stock). It is never again going to be a major sector, but it can still play a pivotal role. We need action to support the private rented sector, but also to protect tenants against unscrupulous landlords and improve their security of tenure. Existing Tenant Relations Officers could be used to license approved landlords to provide assured tenancies and introduce greater accountability to local authorities.

Tackling homelessness

Homelessness is the most potent symbol of social injustice in housing and a symptom of our economic and social failure. It demands an urgent response.

Governments cannot prevent most of the causes of homelessness, which include family breakdown, domestic violence and child abuse. What can and must be changed, however, is the way in which governments respond to these risks, as well as those associated with deregulated mortgage lending and repossessions. At present, people are accepted as homeless if they are literally roofless, if they have a home but are in danger of violence from someone living there, or if they are in temporary accommodation meant for an emergency (such as a women's refuge). Local authorities currently have a duty to find permanent accommodation for people who have become unintentionally homeless, provided that they have 'priority status' (such as having dependent children) as well as a local connection. Other weaker responsibilities exist as well, such as that to provide temporary housing. This legislation has at least secured some rights for some homeless people and, crucially, has stopped children being taken into care simply because their parents were homeless (around two-third of homeless households have dependent children).

The Government's 1994 review of allocations in social rented housing threatens to change this, by removing the duty of local authorities to secure permanent housing for those groups now entitled to it. Instead, councils will only have a recurring responsibility to provide temporary accommodation for up to a year. In effect the rights of the unintentionally homeless would become as weak as the temporary rights of those now classed as intentionally homeless. The inevitable result would be more families spending longer in bed-and-breakfast and other temporary accommodation, with all the damaging effects on children and families that this involves. According to the Audit Commission, bed-and-breakfast hostels offer 'the lowest standards and the highest costs'.[33] The Government's proposals seem to run directly counter to the spirit of the Children Act. While the Government claims that single parents receive privileged treatment if they are homeless, their priority status reflects the fact only that they have children, not that they are without partners. Homeless families with children should not be relegated to temporary accommodation which, even from a Treasury point of view, is a poor deal: the average annual cost of bed-and-breakfast accommodation is £12,200 (and in London £14,600), compared with an average cost of a new local authority or housing association dwelling of £10,800.[34]

Instead, we want to see councils, housing associations and the voluntary housing sectors working in partnership to ensure that the best use is made of existing resources as well as new houses as they are built or refurbished. Organisations of homeless people themselves should be directly involved in the process. *The Big Issue*, for instance, is an extraordinarily successful self-help movement, which not only has a weekly sale of some 165,000 copies but also offers training and advice as well as a source of self-employment. There is considerable expertise in groups such as the Hanover Medical Centre in Sheffield, and the St Dismas Centre in Southampton, which organise health care outreach projects for homeless people. The private rented sector also has a role to play, given its ability to offer quick access to furnished tenancies, provided that the necessary safeguards for licensed landlords are established. Grants to secure tenancies, which have not been available through the Social Fund, would extend security of tenure. There is also a need for legislative reforms, which only central government can make. Minimum requirements include a statutory appeals system and a duty imposed on local authorities to demonstrate that their approach meets standards of good practice. It should also be seriously considered whether the priority-needs qualification can be amended to cover young single homeless people, most of whom are currently excluded.

Housing renewal

The housing problem is one of quality as well as quantity. Over 1.5 million houses have been classed as 'unfit' or of 'sub-tolerable standards', many being damp and highly energy-inefficient. If we do nothing today, more houses will be demolished tomorrow and more people will face homelessness. The community development strategies we proposed will usually include housing rehabilitation (although in Northern Ireland, public housing is generally of higher quality, even in some of the poorest areas). As members of the Miles Platting and Ancoats Development Trust in Manchester told the Commission, better job opportunities would probably lead to people moving away from the area unless they were combined with better housing opportunities as well. The new Housing Companies should therefore develop renewal plans in conjunction with Community Development Trusts, while self-build and self-rehabilitation projects, organised by local co-operatives, offer a small but significant further means of housing renewal.

We are concerned about the dramatic decline in renovation funding over the last decade. If more expensive solutions are to be avoided in future, additional investment is required in the shorter term. One possibility is for the new Housing Bank to offer renovation grants for private housing in serious need of rehabilitation, with the cost of the grant being wholly or partly recovered on the subsequent sale of the property. Improving energy-efficiency should be given particularly high priority, with proper standards incorporated into Building Regulation Standards for all new housing.

Finally, it is intolerable that so many houses lie empty when so many people are homeless. A system of incentives and penalties should be used to reduce the number of unoccupied houses. The renovation grant reform should encourage housing to be brought back into use. Where houses remain unoccupied for a period of twelve months – whatever sector they are in – penalty payments should be introduced and administered along with the local authority property tax.

Advice, advocacy and tenant participation

More information leads to better decisions. That applies both to people as housing consumers and to housing agencies who lend, who allocate and who manage. Irresponsible lending in the 1980s resulted in debt and despair for many lower-income homeowners. Better mortgage advice, along with the broader tenure options endorsed above, is needed.

Local authorities should be given a clear statutory duty to develop local housing information and advice strategies, involving statutory and voluntary providers and developing closer links with commercial providers. Local authority services should become relevant and accessible to people whatever sector they live in: tenants in the private rented sector often experience the poorest conditions and management, yet advocacy services are hardly developed. Independent advice agencies should also be expanded, particularly to offer impartial mortgage advice.

The Tenant Participation Advisory Schemes (TPAS) should be extended to alter the balance of power further in favour of tenants. In parallel, the rights of housing association tenants should be made equivalent to those of local authority tenants. We cannot afford to make the same mistakes of housing management, design and allocation as in the past. To build social justice into housing, we need to ensure that every citizen has access to a home. We are in no doubt about the unfinished agenda we inherit from Beveridge. But we also need to go further, ensuring that housing is affordable, energy-efficient and flexible enough to meet different people's different needs.

Housing for the Future

We need to match housing choice with people's aspirations; and we need housing security in the face of changing economic and employment realities.

- Develop a mortgage benefit to help low income home-owners off benefit and into work (Chapter 6)
- Rebalance housing finance to support bricks and mortar rather than individuals, and promote tenure flexibility
- Develop a national Housing Bank to co-ordinate the investment of private capital
- Start to re-invest receipts from council house sales in building new homes and refurbishment
- Experiment with Local Housing Companies to regenerate social rented housing
- Get homeless families out of expensive and unsatisfactory bed and breakfast accommodation, and into secure housing
- Reduce the number of unoccupied and unsuitable properties
- Promote tenant participation and involvement in decision-making
- Improve energy efficiency

Civic Leadership: Reviving Local Democracy

Social capital is about the strength of communities, and their ability to make a difference to the lives of their members. At the heart of the ability to make a difference, the ability to shape the course of one's own life, is the issue of democracy. From Cape Town to Vladivostock, democracy is on the march; (almost) everyone is a democrat. Yet paradoxically, the traditional institutions of liberal democracy have rarely been under greater scrutiny. Nowhere is this more the case than in the UK, and nowhere is it more true than in relation to the ability of local people to govern their own affairs.

Civic leadership is not a pipedream. Standing on the balcony of Norwich City Hall after a day of visits to successful small businesses and innovative voluntary groups, looking over a thriving market and a busy community, we saw the effect of positive civic leadership and imagined how much more could be done if the talents and energies of local people were given the freedom they deserve. Nor was that an isolated example: on visits all over the country, we have been impressed by the energy and imagination of many local councillors and officers trying to do their best by their communities with little encouragement from national government.

As Professor David Donnison and his colleagues at Warwick University's Local Government Centre have recognised, we need new forms of government able to take a strategic perspective on the problems and able to accommodate the needs of both 'mainstream' and 'marginalised' communities. Donnison argues that we need to mobilise public, voluntary, private and community-based interests to undertake different tasks at different levels:

> [Mobilisation] is a task for civic leaders who have a broad responsibility for the development of their own place and political authority to speak for its citizens. It cannot be tackled effectively by one service, agency or professional working alone, or by focusing only on particular areas of deprivation.[35]

In the nineteenth century, economic and social development were driven locally by civic pride and municipal initiative. Cities such as Birmingham, Leeds, Newcastle and Liverpool were all governed by entrepreneurial civic leaders, determined to build prosperity in their home towns. It was not only the unity of the United Kingdom that ensured its economic strength, but its local diversity. Local government was an enormous economic and social resource.

Over the course of the century, and despite successive reorganisations of local government, the municipal enterprise of the nineteenth century has been dissipated. On the Left, despite the success of 'gas and water' municipal socialism, the Fabian tradition looked to central government for social and economic reform. Meanwhile, on the Right, Mrs Thatcher and her government set out to destroy what they saw not just as bastions of left-wing inefficiency and waste, but also bureaucratic institutions that stifled initiative and enterprise. The logic of deregulation leads Deregulators inevitably to see local government as an interference in the free operation of the market: Deregulators end up as Centralisers. Investors see local democracy as an essential element in social and economic renewal.

The stripping of powers from local government and the reduction in the proportion of local authority funds raised locally have diminished the importance of local government and the local electoral process. We have visited parts of the UK where the turnout in local government elections is below 20 per cent. We have also heard how the 'winner-takes-all' electoral system results in one-party states. Electoral competition should be used to spur good and responsive government.

Only if accountability can be strengthened will people gain rights, not merely as customers but as citizens. That must be the priority for civic leaders, local politicians and council officers. Civic leadership requires the commitment of people who are elected and have a responsibility to consider the whole community. Effective local government also depends upon the contribution of many agencies – including the voluntary sector, the private sector, the TECs and the health services – rather than just particular interests. The alternative is alienation and suspicion in the relationships between citizens, local government and central authorities.

Decentralisation

Unlike most of the UK's European neighbours, we lack a regional tier of government. Centralisation by stealth has removed responsibilities from local councils to Westminster, and to appointed boards (or quangos). Fiscal centralisation has left local authorities with responsibility for just 15p in each pound of their income. Accountability has come to mean accountability of councils to central government, not to local voters.

British government badly needs to be decentralised. Modern societies and economies are simply too complex to be governed effectively from the centre. The renewal of our social capital depends upon effective, imaginative and responsible government at the local and regional level. Because partnership depends on the sharing of contributions, risks and benefits, a weak local government will mean weak local partnerships. But effective local government can make an enormous difference. Much of the strength and resilience of the German economy, for example, derives from its powerful structure of regional and local government, able to build the social and economic network within which small and medium-sized businesses thrive. In any case, Westminster is too burdened to substitute itself for local democracy. Parliament produces an average of thirteen pages of primary legislation and eighteen statutory regulations each day it sits.[36] Central government cannot and should not behave as if it is capable of responding flexibly and decisively to local problems, from school closures to planning decisions. At the same time, MPs are pressed into service as stand-in social workers to overcome the weakness of local government. The principle of subsidiarity, strongly supported by the present Government in Europe, should be applied to the renewal of democracy in Britain; responsibility should be passed to the lowest tier of government at which it can be handled. Of course central government must retain key legislative powers, but neither Whitehall nor quangos have the capacity to perform the important tasks of civic leadership.

In this context, the establishment of central government's Integrated Regional Offices, while a first step in the construction of an effective structure for economic regeneration, looks more like 'Whitehall in the regions' than decentralised government.[37] In Sheffield, for example, we heard how the projects involved in the city's Cultural Industries Quarter are being constrained in their plans for expansion by the narrow investment rules operated by the regional office of the Environment Department. On the other hand, Lancashire Enterprise, one of the most successful of the regional enterprise boards and development agencies established by local authorities in the 1980s, has developed a consultancy role to help build trading relationships, as well as upgrading premises for new and expanding enterprises. It is representative of the best of Continental practice.

We support proposals for the creation of a Scottish parliament and a Welsh assembly. In parts of England, there is also a strong body of support for a regional tier of government; where there is economic, social and cultural rationale for regional government, it should be created. In London, the strategic void left by the abolition of the GLC should be filled by a directly elected assembly. The position of Northern Ireland must also be reviewed: the democratic deficit there has distinct causes and much deeper roots than in Britain, but its resolution is beyond our remit. Throughout the United Kingdom, however, the decentralisation of power and the establishment of new centres of government will require the framework of a Bill of Rights to protect individuals and minority groups against discrimination or injustice.

If tomorrow's councils are to fulfil their partnership role in building economic and social success, they will require greater power and more resources to invest. Local government must clearly act within constraints set by national government, but far too often measures introduced by central government have in fact constituted political manipulation. The consequence of rate-capping, the uniform business rate and other measures that have reduced the autonomy of local government mean that councils cannot be held accountable for the funding of the majority of their actions. Drawing on other European experience, we would like to see local governments in this country given a general competence to undertake any activity that is approved by their electorate and not specifically prohibited by law. We have not tried to carry out a detailed review of the extremely complex issue of local government finance and taxation. It is quite apparent, however, that local councils must have far greater freedom to spend substantial resources in accordance with local priorities, whether this is achieved through local powers of taxation or the assignment of national revenue. As a starting point, councils should be given a new power to seek voters' approval for a limited council tax increase dedicated to a specific purpose.

It is not enough, however, to decentralise power to local government. Local government bureaucracies can also be centralised, inflexible and secretive. Decentralisation is important at the level of the community as well. There are both positive and negative lessons from the London Boroughs of Islington and Tower Hamlets where councils have 'gone local', by establishing one-stop community offices, or devolving spending power to neighbourhood level. More systematic anti-poverty policies are being developed through the National Local Government Forum Against Poverty, drawing on the experience of authorities such as Rotherham. There are limits to how many functions can be decentralised. Diversity means that the activities of some councils will be a nuisance to Westminster; but that is a price worth paying for the revival of local communities.

Public accountability

In 1888, responsibility for the administration of English counties was taken away from the magistrates, an appointed lay elite, and given to elected councils. A century later, a new magistracy is being created in the shape of a non-elected elite which can in no sense be regarded as locally accountable. Black holes of accountability have appeared between citizens and central government. Government responsibilities and the public's right to hold it to account are vanishing into them. As Professor John Stewart has written:

> There is a growing crisis of accountability in the emerging pattern of government. Public accountability has to be reinvigorated, but that cannot be achieved by accountability of an over-burdened centre or by local government in its traditional forms.[38]

Together with the centralising of power in a few hands at Westminster, this growth in appointed bodies at the local level has contributed to a crisis of public accountability. The spread of the quango, whose board members are selected by ministers and not elected by those on whose behalf they act, has seen the removal of local authority representatives from key activities related to housing, health and training. At least £1 in every £5 spent by central government – £50 billion per year – is accounted for by quangos, whose budgets now exceed those of local government. Ministers argue that accountability exists through the ballot box at general elections and in the demands and choices of customers; but this is a complacent and self-serving account of quangos' relation to accountable democracy.[39] It is ironic that just as the more progressive elements of the private sector are moving towards a broader definition of accountability, and are recognising the need to take account of the views of the community, government is freezing the public out from involvement in key decision-making. Public accountability should be an ongoing process, not a periodic event.

The answer is not to turn the clock back to 1979. It is time instead to develop a new accountability for government in the UK. Its first principle must be that the weight of accountability is dispersed and shared by different tiers of government. The second principle should be that accountability is a process of public stewardship. It is not reducible to the management accountability found in the private sector and in the existing Citizen's Charter. The more accountability is seen as a process, a continuing relationship, the less it is served either by the delegated authority of ministers or the rights of 'customers': no one really believes, for example, that the new water companies of England and Wales are held accountable by the customers.

Several local authorities have taken the initiative by developing a scrutiny role on behalf of the public. In Kirklees, for example, the council has established a number of Scrutiny Commissions, to which local agencies give an account of their work. We view this development with great interest, since it begins to redefine the role of the local authority in a way that could be more relevant to local people. The scrutiny activities are not limited to those services directly provided by the council, but are instead part of a broader information and monitoring role for the council. There is no reason why quangos could not come under scrutiny in this way.

However, councils presently have no power to hold them to account. To strengthen public accountability, more fundamental reform is required.

There is an overriding requirement for clear codes of practice governing the proper conduct of quangos, at least equivalent to those applying to local authorities, concerning openness over appointees and their interests. Currently only one in three has its accounts scrutinised by national auditors and fewer than one in ten opens its doors or its accounts by holding any public meetings.[40] The power to replace members of the board and to hold them to account through auditing and possible surcharge procedures should be established. In other cases, there will be persuasive reasons for direct elections. Although voters may object if local elections become too numerous, they may respond positively, for instance, to an opportunity to elect 'health councillors'. If local government were empowered to take an integrated view of services provided in an area, for instance to combine the health and community care functions that are currently separated, some of these problems would be more easily resolved.

The creeping loss of powers to the unelected state diminishes the stake of citizens in the process of governance, and allows the spread of corruption and secrecy. The trend must be reversed. It is a disgrace that the power of appointment, which is crucial, should at present be simply exercised by the Government. One route for reform would be the establishment of a Public Appointments Commission, accountable first to Parliamentary Select Committees, and later, as they are established, to regional tiers of government.[41]

Another possibility is to make greater use of public hearings, initiated when enough members of the public want to raise an important issue with the local authority or health authority. A further option is to use referenda as a consultation process. Several councils have organised referenda on issues from local government reform to the future of water and sewerage. Most recently, Strathclyde Region's referendum on the latter issue attracted a turnout of general election proportions. It was conducted by postal ballot, an approach which has significantly increased participation in New Zealand's council elections.

An innovative idea being developed by Professor John Stewart is the introduction of citizens' panels on the jury service principle. Members of the public would be chosen at random to join a panel which 'shadowed' the work of the health authority or specific local government committees. They could serve as a means of reconnecting the process of governance to public opinion. The purpose is not to replace government by election with that by jury, but to improve the consultation process. People are entitled to expect their elected representatives to take decisions on their behalf and then to be called to give an account. But where representatives can have their efforts supplemented by participative forms of democratic input in between elections, such initiatives can support the work of councillors rather than hinder them. In some instances, the responsibilities of appointed boards will be better conducted through the local authority directly. Alternatively, some local boards might continue to operate, but with their members elected or appointed by the council, rather than by a Secretary of State.

The Commission does not have a remit to review the national electoral system, nor do we make any claims about the effect of different electoral systems on the quality of government. If local government is to have a new importance and greater responsibilities, however, and if a new tiers of government are created in Scotland, Wales and the English regions, then we cannot ignore the inadequacy of a voting system which leaves minorities unrepresented and which may allow one party to achieve almost permanent control of a council on a minority of votes. By improving the incentives for people to vote and councils to be more responsive, electoral reform for local government could be an important way of reviving local democracy.

Improving public services

Public services exist for the benefit of people who use them – both in the limited sense of public service clients and in the broader sense of the wider benefits that accrue to society from effective public education and social services. But public services depend on the commitment and ideas of the people who deliver them, whether civil servants or teachers, social workers or care assistants, doctors or nurses. Public service is an honourable profession, and should be recognised as such. The key elements of public service – trust, recognition, commitment – apply both to the treatment of citizens by public service workers, and the relationship between politicians and managers and their front-line workers.

Citizens are not just passive recipients of public services, but neither are public service workers robots – their energy and ideas are crucial to effective public service. Attempts to give people more influence over how services are run, such as the UK's Citizen's Charter, have so far been founded on a narrow understanding of the public's interests. Contractual accountability usually means choices being made by purchasers rather than the public. We believe that both responsive service to consumers (how housing or public transport is delivered) and public accountability to citizens (the ability to call for more or better housing or public transport) are essential elements in any serious attempt to empower people.

As part of our commitment to achieving a more personalised and relevant welfare state, the views of service users must be sought. Assessments of disability and community care needs are particularly relevant here. Some argue that representativeness cannot be achieved, because unrepresentative 'busybodies' will dominate consultation exercises and therefore participation will always be patchy. Yet some community groups and tenant management organisations have good reason to claim they are more representative than many councillors, often attracting more candidates and a higher turnout than the official local election.

Given the widespread acceptance across Europe of the idea of the Social Chapter of the Maastricht Treaty, there is increasing interest in social and economic rights, to accompany the political and civil rights that exist in all advanced democracies. It is crucial to draw a distinction between substantive service rights and procedural rights.[43] Substantive rights are important in setting a standard below which no citizen should be permitted to fall; rights to an education and to health are examples. Substantive rights do not tell us, however, how education and health care should be delivered. This first set of rights is unenforceable when the demand for public services outstrips resources. If two people need a hip replacement or want to send their child to the same school – and there is only enough money at that time for one operation or space for one pupil – who decides who gets what? Such questions cannot always be settled by reference to legal rights: they are essentially political. It is, however, easier to develop a set of procedural rights – to a fair hearing, to unbiased decisions, to an explanation and to an appeal – as well as rights to information to enable decisions to be made. There is no simple formula for introducing procedural rights in health and social services, but such reform is needed if we are to move from people 'knowing their place' to people knowing their rights and fulfilling their responsibilities.

Second, service-providers need to change their culture of decision-making. In South Glamorgan, the County Council has moved further down this route than most local authorities with its Children and Families initiative. Through a network of local family centres, a closer relationship has developed between the Social Services department and parents. Power and responsibility for service planning and provision is being shared: for example, parents' groups have initiated training in childcare and other skills which could act as stepping-stones to future employment. In Newcastle, the City Council's anti-poverty strategy includes the Family Support initiative. It differs from traditional approaches through its emphasis on prevention, delivering practical services for children, young people and their parents without the need for formal assessments.

These innovative approaches are important because the traditional debate about the options for public service delivery – top-down bureaucracy versus market-led outcomes – neglects what is in fact required: a partnership between the providers of services and the users, whether they are children, disabled people, elderly people or commuters. The partnership must extend between providers to include new recognition of the implications of the 'mixed economy' of public service provision, combining the efforts of public, non-profit and private sectors.

Reviving Civic Leadership

Democracy is the first precondition of change. Local democracy and local civic leadership are the roots of a thriving civic culture. And a thriving civic culture is at the heart of a wealthy society.

- Government in the UK is over-centralised and unaccountable. Power must be decentralised to Scotland and Wales, and where appropriate to the English regions, but local councils must devolve power too
- The power of unelected quangos casts a shadow across the political landscape. Power must be returned to democratically accountable bodies where possible, and unelected bodies must be made accountable
- Public services are a vital foundation of opportunity and security. They exist for the benefit of people who use them; and depend on a strong ethic of public service among the people who deliver them
- New rights for citizens must be matched by a recognition of the function of public service professionals, and their key role in the flexible and empowering public service delivery
- A Bill of Rights should provide a new framework for the exercise of devolved power and protect individuals and groups against discrimination or injustice

Something for something: Citizens' Service for the UK

Unemployment among 16 to 25-year-olds is twice the national average. Almost one million young adults in that age group are neither in work or on a training course, nor in further or higher education.[44] According to the National Children's Home, more than 150,000 16 to 19-year-olds experience homelessness every year.[45] 18 to 20-year-olds earn on average just over half average earnings, compared with 61 per cent in 1979. As many as 2.5 million 18 to 25 year olds did not vote at the last general election.

And legal anomalies plague the development of a coherent youth policy: 16-year-olds can pay taxes but not vote, marry but not get a mortgage.

These figures represent an enormous gamble with our future. If the most enduring adolescent experience is one of exclusion and alienation, a tinder-box of resentment is created. As a report by a coalition of sixteen youth organisations put it:

> Young people are active citizens in society, able and wanting to make an effective contribution to the social, economic and cultural development of the country but denied the right to do so. Our society is one which deters the active participation of young people in the society that they are shaping.[46]

Citizens' Service, our proposal for a new voluntary community service scheme, reflects our ambition of creating a 'something for something' society, rich in civic wealth and social capital, where rights are matched by responsibilities, where mutual respect and individual fulfilment proceed side by side, where independence and mutuality are not opposed but can be combined. New and imaginative ways of giving young people a stake in the system – some power, responsibility, opportunity – are an investment in the parents and employees of the future. The culture of responsibility and commitment at the heart of Citizens' Service must be part of any attempt to regenerate the UK's civil society.

The debate about rights and responsibilities in this country has often assumed a sterile either/or format. Professor T.H. Marshall's famous historical review of how political, economic and social rights have been extended over three centuries focused on rights. Charter 88 has with justification called attention to the rights which British citizens should be able to claim, and others have stressed the welfare rights which could serve as a stronger basis for reshaping the relationship between government and citizens. However, the extension of responsibilities is not high on the agenda. Recent Conservative governments, on the other hand, have preferred to focus on the responsibilities which people have to each other and to the state, but not the responsibilities which governments have to individuals.

The reality is that rights and responsibilities go together. To strengthen social rights (which is essential), responsibilities must be clarified. We believe that opportunities for people and for companies to put something back into the community should be more widely available. We therefore propose a new initiative aimed at extending opportunities and responsibilities to young people, which will benefit both the participants through their personal development and communities through the services they receive. That is why it should be built by extending the work of a number of different organisations such as the Prince's Trust Volunteers and Community Service Volunteers, and including different activities by harnessing local networks rather than laying down a single programme from the centre. Citizens' Service would be a voluntary community service initiative aiming to meet identified needs and to bridge the gap between personal, social and learning skills. It would include strong citizenship and life skills elements, as well as offering income maintenance and, through the Learning Bank described in Chapter 4, credits towards the cost of education and training courses. Opportunities to participate in Citizens' Service should extend beyond school-leavers: there will be places for people who have been out of work since they left school, for student graduates, employees, employers and retired volunteers.

Citizens' Service is not a form of National Service by the back door. Although some people argue for a compulsory national community service scheme for all young adults to ensure that young people from all backgrounds are represented, we do not believe that such an approach is either desirable or necessary. Nor do we propose that Citizens' Service should form part of a sentence imposed by the criminal courts. Quality, not compulsion, will be our recruiting sergeant. Our aim is to attract young people from different backgrounds, with different skills and abilities, to participate on a voluntary basis to meet community service needs. To succeed, it will have to attract and retain people who have few other options as well as those who can choose between opportunities. Compulsion would reduce motivation and commitment; our initiative is designed to tap enthusiasm and latent skills. In the USA, the voluntary national service initiative being developed by the Clinton administration has managed to attract four times as many young volunteers as there are places.[47]

Objectives

The main objectives of Citizens' Service are:

- First, education for citizenship. Citizens' Service would have an intrinsic value in helping people to learn practical life skills. It would include a core educational component which could be completed during the later school years, and for that reason could in the long term become a requirement of the secondary education qualification.
- Second, Citizens' Service would aim to break down social barriers. Citizens' Service would have the potential to put aside other status distinctions by involving people from different communities (and perhaps different parts of the country) in the same projects. There is enormous scope for increasing the social awareness of young people by offering opportunities for collaboration with people they might otherwise never encounter. The barriers of ignorance are very often the barriers of limited experience, for people of all ages and backgrounds. Citizens' Service offers one way of breaking some of those barriers down. Far from being confined to those who are unemployed, it should also attract students before or during their courses, as well as young trainees in employment.
- Third, Citizens' Service should promote the personal development of those taking part, enabling them to extend their self-confidence, acquire new competence and learn to work more effectively with other people. Although different organisations involved in Citizens' Service will have different views about how far it should enable people to work towards recognised qualifications, some Citizens' Service options should certainly include such modules. Even where that is not the case, the process of bringing together young adults to undertake socially useful activities that are now being under-funded or entirely neglected can be a powerful tool for learning, particularly if both the 'service providers' and the 'service users' are involved in shaping the project.

Citizens' Service is designed to offer benefits to young people as well as to the community. Above all, participation must be of intrinsic worth and satisfaction. The Prince's Trust Volunteers, whose participants include young trainees funded by their employers, has found that carefully structured team projects can provide a high level of training and personal development within a relatively short period. But participation should also entitle participants to post-service credits. As part of the new Learning Bank that is at the centre of our commitment to lifelong learning, Citizens' Service participants could have part or all of their higher education tuition fees waived, following the example of President Clinton's plan for the USA. But post-service credits could be used much more widely and could, for instance, offer help with the cost of securing a tenancy, or even driving lessons.

Activities

There is clearly no shortage of socially useful work to be done, but voluntary community service must not be a way of substituting cheaper young labour for the employment of public service professionals. Citizens' Service is not a public works programme. Citizens' Service will be based on local audits of tasks requiring greater investment of time, commitment and money, drawn up by a wide network of public- and voluntary-sector agencies including Community Development Trusts. It will then seek to identify unmet community needs and bring together volunteer commitment to meeting them. Citizens' Service activities would usually be those which the private sector will not do and which the public sector is unable to do. Citizens' Service would aim to strengthen existing services as well as invest in new ones. It would not build a new bureaucracy, but draw upon the wealth of experience which already exists in the voluntary and statutory sectors, with different local and national agencies becoming, in effect, Citizens' Service 'franchise-holders'.

Citizens' Service should offer a number of different activities. The following five are important:

- Community: working with an education, health or local authority, or a voluntary agency or charity in a suitable area.

- Environment: conservation and maintenance of urban and rural public places.
- Security: assisting with community safety initiatives, working with the police and, perhaps, on emergency relief.
- International: giving young people the opportunity to work in a developing country, with the co-operation of existing agencies.
- Skills: where the participant could choose to return to any of these four activities for an extended period, emphasising a specific skill which could link up with training qualifications.

Among the specific tasks often identified as the most neglected are time-intensive caring activities, where personal contact and the commitment to a higher quality of life for service users is vital. The long-established Community Service Volunteers (CSV) and their Retired and Senior Volunteers Programme (RSVP) are among the organisations helping to offer respite care for full-time carers. Citizens' Service could play a vital role in building real care in the community, although volunteers would have to commit themselves for a sufficiently long period to build up the necessary relationship with the person whom they were helping. It is probably the best example of an activity that will require the participation of working-age and retired Citizens' Service volunteers. Although volunteers can never substitute for trained teachers, they can complement their professional work by giving additional, one-to-one help; a number of CSV projects have found that student volunteers can significantly increase reading levels in a short space of time. Volunteers could also help to staff playgroups and holiday schemes. Environmental work, such as maintaining and developing conservation sites and upgrading derelict areas, is another area where a great deal needs to be done, and Citizens' Service could incorporate a substantial 'green' programme. Other areas of service might include mentoring in children's homes and residential long-term care homes, assisting in health service delivery, developing educational programmes for prisoners and making dangerous public places safer.

In order to attract participants from different social, ethnic and regional backgrounds, Citizens' Service should be validated with a certificate showing achievements in both 'hard'and 'soft' skills, which could help to open doors on to further opportunities for learning and work. Citizens' Service needs to establish a high reputation with employers, trainers and educational establishments. The Youth Award Scheme is a framework already established by the University of the West of England for accrediting skills acquired in similar projects.[48] Around 30,000 young people in more than 300 schools and colleges are involved, and the scheme has been recognised by Oxford University as evidence that those gaining the Award have developed valuable social and personal qualities.

To make it work, the *prospect* of Citizens' Service must be introduced at least 3 years before the end of the compulsory schooling period, through social, community or citizenship studies in schools. Participants in Citizens' Service would be involved in outreach work with schools as well as churches, community groups, colleges, universities and in workplaces. To enter Citizens' Service, students would be required to complete a Citizens' Learning Module, aimed at placing school and work-placement experiences into the wider context of what can be expected after school. Its focus would be on practical life skills of value to everyone: learning how to use health services, contacting elected representatives, how the National Insurance system and Benefits Agency works, and what a Citizen's Advice Bureau does, in addition to first-aid training, life-saving skills and the Highway Code. Basic literacy and numeracy education could be included. It would then be the right of every young adult to learn these skills, and their responsibility to know their rights. The module could be completed at a local college where people from other schools would also be participating, combined with visits to statutory and community organisations.

School-leavers, among others, could then be offered the opportunity of undertaking Citizens' Service projects on a full-time or part-time basis. A wide range of programmes should be available, offering different activities for different lengths of time. Some community service proposals specify a one year period of service, while others, such as the Prince's Trust Volunteers suggest that three months may be sufficient to achieve a high level of learning and experience. However, the flexibility of Citizens' Service would be an important quality: weekend, evening, summer holiday or full-time service placements could be undertaken. Our illustrative costings are based on an average participation time of three months.

Finance

The issue of financial maintenance is obviously important if this initiative is not to become a middle-class perk for the 'gap year' between school and university. Except where participants have been seconded by employers, participants should be paid a fair and realistic sum to reflect their contribution: a weekly allowance of £50 plus lunch and travelling expenses might be appropriate. A core feature of successful community service programmes has been a system of credits for use when the period of service ends. If we are serious about creating an attractive Citizens' Service alternative in the UK, appropriate post-service credits must be included.

Adding together the estimated costs of project start-up and post-service credits, the total cost for a full-time three month Citizens' Service placement could be just under £2,000.[49] Considering the negative experience of many young people under the Youth Training Scheme, a 'numbers approach' to building a national Citizens' Service would not be appropriate. Instead, Citizens' Service should offer high-quality learning and service opportunities. Quality rather than quantity of places should be established as the benchmark for success and Citizens' Service should therefore build up gradually over several years, with a goal of perhaps 150,000 places. The aim of Citizens' Service is to attract participants who are in work, out of work and in between (such as students). Employees would continue to be paid by their employers and would therefore probably take part in shorter periods of service; retired volunteers would be paid expenses; participants on Housing Benefit would continue to receive it; and because some of those taking part would already be receiving Income Support, most of their allowance would not represent new expenditure. The precise costs would depend on the mix of unemployed people, students and employees who took part. High quality management and administrative support is also required if Citizens' Service is to succeed; some of this could be provided by 'Third Age' volunteers, including older people seconded by their employers.

There is strong evidence that there would be a significant payback on this investment. Participation in Citizens' Service can be expected to improve employment prospects for unemployed participants and to contribute to community safety through reduced crime. A cautious estimate of total savings amounts to over £70 million after five years, suggesting a net cost of just under £300 million per year.[50] We favour an incremental approach to the growth of Citizens' Service, based on what works best following a piloting stage and this development period. During this time the scope for savings through reduced crime and improved employment opportunities can be more accurately assessed.

To make Citizens' Service work, a number of pilot experiments should be introduced in different parts of the UK, covering different activities. At this stage many of the unanswered questions about Citizens' Service would be resolved. The main 'stakeholders' in the initiative would be involved in designing the projects, not least existing community- and statutory-sector agencies, to overcome any problems of duplicating efforts. It will not succeed unless there is effective monitoring of outcomes and unless quality assurance plays a central part in that evaluation. Voluntary participation should not lead to service recipients experiencing a poor quality or unreliable service. We are convinced that, in the long term, Citizens' Service could make a major contribution to the civic life of the UK.

Conclusion

Traditional institutions, from marriage to the monarchy, are in flux. Some are damaged, some under attack. Institutions matter deeply, and they must fit the times. They can be a force for good only if the values of equity, openness and responsibility pervade their organisation and practice. It is those values that we have sought to advance in this chapter. Although families are changing in form, their central function – the nurture of children – remains unchanged and needs to be properly valued and supported by government. Families themselves are embedded in wider communities which profoundly affect, for good or ill, parents' abilities to nurture their children. Government can never take the place of community: what it can and should do, however, is create political, institutional and financial frameworks which will help local people to rebuild their communities from the bottom up, making them safer places in which to live and generating a better quality of life which can support wider economic opportunities. The development of community banks and credit unions, coupled with substantial reforms to housing, are central to a strategy of community regeneration.

A government that wishes to unleash the energy of people in their own communities must also be willing to devolve some of its own power. The revival of civic leadership, which provided the impetus for social and economic development in the nineteenth century, will be equally vital to national renewal in the twenty-first. That will require greater power and responsibility for elected local councils, as well as the creation of new forms of elected government within the nations and regions of the United Kingdom. Finally, we propose a Citizens' Service which will enable young people, in particular, to give 'something for something' in a programme which will enhance both individual and community development. Change will not bear immediate fruit, but it is essential if the structures of governance in this country are to retain their capacity to shape our future.

Notes

1. Address to Family Welfare Association Colloquium on Poverty and Exclusion, February 1994.
2. John Gray *The Undoing of Conservatism* (London : Social Market Foundation, 1994)
3. Robert Putnamm 'The Prosperous Community : Social Capital and Public Life' *The American Prospect*, 13, Spring 1993
4. Brian Robson et al *Assessing the Impact of Urban Policy* (London: HMSO, 1994)

5. The *Guardian* 15 June 1994
6. For a fuller review of the issue, see Penelope Leach and Patricia Hewitt *Social Justice, Children and Families*, Commission on Social Justice Issue Paper 4 (London: IPPR, 1993)
7. Alan Duncan, Christopher Giles and Steven Webb *Social Security Reform and Women's Independent Incomes* (Manchester: Equal Opportunities Commission, 1994)
8. *Family Policies: A Declaration of Principles* submitted to the Commission by Relate, National Stepfamily Association, One Plus One, Carers National Association, Family Policy Studies Centre and National Council for One Parent Families
9. Michael Young and A. Halsey *The Family Covenant* (London: Institute of Community Studies, 1994)
10. Scottish Law Commission *Report on Family Law* (Edinburgh: HMSO, 1992)
11. David Donnison *Act Local: Social Justice from the Bottom Up* Commission on Social Justice Issue Paper 13 (London: IPPR, 1994)
12. Home Office *Research Findings Bulletin* (London: Home Office, October 1992)
13. Beatrix Campbell *Goliath: Britain's Dangerous Places* (London: Methuen, 1993)
14. Bank of England *Banking Act Report* unpublished, April 1993
15. Paul Henderson *Community Development* Submission to the Commission
16. Tony Gibson *Danger: Opportunity* (York: Neighbourhood Initiatives Foundation/Joseph Rowntree Foundation, 1993)
17. Phil Shiner *Community Empowerment and the Planning System* submission to the Commission
18. Paddy Doherty, speech to Development Trusts Association Conference, 1993
19. Phil Shiner *A Proposal for a National Community Law Service*, submission to the Commission
20. This idea builds on a proposal from Bob Holman for a National Community Development Fund to allocate funding to low-income areas for community activities
21. For further details, see for example Commission on Criminal Justice *Crime and Prejudice* (London: Channel Four Television, 1993).
22. Stephen Thake and Reiner Staubach *Investing in People: Rescuing Communities from the Margins* (York: Joseph Rowntree Foundation, 1993)
23. Ibid

24. Andrew Sentance in *Making it Happen: Finding the Resources for Social Housing* Shelter Seminar Report, November 1993
25. Neville Simms in *Making it Happen* ibid
26. Steven Wilcox and Janet Ford *Working Households: Affordable Housing and Economic Needs* (London: National Federation of Housing Associations, 1994)
27. National Federation of Housing Associations *False Economy - Putting People, Programmes and Private Finance At Risk* (London: NFHA, 1994)
28. A report from the Rowntree Foundation by Steven Wilcox in *Housing Finance Review 1993* (York: Joseph Rowntree Foundation, 1993) proposed the transfer of council housing to local housing companies and estimated this would save the Treasury £16 billion a year. Our proposal differs in that we are not proposing the withdrawal of public investment in social housing. See also Ged Lucas and Brendan Nevin 'A Fairer Firm' *Housing*, July/August 1994
29. National Federation of Housing Associations *False Economy* op cit
30. Kenneth Gibb et al 'Making Housing Pay' in Kenneth Gibb and Robina Goodlad (eds) *Housing and Social Justice* Commission on Social Justice Issue Paper 9 (London: IPPR, 1994)
31. 'Housing: The road to economic recovery' Shelter Conference Report, April 1993
32. Wilcox and Ford *Working* op cit
33. See 'Short-Term Solutions' in *Roof* July/August 1994
34. Shelter *The Costs of Temporary Accommodation Relative to New Build for Local Authorities* (London: Shelter, 1993)
35. Donnison *Act Local* op cit
36. John Banham *The Anatomy of Change* (London: Weidenfeld and Nicholson, 1994)
37. Iain Deas and Eric Harrison, 'Hopes left to crumble' *Local Government Chronicle*, 13 March 1994
38. John Stewart *The Rebuilding of Public Accountability*, unpublished manuscript
39. See John Stewart 'Defending Accountability' in *Demos Quarterly* Winter 1993
40. See *Ego-Trip: Extra Governmental Organisations in the UK and their Accountability* (London: Democratic Audit and Charter '88 Trust, 1994)
41. See Anthony Wright 'Friends in High Places' in *Parliamentary Brief*, 2, 9 (June / July 1994).

42. See John Stewart *Democratic Government or the Growth of Quangocracy,* submission to the Commission

43. Anna Coote *Bridging the Gap Between Them and Us,* submission to the Commission. See also Anna Coote (ed) *The Welfare of Citizens* (London: Rivers Oram Press, 1993)

44. David Blunkett MP, submission to the Commission (February 1993).

45. National Children's Home *The NCH Factfile* (London: NCH, 1993)

46. British Youth Council Looking to the Future: Towards a Coherent Youth Policy (London: BYC, 1993)

47. M. Gray, R. Schoeni and T. Kaganoff *National Service – Designing, implementing and evaluating a successful program* RAND Issue Paper (Santa Monica CA: RAND 1993).

48. 'When A Levels alone are not enough' *The Times*, 29 November, 1993

49. We assume that 10 per cent of volunteers would choose residential placements. Organisations requiring this sort of participation would pay accommodation costs.

50. The Henley Centre *Establishing a National Community Service Programme for Young People – The Costs and Benefits* A Report for Community Service Volunteers (London: The Henley Centre, 1994)

8

TAXATION:
INVESTING IN OURSELVES

We have argued throughout this report that if we want to create new opportunities and build a better society, we must be willing to invest more in ourselves. Our vision of national renewal is long term: we are looking ahead to 2010 and beyond. The strategies we propose are equally long term; it would be impossible to try to put them all into effect at once. Instead, we have distinguished between the goals that society and government should set and the framework we should aim to build in the future, and the short term steps that could and should take us in the right direction. Debate needs to focus on the rights and wrongs of the principles, the objectives and the structure of what we propose; it is only when those large questions are settled – questions about the *direction* in which we want our country to go – that detailed issues of cost can be decided. The traditional British values of pragmatism and empiricism have their place, but vision must come first.

It is in any case impossible to predict now what the state of the economy or the public finances will be by the time of the next general election, let alone by the end of this century. Decisions about priorities and how they should be funded will therefore have to wait and in any case should follow a widespread public debate about the future of this country – a debate which we hope will be stimulated and informed by this report. We have, of course, given examples of the costs of some of our proposals. These are illustrative figures, designed to help people make better-informed judgments about the implications of our proposals. Estimating a possible cost does not mean that a change should be made immediately: even if most people in this country agree with our view of

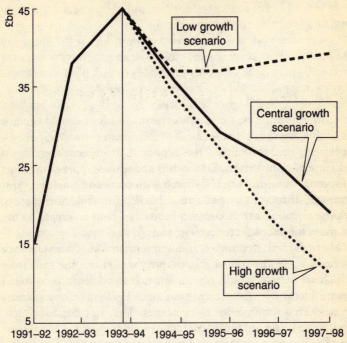

Figure 8.1 – The Growth Dividend
Public Sector Borrowing Requirement

GDP growth from 1993/4: High 3.5%; Central 3.0%; Low 1.8%

Source: *The Independent* 20 June 1994

what is desirable, the UK does not have the resources to do everything at once.

There are many ways to fund the investment that this country needs. An annual government budget of more than £250 billion leaves plenty of room for government to change priorities. Over the last fifteen years, enormous sums have been found for new policies, including £10 billion for inner-city regeneration (most of it, according to a government-sponsored report, largely wasted).[1] The social security budget, which has risen substantially, should in future be reduced: not by making it more difficult for people to claim benefits or by reducing their value, as the present Government is doing, but through the 'welfare to work' strategies which we propose. Contributions from graduates will make it possible, over several years, to expand further and higher education without increased government spending.

Government budgets do not remain static. Figure 8.1 illustrates the increased tax revenues that will flow to government over the next few years if the economy continues to pull out of recession. Private capital should be mobilised for public sector developments, including higher education as well as railways and telecommunications, while new investment funds should become available as part of a co-ordinated European economic policy – provided, of course, that the present Government's policy of refusing to claim certain EU funds is abandoned. Part of the costs of some programmes can be shared with users and employers (for instance, through charges and subsidies for childcare places), while contributions to pension funds can help to create secure incomes for people in retirement and old age.

None the less, taxation is and will remain a substantial source of funding. In the rest of this chapter, we set out the principles which we believe should govern fair taxes and illustrate some of the problems with the present system. In 1979, the Conservatives were elected on a pledge to cut taxes. That has not happened. Today, the vast majority of families, low-income, as well as middle-income – teachers and police officers – are facing higher tax increases than ever before. These taxes are the price of an economic theory that has not worked. Who now believes the claim that income tax cuts would be a miracle cure for the British economy, that by releasing enterprise and removing the dead hand of government, they would make us all better off?

It is, however, important to restate an old principle: taxes are the contribution that we all make towards building a better society. Taxation in a democratic society is based upon consent; it is a desirable good, not a necessary evil. If we want the ends – higher standards in our schools, better health, no more youngsters sleeping in the street, safer communities – we must be willing to pay the means. The public goods we pay for through taxation create social and private benefits – the two should go together for common benefit. Unfairly or excessively levied, taxes

Figure 8.2 – Where the Money Goes
Expenditure by function 1992–3

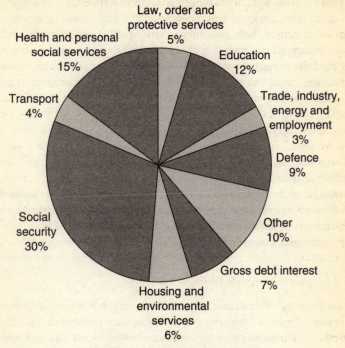

Law, order and protective services 5%

Health and personal social services 15%

Education 12%

Transport 4%

Trade, industry, energy and employment 3%

Defence 9%

Social security 30%

Other 10%

Gross debt interest 7%

Housing and environmental services 6%

General government expenditure
(excluding privatisation proceeds) = £269.2 billion

Source: HM Treasury Financial Statement and Budget Report 1994–5
(London: HMSO, 1993)

are indeed a burden which people rightly reject; but fair taxes, wisely and efficiently used, are a responsibility we should share and accept.

Taxation in the United Kingdom today, however, is neither fair nor efficient. By 1996, the total level of taxes – including VAT, duties on alcohol and cigarettes and National Insurance Contributions as well as income tax – will be higher than for generations. Those on low and middle incomes will bear the burden. But the enormous revenues being raised are not delivering the public goods we all want to see. In the 1980s, tax cuts failed to deliver economic success: in the 1990s, tax rises are the price of economic failure. Figure 8.2 shows where government revenues are spent.

A vicious circle of low economic growth, rising unemployment, falling public revenues, rising public expenditure and, inexorably, rising taxes is bad enough. What makes it even worse is that the taxes are not fairly shared. Of the £31 billion which went in income tax cuts during the 1980s, £15 billion went to the richest 10 per cent of the population.[2]

Principles for Tax Policy

There are, we believe, ten principles which should govern tax policy in this country. We hope that a future government will make clear the principles on which its own approach to taxation rests, so that every member of the community can understand the contribution which they are being asked to make, and hold government to account for its decisions.

1. No taxation without justification

The purpose of taxation is to raise money for activities which cannot be pursued without government action. These include the public contribution to economic investment, as well as enabling people to meet their basic needs and enjoy wider opportunities. Without taxation, we cannot create a better society.

Most people understand and endorse this principle. The *British Social Attitudes* surveys have found consistent support for increased investment in health and education, with nine out of ten people rejecting the idea that spending on these services should be cut in order to help the economy. Ten years ago, a majority of people wanted overall taxes and spending to be kept at the same level or reduced; today, the majority say they would prefer both taxes and spending to increase.[3]

Taxes must be justified in practice as well as principle. Even if people say they are willing to pay higher taxes for better schools or policing, they will only do so if the schools and the community safety programme provide value for money. That is why, in every strategy we propose, we emphasise the need to organise services efficiently, to monitor results and spread best practice.

2. Taxes must be fair

It is easier to say that taxes should be fair than to make them so. But there are three aims of fair taxes. First, people in similar circumstances with similar incomes should pay similar amounts of tax ('horizontal equity'). Second, people who are better off should pay a higher proportion of their income in taxes than people who are worse off ('vertical equity'). And third, no one should pay punitive levels of taxation (there can be no question of returning to the top tax rates of the 1970s as we seek to reduce swingeing marginal tax rates at the bottom).

The financial relationship between citizen and state encompasses, equally, the payment of taxes and the receipt of benefits and services. From the individual's point of view, receiving benefit and receiving a tax allowance may be very different; from government's perspective, however, both have the same effect on public finances. It is yet another defect of our present system of national accounting that Child Benefit, for example (which serves exactly the same purpose as a child tax allowance, only more fairly) is treated as public expenditure, while tax allowances merely count as revenue foregone.

3. Taxes must be acceptable to the public

When people have been told for more than fifteen years that taxation is confiscation, it is surprising that taxation remains as widely acceptable as it does. But in any democracy, a tax which is unacceptable may help to bring down a government or – in the case of the poll tax – a Prime Minister.

If, however, government is prepared to make the case for responsible taxation, to ensure value for money in every public service, to design fair taxes, reform its budget process and give people useful information about how their money is spent, then there is every reason for taxes to be, if not popular, then at least widely acceptable. That will require a transformation of Britain's increasingly corrupt and inefficient culture of government, but we believe it is essential.

4. The connection between taxes and achievements should be as clear as possible

When people do not know where their contribution is going, it is hardly surprising that they object to paying more and more into the black hole of government. We look later at the issue of 'earmarked' or 'hypothecated' taxes. But two general reforms are needed to connect taxes paid and results achieved.

First, we need to build on the present government's Budget reform. Before 1993, government spending was dealt with in the Autumn Statement, after a summer spent horse-trading between ministers. But the taxes needed to finance the spending only came the following April in the Budget. The November 1993 Budget, for the first time, brought income and expenditure together. A future Chancellor should seize this opportunity to promote well-informed national debate about the choices facing the country. A 'Consultative Budget', published perhaps in September, could set out quite clearly the improvements to investment and services which are needed, what they would cost and how they could be funded. A similar process should take place locally. (See Chapter 7).

Second, every citizen should receive at least once a year a simple summary of how their money has been spent. This could be made available with payslips, tax returns, or pension and benefit payments. In future, as government information technology improves, it should become possible to deliver personalised information to more and more people. Although VAT and excise duties can only be calculated on an average basis, income taxes and national insurance contributions are known for each individual who pays them.

5. As far as possible, taxes should contribute to improving the United Kingdom's economic performance and promoting employment

Government is not and cannot be the only source of investment, but its decisions about tax policy can have a major impact on the balance of the UK economy. Although private capital has an important role to play in securing the public infrastructure on which a successful economy depends, it can fulfil this role only if government takes a lead.

If that is to be achieved, however, government must reform its own accounts in order to draw a clear distinction between capital investment and current spending. Every household and business knows the difference between investing in a home and having a holiday, between buying new equipment and paying higher wages. Because government requires citizens to pay taxes, it has an even greater responsibility than families and businesses to manage its income and expenditure properly. Trustworthy national accounts – including a national balance sheet – will make it far easier to judge whether or not taxes and spending are helping or hindering our economy.

Taxation can also help or hinder job creation. The best British employers, like most employers in Germany and many other parts of the EU, regard pension contributions, training budgets and other social costs as a good investment and the mark of a good employer. Throughout the European Union, however, governments are increasingly worried that high social security charges on employees and employers may be contributing to high unemployment. Although the UK has lower charges than almost any other EU country, there is room for further reform here. Over the longer term, we should consider shifting taxation away from work and towards environmental pollution and resource use – 'taxing bads, not goods' – as we discuss below.

6. The structure of tax reliefs and allowances should be made as simple as possible, and used sparingly to pursue policy objectives

Taxes often affect people's choices – for instance, between remaining an employee or becoming self-employed, between different kinds of investment, or between different kinds of payment (such as paying employees through perks which escape National Insurance Contributions). Sometimes the effect of taxation is deliberate, sometimes wholly unintentional. The Business Expansion Scheme, which was designed to help small businesses grow, was also used as a tax subsidy for private rented accommodation (including student colleges) which did nothing to add to the supply of homes for rent.

In line with our previous principle, tax allowances can help to promote investment. But the more government tries to use taxes to pull and push people into behaving in certain ways, the more scope there is for creative accountants to invent new tax dodges and the greater the risk that the tax policy will have completely unintended effects. The simpler the tax system and the fewer the tax reliefs or incentives, the more chance government has of achieving the result it wants.

7. Taxation should respect individuals' independence

Until 1990, a married woman was not recognised as a taxpayer, her income being treated as her husband's. Separate taxation was widely welcomed and must be retained, despite the big gains which it gave to very wealthy couples who could redistribute their investment income between them.

8. Subject to Principle 2 (fairness), taxes should be levied on as broad a base as possible

If taxes are only paid on one kind of income – such as earnings – then higher rates are needed to raise the required amount of revenue. But high rates encourage tax avoidance and increase pressure for tax reliefs; as a result, they need more effort to police them. By having a broad tax base – including consumption as well as earnings, property as well as income – government can raise the same amount with lower tax rates.

But fairness sets a real limit to how far the tax base can be broadened in this way. VAT rates have risen from 8 per cent in 1979 to 17.5 per cent today, and VAT has now been extended to domestic fuel, which was previously exempt. This more-than-doubling of VAT is one of the main reasons why the poorest 10 per cent of people now pay *more* of their income in taxes than the richest 10 per cent. Nor will compensation through the social security system be enough to offset the damage done to the poorest people by imposing VAT on fuel.

9. Taxes should be easy to understand and collect

Despite the costly fiasco of the poll tax, the British tax system enjoys a high degree of compliance. Unlike Italy, for instance, most people in the UK pay all or most of the tax for which they are liable. It is essential to maintain this state of affairs.

Nevertheless, our tax system faces significant problems. It is estimated that tax-avoidance schemes and, worse, illegal tax evasion may cost the country as much as £9 billion a year – the equivalent of about 4p or 5p on the standard rate of income tax. Although there are only 817 Inland Revenue compliance staff, the amount of revenue they raise in a year is six times as much as the money saved by the 780 social security staff dealing with benefit fraud.[4] Clearly, additional staff resources should be invested in tax collection: the House of Commons Public Accounts Committee recently found that the Inland Revenue had failed to collect £2.7 billion of taxes owed, while tax remissions and write-offs have increased significantly for the last four years. Furthermore, the cash-in-hand economy is now estimated to be worth between £41 billion and £56 billion a year, escaping income tax and national insurance contributions completely. Most of this money is, however, spent and at that point, at least, some of it will be taxed through VAT and excise duties.

Unfortunately, very few people understand their income tax. The difference between 'marginal' and 'average' tax rates – although crucial to policy-makers – is particularly baffling to public and press alike. The less important marginal rates (the amount paid out of every extra £ of income) make the headlines; the vital average rate (the total share of income paid in taxes) is ignored. Confusion is so great that in the 1992 general election, the Liberal Democrats' proposal for an extra 1p tax for education was widely thought to mean only an extra penny a week. The proposals we make below for minimum and maximum taxes are designed to help overcome the problem. But again, the simpler the tax system, the easier it will be to explain.

10. The UK tax system should take account of growing capital, business and labour mobility within the EU and global economy

Where taxes (and much else) are concerned, Britain is no longer an island. There is still scope for tax differences within the European Union, but less than there used to be. In particular, the ability of professionals and other highly paid workers to move themselves and their companies from one part of the EU to another sets practical limits to taxation. Some environmental taxes or charges can be introduced at a national level without affecting competitiveness. But others – particularly a general tax on energy use and carbon emissions – could only be introduced across the European Union as a whole (and even then there are fears about the effects on Europe's costs compared with the rest of the world). The British Government must play a positive role in shaping the tax framework for the European Union, instead of passively accepting others' decisions.

Putting Principles into Practice

We have not tried to carry out a detailed analysis of every aspect of the British tax system. Instead, we identify five ways in which the present system falls short of the principles we have set out and suggest options for government to consider. Finally, we consider larger issues about how taxes might develop in future: whether towards 'hypothecation', where specific taxes are linked to specific purposes, or towards indirect and, specifically, environmental taxes.

Problem 1: High tax on low pay

The first unfairness which concerns us is that people start paying income tax on very low incomes (for a single person of working age, £66 a week in 1994/5). National Insurance Contributions start even lower (at £57 a week). In 1949, a married man with two children started paying tax at 103 per cent of average earnings; today he could be paying tax at less than 30 per cent of the average.

The best way of dealing with this problem in line with Principle 2 above (fairness) would be to take as many people on low incomes as possible out of income tax altogether, by raising personal tax allowances (the level of income at which income tax starts to apply) faster than earnings.

An alternative would be to introduce a new starting rate of income tax at, say, 10 per cent. If that were accompanied by further gradations in tax rates higher up, income tax could be more finely tuned to people's different incomes instead of, as now, a single rate applying to the vast majority of people. On the other hand, a 10 per cent starting rate would be of less benefit to the poorest taxpayers who would be better served by an increase in tax allowances which would take them out of tax altogether. At a practical level, the more tax rates there are, the more difficult it is to calculate the right tax on the interest earned on savings. Building societies, for instance, deduct tax at the 'standard' rate of 25 per cent; the excess has to be reclaimed (but often is not) by people who pay at only 20 per cent.

We have also looked at various options for changing the structure of National Insurance Contributions. There is a real problem with the 'entry fee' (currently £1.14 a week or £59 a year) which is effectively charged once an employee's earnings reach the Lower Earnings Limit. Although it would clearly be fairer in principle to exempt earnings below the limit from contributions altogether, the reform would be extremely expensive and would benefit all contributors, not only the low-paid: it is therefore certainly not a priority. The contribution rate itself (now 10 per cent) is low compared with income tax; as with the 'entry fee', cutting it would not only be expensive but would help all contributors rather than focusing on the low-paid.

The second problem concerns the Upper Earnings Limit (£22,360 a year), above which no contributions are payable. Although some people argue that the upper limit is justified, since entitlements under SERPS are based on earnings between the lower and upper limits, others believe there is no justification in principle for a limit which has the effect of making national insurance contributions significantly less progressive than income tax. Whatever view one takes of the principle, there is a strong case for ending the practice of raising the Upper Earnings Limit in line with prices rather than earnings. As a result of this scarcely noticed change, the range of earnings over which contributions are paid – and SERPS entitlements calculated – is falling substantially in real terms. If this process continues, the upper earnings limit – worth around 146 per cent of male average earnings in 1980, and about 119 per cent in 1993 – will be worth 91 per cent of male average earnings by 2015, 79 per cent by 2025/26, and only 58.5 per cent by 2045/46.[5]

Problem 2 : Unfair tax allowances

The second problem is that personal tax allowances (the amount of tax-free income allowed to each individual) are worth twice as much to top-rate taxpayers as they are to the worst-off taxpayers. If someone's income is so low that he or she pays tax only at the present starting rate of 20 per cent, then the tax saved by the personal allowance is only 20 per cent of the allowance's face value. The present single person's allowance of £3,445 is therefore worth £689. For the top-rate taxpayer on 40 per cent, however, the personal allowance is worth 40 per cent of the single person's allowance, or £1,378.

Until recently, all tax reliefs and allowances operated in this way – including tax relief on mortgage interest payments, pension and life insurance contributions, and tax allowances for various investments. To their credit, successive Conservative Chancellors, including John Major, have recognised the unfairness of this system and the incentive it creates for tax avoidance schemes. A process of reform has begun, although the revenue saved has not been used to help people on the lowest incomes. This gradual reform is clearly sensible, although the value of personal tax allowances should not fall below the standard rate of income tax. Depending on the overall state of public finances, the option of transforming personal allowances into a tax credit worth the same to most taxpayers could be combined with our last suggestion – raising the level of the personal allowance – to take some half a million people out of tax and to produce a fairer income tax system.

The present government is also phasing out mortgage interest tax relief (MITR) by freezing the total mortgage on which relief can be claimed at £30,000 as well as by cutting the value of the relief. Formerly available at the top rate of income tax, MITR has already been restricted to 20 per cent and, from April 1995, will be further reduced to 15 per cent. Owner-occupation in the United Kingdom is now so extensive that the original purpose of this tax subsidy, to promote home-buying, has been fulfilled. Furthermore, MITR helps to fuel house price inflation, locking out many first-time buyers and restricting mobility. Depending upon other changes which might be made in the tax system as well as the level of interest rates, continuing to phase it out gradually would release funds for other purposes.

Problem 3 : The effect of taxes on employment

The third problem concerns the effect on employment of employers' national insurance contributions (see Principle 5 above). Employers pay nothing on earnings below the Lower Earnings Limit, after which payments are made at a low rate (3.6 per cent on earnings between £57 and £100) which rises through two further stages to 10.2 per cent on earnings above £200 a week. Because low earnings are taxed at lower rates, there is an incentive to employers to take on the less-skilled workers who are most likely to be unemployed. Indeed, the European Commission is urging other countries to adopt precisely this kind of structure as part of its employment programme. Although the UK already has lower social security contributions than most other EU countries, it is worth considering whether even lower contributions for lower earnings would encourage firms to take on more workers. For instance, at the same time as a national minimum wage is introduced, employers' national insurance contributions could be cut, effectively returning to employers some of the money which the min-

Figure 8.3 – Employer Social Contributions in Europe

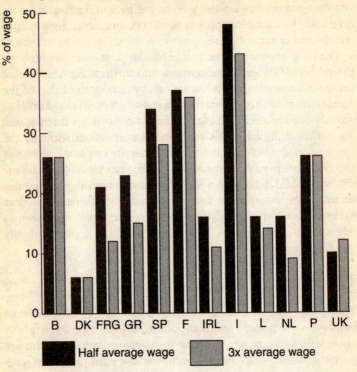

Half average wage   3x average wage

Source: Commission of the European Communities Growth,
Competitiveness and Employment (Brussels, CEC, 1993)

imum wage will save government. As Dr Andrew Britton, Director of the National Institute of Economic and Social Research,
has suggested, contributions should be related to hourly pay
(rather than total weekly earnings) if job creation is to be max-
imised for people with low earning power; this would, however,
require substantial administrative changes for employers.[6]
Figure 8.3 shows how the level of social contributions varies
across the EC. The levies on UK employers are, in comparative
terms, very low.

It must be recognised, however, that the present structure of
employers' contributions, and particularly the zero-contribution

rate, gives employers an incentive to create part-time jobs with very low hours. The Low-Pay Network in Stirling, for instance, found one local employer offering 91 part-time jobs, only four of which paid more than £56 a week. If the same hours had been worked by 28 full-time employees, the Treasury would have gained £40,000 more in income tax and contributions. It may be impossible to encourage job creation at the bottom of the labour market without running into this kind of problem (for instance, turning employers' contributions into a payroll tax on all earnings would deal with the Stirling problem, but destroy the incentive for job creation). If, however, the number of jobs below the contribution threshold grows so rapidly as to erode the national insurance base, government would need to consider abolishing the zero rate, while at the same time reducing other rates so that the overall charge to employers remained the same.

Problem 4: Unequal tax burden

It is clearly wrong that the richest people pay a lower share of their total incomes in direct and indirect taxes than the poorest, and unfair that a millionaire should come into the same tax bracket as the police officer on, say, £30,000. If additional revenue needs to be raised in future to compensate for tax cuts for people on lower incomes or to help fund new programmes, government should consider the option of introducing a new top rate of income tax. Recalling what we said about the Single Market, however, it is important to look at top tax rates, and where they take effect, in other countries.

As Table 8.1 suggests, it would be possible to introduce a new top rate of income tax for very high earners (including bonuses and perks, as well as salaries) without damaging competitiveness. There should be a clear basis for the income level at which any new top rate takes effect; for instance, it could be set at five times average earnings, or designed to affect only a specific proportion of taxpayers, say the top 1 or 2 per cent.

A useful option to consider is a *minimum tax bill* for people on high incomes, either as an alternative to the normal income tax, as in Canada and the USA, or a supplement to it, as in Denmark

Table 8.1: Tax at the Top

Country	Top Tax Rate (per cent)	Threshold (local currency)
France	57	261,300 (francs)
Germany	53	120,000 (D-marks)
Netherlands	60	86,500 (guilders)
USA	40	250,000 (dollars)
Japan	50	20,000,000 (yen)
UK	40	31,600 (sterling)

Source: *Hansard*, 28 October 1993, cols 749 – 750

and Norway. A minimum tax bill would prevent better-off people from using so many tax allowances that they end up paying little or no income tax. The most effective way of ensuring that the very rich pay their fair share of tax is, however, to deal with loopholes such as the use of offshore trusts to escape British taxation.

Government should also consider introducing a *maximum tax bill*, which would set a limit to the proportion of any individual's total income which could be paid in income tax and national insurance contributions combined. What really matters to most people is the total share of their income which they pay in tax – in other words, the average tax rate. A maximum tax bill would reinforce a commitment to fair taxes, while ensuring that any other tax reforms did not impose an excessive burden on any particular group. The maximum tax bill should certainly be no more than 50 per cent.

Problem 5: Unfair taxation on inheritance

People's living standards depend upon their wealth, as well as their income. Taxation on inherited wealth is justified in principle as a way of reducing inequalities, as well as by the need to raise necessary revenues as fairly as possible. The present system of death duties, however, is inimical to social justice. A wealthy person with a good accountant can easily ensure that his estate avoids tax almost altogether, with the result that inheritance tax contributes hardly more than $^1/_2$p on the standard rate of income tax. Professor Cedric Sandford, a UK tax expert, described the current inheritance tax as 'an unseemly lottery with life, a state-created gamble in which the state stands to gain at the expense of heirs of the less fortunate donors'.[7]

The most important inheritance tax exemption covers agricultural and business property. Although the intention is to keep the farm or business intact as a going concern, no tax is paid even if the person inheriting after an owner dies sells out immediately. This loophole could be closed by requiring beneficiaries to retain the property for a minimum period of several years.

The tax exemption for gifts made more than seven years before death discriminates quite unfairly between different recipients. If a parent who gives a substantial sum to his children then lives for at least another seven years, his children pay nothing on their gifts. If he dies the day after making the gifts, however, full inheritance tax must be paid. The former head of the OECD's tax division, Ken Messere, described the present system to us as 'a flagrant example of Conservative administrations' desire to perpetuate wealth inequalities' and recommended that it be replaced by a donee-based inheritance tax. It would clearly be fairer and more efficient to tax all gifts, whenever they were made, with exemptions for small gifts as well as gifts and inheritance between husband and wife, and an overall threshold below which no inheritance tax would be charged. A system of this kind is operated by many other OECD countries.[8]

Hypothecated taxes

In most industrialised countries there is growing interest in the possibility of 'hypothecated' taxes – in other words, taxes earmarked for particular items of expenditure. Supporters argue that hypothecation would make taxation more acceptable by connecting taxes and services or benefits more closely, and making the cost of a service clear. Taxes could more easily be raised for popular purposes, and voters could be given the opportunity to support a new programme along with a new tax to fund it.

Apart from social insurance contributions, where there is a clear link between contributions and benefits, earmarked taxes make the best sense when they are devoted to one-off capital investments. Once the national accounts have been reformed to identify investment clearly, we propose that government establish a National Renewal Fund to help finance major investment projects. Each year, the Budget would allocate a proportion of tax revenues to the Fund. This could come from existing income taxes, or from a less visible tax, such as capital gains tax, corporation tax or death duties, which could have the desirable effect of raising people's interest in how efficiently these taxes work. As with the Budget generally, there should be public debate about how the National Renewal Fund is invested, as well as annual reports about the gains to the country from the investment.

Unlike capital expenditure, however, hypothecating taxes for regular expenditure risks leaving a crucial service vulnerable to a drop in revenue. For instance, if income tax revenues fall because more people are out of work, an education tax would produce less; the schools would have to manage with less money, or the remaining taxpayers would have to pay more, or the government would have to top the education tax up from other revenues – making a nonsense of hypothecation in the first place. The reverse is also possible, with a hypothecated tax producing more money than can actually be spent on a particular service (as happened in some Central London boroughs, where parking-meter revenues may only be spent on more parking spaces but there is nowhere to build them). It is possible to overcome these problems, but only by making hypothecation a cosmetic rather than a real change.

The extension of hypothecated taxes may also increase the pressure for tax reductions to people who opt out of services. Indeed, Deregulators often argue for hypothecation as a half-way house to privatising all government services. The result would, of course, be to deepen social division, leaving public services dependent on dwindling revenues and disconnecting the better-off from the wider community. For those reasons, we do not generally favour hypothecated taxes.

There is, however, a case for earmarking any tax *increase* which government might decide upon, so that citizens know exactly why the increase is needed and how it will be spent. That was the approach taken by the Liberal Democrats with their proposed 1p for education in their 1992 election manifesto, and by the French Government which in 1988 introduced a one-off 'solidarity tax' on people with very high earnings or bonuses, in order to help fund new measures to encourage the unemployed back into employment. From January 1995, the German Government will introduce its 'unification tax' to help fund development in the eastern states. If tax increases are needed, a clear link with the purpose for which they are raised could be part of the far more open Budget process we advocate.

Taxing 'bads' not 'goods'

Throughout the European Union, there is a growing interest in shifting taxation from earnings to environmental pollution and resource use. Jacques Delors' European White Paper on *Competitiveness, Jobs and Growth* suggests that a significant increase in employment could be produced by 'a reduction in employers' social security contributions targeted on categories of workers with a low level of skills [together with] a tax on CO_2/energy rather than VAT being increased'.[9] In Germany the opposition Social Democratic Party proposes reducing social security contributions and making up the lost revenue through environmental taxes and charges. The British Government should take seriously the case for a long-term programme of ecological tax reform.

The general case for taxing 'bads' (pollution) rather than 'goods' (employment) is strong. Since labour is plentiful and natural resources scarce, the present balance of taxation is wrong. A shift away from income and social security taxes could promote employment by making labour relatively cheaper, while properly designed environmental taxes would cut pollution and resource consumption. Industry would have an incentive to find the cleanest, cheapest forms of production and transport, helping to stimulate product and process innovation (although clean technologies could themselves be capital – rather than labour – intensive). Finally, environmental taxes may be more acceptable to people than income taxes.

Environmental taxes are sometimes considered alongside other taxes on consumption, but a general shift from income to consumption taxes would cause large problems in the UK. Using revenues from higher or more extensive VAT to reduce income tax penalises the poor and benefits the rich. Even the poorest people, who pay no income tax, do pay VAT, while the richest people who pay higher income tax generally spend a lower proportion of their income and therefore incur proportionately less VAT. The introduction of VAT on domestic fuel, for example, bears heavily on the poorest 10 per cent of households but has little effect on the richest 10 per cent,[10] while charging VAT on standing charges has little effect on energy consumption.

Nevertheless, the UK, like other highly industrialised nations, has a responsibility towards future generations across the world to reduce its energy use. The Inter-Governmental Panel on Climate Change calculates that a 60 per cent cut in CO_2 emissions worldwide may be necessary to stabilise global warming. A much more modest aim of stabilising CO_2 emissions at their 1990 level by the year 2000 was agreed, by the UK amongst others, at the 1992 UN Conference on Environment and Development at Rio. The European Commission has proposed a combined energy/carbon tax, rising gradually over several years, with compensating cuts in other taxes or increases in benefits. The UK Government has strongly resisted the EC proposal for fear of its effects on industrial competitiveness. The EC itself is now arguing that an EU energy/carbon tax should be levied only if it is also applied throughout the OECD, making the prospect of its early introduction remote. While some exemptions for energy-intensive industries subject to international competition would be needed (and are included in the EC proposal), energy taxation would not significantly increase costs in most industries. Coupled with tougher regulations on fuel efficiency, it would encourage cleaner and more efficient forms of transport, which is now the fastest-growing source of pollution both globally and nationally.

Within the European Union, even allowing for differences in weather, the UK has the lowest standards of domestic energy efficiency (such as home insulation) and a shocking level of 'fuel poverty'. If, however, energy taxes were not only revenue-neutral but offset by grants and installation schemes to save energy at home, the result would be good for individuals, industry and the environment. Although energy-efficiency schemes are not new, few have been energetically implemented by national government. Some local authorities, however, have effective schemes which would serve as models. In Avon, for example, Woodspring District Council will almost halve the energy use and CO_2 emissions in its council houses by 1999, producing warmer, quieter homes which cost much less to heat. It would be environmentally irresponsible for any advanced industrialised country to continue allowing the real price of energy to fall as it did between 1983 and 1990, with average industrial energy prices now well below the 1970 level which predated the first oil price shock. Government should anticipate long-run pressure on real energy prices and must find the most effective ways of ensuring that we can all keep warm while using less energy.

Over the long term, it is likely that continuing concern about unemployment, environmental pressures and the growth of the informal economy will combine to support a shift from taxes on employment towards environmental taxation. Such a shift would have to take place over twenty years or more, and take careful account of the impact on people with average and below-average incomes: there is no case for 'big bang' changes. There is, however, considerable scope for more modest environmental charges and levies, such as landfill levies, effluent charges (particularly on water pollution), environmental taxes on damaging products (such as certain batteries or disposable containers), and road pricing in congested inner cities. All of these can provide powerful incentives to reduce environmental damage, as well as useful revenues.

Notes

1. Brian Robson et al *Assessing the Impact of Urban Policy* (London: HMSO, 1994)

2. *Hansard*, 19 June 1992, cols 688-9

3. Roger Jowell et al (eds) *British Social Attitudes: The 9th Report* (Aldershot : Dartmouth Publishing, 1992)

4. The *Observer*, 17 April 1994

5. *Hansard*, 1 February 1993, col 24

6. Andrew Britton 'Full Employment in a Market Economy' paper for the TUC/Employment Policy Institute conference *Looking Forward to Full Employment*, July 1994

7. Cedric Sandford *Reforming Death and Gift Taxes* submission to the Commission on Social Justice, 1993

8. Ibid

9. European Commission *Growth, Competitiveness,Employment* (Brussels: European Commission COM [93] 700 Final, 1993)

10. M.Pearson and S. Smith *Taxation and Environmental Policy: Some Initial Evidence* IFS Commentary No 19 (London: Institute for Fiscal Studies, 1990)

CONCLUSION:
THE NEED FOR CHANGE

Harold Wilson said of Royal Commissions that 'they take minutes and spend years'. The danger, of course, is that in the period between conception and completion, the world moves on: problems change, new ideas take shape, solutions are undermined and replaced. As the late Peter Jenkins wrote of the 1968 Donovan Commission: 'What would have been unorthodox ten years before, eye-opening to many even when the Commission first sat in 1965, was by 1968 becoming too orthodox – already new theory was lagging behind new practice.'[1]

The task for any Commission such as ours is to take a fresh look not only at the past, but at the future, and to decide strategy accordingly. Rather than start with the here-and-now, the challenge is to stand in the future: to be clear about our values, to understand as best we can the forces shaping change, and to create our own vision of the future. We need a clear sense of direction, coupled with realistic strategies which can enable politicians and people to hold fast to their values in a rapidly changing world.

We have set out to offer a compelling analysis of the challenges facing the United Kingdom, to set a vision of the future and to develop practical strategies which would enable this country to change for the better. We believe that this country's decline is rooted in our failure to come to terms with the economic, social and political revolutions which are transforming the world. That does not mean that our future is determined: the choices we make now, as individuals and as a society, will continue to resonate in ten, fifteen, twenty years' time. In our view, the Investors' future offers the only prospect of economic opportunity, social security and mutual responsibility.

In our proposals for lifelong learning, for full employment in a modern economy and a new balance between paid and unpaid work, for a new social insurance system and secure pension arrangements, for the development of health and community care, and the revival of distressed communities, we have set out the principles and objectives that should guide government over the long term, as well as the steps towards these objectives that can be taken in the short and medium terms. Throughout, we have imagined the United Kingdom as a different sort of country – and then asked how we can bridge the gap between the country we are and the country we would like to be.

Ours is a long term strategy, designed not to amend a few policies but to set a new direction. That is what people want, and that is what the country needs. But the fact that change will take a long time does not mean that there is time to spare; it means that we have to get on with it. Ours is a call for urgent action. The longer the neglect of economic opportunity, social security, and civic health, the longer it will take to turn things round. The more marginalised the poorest, the more we will pay for their inclusion; the more insecure the labour market, the longer it will take for people to embrace change; the more centralised our political structures, the more difficult it will be to bring hope of renewal.

When the challenge is so urgent, our timescale of ten to fifteen years may seem too long. Imagine, however, that fifteen years ago, government had determined to invest the revenues from North Sea Oil in the long-term development of the UK economy; that ten years ago, it had embarked upon a programme to expand nursery education; that a Jobs, Education and Training programme to prevent long-term unemployment had been initiated five years ago, and welfare-to-work reform was already under way. We would not be living in utopia, but this would already be a very different country. What we need from government now is the courage to take steps which will bear fruit beyond the electoral cycle; what we need from all our political leaders is a willingness to help develop a political and economic culture in which long-term strategies can flourish.

We do not have all the answers. But we have learnt a lot over the last eighteen months. Above all, we have been impressed by one thing: that this country, and the communities and individuals that make it up, have enormous potential to surmount problems, resolve conflicts and advance the timeless values of social justice. Those values define our purpose; they infuse our ambition; and they fuel our optimism. The future can be better than the past: it is up to us all to make it so.

Note

1. Peter Jenkins *The Battle of Downing Street* (London: Charles Knight and Company, 1970)

WRITTEN AND ORAL EVIDENCE

Organisations and Individuals Who Contributed to the Commission's Work

Many people helped the Commission, some by submitting written evidence, others by preparing papers, attending seminars or meeting Commission members. We are extremely grateful to them all. Those marked * submitted written evidence.

Dr Sam Aaronovitch, Local Economy Policy Unit, South Bank University*
Janos Abel, Convener, Green Economic Society, London School of Economics*
Ann Abraham, National Association of Citizens Advice Bureaux
Ann and John Abrami*
Acafess Community Trust (ACT)*
Nick Acheson, Assistant Director, Disability Action, Belfast
Advice Services Alliance*
Age Concern*
Professor Peter Alcock, Sheffield Hallam University*
Michael Allott*
Alzheimer's Disease Society*
Hilary Armstrong MP
Rt Hon Paddy Ashdown MP, Leader, Liberal Democrats
Peter Ashby, Full Employment UK*
Association of London Authorities (ALA)*
Association of Metropolitan Authorities*
Ruth Badger, Industrial and Economic Affairs Committee, Church of England

Peter Bailey, Park View School, Birmingham*
John Bald*
Ed Balls*
Terri Banks, Carnegie Inquiry into the Third Age
Dr Nicholas Barr, London School of Economics
Keith Barton, Bacon and Woodrow
Dr Iain Begg, University of Cambridge*
Fran Bennett*
Sarah Benton*
Fred Berry*
Dr Richard Berthoud, Policy Studies Institute
Richard Best, Joseph Rowntree Foundation
Graeme Betts, Coventry City Council*
Rodney Bickerstaffe, Deputy General Secretary, UNISON
Dr R.A. Bischof, Chairman, Jungheinrich UK*
Rt Hon Tony Blair MP
David Blunkett MP*
Selwyn Bowes*
Richard Bramhall*
Linda Bransbury
D. Brennan*
Professor Tim Brighouse, Chief Education Officer, Birmingham
    City Council
Hans Breitenboch*
British Association of Social Workers*
British Council of Churches
D. Bromley*
Clive Brooke, General Secretary, Inland Revenue Staff Federation
Gordon Brown MP
Joan Brown*
Professor William Brown, University of Cambridge*
Keith Burgess, Partner, Andersen Consulting
Margaret Buttigieg, Health Visitors Association
Anne Campbell MP
Carers National Association*
Graham Carey*
Sir John Cassels, Director, National Commission on Education
Caring Costs*

Terry Carlin, General Secretary, Irish Congress of Trade Unions*
Kay Carmichael*
Carnegie Inquiry into the Third Age
John Carr*
Catholic Housing Aid Society (CHAS)
Centre for Micro-Social Change, University of Essex
CHAR (Housing Campaign for Single People)
The Chard Group (Liberal Democrats)*
Child Poverty Action Group (CPAG)*
The Child Psychotherapy Trust*
Children in Scotland*
John Chivers*
Christian Council on Ageing*
Church Action on Poverty
Churches Council for Racial Justice*
Churches' National Housing Coalition*
Citizen's Income Study Centre
Citizen Organising Foundation
Civil and Public Services Association (CPSA)*
Richard Clements, Director, Citizen's Income
David Clinton, Partner, Andersen Consulting
Dr Clough, The Royal Naval School For Girls*
Ken Coates MEP*
Professor Gerry Cohen, All Soul's College, Oxford*
Commission for Racial Equality*
Committee on the Administration of Justice, Belfast
Community Service Volunteers (CSV)*
Paul Convery, Unemployment Unit
Bob Cooper, Director, Fair Employment Commission for
    Northern Ireland
Willy Cooper, Industrial Partnership Association
Yvette Cooper*
Anna Coote, Institute for Public Policy Research*
Jeremy Corbyn, MP
James Cornford, Director, Hamlyn Foundation*
Council for Disabled Children*
Dr Gary Craig, University of Humberside*
Professor Ivor Crewe, University of Essex

Elizabeth Crowther-Hunt, Director, Prince's Trust Volunteers
Professor David Currie, London Business School
Dr Jane Darke, Sheffield Hallam University
Bryn Davies, Union Pension Services Ltd
Howard Davies, Director-General, Confederation of British
    Industry
Ron Davies MP*
Robert Davis*
Professor Nicholas Deakin, University of Birmingham*
John Denham MP
Professor Meghnad Desai, London School of Economics*
Development Trusts Association
Donald Dewar MP
Andrew Dilnot, Director, Institute for Fiscal Studies
Disability Alliance
Disablement Income Group*
Richard Disney, Institute for Fiscal Studies*
Professor David Donnison, Centre for Housing Research and
    Urban Studies, University of Glasgow*
Professor Ronald Dore, London School of Economics
Angela Eagle MP
Dr John Eatwell, Trinity College, Cambridge*
John Edmonds, General Secretary, GMB
Elizabeth Edwards*
Helen Edwards, National Association for the Care and
    Resettlement of Offenders (NACRO)
Dr Patricia Elliott and Mr C. Dale*
Equal Opportunities Commission*
Richard Excell, Trades Union Congress
Dr Jane Falkingham, London School of Economics
Derek Fatchett MP*
Family Policy Studies Centre
Family Service Units*
David Faulkner, St John's College, Oxford*
Dr Anthony Fielding, Sussex University
Frank Field MP*
Adrian Fisher, Minotaur Designs*
Francis Fitzpatrick

John Foster, General Secretary, National Union of Journalists
Rt Hon Reg Freeson*
Michael Frye, Chairman, Elliott plc
Furniture Resource Centre Limited, Liverpool
Jeffrey Gates, formerly counsel to the US Senate Committee on
    Finance
John Gazder and Barry Yates*
Luke Geoghegan
Professor Jonathan Gershuny, University of Essex
Kenneth Gibb, Centre for Housing Research and Urban Studies,
    University of Glasgow*
Dr Tony Gibson, Neighbourhood Initiatives Foundation
Professor Anthony Giddens, University of Cambridge*
Glaxo Pharmaceuticals (UK)
Andrew Glyn, Corpus Christi College, Oxford*
Dr David Goldblatt, The Open University*
Professor Harvey Goldstein, Insititute of Education
Robina Goodlad, Centre for Housing Research and Urban
    Studies, University of Glasgow*
Bryan Gould
David Grayson, Business in the Community
Paul Gregg, National Institute of Economic and Social Research*
Ross Gregory*
Steve Griffiths, GRIC*
Professor A. H. Halsey, Nuffield College, Oxford*
Dr Jeremy Harbison, DHSS, Belfast
Roy Hatfield, Partnership Marketing Limited*
Chris Hayes, The Prospect Centre
Josephine Hayes, Women Liberal Democrats
Bryan Heading
Paul Henderson, Community Development Foundation*
Melanie Henwood
Josh Hillman, National Commission on Education
Dr John Hills, London School of Economics
Bronagh Hinds, Director, Ulster People's College
Gina Hocking*
Jonathan Hoffman, Director - Economics, CS First Boston
E. Hollis*

Baroness Hollis
Professor Martin Hollis, University of East Anglia*
John Hollyoak*
Bob Holman, Family Action in Rogerfield and Easterhouse, Strathclyde*
Gerry Holtham, Director, Institute for Public Policy Research
Elisabeth Hoodless, Director, Community Service Volunteers
Sandra Horley, Refuge
John Hutton MP
Independent Pensions Research Group*
International Black Women for Wages for Housewives*
Christine Jackson*
Lord Jay*
Diana Jeuda, Research Officer, USDAW
Alan Jinkinson, General Secretary, UNISON
Joel Joffe, formerly Deputy Chairman, Allied Dunbar*
Paul Johnson, Institute for Fiscal Studies*
Dr Paul Johnson, London School of Economics
Carolyn Jones, Institute of Employment Rights
Douglas Jones*
Jack Jones CH
M. Jones, Sun Alliance Group
Professor Bill Jordan, University of Exeter*
Professor Heather Joshi, City University
Roger Jowell, Social and Community Planning Research
Louis Juliene, Federation of Black Housing Organisations
Dharminder Kang, Andersen Consulting*
Geoffrey Kangley*
R. O'Kelly*
Charles Kennedy MP
Kids' Club Network*
C. Kilkenny*
Tim Knight*
Dr Marion Kozak, former Director, Daycare Trust*
Labour Finance and Industry Group*
Labour Housing Group*
The Labour Land Campaign*
Labour Party Local Government Team*

Labour Social Security Campaign
Labour Party Standing Committee on Equalities*
Gavin Laird, General Secretary, Amalgamated Engineering and
    Electrical Union (AEEU)
Sean Lance, Executive Director (Europe), Glaxo Holdings plc
Professor Hilary Land, Royal Holloway New College*
Allan Larsson, formerly Finance Minister, Sweden
Law Centres Federation*
Professor Julian Le Grand, London School of Economics
Lesbian and Gay Employment Rights (LAGER)
Joan Lestor MP
Professor Jane Lewis, London School of Economics
D. K. Lichfield, Urban Environmental Development Planning*
David Lindsay, CESPA
Lothian Social Policy Group*
Tony Lynes
Roger Lyons, General Secretary, Manufacturing Science Finance
    (MSF)
Inez McCormack, NUPE/UNISON, Belfast
J. McCusker, General Secretary, Northern Ireland Public Services
    Alliance (NIPSA)*
John Macdonald, Scottish CAADE*
Perry McDonnell, Deputy Chief Exxecutive, Training and
    Employment Agency, Belfast
Steven McEwen
Dr Stephen Machin, London School of Economics*
Alastair McIntosh, University of Edinburgh*
Ken MacIntyre*
Andrea McKeown*
Manchester City Council, Welfare Rights Unit*
Howard Mann
Dr Kirk Mann, University of Leeds*
Dr Alan Manning, London School of Economics*
Alan Manning, North-West Regional Council, TUC
Manufacturing Science Finance (MSF)*
Dr Alan Marsh, Policy Studies Institute
Tony Marshall
P. Martin

Nick Mays, Queen's University of Belfast
Professor James Meade, University of Cambridge*
Mediation UK*
Hugh Mellor*
Richard Merritt, Chester, Ellesmere Port and Wirrall TEC*
Merseyside TEC*
Ken Messere, Head of Fiscal Affairs Division (1971–1991),
    OECD*
Dr Hilary Metcalf, Policy Studies Institute*
H. Meyer*
Alun Michael MP
Alan Milburn MP
Gloria Mills, UNISON
John Mills, Treasurer, Full Employment Forum*
Andre Minuth*
Tariq Modood, Policy Studies Institute*
Angela Monaghan, Director, Development Trusts Association
John Monks, General Secretary, Trades Union Congress (TUC)
Dr Pamela Montgomery, Equal Opportunities Commission for
    Northern Ireland
Bill Morris, General Secretary, Transport and General Workers
    Union (TGWU)*
Mo Mowlam MP
Sir Claus Moser
Professor Alan Murie, Heriot Watt University*
National Association for the Care and Resettlement of Offenders
    (NACRO)*
National Association of Councils for Voluntary Services
    (NACVS)
National Association of Health Authorities and Trusts (NAHAT)
National Consumers Council*
National Council for One Parent Families*
National Council for Voluntary Organisations
National Council of Voluntary Child Care Organisations*
National Family Trust
National Federation of Housing Associations*
National Federation of Post Office and British
    Telecommunications Pensioners*

National Institute for Social Work
National Pensioners Convention*
National Stepfamily Association*
National Unemployed Centres Combine
National Union of Civil and Public Servants (NUCPS)*
Dr S Necmi*
Dr Brendan Nevin, University of Central England*
John Newbigin, Enigma Productions*
Mick Newmarch, Chairman, Prudential
Paul Nicolson*
Paul Noonan, Belfast Travellers Education and Development
    Group*
Northern Ireland Council for Voluntary Action (NICVA)
Steve Nuttall, Mercantile and General Reinsurance
Occupational Pensions Advisory Service*
Michael O'Higgins, Partner, Price Waterhouse
One Plus One*
Eileen Orford, Tavistock Clinic
Professor Paul Ormerod, Chair, Full Employment UK
Herman Ouseley, Chairman, Commission for Racial Equality
Robert Palmer, Glasgow City Council*
Parents Against Injustice (PAIN)*
Jennifer Park*
Hermione Parker*
Parliamentary Labour Party Education Committee
Parliamentary Labour Party Health Committee
Parliamentary Labour Party Social Security Committee
Parliamentary Labour Party Women's Committee
Bharti Patel, Low Pay Unit Research Trust
Raj Patel, ASHRAM, Birmingham
Keith Bedell-Pearce, Prudential
Daniel Pearce*
Michelle Pearce*
R. Pengelly*
Pensioners Liaison Forum
Professor David Piachaud, London School of Economics*
Chris Pond, Director, Low Pay Unit*
Dr Anne Power, London School of Economics

John Prescott MP
John Prevett, Bacon and Woodrow
Prince's Trust Volunteers*
Ashley Pringle, City of Edinburgh District Council*
Priority Area Development, Liverpool*
Prisoners' Opportunity to Work
Owen Prosser*
Dr David Purdy, University of Manchester*
Sandy Rally*
Nick Raynsford MP
Genevieve Reday-Mulvey
Brian Rees*
C. Regan*
Relate: Marriage Guidance
Religious Society of Friends*
Resource Use Institute Ltd
Claudia Riley-Searle, Principal Economic Development Officer,
    Wandsworth Borough Council
James Robertson, New Economics Foundation*
Ann Robinson, Spastics Society
B. Rofe*
Jeff Rooker MP
Donald Roy*
Royal Institute of Public Health and Hygiene*
Gordon Rudlin*
David Sainsbury, Chairman and Chief Executive, J. Sainsbury plc
Professor Cedric Sandford*
Phillippe Sands, King's College, London*
Tom Sawyer, Assistant General Secretary, UNISON
Scottish Association of Sign Language Interpreters*
Scottish Council for Single Parents*
Scottish Low Pay Unit*
Scottish TUC
Paul Seymour, Continuing Care Conference
Tom Shebbeare, Director, The Prince's Trust
Barry Sheerman MP
Rt Hon Robert Sheldon MP*
Shelter*

Phil Shiner, Birkenhead Resource Unit*
Alan Sinclair, Chief Executive, The Wise Group
Single Homeless in London (SHIL)
David Skidmore, Secretary, Board of Social Responsibility,
    Church of England
Alan Smith, Granby and Toxteth Taskforce, Liverpool
Chris Smith MP
Professor Dennis Snower, Birkbeck College
Society of Labour Lawyers*
Spastics Society
Sarah Spencer, Institute for Public Policy Research
Ken Spours, Institute of Education, University of London*
Vivien Stern, Director, National Association for the Care and
    Resettlement of Offenders*
Professor John Stewart, University of Birmingham*
Stonewall Group*
Strathclyde Early Years Voluntary Sector Forum*
Radiance Strathdee, Centrepoint
Jane Streather, Newcastle City Council*
Vimla Suppiah, Health Visitors Association
Holly Sutherland and Moira Wilson, University of Cambridge*
Adam Swift, Balliol College, Oxford
Tavistock Institute*
Ann Taylor MP
Gil Taylor*
Dr Stephen Thake, Queen Mary & Westfield College, University
    of London*
Stephen Tindale
Professor Peter Townsend, University of Bristol*
Trades Union Congress (TUC)*
Transport and General Workers Union*
Transport and General Workers Union Retired Members
    Association Wales*
Tribune Group of Labour MPs
Owen Tudor, Trades Union Congress (TUC)
Mary Tyler*
Tony Uden, National Organisation for Adult Learning
Union of Communication Workers (UCW)*

Union of Shop, Distributive and Allied Workers (USDAW)*
UNISON*
Professor John Veit Wilson, University of Northumbria*
The Volunteer Centre UK*
Wages for Housework Campaign*
Wales TUC
Professor Alan Walker, University of Sheffield*
John Ward, Opera North*
Sue Ward, Independent Pensions Research Group
Paul Warren, University of Strathclyde*
Roger Warren-Evans*
Dr Stephen Watkins, Medical Practitioners Union*
Caroline Welch, Low Pay Unit
Welsh Pensioners' Convention
Bengt Westerberg, Swedish Minister of Health and Social Affairs
Rose Wheeler, Rotherham Commission on Social Justice,
    Rotherham Borough Council*
Ed Whitehouse, Institute for Fiscal Studies
Malcolm Wicks MP
Steve Wilcox, University of Wales
Dr Susan Willett, King's College, London*
John Wills*
Richard Winston*
Sally Witcher, Director, Child Poverty Action Group
Adrian Wood, University of Sussex*
Mike Woodhouse, Chairman, The Prince's Trust Volunteers
Work Base Training*
Working For Childcare*
Arthur and Margaret Wynn*
Keith Yates, Central Regional Council, Scotland*
Michael Yates, Andersen Consulting*
Lord Young, Institute of Community Studies*

COMMISSION TERMS OF REFERENCE

To consider the principles of social justice and their application to the economic well-being of individuals and the community;

To examine the relationship between social justice and other goals, including economic competitiveness and prosperity;

To probe the changes in social and economic life over the last fifty years, and the failure of public policy to reflect them adequately; and to survey the changes that are likely in the foreseeable future, and the demands they will place on government;

To analyse public policies, particularly in the fields of employment, taxation and social welfare, which could enable every individual to live free from want and to enjoy the fullest possible social and economic opportunities;

And to examine the contribution which such policies could make to the creation of a fairer and more just society.

COMMISSION PUBLICATIONS

Interim reports

The Justice Gap
Discussion Paper 1
July 1993 ISBN 1 872452 67 1 £3.50

Social Justice in a Changing World
Discussion Paper 2
July 1993 ISBN 1 872452 68 X £3.50

Issue Papers

1. *Social Insurance: Reform or Abolition?*
   Fran Bennett
   Nov 1993 ISBN 1 872452 72 8

2. *Making Sense of Benefits*
   Nov 1993 ISBN 1 872452 73 6

3. *Work and Welfare: Tackling the Jobs Deficit*
   Edward Balls and Paul Gregg
   Dec 1993 ISBN 1 872452 75 2

4. *Social Justice, Children and Families*
   Patricia Hewitt and Penelope Leach
   Dec 1993 ISBN 1 872452 76 0

5. *Racial Equality: Colour, Culture and Justice*
   Tariq Modood
   Jan 1994 ISBN 1 872452 79 5

6. *Dignity not Poverty: A Minimum Income Standard
for the UK*
John Veit Wilson
Feb 1994 ISBN 1 872452 81 7

7. *The Pensions Dilemma*
Paul Johnson
Mar 1994 ISBN 1 872452 80 9

8. *Integrating Taxes and Benefits?*
David Clinton, Michael Yates, Dharminder Kang
Apr 1994 ISBN 1 872452 82 5

9. *Housing and Social Justice*
Edited by Robina Goodlad and Kenneth Gibb
May 1994 ISBN 1 872452 85 X

10. *Citizens' Service*
James McCormick
May 1994 ISBN 1 872452 87 6

11. *Flexibility in Work and Benefits*
Eithne McLaughlin
June 1994 ISBN 1 872452 88 4

12. *Disabled People and Social Justice*
Bert Massie
June 1994 ISBN 1 872452 90 6

13. *Act Local: Social Justice from the Bottom Up*
David Donnison
July 1994 ISBN 1 872452 92 2

Issue Papers are available at £2.95 each, or £20 for the full series.

UK Income Distribution Poster   £4.95

The Right of Every Citizen Video   £5

All available from the Institute for Public Policy Research (IPPR),
30-32 Southampton Street, London WC2E 7RA

Commission Outreach Visits

The Commission made 11 outreach visits, and saw the following organisations or their representatives:

Glasgow: 17 February 1993

Family Action In Rogerfield and Easterhouse (FARE)
Strathclyde Poverty Alliance
Scottish TUC
The Wise Group
University of Glasgow (Open Forum)

Birmingham: 19 March 1993

Dartmouth High School
Birmingham Settlement
Handsworth Single Homeless Housing Association
West Midlands Low Pay Unit
Handsworth College
Asian Resource Centre
Heartland Urban Development Corporation
University of Birmingham (Open Forum)

Newcastle: 25–26 April 1993

Tyneside Training and Enterprise Council
Tyne and Wear Development Corporation
Nissan UK
Norham High School
North Tyneside Childcare Network

Meadowell Resource Centre
Newbiggin Hall Project
Newcastle City Coucil
Money Matters
University of Newcastle (Open Forum)

Southampton: 25 May 1993

Southampton Cargo Handling
Southampton TGWU
Southampton City Council
St. Dismas Health Care for the Homeless Project
Hampshire Training and Enterprise Council
Eastpoint Centre
Southampton University (Open Forum)

Nottingham: 16 June 1993

Nottingham Citizen's Advice Bureau
Nottinghamshire Police
Nottingham City Council
East Midlands Electricity
32 Waterloo Road, (Homeless Young Persons Project)
University of Nottingham (Open Forum)

Sheffield: 13 October 1993

Alzheimer's Disease Society
Hanover Medical Centre
Sheffield Area Health Authority
Sheffield Family Health Services Authority
Sheffield and District Afro-Caribbean Community Association
    (SADACCA)
Sheffield City Council, Family & Community Services
Cultural Industries Quarter
University of Sheffield (Open Forum)

Belfast: 4 November 1994

Belfast Action Teams
Ardoyne/Oldpark : The Flax Trust; Concorde Community

Centre; Wishing Well Family Centre; North Belfast
Community Development Centre
Lower Falls/Lower Shankill : Townsend Enterprise Park
Rathcoole : Newtownabbey Citizen's Advice Bureau; Rathcoole
Youth Centre; Bytes for Belfast project; Rathcoole Community
Group
Ardmonagh Family Centre, Turf Lodge
Northern Ireland Women's Aid Federation
Queen's University of Belfast (Open Forum)

Cardiff: 14 December 1993

South Glamorgan County Council (Social Services Committee
and Officers)
Ely Family Centre
Llantwit Major Family Centre
Trowbridge Family Centre
Wales TUC
University of Cardiff (Open Forum)

Manchester: 16 February 1994

Miles Platting and Ancoats Development Trust
Manchester City Council Social Services
Church Action on Poverty
Manchester Training and Enterprise Council
Manchester University (Open Forum)

East Anglia: 17 March 1994

Listawood Magnetics, Harpley
Norwich City Council
Litcham High School
Bowthorpe Development – Chapel Break Village Hall
Norwich Advice Services
Advice Arcade
St Martins House for the Homeless
University of East Anglia (Open Forum)

London: 22 April 1994

The Big Issue
Mulberry School
Bootstraps Enterprises
Prince's Youth Business Trust

The Institute for Public Policy Research

The Institute for Public Policy Research was founded in 1988 to provide an alternative to the free-market think-tanks. In addition to the Commission on Social Justice, its work is organised into five programmes: *New Economy*, a quarterly journal which brings to the lay and expert reader debate on the latest economic thinking; *Social Policy*, which is exploring how individuals and communities can take charge of their own services and their own lives; the *New Europe*, which examines constitutional, legal and institutional changes necessary to secure democracy, prosperity and peace in Europe, East and West; *Democracy and Human Rights* which examines questions of rights, responsibilities, power and accountability in the UK and beyond; and *Media Policy*, which will propose policies for a sector vital to our economy as well as our democracy.

The Commission will retain a small staff at IPPR to disseminate material and develop the policy ideas set out in this report. To contact the Commission, or to receive a full IPPR publications list, please write to or telephone:

Commission on Social Justice
IPPR
30-32 Southampton Street
London WC2E 7RA
(tel: 071 379-9400; fax: 071 497-0373)